CW00766292

FORENSIC ARCHITECTURE

Forensic Architecture

VIOLENCE AT THE THRESHOLD OF DETECTABILITY

Eyal Weizman

ZONE BOOKS · NEW YORK · 2017

Printed in Belgium.

Distributed by The MIT Press,
Cambridge, Massachusetts, and London, England

Library of Congress Cataloging-in-Publication Data
Names: Weizman, Eyal, author.
Title: Forensic architecture : violence at the threshold of
    detectability / Eyal Weizman.
Description: Brooklyn, NY : Zone Books [2017] | Includes
    bibliographical references.
Identifiers: LCCN 2016050515 | ISBN 9781935408864 (hardcover)
Subjects: LCSH: Forensic sciences. | Forensic anthropology.
    | Human rights. | Architecture — Political aspects.
Classification: LCC GN69.8 .W45 2017 | DDC 614/.17 — dc23
LC record available at https://lccn.loc.gov/2016050515

Contents

Preface

FORENSIC ARCHITECTURE — the investigative practice that this book introduces — refers to the production of architectural evidence and to its presentation in juridical and political forums. It regards the common elements of our built environment — buildings, details, cities, and landscapes, as well as their representations in media and as data — as entry points from which to interrogate contemporary processes and with which to make claims for the future.

Forensic Architecture is also the name of a research agency I established in 2010, together with a group of fellow architects, artists, filmmakers, journalists, scientists, and lawyers. We undertake independent research or act on commission from international prosecutors and environmental and human rights groups to investigate state and corporate violence, especially when it bears upon the built environment. The agency produces evidence files that include building survey, models, animations, video analyses, and interactive cartographies, and presents them in forums such as international courts, truth commissions, citizen tribunals, human rights and environmental reports, and, on one occasion, in the UN General Assembly.

We use the term "forensics," but we seek, in fact, to reverse the forensic gaze and to investigate the same state agencies — such as the police or the military — that usually monopolize it. For this purpose, our investigative work tends to exceed the procedural limitations and necessities of the legal forums in which we present. We locate incidents in their historical contexts and pull from their microphysical details the longer threads of political and social processes — conjunctions of actors and practices, structures and technologies — and reconnect them with the world of which they are part. We also try to use our investigations as an opportunity to embark upon longer-term theoretical and historical inquiries about the relations between architecture, media, and violence, which we make public in exhibitions and texts, such as this book. Architecture, in our practice, to paraphrase Carlo Ginzburg, is "not a fortress but a port or an airport, a place from which we leave to other destinations."[1]

Following an introductory chapter that presents, by way of a historical narrative, the forensic condition of "the threshold of detectability"—a concept central to our understanding of the challenges and limitations of our practice—the book proceeds in three parts. The first, "What Is Forensic Architecture?" is, as its title suggests, a kind of practical manual. Its aim is to outline the methods, assumptions, and critical vocabulary relevant to the field, but also to discuss its constraints, potential problems, and double binds. The issues discussed in this part are interspersed with brief examples from the investigations our agency has pursued in various places worldwide as well as relevant reference materials.

The second part of the book, "Counterforensics in Palestine," presents a sequence of recent investigations in Palestine—a place where the trajectory that led to the establishment of forensic architecture had its origin. It describes the way our practice evolved in relation to recent political challenges and to changes in the nature of human rights that have seen the most relevant evidence increasingly produced by the people experiencing conflicts firsthand.

In the third part of this book, "Ground Truths," the site that typically organizes the optics of forensic architecture has grown to the size of a larger territory, perhaps even to that of the planet, which appears as simultaneously both a construction site and a ruin. The investigation at the center of this part was presented in a citizen-organized truth commission on the site where the Bedouin village of al-'Araqīb on the northern threshold of the Naqab/Negev Desert, a place of habitation that was destroyed and rebuilt more than one hundred times. Part 3 connects the history of this local land struggle to larger-scale and longer-term environmental transformations, to desertification and climate change along desert thresholds worldwide, and to the conflicts that such changes have provoked.

Despite there rarely being a simple "who dunnit" logic to our investigations, accounts of the cases presented in this book follow something of the convention of the detective genre, to the extent, at least, of having two entangled plots: one involving the crime in the past, the other the investigation in the present. The two plots connect with the evidence, whether material, testimonial, or media-based. Both "forensics" and "architecture" refer to well-established disciplinary frames. Brought together, however, they shift each other's meaning, giving rise to a different mode of practice.

Architecture turns the attention of forensics to buildings and cities. Forensics turns architecture into an investigative practice, a probative mode for enquiring about the present through its spatial materialization. It demands that architects focus their attention on the materiality of the built environment and its media representations. It also, importantly, challenges architects to use their disciplinary tools to make claims publicly and politically in the most antagonistic of forums.

At the Threshold of Detectability

THE NEW MILLENNIUM began with a bizarre legal battle. The David Irving trial, which unfolded at the English High Court between January and April 2000, involved one of the most detailed and intense presentations of architectural evidence undertaken in a legal context—drawings, models, aerial and ground-level photographs of buildings—as well as aggressive cross-examinations of it. The case involved a libel suit filed by David Irving against an American historian, Deborah Lipstadt, and her publisher, Penguin Books, for calling him "one of the most dangerous spokespersons for Holocaust denial" and a falsifier of history.[1] Awkwardly, the process forced the veracity of the events of the Holocaust to be put on trial, subject not to historical methods, but to legal rules of evidence.[2] On the tenth and eleventh days of the trial, January 26 and 27, the legal debate revolved around the architecture of one of the gas chambers—an underground structure that was part of Crematorium II in Auschwitz-Birkenau, the deadliest of the five Auschwitz crematoria, where in a space of 200 square meters, approximately half a million people were killed.

It was also one of the only structures related to the extermination process whose destruction was incomplete. There were, in fact, two stages in the attempt to destroy Crematorium II. After the extermination process was stopped in November 1944, SS operators attempted to erase the evidence for the killings by dismantling the gassing instruments. On January 20, 1945, after most of the camp already had been evacuated, Crematorium II, along with all other Auschwitz crematoriums, was dynamited. The concrete roof of the underground structure was supported by seven columns. The demolition team might have placed dynamite next to all of them, but only six detonated. The concrete roof snapped around the single surviving column at the southernmost end of the structure and remained held up like the peak of a devastated tent. This detonation failure made it possible, decades later, for Holocaust deniers, or negationists, as they were sometimes referred to, to enter a small part of the original chamber. On one occasion, Fred Leuchter, a former US penal system execution specialist, was smuggled in there to chisel out concrete samples from the interior and check for cyanide traces (as depicted in Errol Morris's documentary *Mr. Death*). That random samples taken more than four decades after the last gassing didn't contain the level of cyanide that Leuchter would have expected to find in an execution gas chamber in the United States proved nothing, but was presented by Irving as an argument to counter the determination that the building ever functioned as a homicidal gas chamber.[3]

Many of the other details of the structure were subjected to close scrutiny. One, however, became the center of debate. Irving, representing himself, focused the cross-examination of the expert witness facing him — an architectural historian specializing in the history of Auschwitz, Robert Jan van Pelt — on the existence of four small holes in the ceiling of the concrete roof of the structure.[4] According to the few surviving witnesses, both victims and perpetrators, it was through short chimney shafts connected to these holes that the Zyklon B canisters containing cyanide were introduced into the room.

Robert Jan van Pelt pointing to the ruins of Crematorium II in Auschwitz-Birkenau. The gas chamber is on top, and the arrows point to the probable location of the holes in the ceiling.
HOLOCAUST HISTORY PROJECT, 2000

Van Pelt had been studying the architecture of Auschwitz since the late 1980s. His analysis concentrated on the surviving plans, in which he read not only the meaning of lines drawn, but also traces of those erased. On one occasion, he noticed razor-blade erasure marks around the icon that architects use to mark doorways — a quarter circle — on the tracing paper on which the Crematorium II was drawn. In 1942, when the morgue that occupied this building was turned into a gas chamber, the direction of the door hinges had to change. When the bodies inside the room were pressed against the doors, they could no longer be opened inward, and the door had to open toward the outside. This erasure thus confirmed the beginning of a process of industrialized mass killing.

In the trial, Judge Charles Gray addressed van Pelt directly: "You have not seen any holes in the roof, have you, in the...when you went there?"[5] Van Pelt answered in the negative. His expert report, submitted to the court in advance of the trial, presented convergent photographic and testimonial evidence for the existence of the holes, but it conceded that "these four small holes...cannot be observed in the ruined remains of the concrete slab." He explained that finding the holes was impossible due to the state of the roof. Not only had the concrete roof slab broken and crashed as a result of the explosion, but it was exposed to the elements in the following fifty-six years. He also suggested that it would have been logical for the Nazis to backfill the holes with concrete before they evacuated the camp in November 1944, in the same way that any murderer would get rid of a gun. Irving claimed that it was impossible to condemn the Nazis (and him) without producing the weapon itself. Traces of the holes would be discovered in an examination that was undertaken a few years later,[6] but in 2000, the court heard the following exchange.

IRVING You do accept, do you not, that the whole of the story of the 500,000 people killed in that chamber rises or falls, rests or falls on the existence of those holes in that roof?

VAN PELT No.

IRVING [Without it] we only have the eyewitness evidence.

VAN PELT I disagree with that. The whole story rises and falls on the evidence that this room was a gas chamber, which is a slightly different issue.[7]

At the end of this cross-examination, Irving offered van Pelt nothing less than a deal:

IRVING   And you do accept, do you not, that if you were to go to Auschwitz the day after tomorrow with a trowel and clean away the gravel and find a reinforced concrete hole where we anticipate it would be from your drawings, this would make an open and shut case and I would happily abandon my action immediately?

VAN PELT   I cannot comment on this. I am an expert on Auschwitz and not on the way you want to run your case.

IRVING   There is my offer. I would say that that would drive such a hole through my case that I would have no possible chance of defending it any further.[8]

Irving seemed to enjoy the pun — "I am going to keep on driving holes in this case until your Lordship appreciates the significance of the holes, or their absence"[9] — but there was also some logic, albeit a hermetic and elliptical one, to his argument: without these holes, the cyanide in Zyklon B canisters could not have been introduced into the room, and without cyanide, the room could not have functioned as a gas chamber. In that case, the witnesses were either deluded or lying. If the structure was not a gas chamber, Auschwitz could not have been a death camp. Without Auschwitz as the functional and symbolic center of the extermination process, the Holocaust, as a premeditated industrialized policy of racially motivated killing, could never have happened. "No holes, no Holocaust" already had been the formulation of master denier Robert Faurisson for several years.[10] And if the Holocaust didn't happen, Irving could not be accused of falsifying history — *quod erat demonstrandum*!

While Irving was satisfied with proclaiming the Nazis innocent of genocide and himself a victim of libel, the cascading linear logic of denial was extended by some groups that, since the US designation of the Pol Pot regime as genocidal, supported Holocaust denial as an anti-imperialist practice. Without the Holocaust, the entire apparatus of "Western democratic

Fredrick Töben, an Australian Holocaust denier, going through a break in the roof of Crematorium II at Auschwitz-Birkenau. He is trying to demonstrate that the opening was too large to have been one of the lethal holes. FREDRICK TÖBEN, "TO THE MANNHEIM JAIL: JUSTICE AND TRUTH IN CONTEMPORARY GERMANY," *JOURNAL OF HISTORICAL REVIEW* 20.3 (2001), AVAILABLE AT COMMITTEE FOR OPEN DEBATE ON THE HOLOCAUST, CODOH.COM/LIBRARY/DOCUMENT/2978

Robert Jan van Pelt pointing to the roof of the gas chamber in Crematorium I, captured on an aerial photograph by an Allied reconnaissance mission on August 25, 1944. This image is rotated 90 degrees counterclockwise in relation to the previous aerial image.
EYAL WEIZMAN

post–World War II imperialism"—the Fourth Geneva Convention, the 1948 Universal Declaration of Human Rights, the concept of genocide, the United Nations as a system aspiring to manage conflict and maintain international order—would stand on nothing, they believed.[11]

NEGATIVE POSITIVISM

Staking the nonexistence of the Holocaust on holes in a fragmented and almost pulverized concrete slab and imbuing a single architectural detail with such overarching geopolitical significance might appear to be a desperate act—but the use of material evidence to negate survivors' testimony was by then the established method of Holocaust deniers. Witness testimony, Faurisson—in whose footsteps Irving was following elsewhere claimed, produced "too much metaphysics, not enough materialism" and lacked the power of the thing in itself.[12] Even van Pelt felt compelled to admit that "Faurisson made a very radical, but also perverse, epistemic shift" in Holocaust history "from various classes of evidence in which eyewitness testimony has a place to considering material evidence," because "in terms of Holocaust historiography [he] forced us to look at a much larger body of evidence."[13]

A similar approach in 1983 brought Irving some fame for being the first to identify as fake the "Hitler Diaries," which had been bought by the German magazine *Stern* for a huge sum—after several of their pages had been authenticated by distinguished historians who focused their analyses on issues of style, voice, and historical fact. From the floor of a pressroom at the publishers' headquarters in Hamburg, into which he was smuggled uninvited, Irving shouted: "Check the ink!" before being thrown out.[14] The ink was dated to the 1950s.

In the London trial, it was not ink, but architecture — or more precisely, the absence of a particular piece of material-architectural evidence — that Irving sought to mobilize against human testimony. It was not positivism that led him to insist on materiality — there would be nothing wrong with adding a material dimension to other evidentiary techniques — but rather negation, which fundamentally meant negation of the ability of witnesses to speak to history at all. Posing matter against memory, he seemed to advocate a history without witnesses and beyond language.

Because the evidence concerned not only matter, but its absence — the absence of holes — the issue revolved around a rather confusing absence of an absence.[15] The fact that the holes could not be found was presented by Irving as "negative evidence" for the process of extermination. "Negative evidence" is an oxymoronic term that legal professionals and scholars employ when the very absence of material evidence is used as evidence in its own right. In legal terms, it is a kind of antibody meant to disrupt and dismantle the assemblages of evidence on which cases rest. Defense teams mobilize negative evidence to disrupt prosecution cases: despite overwhelming converging evidence, they hope a crime cannot be proved if there is no body or no weapon, or, as in our case, if there are no holes. For prosecutors, on the other hand, negative evidence can also indicate that evidence was destroyed and that this act of cover-up might be considered incriminating evidence in its own right.[16] By blowing up the building, the Nazis were engaged in Holocaust denial, but inadvertently confirmed that a crime had taken place inside.

TOWARD A FORENSIC ARCHITECTURE

Harun Farocki's 1989 film *Images of the World and the Inscription of War* presented an inadvertent prequel to this story. On a cloudless day, August 25, 1944, a US reconnaissance mission was sent to photograph a petrochemical factory — Monowitz-Buna — located next to the Auschwitz-Birkenau extermination camp. The five-by-three miles of ground territory captured by one of the 35-millimeter negatives shot by a US Air Force Mosquito plane included the roof of Crematorium II, somewhere close to the edge of the frame in the lens's area of barrel distortion. The fact that this image, along with a few other aerial photographs from the spring and summer of 1944, captured the crematorium was noticed only in 1978, by two CIA image

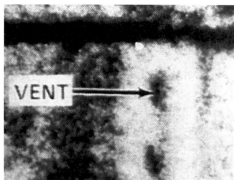

Harun Farocki, *Images of the World and the Inscription of War*, 1989.

analysts named Dino Brugioni and Robert Poirer. When the image was enlarged, Brugioni and Poirer spotted four blurry marks on the roof of the crematorium building and simply annotated them as "vents."[17] These were the small chimney shafts that led to the infamous holes.

Irving claimed that the film on which the shafts were recorded was inauthentic. When he looked at it under high magnification, he noticed a strange interference pattern at the place where the vents were marked.[18] This, he claimed, indicated that the negative had been tampered with by the addition of "brush strokes" sometime after the film was shot.[19] But the court was also provided with a report prepared shortly before the trial by Nevin Bryant, "supervisor of cartographic applications and image process- ing applications" at NASA's Jet Propulsion Laboratory in Pasadena, Cali- fornia, and an expert in the analysis of aerial and satellite images.[20] Bryant used state of the art digital magnification to peer into the molecular compo- sition of the film. At stake was the way in which the photographic process captured and recorded objects on the scale of the silver halide crystals or "salts" that make up the chemical composition of the film. Film resolution depends on the distribution and the ranges of sizes of these grains. Bryant determined that from the altitude of 15,000 feet and at the resolution of the negative, a single grain represented an area of about half a meter square on the ground. He suggested that the interference pattern identified by Irving was a phenomenon that occurs at the level of the grains in the emulsion of the film when images of objects on the ground are captured at or close to the size of the grains in the film. The same kind of interference patterns occurred also in another part of the same roll. The photograph there cap- tured a group of prisoners being marched within the camp. Irving referred to these interference patterns as "brush strokes," as well. Responding to the judge's request for clarifications, van Pelt quoted Bryant's conclusion: the interference pattern was caused when "the size of a head of a person is the same as the size of a grain in the emulsion of the film, and the result of that was that [of] a *moiré effect*, which occurs also in the newspaper when you photograph a picture which has been screened twice."[21] That the indivisible unit of photography represents half a meter square of ground, roughly the same as the size of a person seen from above, is a coincidence that continued to haunt the practice of forensic architecture, as I will explain later.

The shafts on the roof of Crematorium II were also the same size, half a meter by half a meter. It was the shadow cast on that cloudless day that created the blurred interference pattern.

When the size of an object recorded on the negative—here, a person or a shaft—is close to the size of the material element that records it—the single silver salt grain—it is in a condition that I refer to throughout this book as the *threshold of detectability*: things that hover between being identifiable and not. They leave a chemical signature on the negative, but cannot be verified. At the threshold of detectability, both the surface of the negative and that of the thing it represents must be studied as both material objects and as media representations.[22] In other words, this condition forces us to remember that the negative is not only an image representing reality, but that it is itself a material thing, simultaneously both representation and presence.[23]

As the cross-examination went on, it became clear that against the linear argument mobilized by Irving's negative evidence, van Pelt had woven a complex and overwhelmingly convincing network of converging evidence, both for the existence of the holes and for the entire operation of the structure as a death chamber. These included architectural plans, letters, diaries, logbooks, testimonies, and ground-level photographs.[24] Irving lost the trial and later also lost the appeal. My aim here is not to reopen the case, but to show how it turned on the condition of the threshold of detectability. It also demonstrates the ongoing tension between testimony and evidence—material and linguistic practices, subject and object— and the complex interdependencies between violence and the negation of evidence that are central to the field of forensic architecture. I also begin this book with the Irving trial because it serves as a warning: an independent forensics analyst challenging officially sanctioned truths with the typically limited means afforded to activists is not a guarantee of progressive politics.

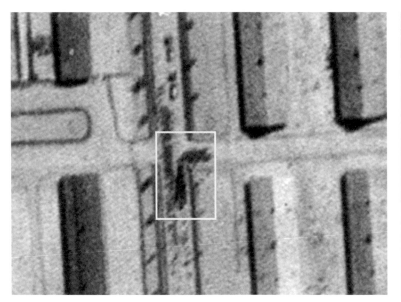
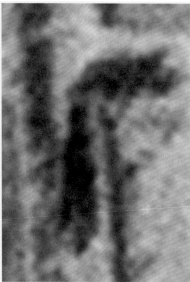

A group of prisoners being marched through a gate in Auschwitz, U.S. Air Force, 25 August 1944. As the prisoner group turns 90 degrees, the narrow neck seems to be a gate. There is another group of prisoners moving along the main north-south route. The size of the head of a single prisoner is the same as that of a single silver salt particle in the film. COURTESY OF NEVIN BRYANT, NASA

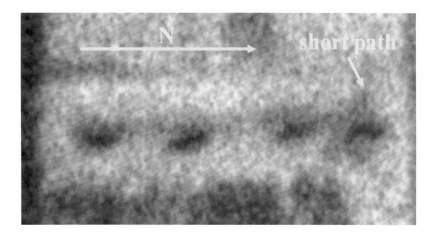

The roof of Crematorium II, rotated 90 degrees clockwise in relation to the first image on page 17, Auschwitz-Birkenau. US Air Force photograph, August 25, 1944. Nevin Bryant explained that the four dark areas are the shadows cast around the Zyklon B chimneys. He identified the short interference path next to the rightmost hole as a person, possibly a member of the SS, standing on the roof. It is possible that gassing was going on at the time when the image was taken. COURTESY OF NEVIN BRYANT, NASA

I recalled the story above about the holes and the Irving trial when Forensic Architecture began its investigation of Western drone strikes.[25] At the end of 2011, we were commissioned by several organizations: Ben Emmerson, the UN Special Rapporteur on Human Rights and Counter-Terrorism, asked us to investigate a number of strikes for a report on drone warfare in Pakistan, Afghanistan, Yemen, Somalia, and Gaza that he eventually presented at the UN General Assembly; the Pakistani human rights lawyer Shahzad Akbar asked us to prepare evidence for a legal action he presented to the UK Court of Appeal; and the UK-based Bureau of Investigative Journalism asked us to collaborate to uncover patterns of drone strikes in built environments.[26]

The reason we were commissioned (despite having only recently been formed) was that for several years drone strikes had shifted from targeting vehicles along roadways to targeting buildings in dense urban environments. The evidence had an architectural dimension, and there were no other organizations providing architectural analysis. Two years into the drone campaign, the Taliban forces in the Federally Administered Tribal Area (FATA) on the Pakistani frontier with Afghanistan learned to avoid, or at least to minimize, traveling between remote bases and moved into towns and cities. The CIA killer drones followed them there.[27] While testimonies and evidence of civilian casualties in the towns of FATA started to emerge, the CIA was still persistent in denying that its drone campaign was taking place at all.

However, a particular type of evidence also started to emerge. The effect of drone strikes on buildings had a distinct signature — small holes in the roof. The targeted building would remain intact, except for a hole that the missile had pierced on its way in to detonate within a room inside the structure.

These holes, our study later established, were the result of the kind of missiles employed in these strikes. As long as drone strikes targeted vehicles, the CIA munitions of choice, primarily Lockheed Martin Hellfire antitank missiles, would do.[28] Since 2007, the US had invested millions in modifying these missiles for the task of striking buildings within urban environments. The "Romeo" Hellfire II or AGM-114R was tested in 2009 and put into action in 2010. It was, in fact, a counterarchitectural technology. One of the important developments introduced in this model of the missile had to do with improving its charge and delay fuse. A few

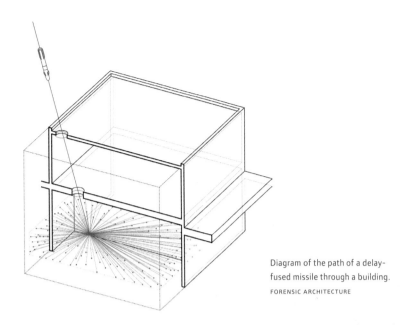

Diagram of the path of a delay-fused missile through a building.
FORENSIC ARCHITECTURE

milliseconds delay between first impact on the roof and detonation, which could be differently set for each strike, allows a missile to break through several layers of roof, walls, and floors made of adobe, brick, or concrete before detonating in a room deeper within the structure, where a payload of hundreds of lethal steel fragments is designed to destroy flesh, but leave the structure intact. Most other airborne munitions detonate upon impact, leaving most of the blast force outside the structure. To ensure the deaths of the people inside, large payloads are needed to bring the structures down.

The apologists described their drone missiles as a "humanitarian technology" because they saved lives and produced less collateral damage than those authorized and used by other military planners.[29] The argument rested on the idea that they are "saving people" from what the United States otherwise would have done to them. The "humanitarian violence" of drone warfare could thus be presented as one that both kills and saves.

The critics of drone warfare objected to the Pentagon's account of the missiles' accuracy (deviation from aiming point) and precision (dispersion of damage).[30] They were not always as accurate and precise as they cleaimed to be. However, in general, criticism of covert drone warfare shifted between two seemingly contradictory positions: it was both too precise, allowing operators to kill from half a world away, and not precise enough, unable to distinguish between civilians and combatants.

Traces of roof-penetrating munitions. Tuffah, Northern Gaza, 2009. Being able to study similar strikes in Gaza assisted the analysis undertaken remotely in Pakistan. KENT KLICH

A man is seen through a hole made in his roof by a US drone strike in Damadola, Bajaur region, Pakistan, on January 13, 2006.
© TARIQ MAHMOOD/AFP/GETTY

The issue, we believed, related to the fact that decisionmakers authorized their use because drone munitions were perceived as highly precise. Like other techniques and technologies of the "lesser evil," the perception that drone munitions could be precise was an important factor in allowing for drone strikes to be continually authorized in densely inhabited civilian areas, in markets, in homes, in mosques, and in schools, leading, cumulatively, to the proliferation of civilian casualties. Of the 380 strikes that one of our partners, the Bureau of Investigative Journalism (BIJ), recorded in Pakistan from 2004 and 2014, we have established that more than 234, or about 62 percent, were targeted domestic buildings. The holes in the roofs across FATA thus demonstrated the relation between the microscale technology of drone missiles and their effects on a larger territorial scale in an extended campaign that according to the BIJ, by the end of 2014 resulted in as many as 1,614 civilian casualties in Pakistan alone.[31]

However, the confirmation of such architectural traces of drone missile strikes was not easy to come by. The areas where drone warfare took place were made inaccessible to journalists and human rights investigators from

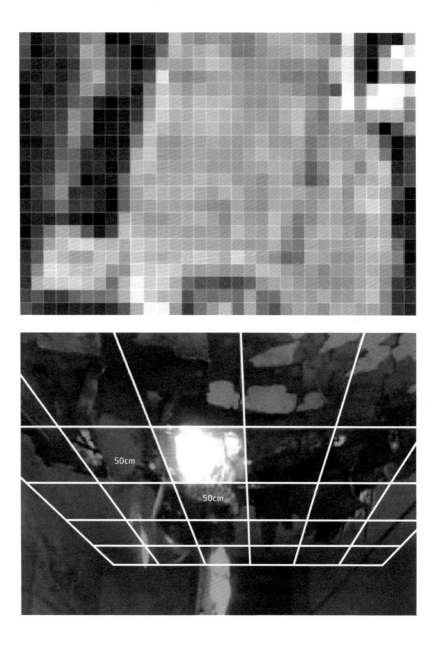

TOP: An enlargement of a satellite image at the presumed location of a March 30, 2012, drone strike in Miranshah, FATA, Pakistan. We were unable to identify the hole in the roof because it is smaller than the size of a single pixel. BOTTOM: The hole in the roof through which the drone missile entered the same building.
DIGITALGLOBE, MARCH 31, 2012; MSNBC BROADCAST, JUNE 29, 2012

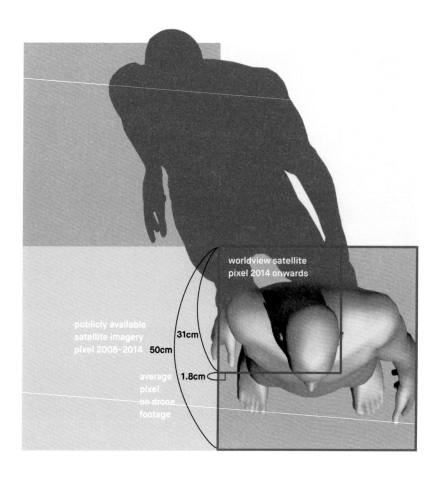

worldview satellite
pixel 2014 onwards

publicly available
satellite imagery
pixel 2008–2014 50cm

31cm

average
pixel
on drone
footage

1.8cm

The photographic modulor: pixel sizes
in relation to the dimensions of the
human body. FORENSIC ARCHITECTURE

Pakistan and worldwide; as such, there were very few images in public circulation. The most common way to investigate would have been satellite images. From their perspective, however, the hole in the roof was smaller than the area captured by a single pixel in the resolution to which publically available satellite images were degraded.

This resolution posed a digital version of the problem that had emerged with the silver salt particles in the negatives of the 1944 reconnaissance photographs of Auschwitz. In both cases, the hole indicated that the room under it was an execution chamber, and in both cases, such holes and the violence they evidenced were at or under the threshold of detectability. The point here is not to compare attempts to exterminate a whole people in gas chambers to a secret and largely illegal assassination war conducted in civilian areas, but to show that the forensic-architectural problem was analogous in the sense that it forced us to examine the relation between an architectural detail, the media in which it could be captured, a general policy of killing, and its acts of denial.

Unlike the randomly disturbed grains of analog photography, digital images, such as satellite images, are divided into a grid of equal square units, or pixels. This grid filters reality like a sieve or a fishing net. Objects larger than the grid are captured and retained. Smaller ones pass through and disappear. Objects close to the size of the pixel are in a special threshold condition: whether they are captured or not depends on the relative skill, or luck, of the fisherman and the fish.

Throughout recent decades, the resolution in which satellite images were made publically available gradually improved. In the 1970s, the first of the Landsat earth-observation satellites beamed back images of the earth at 60 meters per pixel. Small villages were swallowed in the single monochrome square. In the 1980s, the pixel size was reduced to 30-meter squares, then, at the turn of the 1990s, it was down to 20.[32] At that resolution, as architect Laura Kurgan has explained, human rights violations begin to be recognizable as environmental transformation: one can see, for example, the traces of mass graves in agricultural fields; however, buildings and neighborhoods are captured as an undifferentiated mass. At the turn of the millennium, individual buildings came to be differentiated at 2.5 meters per pixel, then a few years later, the publically available images sharpened further to 0.5 meters per pixel. However, this gradual process of the earth's coming into focus was then halted. The pixel resolution of contemporary, publically available satellite images is not only a product of optics, data storage, or bandwidth capacity, but of legal regulations that bear upon political and even geopolitical rationales. Throughout the height of the drone campaign and for the entire duration of our investigation, the resolution at which satellite images were made publically available was legally kept at 0.5 meters per pixel, with each pixel representing half a meter by half a meter of ground's surface — incidentally, also approximately, the same ground surface area captured by a silver halide grain in the analog aerial images debated in the Irving trial.

The reason for halting the process of improving the resolution of publically available satellite images was that at 0.5 meters, the pixel resolution corresponds to the dimensions of the human body — an area 0.5 meters by 0.5 meters is roughly the size of the human body as seen from above. As such, the pixel could be thought of as analogous to what Le Corbusier called a "modulor" — a system of proportions and measurements that relate to the human body.[33] The satellite images' modulor was not meant to help organize space, but rather to remove the human figure from representation. The human body was now drowned within the pixel resolution available to independent groups to analyze human rights violations.

The 0.5-meter resolution was selected as a limit for publically available

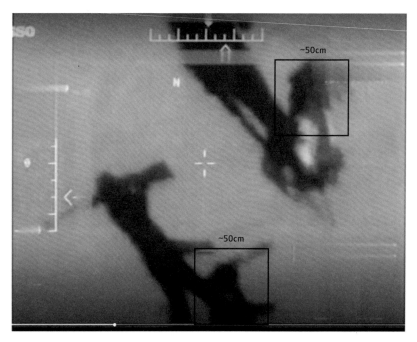

Leaked footage from Italian military drones flying in Iraq — originally published in December 2015 in *L'Espresso* — helped us estimate that the rough pixel resolution of these drone-mounted cameras is between 1 and 2 centimeters per pixel. The black squares on this image, marking the size of a single pixel in a satellite photograph at the time we undertook our investigation, contain 1,681 pixels in this image. *L'ESPRESSO*

images because it bypassed risks of privacy infringement when recording people in public spaces, much in the same way that Google Street View blurs the faces of people or car license plates. But the regulation also has a security rationale: important details of strategic sites get camouflaged at the 0.5-meter resolution, as are the consequences of violence and violations such as drone strikes on buildings.

In a further radicalization of the geopolitics of resolution, US satellite image providers make an exception to the 0.5-meter rule in Israel and the Palestinian territories it occupies. An amendment to the US Land Remote Sensing Policy Act of 1992, which established the permitted resolution of commercial US image satellites, dictates that these areas are shown only at a resolution of 2.5 meters (later effectively eased to 1.0 meter per pixel), a resolution at which a car is depicted as two pixels and a roof, another common target, is depicted by four. The screen thus placed over Israel's violation of Palestinian rights in the West Bank and Gaza contributed to Turkey's decision, after the Gaza Flotilla incident of May 2010, to send its own image satellite into space and make available 0.5-meter-per-pixel images of Palestine/Israel.[34] Eventually, in June 2014, the 0.5-meter limit was changed to 31 centimeters per pixel after an appeal from a commercial satellite company to the US Department of Commerce convinced them that a person could still not be recognized at this resolution—a change that, again, applied in all places but Israel.[35]

The resolution of satellite images also has direct, if inadvertent, consequences for our ability to investigate drone strikes. Although at a resolution of 0.5 meters (in use until the end of our investigation in early 2014) the general features of individual buildings can be identified, a hole in a roof—the signature of a drone strike, often no wider than 30 centimeters in diameter—would appear as nothing more than a slight color variation, a single darker pixel, perhaps.

UN bodies—primarily through the UN satellite analysis unit of UNO-SAT—tend to undertake investigations by studying before-and-after satellite images. Because satellite images render people invisible, the scale of analysis shifts to architecture or to the environment—to buildings and ruins or cities and landscapes. The analysis depends on what difference can be detected in a before-and-after image. But when examining sites known to have been struck by drones, no such difference is noticeable. This might give another meaning to the helplessness captured by the term "UN resolution."

US agencies are not limited to the satellite image resolution that the public is. The resolution of cameras on US spy satellites is much higher.

The satellites of the Pentagon's Keyhole program can see to a resolution of about 15 centimeters, or 6 inches, per pixel, but these are not available to the public or to human rights groups.[36] The United States can also use other platforms, such as airplanes and drones, to peer into the territory of the publically available pixel. The optical resolution of military drone cameras is still kept secret. Former operators have said that the images are sharp enough to identify individuals by their faces. Others have said that the resolution is not sharp enough to differentiate between children and adults and that spades could be mistaken for guns. The images and footage that have been made public recently seem to be in high resolution and in color, but examples of visual misidentification abound — in Gaza, medics loading gas canisters were attacked when the Israeli military mistook the canisters for missiles.[37]

The difference in resolution demonstrates the imbalance of power. While the human body is the scale to which drone optics are calibrated, it is the very thing that publically available satellite images are designed to mask.[38]

In contemporary conflicts, both the killing and its investigation are image-based practices. However, investigating drone strikes by analyzing satellite images inverts one of the foundational principles of state forensics as practiced since the nineteenth century, namely, that to resolve a crime, the investigator, the police, must be able to see and know more than the perpetrator, the criminal, to have better access to vision and to historical and comparative data. This principle led to the introduction of photography, chemistry, and fingerprinting to police work, notably by such pioneers as the Italian criminologist Cesare Lombroso, the Swiss forensic photographer Rudolphe A. Reiss, and the French police officer Alphonse Bertillon.[39] In our case, however, it is the killer who has had access to better optics, data, and information than the investigators.

This inversion is nested in another: in police work, the state investigates the crimes of individuals, but here, a state is the alleged criminal, undertaking both secret assassinations and their denial, and individuals and independent organizations undertake the investigations. The visual spectrum between the high resolution used for killing and the low resolution available for monitoring the killing is the space exploited by deniers. The practice of counterforensics at the heart of this book has to engage a condition of structural inequality in access to vision, signals, and knowledge, and to find ways to operate close to and under the threshold of detectability.

The threshold of detectability intersects with other important threshold conditions, both territorial and juridical. Targeted assassinations almost exclusively take place in particular kinds of place — frontier regions such as those of FATA, on the border region between Pakistan and Afghanistan, or in Northern Yemen, Somalia, and Gaza that are all, to a lesser or greater extent, outside the effective control of the states in which they exist.

Between June 2004 and 2014, FATA was the central focus for the drone campaign. It is an area governed under the Frontier Crimes Regulations (FCR), a vestige of British colonial rule that in 1901 rendered the region extraterritorial to the Raj — physically within its borders, but outside its full jurisdiction. In FATA, the juridical rule of law was replaced by regulations and executive rule. On the one hand, under this regime, the area benefited from limited local autonomy, but on the other, it was subjected to collective punishment if individuals or organizations were perceived to be threats to state security. Villages were destroyed, and mass exile and imprisonment were enforced without judicial oversight or the possibility of appeal. This extraterritorial condition was retained by Pakistan after independence in 1947, and although the regulations were continually revised, FATA is still considered exceptional in relation to the rest of the country. It is also outside the threshold of its civic responsibility: Pakistan's central government is still not obligated to provide infrastructure, such as schools or hospitals, for FATA's seven million residents. Child mortality and levels of illiteracy there are the highest in the country.

The maintenance of the region's extraterritorial status, now against the will of most of its inhabitants, has been essential in the pursuit of the drone campaign. People cannot be detained and brought to trial because, according to the Pentagon legal advisers, targeted assassinations can be permitted only if they are undertaken as imminent self-defense and where "a viable arrest opportunity" does not exist. The United States thus repeatedly has referred to FATA as "lawless" in order for violence to be legitimately imposed from the outside, and this without noting the role both it and Pakistan have played in imposing that very status. It is thus precisely the closing of juridical options that opened the door to targeted assassinations.[40]

The extraterritorialization of FATA also enabled a peculiar temporal inversion. According to US executive regulations, targeted assassinations cannot be justified as retributions for crimes that individuals have perpetrated in the past—this is the role of the judiciary and requires habeas corpus, the presentation of evidence, and a fair trial—but rather can be employed only in a predictive manner in order to stop "imminent attacks" that otherwise would be committed in the future. Gradually, the category of imminence has become elastic and its applicability has been pushed back in time, losing its sense of immediacy.[41]

Predictive forensics—the futurology of contemporary warfare—studies the future mathematically by using tools that most closely resemble those of risk management by financial or security companies and those employed in marketing.[42] The pattern analysis undertaken by the CIA in Pakistan and Yemen scans various bits of data about people's lives—for example, their movement along certain roads determined by the Pentagon to be "toxic," telephone calls to specific numbers, congregation in particular religious buildings—for patterns that might "correspond to a 'signature' of preidentified behavior that the United States links to militant activity."[43] Until 2015, when this process, referred to as "signature strikes," was officially discontinued, the CIA assassinated people who were determined by an algorithm to pose an "imminent risk," without their identities or names being known.

The legal extraterritorialization of FATA is enforced by an old-fashioned territorial siege. FATA is officially considered a "Prohibited Area" that nonresidents require special permission to enter. Pakistani military checkpoints established along the border of the region filter movement in and out of it. But it is not only suspected militants whose movement is interrupted. These military checkpoints, along with others established by the Taliban themselves, also disrupt the movement of journalists and human rights researchers, and informal regulations intercept the bringing in and taking out of electronic equipment, including mobile phones, cameras, and navigation equipment.

These checkpoints are thus part of a media siege, which in the early years of the campaign was largely successful—only a few photographs and eyewitness testimonies were made available outside of these regions. So while other conflicts, in Syria, Ukraine, and Palestine, for example, generated massive amounts of images and data, the ones in FATA, much like those in parts of Yemen and Somalia, remained in the shadows in both social and mainstream media. In the early days of the drone campaign, this fact helped Pakistani and US spokespersons deny that it ever existed and misleadingly claim that the casualties of drone strikes died instead in "bomb-making accidents."[44]

Thereafter, when the facts of the campaigns could no longer be refuted, the form of denial employed by US agencies took the form of the "Glomar Response," so named for the *Glomar Explorer*, a ship built by the CIA in the 1970s to recover a Soviet nuclear submarine that had sunk in a deep area of the Pacific Ocean and operated under a cover story that it was a marine geology research vessel. Under the terms of the Glomar Response, US agencies "neither confirm nor deny the existence or nonexistence" of such covert activities and of documents requested under freedom of information acts. Simply to say, "This is untrue" or "This did not happen" requires a plausible counternarrative. Glomarization, however, is a form of denial that aims to add no information whatsoever. Everybody knows, not least the people terrorized by airborne violence, that drones constantly hover over their cities, but Glomarization is a form of denial that enabled the continuation of the assassination campaign: it allowed the United States to avoid questions about the legitimacy of its preferred mode of killing and the Pakistani government to deflect protests over its collusion. Glomarization continued even after Obama publically acknowledged, in 2012, the existence of the covert drone campaign in Pakistan.

Glomarization is not only a rhetorical formulation, however; it is also based on a territorial blockade meant to make unavailable access to ground-level images and testimonies and on the fact that traces of the violence cannot be identified in the resolution of available satellite images. The resolution of satellite images themselves often can "neither confirm nor deny the existence or nonexistence" of holes in roofs that would otherwise constitute evidence of drone strikes.

Drone strikes can thus be understood not as a direct, linear relation between a drone, via a missile, and a target, but rather as a set of operations enabled by the production of thresholds — territorial, juridical, and visual. Juridical thresholds extraterritorialize entire territories, physical thresholds filter the movement of people in and out of regions, and photographic thresholds filter objects in and out of visibility.[45]

Pattern analysis can also be used as a counterforensic technique by investigative journalists and human rights groups seeking to unveil some aspects of state violence. In 2012, Forensic Architecture was asked by the BIJ to analyze patterns of CIA drone strikes in FATA/Pakistan. Our analysis sought to examine the relation between strikes on buildings and civilian casualties. The research was based on an extensive database compiled by the BIJ that logged in thousands of news reports, witness testimonies, and field research on drone strikes between 2004 and 2014.[46]

We trawled through the BIJ's archive, looking for and tabulating spatial information that had not been previously looked at by them. We entered each incident into a new database that had multiple categories and tags: space/time coordinates, target type — domestic, public, religious, and commercial buildings, outdoor gatherings, or vehicles — and the extent of death, injury, and structural destruction caused. An interactive cartographic platform then spatially visualized the relations between hundreds of strikes. Different patterns, relations, and trends emerged across this aggregate data, helping to reveal relations between a large multiplicity of separate incidents that otherwise had not been obvious. We could notice a distinct escalation in targeting buildings and an increase in civilian casualties immediately after the December 2009 suicide attack in the CIA's Camp Chapman, for example.

Our pattern analysis also demonstrated the way in which the Taliban's tactics evolved in reaction to US strike policy and adapted to the hunter algorithms behind the CIA's signature strikes, with the result that both hunter and prey coevolved. Accordingly, the Taliban shifted their pattern of movement in space.[47] Adapting to CIA targeting patterns was the reason the Taliban retreated into the cities.

As strikes shifted away from vehicles, the analysis showed that domestic buildings became the most frequent targets and that the number of civilian casualties consequently grew. In total, our analysis with the BIJ revealed homes were the target of 61 percent of all drone strikes in Pakistan, and it was in their homes (often misleadingly referred to by Western media as a "compounds") that most civilians were killed. The shift in the pattern of targeting was supported by the development and introduction of the new generation of missiles with improved capacity of penetrating walls and roofs.[48]

RIGHT: Casualty heat map of drone strikes in FATA/Pakistan, 2004–14. FORENSIC ARCHITECTURE WITH THE COLLABORATION OF SITU RESEARCH

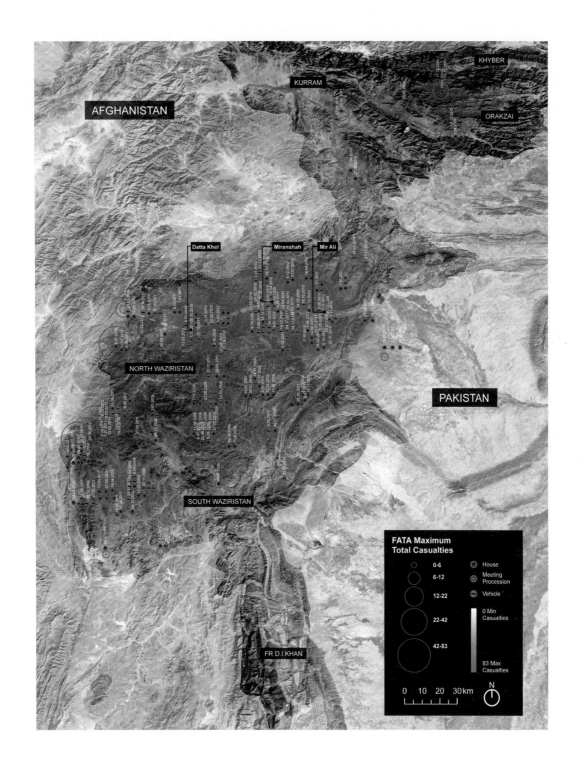

AFGHANISTAN

KHYBER

KURRAM

ORAKZAI

Datta Khel

Miranshah

Mir Ali

NORTH WAZIRISTAN

PAKISTAN

SOUTH WAZIRISTAN

FR D.I.KHAN

**FATA Maximum
Total Casualties**

0-6

6-12

12-22

22-42

42-83

House

Meeting
Procession

Vehicle

0 Min
Casualties

83 Max
Casualties

0 10 20 30km

N

Investigating a number of drone strikes, we sought to engage the testimonies of people who experienced drone strikes first-hand. I will recount only two such cases, each involving another form of testimony. The first involves analysis of video testimony shot in the aftermath of a drone strike by an unidentified person and smuggled out through the blockade that cordoned FATA off. The second involves using architectural modeling as a way to enhance the testimony of a survivor of a strike who managed to escape the region and return to Europe.

Both these testimonies added precious information where there was little else, but also had the potential to confront sovereign denial with the moral force of first-hand experience. They also had another aspect in common: both testimonies involved risk-taking by the people who spoke out. As such, they exemplified the power of *parrhesia*, a classical Greek term that Michel Foucault took to mean the courage to risk one's life in order to speak an unpopular truth. *Parrhesia* "demands the courage to speak the truth in spite of some danger. And in its extreme form, telling the truth takes place in the 'game' of life or death."[49]

The video testimony was recorded using a handheld camera, likely a mobile phone, in the aftermath of a March 30, 2012 drone strike in Miranshah, North Waziristan, FATA, one in which four people were reportedly killed. It was a rare piece of evidence, one of very few videos documenting a site destroyed by a drone strike to be made available outside of Waziristan, and it had to be physically smuggled out to be seen. NBC screened forty-three seconds from it. Amna Nawaz, NBC's Islamabad bureau chief, who obtained the video clip, explained how they got the video to their Islamabad offices. "In order to take this piece of video out, we actually had to take a couple of weeks to move the video from place to place until it was safely in the hands of somebody we knew can transmit it back to us."[50] When screened, the video showed a rather indistinct architectural ruin, confirming only its own destruction.

Photography theorist Ariella Azoulay urges us to study the circumstances by which images are produced, broadcast, viewed, and acted upon, as well as to follow the set of relations that the photograph establishes between the people photographing and the spaces and subjects photographed. In this case, such relations extended to those moving and smuggling the footage, those broadcasting it, those looking at it, and those, like us, modeling and helping to decode it.[51]

The aftermath of the March 30, 2012, drone strike in Miranshah, North Waziristan. The size of the dark area around the window opening suggests the videographer shot from some depth within the room. MSNBC, JUNE 29, 2012

The video clip had two distinct sequences, each shot in a different room. The first was shot out of an unfenestrated window opening on the third floor. Out of the window we could see the destroyed roof of a lower building, two stories high, located in a dense market street and surrounded by what seemed to be residential and commercial buildings.

The roof seemed badly damaged, likely because it was struck by several missiles. The video clip's second sequence showed the interior of a room in the damaged building bearing hundreds of blast marks on the walls. There was a distinct hole in the ceiling through which the missile entered and where sunlight now poured in. While the first room revealed something about the videographer, the second revealed something about the people killed in the blast.

In the first sequence, a large part of the image was masked by the window frame and the wall around it. This space around the window opening was rendered dark because the light meter was calibrated to the sunlit outside. However, it was not dead information. Its changing position and

A collage pieced together from individual frames extracted from the footage allowed us to identify distinct features of the building that would later help find the building in a satellite image of Miranshah. On the left, closest to the videographer, is a series of beams that fanned out in a radial pattern, and there is a distinctly visible higher building on the left side of the building near the bend in the road.

FORENSIC ARCHITECTURE WITH THE COLLABORATION OF SITU RESEARCH

proportion from one video still to the next helped us reconstruct the videographer's movements inside the room. The videographer moved from right to left and from as far as a meter away from the window to as close as a few centimeters from it, all the while panning to capture the full extent of the ruin outside, and this without ever crossing the window line. In this way, the videographer would have remained invisible to a person standing at street level outside and also to anyone looking from above.

Cameras record from both their ends: the objects, people, and spaces their lenses capture, as well as the position and movements of the invisible

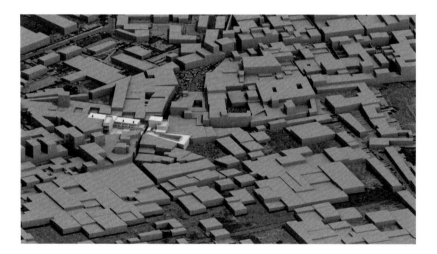

TOP: Comparing similar elements in the video and the satellite photograph, we were able to locate the targeted building within the city of Miranshah. BOTTOM: By analyzing video and satellite images of the scene and the shadows cast in them, we were able to build a computer model of the targeted building (in white) and the market area around it (in gray).

photographer. Blurs are important in revealing things about the photographer. Rushed and erratic camera movements might indicate the risk involved in taking some images. A blur is thus the way the photographer gets registered in an image. As such, looking at blurry images is like looking at a scene through a semitransparent glass in which the image of the photographer is superimposed over the thing being photographed.

Similarly, the concrete window opening captured in the image frame may have recorded the videographer's sense of danger and that the danger was perceived to come from outside. It might be that the videographer feared being seen filming by locals or by US drones overhead. Drones sometimes strike the same spot twice, killing first responders and people gathering in proximity in a process known as "double tap."[52]

The second room captured in the video clip was the one in which people were reportedly killed. The hole in the ceiling is where the missile entered the room. The wall was scattered with hundreds of small traces from the explosion. These were caused by the metal fragments that the blast propelled outward. We inspected the interior wall and marked each one of the traces of the blast. Each fragment hit the wall at a different angle, allowing us to reconstruct the location and height of the blast. That the missile was detonated in midair confirmed it was a delay-fuse missile, likely the "Romeo" Hellfire II AGM-114R mentioned above. After marking all the traces, we also noticed two distinctly shaped areas in which there weren't any traces. If there were people in the room, their bodies would have absorbed the fragments and stopped them from reaching the wall. It is thus possible that the blank spots were the "shadow" of the casualties. In this case, the wall functioned as a photographic film, with the people exposed to the blast recorded on the wall in a similar way in which a photographic negative is exposed to light. It is an analogous process to the one in which the bodies of residents of Pompeii were exposed to the ash layer of Vesuvius or the way in which in Hiroshima, the nuclear blast left a shadow of a man on the steps outside the Sumitomo Bank.

The interior walls in the room in the building in Miranshah thus functioned as recording devices. It was through a process of double photography — the video stills of the room were photographs of a photograph — that the human bodies destroyed by the drone strike, which otherwise disappeared in the pixels of satellite images, could be made present. These shadows connected a representation of dead bodies with that of a destroyed building.

The still frames representing the interior of the targeted building from the MSNBC footage. The interior footage allowed us to reconstruct the location of the blast within the room targeted. MSNBC, JUNE 29, 2012

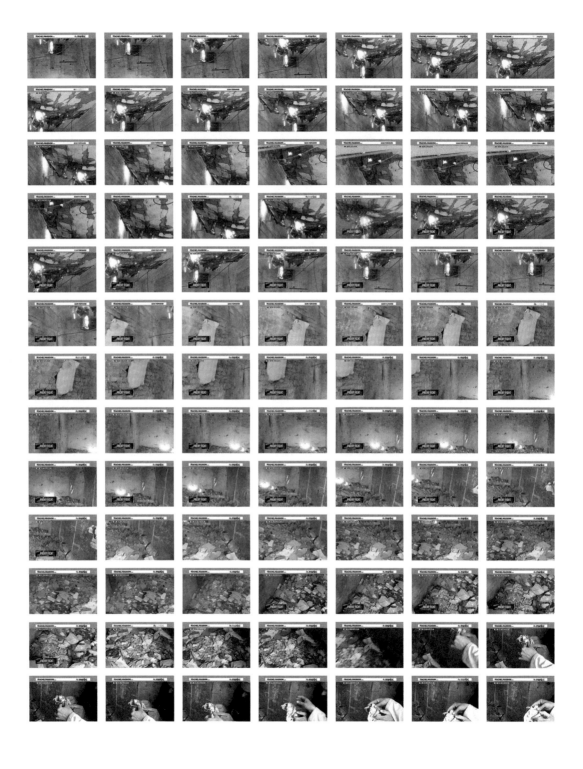

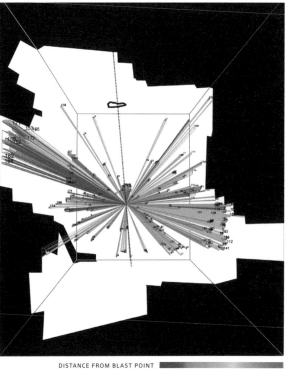

DISTANCE FROM BLAST POINT

LEFT: All the video still frames from the interior of the room combined into a single panoramic collage. The parts in black are those not caught on video. We marked all identifiable blast traces on the wall. RIGHT: A reconstruction of the trajectories of shrapnel and the location of the blast. The different colors indicate distance from the blast point. FORENSIC ARCHITECTURE

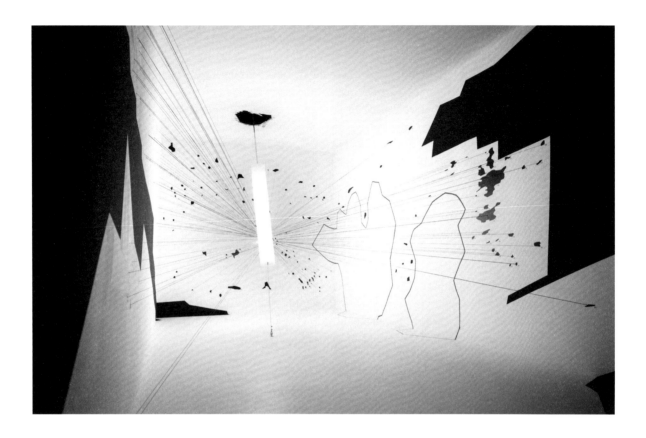

A full-scale reconstruction of the targeted room
in which the blast occurred, enabled by the occasion
of the 2016 Venice Biennale of Architecture. This
model allowed us to verify the blast point. Where the
distribution of fragments is of lower density, it is
likely that people absorbed them. The red lines mark
the likely places where people were hit. This room/
model is a spatial representation of video footage.
FORENSIC ARCHITECTURE; PHOTO: MATTHIAS BÖTTGER

THE ARCHITECTURE OF MEMORY

The second case dealt with another limit condition of testimony: a survivor's memory. Responding to a request from the European Center for Constitutional and Human Rights (ECCHR)—a German human rights group—we traveled to Düsseldorf in Germany to meet one of the few witnesses of a drone strike who had made her way back to Europe. She was a German woman who wanted to publicize the event she had witnessed, but who was also keen to remain anonymous. Several years earlier, she had moved to Pakistan with her husband and his brother. On October 4, 2010, she was at her home on the outskirts of the town of Mir Ali, North Waziristan, when it was struck by several missiles. The attack killed five people, some of them suspected terrorists. The witness returned to Germany, where she and her husband were subjected to long interrogations by the security services. A few months later, she started speaking publically, first to the human rights advocates and lawyers of ECCHR and later in the media. Her aim was to advocate against the continuation of drone strikes and the German intelligence agency's involvement in providing information that facilitated them and to communicate, through her personal story, the reality of living under drones. However, some of the details of the strike were obscured in her memory.

When delivering testimony, victims of extreme violence must recall and reconstruct the worst moments of their lives, moments when they were physically hurt or experienced, at close hand, the loss of loved ones. Victims might remember what happened before a traumatic incident or after it, but the closer one gets to the essence of a testimony, to the heart of the most violent incidents, the more elusive memory can become. Such testimonies are rarely straightforward records of events and cannot be interpreted

LEFT: The computer modeling of the site and event of the strike in Mir Ali on October 4, 2010, took one full day. RIGHT: The witness chooses objects to be located within the model of her house. FORENSIC ARCHITECTURE

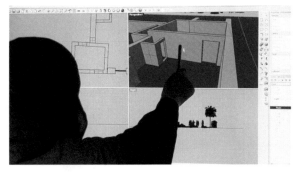 

only for what exists in them, but, significantly, for what is missing, distorted, or obscured. Such testimonies are often riddled with memory loss, resulting in lacunas, contradictions, and blackouts. It is this dimension of victim testimonies that led deniers of all sorts of cases of historical violence to denigrate them and to consider them wrong or biased and thus invalid. But these memory gaps are somewhat analogous to disruptions and blurring in the video images discussed above. What blurs and masks part of the evidence reveals something else. In their book *Testimony*, Shoshana Felman and Dori Laub explained that it is often in the failings and shortcomings of memory — in the silence, confusion, or outright error — that the trauma of the witness and hence the catastrophic character of the events they experienced are inscribed. Paradoxically, it is testimony's imperfections that bear witness to the fact of violence.[53]

Together with the witness from Mir Ali, we decided to try another route to memory. We would help our witness build a digital model of her house. She would build it as she remembered it and in as much detail as she could provide. We would not make any predeterminations regarding what is important to model, but furnish the model with all objects she could tell us about — doors, windows, rooms, furniture, utensils, and other objects — in as precise a way as possible. We would then try to position her point of view within this virtual environment, allowing her to walk through the spaces where the event took place. The presence of her lawyer, Andreas Schüller, from ECCHR, gave our witness confidence to speak. A German-speaking architect, Reiner Beelitz, digitally constructed the house as fast as our witness described it, employing the same software used by architects to present clients with a quick impression of an interior design.

The witness seemed empowered in directing the reconstruction process. Slowly, as she was sizing the rooms, locating the windows and doors, and

LEFT: The first location of the fan within the model of the house.
RIGHT: The second location of the fan in the model. FORENSIC ARCHITECTURE

placing mundane objects in this virtual environment, she started narrating fragments of life in this house and some of the aspects of the incident itself.

Here, the role of architecture was not that of material evidence. We had no access to the site, no ruins to study, and no photographs except a satellite image that showed nothing except the blurred contours of her house. Architecture, in this investigation, functioned as a mnemonic technique, a conduit to testimony. The model was a stage on which some of her memories could be accessed and performed.[54]

An important reference point in our work was the classic and medieval tradition of mnemonic techniques as told by Frances Yates in *The Art of Memory*. The ancient and lost art reserved a special place for architecture as a medium for establishing relations between memory, narrative, and destruction.[55] The technique, made famous by the rhetoricians and orators of antiquity such as Cicero and Quintilian, advised orators tasked with remembering long and complex speeches to commit the spatial arrangement of known buildings to their memory or to construct new ones mentally. Every room in these buildings was to be furnished with objects relating to the issues that the orator needed to bring up — a fountain, a dagger, a plant, a chair, or a bed. In delivering the speech, the orators would imagine themselves walking through the building, passing through corridors, traversing courtyards, opening and closing doors, encountering objects, and in this way recalling different issues and ideas. The same building could be used for different speeches. All that was necessary was to remove one set of objects and bring in new ones, then "walk" through the building again.[56]

WITNESS   Here was a big heavy iron door like on the other side. Correct. I would widen it a bit more. Yes, it is okay like this. Stop. I now remember. The door was over here and the window on this side. Can I see it from above?

LAWYER   Does this visualization help to remember what happened two and half years ago?

WITNESS   It helps me a lot. Without the plan I could have not remembered it like that.

The witness from Mir Ali and a female friend were in the house the evening it was struck. A group of men, some of them guests unfamiliar to the two friends, had just sat down to eat when a number of missiles landed. The witness's son, age two, was outside the compound walls with his father. "While we were eating," the witness recalled, "we heard a very loud bang. The house shook, and a lot of earth fell on us from the roof... everything was covered in thick smoke." She did not see the missiles land, but heard them and then screams, followed by the smell of burned flesh and smoke, and then she heard the weaker moans of the dying. She ran outside. Later, she returned to the house. In the courtyard, she saw "a big black hole where the missile hit. Everything was burned. There were pieces of cloth, and metal from the rocket." Her brother-in-law was killed, along with at least four others.

Elements modeled in the reconstruction that were significant to the investigation included toys and a child's walker that we located, according to her testimony, in the open courtyard. These, when seen from above, should have indicated to the drone operator that a small child, the witness's son, was in the premises when it was attacked. There was also, significantly, a fan. During the modeling process, the witness returned to it again and again. She seemed uneasy about it, repeatedly adjusting its location. Initially, she placed it as a ceiling-mounted ventilator. Later, she asked to place it as a freestanding fan inside the room. A few moments later, she again shifted its location, taking it outside and placing it within the small courtyard for the women. When "walking" through the model in the digital aftermath of the strike, she mentioned that she had found human flesh on the fan's blades. Here, architecture and memory got entangled in a way that cannot be easily divided into subject and object, testimony and evidence, matter and memory.

WITNESS   And the fan is still missing. Yes, in the courtyard, at this position here.
LAWYER   A standing ventilator?
WITNESS   Yes, standing and with a round shape…I found burned pieces of flesh and
           hair in the fan.

The interior courtyard with the fan and the child walker, modeled and rendered according to the description of the witness.
FORENSIC ARCHITECTURE

PART ONE   What Is Forensic Architecture?

FORENSIC ARCHITECTS deal with "the application of architectural facts to legal problems," as one practitioner puts it.[1] These facts, according to a firm providing such services, are the "cause and origin of architectural defects such as construction, windows, wall and roofing failures; floor problems; accessibility issues and architectural design errors."[2] The legal context is most often an insurance dispute, for which forensic architects provide reports or testimony under oath.[3] There were building surveyors for almost as long as there were builders, but according to Dale Paegelow, a forensic architect who in 2001 self-published something of an introduction to the practice, the term "forensic architecture" emerged only in the early 1980s.[4] It is hard to verify this claim or information regarding the number of practitioners who refer to themselves as "forensic architects," because there are no professional registration bodies, no courses in the subject, and there is no official accreditation. However, judging by the number of corporate firms that have recently started advertising forensic services, their numbers seem to be growing, something that might indicate the expanded role of insurance in the actuarial and litigational culture of the contemporary building industry. Structural and infrastructural analysis are also key to risk analysis in its evaluation of damage yet to come — "low-probability, high-impact disasters" — caused by the forces of man, nature, or, increasingly, their combination.[5]

Because forensic architects are the students of architectural failure and because their service is often mobilized on behalf of clients and against designers, they are not particularly popular in architectural circles. The practice occupies a marginal place in the professional landscape and is ignored by virtually all architecture schools worldwide. For architects, building surveying might seem too ordinary and unimaginative a practice, but surveyors understand a fundamental thing about buildings often lost on architects: buildings are not static entities. Rather, they continually undergo dynamic transformations. These transformations are not aberrations of an ideal state embodied by the hard lines of a drawing, but are inherent to all built structures. Each of the different materials of which a building is composed—steel, plaster, stone, glass, concrete, wood, and, increasingly, plastic and silicon—constantly permeate, move, and adjust in response to environmental forces. Shifts in weight distribution—indicative of changes in the way a building is used—affect the levels of floors and beams. Computers and servers generate excess heat that affects ceiling panels, bending them out of their clips or screws.

Questions regarding the structure—often understood as "the bones" of a building—are not the only ones that concern forensic architects. The performance of ever more intricate mechanical, electronic, or infrastructural systems is increasingly subject to the study of flows and blockages. Records of the atmosphere's interaction with buildings are deposited in layers of dust and soot on their façades, and their microstratigraphy can provide a rich archaeological resource for a study of urban air, containing information regarding changing levels of CO_2, lead, or toxins in the atmosphere—a vestige of a history of industrialization, transportation, and attempts at regulating them.[6] Some of a building's transformations occur well below the threshold of human perception and along extended time scales: it takes years for an air bubble trapped between a wall and a fast-drying paint to make its way up the building facade. Its expansion and contraction, the path and the speed of its crawl, indexes year-to-year changes in temperature and humidity, changes in the climate and efforts to regulate it.

Building surveyors might not always, or not yet, be so tuned to the sentient materiality—indeed, the hyperesthesia—of buildings. Still, they do understand decay as a process of form making that shapes the building beyond the control of the architect and often despite it. If material deformations are a building's response to changing environmental force fields, then, inversely, the formal mutations a building undergoes are processes of recording: *deformations* as matter *in formation* are also *information*. From this perspective, buildings are not only objects to be repaired, restored, and lived in, but also sensors of the environment outside themselves (and this before and regardless of the digital computerized sensors of smart buildings that might be placed within them).

Every material object can be read as a sensor, but buildings might be among the best sensors of societal and political change. There are several reasons: buildings are immobile, anchored in space; they are in close and constant interaction with humans; they are exposed both to the elements outside them and to an artificially controlled climate within. And this besides embodying, of course, the political, social, strategic, and financial rationalities that went into their conception.

Architecture and the built environment thus could be said to function as media, not because photographs of buildings might circulate in the public domain, but because they are both storage and inscription devices that perform variations on the three basic operations that define media: they sense or *prehend* their environment, they hold this information in their formal mutations, and they can later *diffuse* and externalize effects latent in their form.[7]

However, the built environment is not only a passive sensor of environmental and political change. It interacts with and affects the very processes it records. For one example, buildings record the climate but the energy they consume is also among the biggest contributors to climate change.

Buildings and cities, some geologists lately have suggested, have added the most recent layer to stratigraphy that makes the rock record of the earth. Spread the material that composes them evenly across the dry surface of the earth, and it would pile almost a meter high. When seismic events take place, the human-made crust of the top surface might crack like all the other layers. Moving through the deep surface of the earth, supersonic cracks tear through not only rock but also the thickness of the atmosphere as if it were a solid medium. Geologists depend on earthquakes to reveal hidden layers of rock. A structural crack reveals information about the way a building was assembled, otherwise buried under stucco or cladding. Cracks are material events that emerge as the result of force contradictions. They progress along paths of least resistance, exploiting and tearing through different material substances where the cohesive forces of aggregate matter are at their weakest. Each crack is a unique result of a specific disposition of a force field and material irregularities on the micro level. Cracks can move slowly, linger for years in a state of potentiality, or accelerate and tear a building apart when force contradictions can no longer be absorbed. Leonardo Da Vinci filled his notebooks with the studies of cracks. In giving practical advice to builders, he mapped the conditions that produced them — an interaction between topography, the rock on which the building rests, its orientation to the sun, the materials used, the construction process, and errors in its construction. It is cracks rather than buildings that are the most precise records of their environment and its changes. Elsewhere, he recommended staring at cracks for training the imagination.[8]

In considering buildings as historical documents, forensic architecture has a claim to the history of architecture, especially at a time when the field has largely disavowed the materiality of buildings in favor of the history of architectural practitioners and the documents that they leave behind.[9] It can also potentially extend architecture's historiographical methods, because it gives accounts of the history of buildings as material things beyond the history of their human conception with a biography that is beyond that of an architect.[10] What forensic architects call "the structural history" of a building includes terms such as "environmental root causes," "architectural pathologies," "crises," "building failures," and "transformative structural events" that almost comically connect the material history of buildings with the conceptual terms of "historical materialism."

It is in this way that forensic architecture is able to invert phenomenology's categories of perception and experience: it is not concerned with how we might experience a building, but rather, fundamentally, with how a building might experience its users, how it might sense the way they move and act within and around it. This is not to make an anthropomorphic point: buildings sense not in a human, but rather in a building sort of way. The same principle, as I will later show, can also be extended to built environments and larger territories across the dry surface of the earth. They also act as political sensors to be read.

Forensic architects employ buildings as instruments of historical measure, but reading environmental, historical, and political processes from built form is never straightforward. What could be learned from the processes of degradation or from the traces of violence is partial and murky. If they are to be considered as sensors, buildings should be understood as chaotic, nonlinear ones, with inscription being weak and the reading process always indeterminate. The dynamic transformation of their composite materials, which sometimes perfectly align, most often not, is not linear and therefore cannot translate environmental forces into material transformations in the same fashion that quicksilver in thermostats, for example, translates temperature into volume. Buildings register some forces and erase others, and any attempt at interpretation must acknowledge the limits of material registration and requires careful reading against other data. To read buildings as sensors, we need other sensors — optical, chemical, and photographic — and these are themselves conditioned in all sorts of other ways.

As a historical method, forensic architecture, as currently practiced, is limited in other ways, too. The causal threads that building surveyors currently take into account for the purpose of insurance cases, for example, are extremely short and close at hand. When surveyors study cracks or other failures in the structural history of buildings, they interpret their findings in relation to a narrowly circumscribed set of structural conditions in which material deformations are traced back only to the most proximate of physical causes, leaving out other causal relations.

CRACKS: LINES OF LEAST RESISTANCE

On April 23, 2013, cracks appeared in the floors and walls of a building used by the Rana Plaza factory, a garment industry "sweatshop" located in the deregulated Export Processing Zone (EPZ) of Dhaka, Bangladesh. Municipal building surveyors came to inspect. They photographed and marked the cracks with thick felt-tip lines and recommended the factory's closure. A crack is merely the potential for something to occur. It might linger for years or expand suddenly and tear a building apart. The Rana Plaza factory's owners, hard pressed to deliver goods cheaply to Western labels on contract, assessed the risk of collapse in relation to the risks of delay on contractual obligations. The management, located off site, ordered the workers in. At 9:00 a.m., an hour after the start of work, the cracks expanded, cut through the building, and brought it down. More than 1,127 workers, mostly women, died and a further 2,500 were injured. It was the deadliest accidental structural collapse in history.

The legal process dealing with the collapse involved building surveyors both as witnesses and among the accused. But the trial engaged only the construction quality of the building, the thickness of reinforcing bars in the concrete columns, the floors illegally added, and the loads of the industrial machinery that the building was never designed or given permits to hold. However, the collapse also exposed a form of economic violence. Dhaka-based architect Sujaul Khan explained that it was created by "a combination of two failures: the failure of the construction of the building" and a political failure to protect workers from exploitation. The trial addressed only the first of these. Left out of the trial were the factory owners, who through a tangle of subcontracting chains to multinational corporations, had brought prices down and productivity up through deregulated labor conditions that helped feed an endless appetite for cheap fashion.[11]

In 2008, cracks started to appear in homes, public buildings, and streets in Silwan, a Palestinian neighborhood located next to the Old City of Jerusalem. In 2009, the floor of a UN girls school collapsed; in 2010, cracks appeared in the main street; and in 2011, serious damage was inflicted to the ground near Ain-Silwan Mosque. Shortly beforehand, a Jewish settler association called El-Ad had started the illegal excavation of tunnels through parts of an Iron Age site it believed to be the biblical "City of David," claiming its subsoil to be a holy site and those surface dwellers above it "squatters" to be displaced. This excavation, undertaken beneath the Palestinian homes without the consent and regardless of the protests of their owners, was echoed above ground, with El-Ad supporting settlers seizing or fraudulently buying,

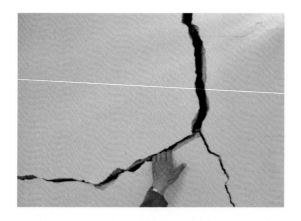
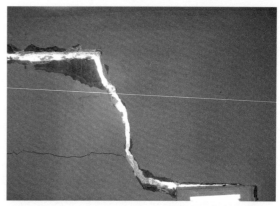

inhabiting, and fortifying residential buildings throughout the neighborhood. What started as illegal excavation turned into a project funded and recognized by the Israeli Antiquities Authority and the municipality of Jerusalem.

The tunneling displaced layers of Muslim archaeology deemed irrelevant by the diggers. It also removed layers of aggregate earth that normally would have absorbed vibrations underneath building foundations. Small seismic cracks that might begin in the limestone bedrock could now shoot up though archaeological strata to the surface, splitting the old, battered asphalt of roadways never maintained by the municipality. The cracks continued moving through the neighborhood's buildings, appearing and disappearing as they cut through different material elements. One crack might enter a building's foundation, crawl up a concrete column, moving along paths of least resistance, finding uneven or imperfect parts of the concrete casting, perhaps the place where a forty-year-old cigarette butt might have been thrown into the cement mix during the process of construction.

In 2008, a case was presented in the Jerusalem District Court and later in the Israeli High Court. Photographs of the cracks were presented. The historical and political context of the ongoing occupation of Palestine, above and below the surface, was mentioned, but never heard. After ordering a short suspension of the excavation, the High Court rejected the residents' petition, accepting the state's claim that the cracks were unrelated to the excavation, but likely the result of "poor and illegal construction" (without permits, there is hardly any "legal" construction possible) and authorized the continuation of the subterranean colonization.[12] On a recent visit to the site, Jerusalem's major said: "When you stand in the City of David we see layer after layer of foreign occupation, and when we reach the bedrock — there we find the Jewish layer. After the heads of states visit here there would be no doubt who are the true owners of this city."[13]

LEFT: Cracks in a house in Silwan. RIGHT: Cracks in a house in Silwan, East Jerusalem. This photograph was submitted to the Jerusalem district court in 2008 and later to the High Court of Justice. LEFT: GADI DAGON; RIGHT: SILWANIC.NET

CONFLICT SURVEYORS

The challenge of this book is to demonstrate the ways in which forensic architecture can exit the specialized framework of insurance disputes and extend the lines of causality originating from architectural failure.[14] One of the most important contexts in which an expansion of the terms of forensic architecture is relevant and urgent is that of armed conflict. Because most warfare now takes place in urban environments, homes and neighborhoods bear the consequences. Buildings can thus become the medium upon which traces of fighting are left and from which incidents can be reconstructed.

An explosion causes a rapid release of energy in several forms: sound, heat, and shock waves. Highly compressed particles of air propagate radially outward from the explosive source at supersonic velocities. Walls bend inward and break, initiating a progressive collapse. Air rushes in to fill the vacuum, carrying high-velocity lethal debris and flying bits of glass.[15] Most people dying in contemporary conflicts die in buildings, primarily in homes.[16] When the dust settles, the way it has settled can become evidence.

But the built environment cannot merely be considered as the location of conflict or its incidental, collateral damage. Rather, urban and environmental destruction is often the very target of violence. The transformation of the environment, buildings, and infrastructure is a means of exercising control, facilitating displacement, or offering resistance. Architectural analysis can provide an alternative pathology of contemporary conflict because it enables a different perspective on the context and conduct of armed conflicts.

Cities are composite assemblies of structures, infrastructure, and technologies, of social and political structures, with some plant and animal life, as well. These elements are in continuous interaction, sometimes in conflict or competition with each other. Warfare in urban environments is equally complex. It is not always manifested as a clash between two armies in a built-up area, but as a set of asymmetrical and diffuse encounters between large multiplicities of groups — militaries and guerilla forces, often different and rivaling, contract security providers, NGOs, and media organizations — in an environment that is largely civilian and with repercussions that are immediately political.

The urban environment is highly sentient in both material, analogue, and digital terms. It is a dense media environment saturated by optical and other sensors' photographs, noise, meteorology and pollution detectors, security cameras, fixed-orbit and image satellites, and smart phones. A conflict involves thousands, sometimes tens of thousands, of people entering into an unfamiliar environment that is also home to hundreds of thousands, sometimes millions of people. When this takes place, all elements of the city start recording, each in its own way. Buildings record vibrations and the force of impacts. Plants record—crushed fields around a city's agricultural outskirts register the movement of military vehicles on them when they stop photosynthesizing, a signal that is captured by remote sensors orbiting above and beamed back to earth. Air-quality sensors pick up increases in traffic as tanks roll in or refugees escape. People remember—in processes that, as I have already shown, are often complex and not straightforward—and increasingly use their camera phones to record the events around them, uploading images, sound, and video online. Each of these sensors is indeterminate, and patient investigative labor has to be invested in reading anything from them and then later also in cross-referencing and pulling the data together.

In this context, the work of forensic architects might seek to adopt the imaginary gaze of a future archaeologist looking back at the present. The archaeology of the present is not only physical, but requires all sorts of digital sensors. As in archaeology, rarely are single buildings significant in themselves. They are rather entry points through which one must navigate, connecting and composing sets of relations between different structures, infrastructures, objects, environments, actors, and incidents. "Evidence assemblages" must necessarily establish relations between, say, digital photographs, material ruins, remains of ammunition, and human testimony.

The "architecture" in "forensic architecture" thus means several distinct things: architecture is alternately the object of investigation, the method of research, and the mode of presentation. The first is the most obvious: the bruised materiality of buildings is at the focus of our investigations. Architecture in this context is what lawyers call the "primary evidence." But in the forensic context, architecture can also be a mode of research, the means of locating disparate bits of evidence and data and composing the relations between them in space. In this context, architecture is considered as "secondary," or "illustrative evidence." Though forensics is generally understood as a shift away from the ambiguity of testimony toward material evidence, forensic architecture, as we have seen in the Introduction, can help create a synthesis between testimony and evidence. The architectural models we construct, often made together with witnesses or victims of violence, help people recall incidents obscured by the experience of extreme violence and trauma. Architecture in this context becomes a mnemonic device. Architecture can also be useful as a mode of presentation: architectural models and animations, even if of complex events, are usually intuitively understood by both legal professional and the general public.

If the figure of the detective was nineteenth-century literature's response to the conception of the modern metropolis as a crime scene, the building surveyor might be the indispensable figure to address the prevalent condition of urban life as urban conflict. If understanding the environmental logic of contemporary conflict requires a building surveyor, however, it must be a building surveyor of a different kind: the survey can no longer be immediate and haptic; the trained surveyor's eye and the notepads on which observations are recorded must be complemented by media, data, and remote sensing technologies, and the lines of causation must splinter into causal fields that extend to politics, the environment, economy, and law.

Staro Sajmište (the Old Fairgrounds), on the outskirts of Belgrade, was inaugurated in 1938 as the site of an international exhibition. A series of pavilions — each representing a state or a company — was built around a central tower. At the end of 1941, following the German occupation of the kingdom of Yugoslavia, the fairgrounds reopened as the Semlin concentration camp, where both Jews and Romas were detained and murdered, the former in the first systematic use of gas vans. The site later became an internment camp for Communists, partisans, Chetniks, and other "enemies of the state." The logic of visibility that dictated the layout of the exhibition site also suited the panoptic regime of the camp. No major structural transformation was necessary, except for a high fence that was erected around the compound. After the war, the remaining structures of the Sajmište complex became the home of several generations of people and included artists' studios, workshops, and small industries. The fence around the former camp area was taken down. Some of the abandoned structures were occupied by a Roma community that included survivors of the Nazi persecution and their decedents. Since the war, Belgrade's urban expansion has placed Staro Sajmište at the heart of the city as a kind of extraterritorial island in which alternative culture could flourish.

The Semlin camp within the fairground structure, Belgrade, RAF, 1944. The tower is at the center and the pavilions all around. Bomb craters — the result of the allied bombing of Belgrade — can be seen within and around the camp.
IMAGE COURTESY OF JOVAN BYFORD

Recently, another transformation of the site was announced: its planned conversion into a Holocaust memorial center and a museum. One of the reasons was that as a candidate country for admission to the European Union (EU), Serbia was required, among other things, to abide by the Stockholm Declaration, which demands "the adequate commemoration of the Holocaust sites on its territory." The impending transformation would turn the site back into an exhibition ground, and the fence would have to be erected once more, now to protect the museum. Disturbingly, these plans necessitated the displacement of local communities including, perversely, the Roma people who were themselves victims of the Nazis. The first evictions began in the summer of 2013. It is an unacceptable contradiction, we thought, to see a Holocaust memorial built on forcefully cleared ground. Forensic Architecture's investigation of the site was part of an attempt to help the residents protect their homes in the belief that commemoration does not necessarily contradict ongoing inhabitation.

In the spring of 2012, in an investigation coordinated by Susan Schuppli, Forensic Architecture collaborated with forensic archaeologist Caroline Sturdy Colls and the Belgrade-based Monument Group in undertaking a study of the remnants of the site, above and below ground. Sturdy Colls, in previous years, had developed a method of "noninvasive" archaeology involving the use of remote sensing and ground-penetrating radar (GPR), an instrument that transmits pulses into the ground to a depth of up to fifteen meters to detect minute differences in densities. In the fuzzy three-dimensional model of the subsoil she produces, one can identify irregularities in soil structure indicating buried objects and voids. Subterranean objects do not have

Staro Sajmište, extent of the area surveyed, 2012. 3D laser scan data. The brown/yellow parts of the photographic point cloud are the result of the scan. The rectangular surfaces in blue are GPR scans of the subsoil. The features and areas captured are: 1. Central Tower (incl. areas A, B); 2. Italian Pavilion; 3. Spasic Pavilion; 4. Hungarian Pavilion; 5. German Pavilion (incl. Areas C, E, I).
FORENSIC ARCHITECTURE, SCANLAB, AND CAROLINE STURDY COLLS

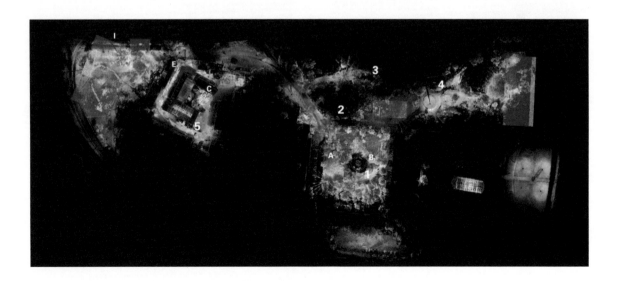

sharp, clear borders. They are made visible only as a gradual increase in the density of the medium of the earth. Their identification often depends on probabilities and interpretation. Objects can be confirmed only when excavated, cleared of their excessive earth, and their borders reestablished, but much information is lost. This is the reason that Colls's remote sensing archaeology has been used in examining Nazi concentration camps in Poland, where rabbinical authorities forbid material exhumations.

The survey included also work with ScanLAB, a London-based laser-scanning practice that recorded the entire site aboveground. When a laser beam hits an object, it returns the signal to record the location of a point. A point cloud is a spatially distributed group of coordinate points that produce a photographic space within which one can navigate virtually.

The aboveground and underground scanning resulted in an archaeological report that presented the site as a long process of ongoing transformations, encapsulating all its periods of use, structural additions, and alterations without privilege. The constant transformations, deformations, restorations, and conversions captured the unique history of the site.

The report confirmed a counterintuitive fact: Staro Sajmište stands today thanks to its ongoing inhabitation, which has sustained it for the past sixty years.

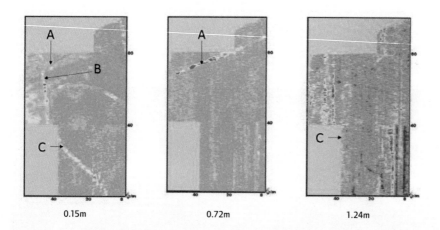

0.15m   0.72m   1.24m

Survey Area I. A GPR survey undertaken in search of mass graves (none were identified). Feature A is likely a water pipe from the era of the camp. Feature B is a path bisecting the survey area. Feature C, is likely a back-filled ditch, but its purpose is unclear. Colls explained that its form and depth are also consistent with buried structures of much earlier periods, such as a tumulus, or a Neolithic round barrow—a mound of earth and stones raised over graves—specimens of which are known to exist in the region. This feature, if indeed correctly identified, predated all other periods and complicated the history of the site.
FORENSIC ARCHITECTURE, CAROLINE STURDY COLLS

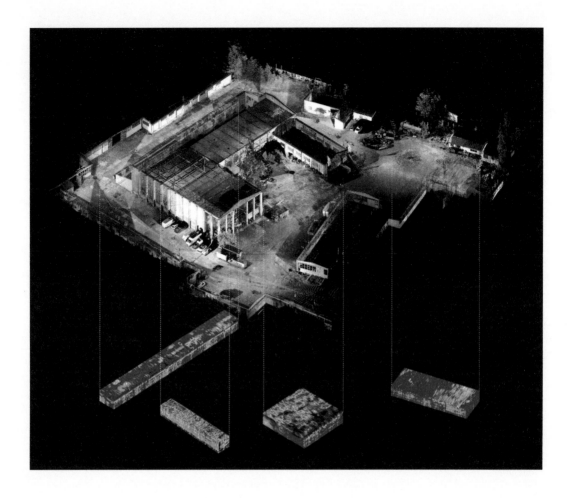

German Pavilion, 2012. Vertical section through 3D laser scan and GPR data. The photographic point cloud is the result of the scan. The rectangular surfaces in blue are GPR scans of the subsoil. The GPR survey established the presence of two buried structures from the camp period, now in-filled, as well as the sewage system on the bottom right. Sewage is important because following it allows us to connect contemporaneous structures. FORENSIC ARCHITECTURE, SCANLAB, CAROLINE STURDY COLLS

As Sturdy Colls put it: "the people who have lived in these buildings have played a role in preserving them. Many of these buildings wouldn't be here if people hadn't lived in them." On October 5, 2013, we convened a public forum to present the archaeological report inside one of Staro Sajmište's most infamous structures — the former structure that at the time of the fair was the German pavilion and that during World War II had served as accommodation for the camp's inmates. In this context, we also introduced a proposal titled "Living Death Camps" in which rather than evict the people living and working in Staro Sajmište, commemoration would be best served by supporting the community and its material necessities of ongoing life.[17]

This book records the work of the research agency known as Forensic Architecture. Although the name refers to the work of building surveyors, our agency is composed instead of an interdisciplinary team of architects, filmmakers, artists, scientists, and lawyers. Our products are evidence files in the form of building surveys, physical or digital models, animations, video and maps of various forms. When we work in a legal context, it is often for prosecutors in international law or human rights cases, but our work is not limited to the legal domain—we also produce evidence for citizen-organized truth commissions and tribunals and human rights and environmental protection agencies. Our investigations seek to extend beyond the procedural limitation of each of the forums in which we are asked to present evidence. We try to present incidents in their historical and political contexts—to reconstruct around them the world that made them possible. A full account of our investigations is on our website. Summaries of a few of them have been reproduced as short texts here.[18]

We use the term "forensics," but our work actually seeks to invert forensics as currently practiced and return the forensic gaze, otherwise the mode by which state agencies, such as the police or the secret services, survey the people they seek to put under control. We use forensic architecture to monitor state agencies (and sometimes corporations), challenge their claims and, as much as possible, their near monopoly on information in war. The inversion of the forensic gaze is captured in a neologism that Thomas Keenan, following Allan Sekula, called "counterforensics."[19] The state has monopolized both killing and identification; hence, counterforensics turns the state's own means against the violence it commits. While forensics is a state tool, counterforensics, as we practice it, is a civil practice that aims to interrogate the built environment to uncover political violence undertaken by states. The call to "take over the means of production" means for us to take over the means of evidence production. Here, forensics is not only the technical, neutral domain of expert specialists, nor is it the application of empirical science within a well-established court system and its protocols, but instead an engaged civil practice that seeks to articulate public claims using architecture.

Turning forensics against the state is essential because of the intertwined nature of state violence, which, as previously mentioned, is both violence against people and things and also against the evidence that violence has taken place at all. It is important to confront secrecy and denial not only for the sake of historical truth, a reckoning with the deeds in the past, but because they give legitimacy to state violence and are the conditions that enable its ongoing perpetration.

To salvage the word "forensics" and wrest it from the grip of state agencies and bureaucratic processes, we found an important operative concept in *forensis*, Latin for "pertaining to the forum" and the origin of the term "forensics." When the Roman orators of the first and second centuries — Quintilian and Cicero, for example — used the term, they referred to more than just the legal sphere.[20] The forum was a chaotic and multidimensional domain of economy, circulation, politics, and judgment in which both people and things participated and were presented. Small things, such as coins or daggers, could be physically displayed, but things abstract, far away, or too large, such as rivers, territories, wars, towns, famines, or empires, had to be made vivid by the power of representation or aural demonstration — by what Quintilian referred to with the rhetorical trope of "prosopopoeia" — the attribution of a voice to inanimate things.[21] In discussing "giving a voice to things to which nature has not given a voice," he wrote of the power of prosopopoeia not only as having the power to "evoke the dead, as forensic pathologists still do in courts today, but also as "giving voices to cities and states," something that is directly relevant to the practice of forensic architecture.[22] Conviction, he believed, requires not so much the objective weighing of facts as the placing of an invisible reality before the public's eyes — something achieved by what he called *energia*, "vigor of style" — a manner of presentation "in which the truth requires not merely to be told, but to a certain extent obtruded."[23] Today, contemporary modes of prosopopoeia and energia animate material objects by converting them into data or images and placing them within a narrative. Despite its origins in the imperial context of Rome, we found in *forensis* a productive category that helped us define our practice as a mode of public address and a means of articulating political claims using evidence grounded in the built world — which is most of the world, by now.

The problem in the history of forensics as a term and as a practice is that throughout the process of its modernization, it followed a trajectory of linguistic telescoping. The forum for its use gradually started referring exclusively to the courts of law and "forensics" to the use of science, primarily medical science, in them. The critical dimension of *forensis* — its public, political element — was lost in the process. Forensics has instead become the art of the police. Indeed, the modern history of forensics is the history of the techniques by which state agencies monitor, survey, and govern their populations, enforce order, and regulate deviations. Its spectrum extends from the nineteenth-century pseudosciences of phrenology, through the biometrics of fingerprints, Alphonse Bertillon's type police, and the colonial archives, to the image surveillance, digital eavesdropping, and pattern analysis of the present moment. It is in this way that forensics embodies what Allen Feldman has called the "police concept of history."[24]

Forensics has three sites of operation, namely, the *field*, the *laboratory* (in our case, it would be the *studio*), and the *forum*. The field is the site of investigation. It is the place where violence takes place and where traces are left. The lab is where material is processed and composed into evidence, and the forum is where it is presented.

Sometimes we must follow these spatial, institutional, and epistemic designations, namely, collect evidence in the field, process it in our studio, and present it in institutions of bureaucratic justice such as international and national courts and tribunals or the UN. Civil practice can of course also be performed in state and intrastate institutions, but in practicing civil forms of *forensis*, we cannot always rely on such forums. None of these forums is universally accessible—all are conditioned by institutional, legal, political, and geopolitical considerations. We can thus not limit the presentation of our evidence to any single context, but must seek to migrate it between several different forums. At other times, we must search for alternative, informal forums. Tactical and operative, they can take place in the field and on the street. At yet other times, when the necessary forums do not exist, we must conceive, assemble, or construct new ones. (See Part 3, "Ground Truths.") In the latter case, we have used the literal meaning of the term "architecture" in "forensic architecture" — we have designed and built places of assembly where there were none. The stereoscopy of forensic architecture has in this case simultaneously looked backward and forward—to debate events in the past, it assembled forums in which this can happen.

The general aim, whether we can yet achieve it or not, is to erode the differences between the domains of field, lab, and forum. In the field, rather than evidence being assembled by professional human rights workers traveling to examine what has occurred on the ground, there is now a multitude of independently generated and processed evidence, such as filmed and written testimonies posted on blogs or social media websites. This material is produced on the terms of those experiencing violence. The field is also not a neutral, abstract grid on which traces of a crime can be plotted out, but is dynamic and elastic, a space that is shaped by conflict and violence and that also shapes the conflict that takes place in the forum.

The laboratory itself gets diffused when stages of investigative work — the exposure, documentation, collation, validation, and analysis of evidence, using satellite images or video analysis — is crowd-sourced. In this context, the classic terms of verification, expertise, provenance, and the chain of custody are replaced by the multiple checks on truth and accuracy provided by the crowd. Such forums also allow us to develop our open-source crowd-sourcing software, PATTRN, to support such developments. (See pp. 116–17.)

Finally, forums are no longer confined to arenas such as buildings, but become increasingly diffused across a wide spectrum of channels and media forms. We share the techniques we develop, publically on our website and in workshops with activists. Exhibitions in cultural, architectural, or art institutions allow us to present our work in its historical and theoretical context and to generate debate around these issues.

Forensic speech is traditionally undertaken as a relation between three elements: an object or a building "made to speak," an expert who functions as the translator from the language of objects to that of people, and the forum or assembly in which such claims can be made. To refute a forensic statement, it is necessary to dismantle this triangle of articulation, which means to demonstrate that the object is inauthentic, that the interpreter is biased, or that the translation is unfaithful.[25] But the relations between these component parts have themselves become complicated. Objects are animated in the process of presentation; skulls, buildings, and ecosystems are referred to as if they were human subjects; the interpreters,

Forensic anthropologist Fredy Peccerelli demonstrates the impact of a bullet fired from a gun on a skull. When a gunshot hits a skull, he told us, the speed of the cracks tearing round the circumference of the skull is faster than that of the bullet, so they beat it to the other end. Upon exit, the bullet impacts an already cracked surface.
STILL FROM PAULO TAVARES AND EYAL WEIZMAN, *THE MINERAL GEOLOGY OF GENOCIDE,* 2012

meanwhile, are no longer necessarily human experts, but automated or semiautomated technologies of detection, calculation, and imaging, while the forums expand to a multiplicity of modes of articulation.

Although forensics is associated with the horror of crime-scene investigations, with dead bodies and destruction, as a mode of public presentation, it can sometimes be reminiscent of the genre of comedy. To say that something is comic does not necessarily mean it is funny. Forensics is comic because it enacts a fantasy distinct to the genre: that of speaking, acting objects. Evidence never speaks for itself, but speak it does, through its surrogate experts. Forensics is the mode by which the present theatre of horrors is performed by objects in front of a public. Comic moments—a man speaking to a skull and expecting it to speak back, say—can obviously exist in the greatest of tragedies, and forensic anthropologists presenting human remains in court continuously perform variations on this trope. They treat human remains as if they were witnesses, presenting themselves merely as translators or interlocutors. In our presentations, we similarly often employ figures of speech that animate the inorganic, make claims with and pose questions to objects large and small, ventriloquize not skulls, but physical and digital objects—buildings, neighborhoods, software, territories, and digital networks.

COUNTERFORENSICS

The advance of state forensics has also given rise to a multiplicity of counterforensic techniques that seek to hide from, evade, or disrupt the ability of states and corporate entities to collect traces. These extend from migrants using razor blades, fire, or acid to destroy their fingerprints to avoid identification and deportation to forms of digital camouflage against computer surveillance. In all these cases, counterforensics seeks to understand and map the logic of surveillance—investigate the means of state investigations—in order to be able to interfere with, camouflage itself from it, or render it inoperative.[26]

This depends on both opacity and transparency, with the former being the condition for the latter: camouflage from state and corporate surveillance, data protection, and anonymization, as anyone working in this field knows well, is the necessary prerequisite for the exposure of political crimes.

In addition to investigating the means of state investigations, forensic activists must examine the politics of the forums in which evidence is presented. No forum is neutral. Each is a product of and situated within a specific political reality, and each operates according to different sets of protocols. Each forum differently frames evidence's condition of visibility — what can be said, shown, and heard. Internal autocritique of our own actions and decisions is essential to mitigate collusion and determine when we might need to change course. While courts are important sites of political struggle and for gathering historical research, the danger is that a legal process can also sometimes supplant political action.

We must also learn to engage critically with the juridical and normative frames of human rights and international humanitarian law (IHL or "the laws of war"). Such frames cannot by themselves address systemic or structural violations. Merely insisting on normative regulation can end up reinforcing the status quo. Defending rights from within existing social, political, and legal frameworks can be counterproductive if the struggle is to replace the powers that have established these frameworks in the first place.[27] The legal cases are only as good as the political processes of which they are a part. Furthermore, unlike in the context of domestic criminal law, in which evidence is presented in existing and well-established forums, in the context of state violence, jurisdiction does not always exist, and often there are no obvious forums to address.[28] Most of our investigations take place in frontier zones with conditions of extraterritoriality that are outside established state jurisdictions and their frames of criminal justice. These are sites where sovereign jurisdiction is unclear (such as in the Mediterranean Sea), has disintegrated (as in some parts of Somalia or Yemen, where militants headquarter and drone assassinations take place), or has been suspended and is under siege (Waziristan, Gaza, the West Bank, or the remote highland frontiers of Guatemala in the 1980s). To that extent *forensis* is forensics where there is no law.

Those who confront political injustice in the name of the principles of international law and human rights also need to be cognizant of the way these laws and directives can themselves become instruments of war. Historically, human rights and international humanitarian laws were formulated by states and promoted by organizations such as the United Nations and the International Criminal Court or the International Committee of the Red Cross (ICRC) in order to regulate and moderate the way militaries wage wars. Interpreted and repurposed by military lawyers, however, these legal codes might also become the means by which militaries design and dispense violence. The strategic benefit that militaries can claim from moderation is understandable: Western militaries, increasingly bogged down by a raft of urban insurgencies, are keen to minimize civilian casualties on occasions when they believe that moderation might allow them to govern populations more efficiently or to win over the "hearts and minds" that have continually eluded them since the Vietnam War. But legal advice and court rulings on some forms of torture, targeted assassinations, and settlements in Israel, have given these forms of violence some legitimacy in the name of humanitarian principles.[29] In some historical circumstances the ethical power of human rights claims also involves the dangers of advocating Western military intervention, purportedly to stop mass atrocities.

Indeed, new frontiers of military practice are being explored via a combination of legal and military technologies that use the law as a weapon of war. There are multiple ways in which contemporary warfare is conditioned and empowered by legal and regulatory principles, rather than simply contained and justified by them. A statement recently made by Stephen Preston, the Pentagon's general counsel, exemplifies the advantages of legal warfare:

> We know that the law of war poses no obstacle to fighting well and prevailing. Nations have developed the law of war to be fundamentally consistent with the military doctrines that are the basis for effective combat operations. For example, the self-control needed to refrain from violations of the law of war under the stresses of combat is the same good order and discipline necessary to operate cohesively and victoriously in battle.[30]

These points above are only some of the ways by which human rights principles, generally understood as counterhegemonic instruments for addressing historical injustices, can be deployed to enhance and legitimize domination and violence. It is our opinion that legal and human rights activism should confront and limit military and state power, not become instructions for exercising it.

Forensic warfare, waged by militaries, does not use the law only as an instrument of war, but also extends the conflict into the quasi-juridical domain, where legal categories are employed in a battle over legitimacy. States can mobilize large resources to construct their claims. Militaries maintain their technological and optical advantage and make public every image and bit of footage that serves their aim and deny access to the rest under a variety of "national security" rationales. Through their press offices or websites, Western militaries frequently upload battlefield videos shot from airplanes, drones, or warheads. These highly selective and vetted perspectives on the battlefield always highlight the violations committed by the other side or moments when the military is seen caring for civilians. At the same time, these very militaries work hard to disrupt the possibility of anyone else monitoring their own violations.

The emergence of international tribunals throughout the 1990s — the International Criminal Tribunal for former Yugoslavia (ICTY) in 1993, the International Criminal Tribunal for Rwanda (ICTR) in 1994, and the International Criminal Court (ICC) in 1998 — not only provided some of the first forums for international criminal legal process after the Nuremberg trials in 1945 and 1946, but has also led to the popularization of the principles of international law. Different parties to a conflict started mobilizing legal categories such as "war crimes" or "disproportional attacks" as slogans. The form of legal activism that emerged in the shadow of "forensic warfare" has been referred to by Western militaries and security think tanks as "lawfare," which they define as "the strategy of using — or misusing — law as a substitute for traditional military means." Lawfare it is argued, has become "an indelible feature of 21st-century conflicts."[31] It is a kind of warfare, they explain, that takes place above the level of the state, in international institutions, and below it, in forums of civil society. This development has made Western states and their militaries vulnerable in the very fields and forums they imagined to control.

War, law, and politics thus do not occupy separate spheres, but rather overlap and interact with each other. International law, human rights principles, and the systems of institutions that exercise and enact them have become part of political struggles, a battlefield on which the law is used by both sides. This fact is bound to disappoint those who imagine that law equals justice. Instead of feeling betrayed by the law, when it provides no remedy, it is more useful to see it as a tool whose effects can be captured by Plato's notion of a *pharmakon*, a substance that is both a cure and a poison. Activists must negotiate these problems by recognizing both the potential and the dangers of human rights principles and of international humanitarian law and be vigilant and realistic about what is possible to achieve with them.

In *forensis*, then, we find both an operative concept and a critical practice — the word critical here indicating something that is vital and dynamic as well as our willingness to interrogate our own position. Our investigations have subsequently simultaneously aimed at state violence both on the battlefield and as embedded in the law.

In the early hours of January 9, 2009, a missile was fired at the Salha family home in Beit Lahiya, northern Gaza. The charge penetrated the roof and landed on the floor in one of the rooms. Three minutes later, a bomb struck and destroyed the house. Six people were killed, all women and children. The first strike was "a knock on the roof," one of several methods — telephone calls, SMS messages, leafleting, and warning shots being others — used by the Israeli Army to warn Palestinian residents of an imminent attack. The warnings began after advice from Israeli military lawyers specializing in international humanitarian law as a way of legitimizing bombing in civilian neighborhoods. Once a warning is delivered, Palestinians have a choice: risk an escape outside or stay. Israeli lawyers and spokespersons justify large civilian death tolls by claiming that such warnings were delivered and implying that they shift the responsibility for their own death to the people warned. But these warnings, though following the dry letter of the law, can be part of the problem and exemplify the danger of using the laws of war as strategic manuals. Warnings are in effect used to clear entire areas and create "sterile combat zones" in which anyone who remains is no longer protected as a civilian, but rather subject to a shoot-to-kill policy. According to legal advice given to the military in 2008, warnings render the killing of people who do not heed them legitimate, because by not evacuating, they could be designated as "voluntary human shields." The military has since withdrawn this line of legal reasoning, but still goes on employing warnings in a manipulative manner, and warning missiles still lead to the death of dozens of civilians within their homes.[32]

Forensic Architecture's investigation of warning strikes was undertaken together with the Palestinian, Gaza-based, human rights group Al Mezan, as part of the UN's Special Rapporteur on Human Rights and Counter-Terrorism report on drone warfare.[33]

On Wednesday, August 28, 2013, we interviewed two of the surviving members of the Salha family in Gaza, Fayez Salha and his son Noor Salha, by live satellite link from Al Jazeera's London studios. (Al Jazeera was then preparing a documentary on the work of Forensic Architecture and made their infrastructure available.) Together with Fayez and Noor Salha, we built a digital model of their home. The model helped the father and son reconstruct the events of that fateful night, and the two went on sketching elements of the incidents on printouts of this model.

At 3:00 a.m., a blast woke the family up. Noor saw smoke coming from the library. The family thought they were under attack. Noor's mother, Randa Salha, called her husband, Fayez Salha, who was on duty as the guard of a UN school. Fayez Salha:

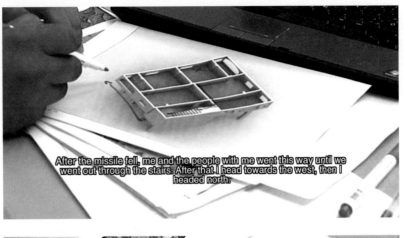

After the missile fell, me and the people with me went this way until we went out through the stairs. After that I head towards the west, then I headed north.

Printouts of the model of the Salha family home on which Fayez Salha and Noor Salha sketched the path of Noor's movement as well as the names of those killed in the place their bodies were found.

FORENSIC ARCHITECTURE

"She called me on the telephone and told me that the house had been hit, so I told them to get out of the house and head toward the closest school." What the family members did not know was that from the moment of impact, they had a mere three minutes before the house was to be destroyed. After moments of terrified confusion, they began to leave. Losing precious time, the family gathered by the stairs, ready to leave, but, according to Noor, his mother wanted the family to separate into two groups. Noor Salha: "We separated into two groups, following the order of the Zionists [The Israeli military], who insisted there should be no more than five or six people together in the street at one time." Noor left the house with four of his relatives in the first group. They were the only ones to survive. As Randa Salha led the second group of six down the stairs, the bomb hit. They were all killed.

Whether searching for historical traces in the materiality of buildings or of bones, the prospect of a political activism that relies on technology and incorporates scientific investigation often raises concerns about the "power" or "tyranny" of experts, about the dangers of becoming detached from direct experience and of replacing unmediated empathy with the cold, misanthropic gaze of the natural sciences. However, throughout our investigations, the experts we encountered were nothing like the authoritarian figures who are featured in such concerns.[34] Rather, they often were part of a network of independent and sometimes also politically vulnerable organizations. Many worked voluntarily because they were motivated by political commitments.

Although expertise is often understood to be preconditioned on a position of neutrality in relation to the subject matter investigated, neither we nor any of our collaborators ever have claimed such a position. No uninvolved investigator would have bothered to go the lengths we have without being committed to the victims whose truth was being undermined or denied. In this form of "engaged" objectivity, political motivations must not be an obstacle to gathering knowledge, but rather the precondition for attaining it.

The experts for the state whom we encountered — lawyers, researchers, or propagandists for hire — were also politically and ideologically conditioned, they worked in support of the state's hegemony in matters of evidence, and generally had better access to resources, technology, and imagery to promote their aims. There was no question of political neutrality on either side, although often when working for the status quo, those confronting us would understand their positions to be neutral because the existing state of affairs seemed to them to be natural. The concept of *forensis* is a good model for connecting political practices and activism, because it is structured by the necessity of taking sides, of fighting for and defending claims. Having an axe to grind should sharpen the quality of one's research, rather than blunt one's claims.

Wearing one's political passions too openly, however, can make one vulnerable, as I keep on being reminded whenever past statements, publications, or even petitions I signed are mobilized against the investigative work of Forensic Architecture by those finding ad-hominem attacks to be more efficient than confronting our findings.[35] Likewise, some theoretical formulations on the topic of "forensic aesthetics" or the "necessity for the truth to be produced and staged" (as developed throughout this and previous books) might leave one exposed on the witness stand, as a British barrister with whom we worked and to whom I once presented a book on the subject of forensic aesthetics sarcastically commented: "Just please don't repeat that on the stand." The words "aesthetics" and "art" are associated in the legal context with manipulation, emotional or illusionary trickery, and certainly with a lack of seriousness that might divert the quest for truth away from supposedly unmediated experience. Aesthetics is antithetical to the legal conception of truth as simple and objectively given, he explained. All forensic practitioners are keenly aware of that paradox: we know how essential aesthetics and the imagination are to the investigative and interpretative labor necessary to ascertain the most simple of facts, as well as to the production and presentation of a truth claim, but likewise, how important it is to refer to the truth as something much more obvious, something that is simply there.

There is another reason why our reports have been challenged and on one occasion suspended (pending a further decision that never arrived, see "White Phosphorous" below). Attorneys for the state claimed that architects do not possess the "relevant expertise in relation to conflict analysis."[36] We argued in response that architecture is a crucial analytical frame to apply when buildings, ruins, and cities are concerned. Similarly, we argued, at a time when there are so many images and so much footage coming out of war zones, the work of the image practitioners on our team — the filmmakers, photographers, and artists — is evidently essential.

Another set of objections was articulated on technical grounds. The material we produced did not always have precedents in being previously admitted as evidence by legal forums. Presentation of new evidence from sources such as those derived from new media, video analysis, interactive cartography, animations, and simulations almost always encountered objections, and when admitted, it was only after some struggle. We learned to prepare our evidence files to show both what we know and how we got there. Whenever such struggles had to be fought, they were worth fighting for reasons beyond introducing a bit of evidence that would make a specific point in a specific context, because when courts did admit such analyses, they also created precedents that would potentially allow others and us to present such work in the future, something that could expand what might be considered as evidence.

During the 2008–2009 Gaza conflict, photographs and videos recorded a hitherto little-known type of airborne munitions — low, luminous clouds, often less than 100 meters above the rooflines, appearing together with the thunder of an explosion. The clouds' multiple smoke tentacles then descended slowly to the ground in a conelike fashion. Other photographs taken from the ground showed the cloud tentacles burning through all surfaces they encountered, including skin and bone, causing death and severe injuries and often igniting secondary fires of the kind that couldn't be put out with normal fire extinguishers. Inhaling the fumes was toxic.

These strange clouds were the result of white phosphorus shells fired from artillery batteries into the cities and camps of Gaza. Each cloud could envelop an entire neighborhood. On one occasion, they set ablaze a United Nations school where civilians were seeking shelter. Israel initially denied the use of such munitions — "We categorically deny the use of white phosphorus"[37] — but when many images of the clouds started circulating in the public domain, they could no longer deny the existence of white phosphorus's existence and claim that the military uses it only "in compliance with international law" as a "smoke screen" to mask force maneuvers in uninhabited

The height of burst of the M825 WP projectile is established by using urban structures as reference measures. Rafah, Gaza strip, January 11, 2009.

IYAD EL BABA/UNICEF, FORENSIC ARCHITECTURE WITH THE COLLABORATION OF SITU RESEARCH areas. However, it was employed over civilian neighborhoods at night, when smoke screens would be useless, and at times when there were no forces anywhere on the ground, rendering the military explanation ridiculous.

Our investigation was undertaken on behalf of the human rights group Yesh-Gvul as part of a concerted civil-society action demanding the banning of white phosphorus munitions.[38] The case demanded a reconstruction of the general features of this form of munitions. We studied many videos of white phosphorus blasts over Gaza, as well as over Fallujah in Iraq, where US forces used it in 2004. The data were integrated into a parametric model that simulated the burst of such projectiles over urban environments. Our analysis showed that the shell explodes at the height of 50 to 120 meters over the surface, where it releases 116 felt wedges soaked in white phosphorus, which starts burning upon contact with oxygen, producing tentacles of thick white smoke. The smoke cloud descends onto the ground in an elliptical form that covers up to 30,000 square meters. We concluded that in the 2008–2009 Gaza conflict, white phosphorous was likely used to harass and terrorize, rather than as a smoke screen.

We presented our report during the Annual Meeting of State Parties to the Convention on Certain Conventional Weapons (CCW) in the United Nations Office at Geneva on November 12, 2012. It was also presented to Israel's High Court. The Israeli attorney general, who could not refute the findings, concentrated on issues of admissibility. "The responders objected" to the report, the judges wrote in their verdict, because "the architectural expertise of the team preparing it was irrelevant to the question of the legality of munitions containing white phosphorous."[39] On April 25, 2013, while the matter was being argued, the military issued a declaration stating that it would cease to use white phosphorus shells in populated areas—thereby yielding to the demand of the petition. A senior military commander explained that they had done so because white phosphorous "doesn't photograph well."[40] On March 5, 2013, the court dismissed the petition without ruling on the admissibility of our report. White phosphorous munitions have not been used in Gaza since. Other munitions have.

Francesco Sebregondi, who coordinated this research for Forensic Architecture, presenting the report "The Use of White Phosphorus Munitions in Urban Environments: An Effects-Based Analysis" at the United Nations Office at Geneva during the Annual Meeting of State Parties to the Convention on Certain Conventional Weapons, November 12, 2012. FORENSIC ARCHITECTURE

Forensic Architecture is part of a broader development that I'd like to refer to as the "forensic turn," a turn of human rights to forensic methods practiced as counterforensics. Among the first practices that could be called counterforensic was undertaken by the "gravediggers" of Argentina, activists who exhumed and analyzed the bodily remains of the victims of political repression. In 1984, a group of Argentinean students established the Equipo Argentino de Antropologia Forense (EAAF) to look for "the disappeared" (*los desaparecidos*), victims of the decade-long "dirty war" during which thousands of political activists, dissidents, and other opponents of the regime, as well as those merely imagined to be so, were kidnapped and murdered by Argentina's security services. The logic behind the emergence of EAAF was simple: the former generals in the military government that overthrew the Perón government, amnestied in a process that they themselves instituted before the transition to civilian rule in 1983, persisted in denying that they had kidnapped and killed their victims and obviously did not reveal their fate. The students of EAAF set out to make the disappeared present by digging them out of unmarked graves and analyzing and identifying their remains, presenting this osteological evidence in the judicial processes against the former military leadership that had finally begun. Ultimately, they sought to bring closure to the families and to hand them over the remains for proper burial. With some notable exceptions, until the EAAF began its work, the mass graves of the victims of political violence were often the sites of religious or national ceremonies and were rarely seen as a historical resource for legal research and advocacy.[41]

The group was trained by Clyde Snow, a celebrated forensic anthropologist known for many high-profile cases including — as Thomas Keenan and I wrote in a book dedicated to his work — the identification of the remains of fugitive Nazi Joseph Mengele in Brazil at roughly the same time. Snow's work in South America helped develop procedures for identifying missing people.[42] Mengele was only the most celebrated of tens of thousands of missing people in South America at the time. In a strange twist of historical irony, it was the forensic procedures developed for the identification of this arch perpetrator of Nazi atrocities that contributed to the effort to identify the missing victims of Argentina.

While exhumations in the mid-1980s started in a spontaneous fashion by groups committed to the exposure of state violence, within less than a decade the demand for the practice increased, becoming professionalized and institutionalized as it started receiving considerable international funding. Exhumation teams grew and started to include a staggering array of practitioners: forensic archaeologists, anthropologists, pathologists, dental experts (odontologists), biodata technicians, DNA specialists, statisticians, ballistic experts, crime-scene photographers, and even experts able to identify mass graves by studying the type of insects that settle there.[43] This international group of "gravediggers" moved from place to place: from Chile to the former Yugoslavia, Poland, Cambodia, Iraqi Kurdistan, Afghanistan, Sudan, Rwanda, Honduras, and Cyprus. The global proliferation of exhumation practices mirrored the universal experience of state violence in which the common grave has become the common ground.[44]

Luis Moreno Ocampo, at the time, the deputy prosecutor of the Argentinean junta trials, who had made much of the legal use of osteological evidence, has recently provocatively suggested that as chief prosecutor at the ICC, he often dreamed of "a trial without witnesses" in which the judicial process is performed by matter and images alone.[45] This nightmarish scenario is impossible, for the time being, at least, because material evidence requires an expert witness to present it to the court. Matter becomes evidence only when channeled through the language of the expert.

In societies recovering from dictatorships, the exhumation and identification of victims of political violence is used in the context of transitional justice to reestablish social bonds; in other locations, they are tools for ongoing political struggles. In this context, most often, exhumations have to be undertaken in a clandestine fashion, in processes involving no or few laboratory protocols and sometimes by assuming personal risks.

Such is the case with the exhumation of Kurdish civilians and guerrillas killed in recent decades by the Turkish military. Many of these grave sites are ignored, built upon, planted over, or turned into dump yards.[46] When such mass graves are known to exist, but are unacknowledged or officially denied, they operate as instruments of state terror.

Clandestine exhumations are taking place in eastern Turkey by groups looking to find the mass graves from the time of the Armenian genocide and in Russia in search of victims of Stalinist terror. In Spain, the first exhumations of the common graves of Republicans and other perceived enemies of the Franco regime started only a decade ago, sixty years after the end of the civil war and twenty-five years after the restoration of democracy as a civil-society initiative by groups of political activists committed to "historical memory." Such exhumations continually encounter controversy and disruptions on institutional and societal levels and have been stopped countless times in response to legal and political challenges.[47] Civil-society forensic groups also emerged in Mexico in search of the disappearances related to the narcowars and migration. Relatives of the victims founded action groups that have identified dozens of common graves without support from Mexican authorities and often against their explicit prohibitions.

THE ERA OF THE WITNESS

While in juridical history, physical evidence and witness testimony were always intertwined in different ways, the human rights movement has reserved a special place for the testimony of survivors. Testimony has been seen as charged not only with an epistemic value with which to reconstruct histories of violence, but also with an affective ethical and political force.[48] It is thus not treated as a simple matter of positive truth. It is not only what the victims say that is important in reconstructing histories of violence, but also all the things that interrupt their testimony—the confusion, error, and contradictions—that are understood to be ethically and politically significant and also laden with information.

It is interesting that in a way similar to the forensic turn's origins in the search for Mengele—the identification of his bones and the media attention around it resulted in an increased public recognition of the work of forensic specialists—the emergent cultural sensitivity to victims' testimony was linked to the discovery of another notorious Nazis escapee in Argentina, Adolf Eichmann. It was in the context of the Eichmann trial in Jerusalem that victims first gained their place as legal witnesses, playing a central role in the context of an international process involving crimes against humanity—in Nuremberg, the US prosecutor, Robert H. Jackson, was wary of letting survivors speak—but the 1961 Jerusalem trial was credited with the inauguration of the "era of the witness."[49] Indeed, the decades that followed the trial in Jerusalem have seen the foregrounding of the narratives of victims in human rights, arts, and the media. Testimony also reshaped sensibilities throughout Western culture, exercising a decisive cultural, aesthetic, and political influence on the visual and conceptual arts and documentary practices.

The value given to testimony was central to the advent of human rights groups such as Amnesty and Human Rights Watch in the 1960s and 1970s, respectively. Testimony fulfilled a historical role in relation to two general

Three-dimensional LIDAR scan of an exhumation site outside the village of San Juan Cotzal, Guatemala, 2015. UNKNOWN FIELDS DIVISION, SCANLAB, AND FORENSIC ARCHITECTURE

contradictions that shaped that period, as Michel Feher explained in relation to this project.[50] The first was the political versus the humanitarian. In the post-1968 period, a creeping despair of the European Left about the Soviet Bloc was compensated for by the surge in humanitarian activism as exemplified by the formation of groups such as Médecins Sans Frontières (MSF) in the early 1970s. These doctors thought that it was delusionary and dangerous to support any of the ideological systems clashing during the Cold War. The only thing left to do was to alleviate the suffering of victims and in the process become witnesses to it. Instead of working for political change, the emergent sensibility of the "era of the witness" asked the public to express empathy with victims, resulting in individuating and thus depoliticizing complex collective histories.

Memory emerged as an important cultural force in the 1970s as a means to challenge official written history and open up the historical record to voices henceforth excluded from it. This suited the aims of human rights organizations, committed as they were to the plight of individuals against the arbitrary violence of repressive states. Testimony is tasked with more than revealing and authenticating claims of historical injustice. The validity of testimony in the context of war crimes stems from the capacity to speak in the face of the horrors of totalitarianism. Ethical, rather than only epistemic, the function of testimony in such situations is primarily in its delivery.[51]

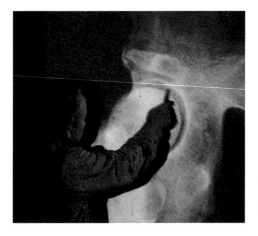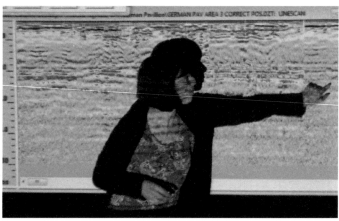

LEFT: Forensic anthropologist Clyde Snow presenting a slide of Josef Mengele's skeleton which he examined in 1985. RIGHT: Caroline Sturdy Colls presenting an analysis of GPR data collected in Staro Sajmište, Serbia, 2012. LEFT: STILL FROM *JOSEF MENGELE: THE FINAL ACCOUNT* (1998), DIRECTED BY DAN SETTON

The "forensic turn"—the emergent cultural and juridical sensibility of the probative value of physical evidence, primarily bones, but also other classes of material evidence—has started to challenge the existing epistemologies and ethical positions of the human rights movement, especially with regard to witness testimonies. However, forensic methods were complementary to human testimony, not antithetical to it. Architecture, for example, can provide more than just investigative tools for the production of measured evidence. It can also be used as a mnemonic device for enhancing memories obscured, hidden, or distorted by the experience of extreme violence and trauma. The memory of horrifying experiences can sometimes remain inaccessible; at other times, they can not be kept out of consciousness, with much more mundane events interpreted as their constant repetition. Testimony after the "forensic turn" had returned as a material, sometimes architectural practice.

The "forensic turn" was not a decisive break from the melancholia of the "era of the witness." Rather, the turn to the material object that emerged with the opening of human rights trials in Argentina and later in relation to the former Yugoslavia and Rwanda did not provide a simplified alternative to the complexities, uncertainties, and ambiguities of the human subject and that of language. The construction, presentation, and contestation of material and image evidence, like all findings in the natural sciences, are qualified by indeterminacies, contradictions, margins of error, and probability calculations. Expert forensic testimony, like any other human testimony, is prone to errors. Presenting evidence in these contexts is not what we understand, with much justifiable suspicion, as "positivism"—the desire to overcome language through materiality and to hold reality to be knowable without any intermediaries—but the art of making claims using matter and media, code and calculation, narrative and performance.

The forensic turn's sensibility to matter and digital codes is not evident in police and military work alone, but has also permeated general culture, high and low.[52] From philosophical movements such as object-oriented ontologies to the forensic crime series on television, attention has shifted from the physiological intricacies of the subject position to narratives led by things, traces, objects, and algorithms.

Bones are a special order of things, still haunted by the subject, and they thus provide the link between subject and object testimony and evidence. The forensic presentation of osteological evidence inherited much of the sensibility associated with victim testimony and has tended to mimic witness positions by adopting its ethical overdetermination. Snow's most famous statement, "bones make great witnesses," and similar statements by other gravediggers such as William Haglund blur the border between the living and the dead, between objects and subjects, image and materiality, people and things.[53] Snow has referred to the method by which missing people are identified as "osteobiography"—the biography of bones.

Animating objects such as bones exemplifies the life-giving metaphor of forensics. Rather than concentrating on the moment of death and the method of killing, osteobiography is concerned with establishing the identity of missing persons by comparing the events of their life to material traits such as the form and texture of bones and fractures in them. Bones are under a continuous process of exposure to various life conditions: habit, labor, health, accidents, location, violence, nutrition, and ancestry, as well as to distinct environmental conditions typical of different geographies, such as temperature and humidity. These influences are inscribed on a surface that is not neutral or passive, but rather one that is mutating, growing, and contracting. Bones can heal and repair, erasing and retaining traces in the process.[54]

As a technique for identifying human remains in mass graves, however, osteobiography was short lived. The physical examination of bones was phased out in the 1990s, when handling large numbers of DNA tests became possible. Identifying the exhumed victims of the two distinct genocides of the 1990s—Rwanda and Yugoslavia—employed genetic databases to deal with much larger numbers of bodies than had been dealt with in Argentina and sometimes more complex sets of technical problems. For example, after the exposure of mass graves in Srebrenica in late 1995, the Serbian forces that perpetrated the killing employed bulldozers to exhume these graves and hastily rebury hundreds of bodies in several secondary graves. These graves were in turn also exhumed, and the remains were reburied in several tertiary graves. Remains of some individual bodies needed to be reassembled from several grave sites—in one case, remains of a single body were found in seven separate locations—spread over an extended geographical area.[55]

Though made redundant in the context of mass exhumations, some of the principles of osteobiography nevertheless came to inform the conception of forensic architecture, which was similarly tuned to the materiality and texture of a building as a surface upon which events get imprinted and upon which process becomes form.

In April 2011, I traveled to Dublin to interview Clyde Snow. He was there on a short holiday. I wanted to ask him about his Mengele investigation in preparation for Thomas Keenan's and my book on the subject. Snow was surprised by my curiosity. After granting a generous interview, he wondered why an architect should take interest in a case long closed. I told him about Forensic Architecture, which had then just been established. "Then you must go to Guatemala!" he said, where he suggested our time would be better spent helping the forensic teams of the Fundación de Antropología Forense de Guatemala (FAFG), which he helped establish, locate and analyze the remnants of indigenous homes destroyed during the genocidal campaign of the early 1980s in the west Guatemalan highlands. We went there and joined the investigation. (See pp. 121–24.) Some of the rural villages of the Ixil Maya had disappeared completely, the organic materials that composed their buildings were consumed by the cloud forest. Only the plants were left, to be read as traces of built form and formerly inhabited areas. Exhumations and archaeological investigations were undertaken then in preparation for the prosecution of military dictator General Efraín Ríos Montt, whose military rule brought unprecedented violence and terror to rural Guatemala in 1982–83. "When you are trying to tell a story, the architectural evidence is as essential as the osteological one," Snow said.[56]

SAYDNAYA: INSIDE A SYRIAN TORTURE PRISON

In 2016, Forensic Architecture was commissioned by Amnesty international to help reconstruct the architecture of Saydnaya, a secret Syrian detention center, from the memory of several of its survivors, now refugees in Turkey.[57]

Since the beginning of the Syrian crisis in 2011, tens of thousands of Syrians, including protestors, students, bloggers, university professors, lawyers, doctors, journalists, and others suspected of opposing the Assad government have disappeared into a secret network of prisons and detention centers. Amnesty International researchers estimated that 17,723 people have died in custody in Syria since the crisis began in March 2011.[58] Saydnaya, located some twenty-five kilometers north of Damascus in an East German–designed building dating from the 1970s, is one of the most notoriously brutal of these places.

Since 2011, Saydnaya has become the final destination for many prisoners who have already passed through a series of other interrogation and detention centers. In it, prisoners no longer face interrogations. Torture is widely and brutally used not to obtain information, but in order to terrorize and often kill detainees.

The Syrian government does not provide information about prisoners' whereabouts and often denies that detainees have ever been arrested. People are simply "disappeared" — killed or dying in secret. In recent years, no visits from independent

Salam Othman, one of the witnesses, reconstructs the architecture of the Saydnaya Prison. FORENSIC ARCHITECTURE

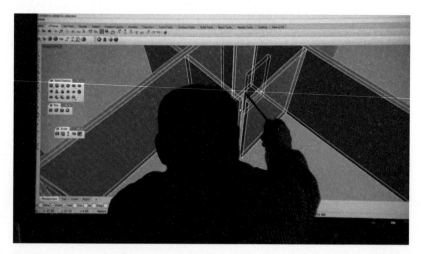

Jamal Abdou recontrscuts the bathroom/toilet area with a group cell. FORENSIC ARCHITECTURE

journalists or monitoring groups that report publically have been permitted to the prison. As there are no recent photographs of its interior spaces, the memories of Saydnaya survivors are the only resource with which to recreate the spaces, conditions of incarceration, and incidents that take place inside.

In April 2016, a team of Amnesty International and Forensic Architecture researchers traveled to Turkey to meet a group of survivors who have come forward because they wanted to let the world know about Saydnaya. Our aim was to help them reconstruct and model the spaces of the prison and some of the events and incidents that took place there. Every witness left with us several deposits of memory that they wanted recorded in detail. However, the process of recollection and reconstruction was not straightforward. In Saydnaya, witnesses were kept in a state of constant disorienting sensory deprivation. Their experience of the prison was at the threshold of both vision and sound: prisoners were blindfolded or forced to press their hands against their eyes while being led into the dark cells. They were forbidden to utter any sound, to whisper, speak, or scream. Because both vision and sound were at liminal states, prisoners' spatial perception was undertaken through detection of differences in temperature, moisture, light, vibrations, and echoes. The modeling process sought to interrogate these sensory thresholds when all memories are conditioned by a state of extreme deprivation.

During the process, the relation between architectural modeling and memory was twofold. On the one hand, the model was a product of memory, a representation of the spaces of the prison as witnesses remembered and described them to us. This model and the description of events within it can potentially become a piece of evidence in a subsequent trial if one ever takes place. On the other hand, the model-building process helped induce further recollections. As they measured rooms; located windows, doors, and objects in their places; experienced the virtual environment of their cells at eye level; and reconstructed the acoustic properties of the building, witnesses had some recollection of events otherwise obscured by violence and trauma. Architectural modeling thus bridged the otherwise separate and distinct functions of testimony and evidence and captured the space between sound and vision.

Memories of violence are rarely straightforward records or internalized representations that are stored in an orderly manner and easily retrieved. Memory, like matter, is plastic, continuously morphing, and affected by violence. Recall could be inaccurate,

If it's so quiet and you're not allowed to speak,
do you hear anything?

TOP: Salam Othman undertakes acoustic reconstruction and modelling. BOTTOM: The image has been rendered to his description. FORENSIC ARCHITECTURE

prone to distortions, and vulnerable to memory contamination. Our colleagues in the Forensic Psychology Unit at Goldsmiths, University of London, advised us that recollections of horrifying experiences might emerge as a result of an indeterminate cognitive process that is triggered by momentary, unpredictable relations — a distributed process that includes bodies, spaces, sounds, and objects. The model as we have conceived it, based on this advice, created the possibility for some of these relations and for recall to occur in a virtual space.

The model-building process also turned the witnesses into active participants in the project. They described in minute detail the cells and other areas of the prison, including stairwells, corridors, gates, doors, windows, bars, and hatches, to an Arabic-speaking architect on our team — Hania Jamal — who constructed computer models of these spaces and elements while they described them to her. They also reviewed and corrected their own and their peers' models. Witnesses then further located and put into relation different elements and characters, such as guards and fellow prisoners, and objects, such as floor tiles, blankets, food bowls, bars, and torture instruments, inside the model as they recreated specific incidents. As the model became increasingly detailed, it was rendered to give an eye-level impression of the spaces, and witnesses could locate themselves virtually within it; experiencing spaces and zooming into elements in them induced further recollections.

As I mentioned, vision was extremely restricted. There was little natural light, and prisoners were made to cover their eyes whenever a guard entered their cell. Most of their movement through the prison was undertaken while blindfolded. Some detainees saw only the floor tiles through a thin sliver under sacks pulled over their heads or noticed only the contrast between darkness and light as they were moved past windows. Furthermore, sound was also restricted: speaking was prohibited, including inside the cells, and prisoners were even forbidden to shout in pain when being beaten and tortured. Detainees in Saydnaya thus developed an acute sensitivity to minute variations and nuances in vision and sound.

To capture their auditory memories, we solicited "ear-witness testimony" and reconstructed elements of the prison's architecture through sound. Lawrence Abu Hamdan, a sound artist and audio investigator on our team, reconstructed ambient and contextual background sounds as another gateway to recollection. Echo and reverberation modeling helped confirm the size of spaces such as cells, stairwells, and corridors, as well as to reconstruct some incidents within them. Abu Hamdan explained that just like a sonar, "the sounds of the beatings illuminated the spaces around them." Witnesses described the way water pipes and air vents amplified and transported sound across the building and said that the guards sometimes tortured people next to these infrastructural systems for the sound of the beatings to flow throughout the building without anyone knowing where it came from. Sound was the

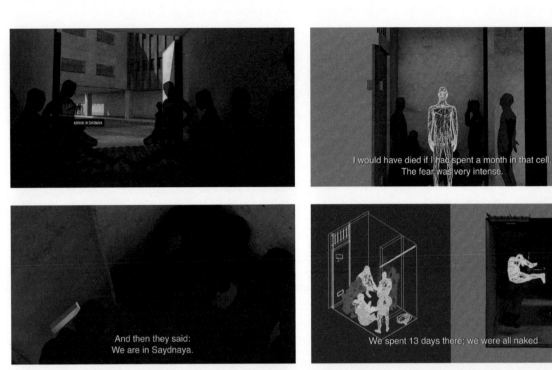

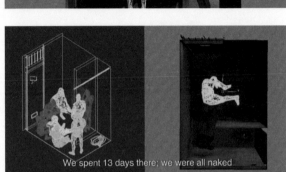

I would have died if I had spent a month in that cell.
The fear was very intense.

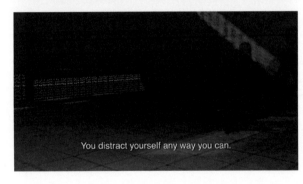

And then they said:
We are in Saydnaya.

We spent 13 days there; we were all naked

You distract yourself any way you can.

Sadynaya, inside a Syrian torture prison, 2016.
FORENSIC ARCHITECTURE AND AMNESTY INTERNATIONAL

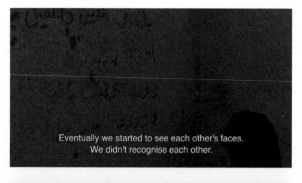

Eventually we started to see each other's faces.
We didn't recognise each other.

As it's made of copper
and we could write on the wall with it.

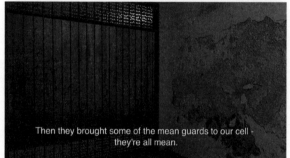

Then they brought some of the mean guards to our cell -
they're all mean.

And sometimes we can hear the wind moving softly
through the branches.

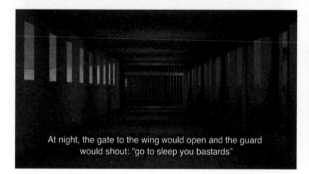

At night, the gate to the wing would open and the guard
would shout: "go to sleep you bastards"

Because in Sadnaya you never want to wake up.

Sadynaya, inside a Syrian torture prison, 2016.
FORENSIC ARCHITECTURE AND AMNESTY INTERNATIONAL

guards' weapon of torture, because they knew that "one person being tortured is like everyone being tortured."[59] The guards, he explained, were the masters of sound and controlled the acoustics of the space.

We cross-referenced the individual spatial and audio testimonies to construct an overall model of the building. Whenever we identified potential errors or contradictions between different accounts, we carefully tried to resolve them, but we also made a note and modeled what we knew to be divergences. Errors, contradictions, and lacunas are enriched with information, because they reveal something of the experience of a detainee and their psychological condition. Such distortions thus contain more information than a measured architectural rendering and could themselves be considered as evidence in their own right.

Each witness had "blanked out" different parts of the building. Some of them described certain spaces as being much larger, corridors as longer, staircases as higher, sounds louder, and the building as having more floors than we knew it to have. The number of certain architectural elements, such as metal gates and doors, also multiplied. The sounds made by cars and tracks, and bread boxes thrown about the corridor, were amplified due to fear and hunger.

The model thus emerged not as a reductive synthesis, but as a description of both the building as we know it to be and also of the unresolvable spatial distortions, blank spaces, and gaps that recorded prisoners' experiences.

Witness accounts were almost always narrated to us as autonomous and self-contained moments outside a coherent narrative and the flow of time. This sense of timelessness, familiar to all prisoners, made us turn away from describing the prison experience as a diary of incarceration. Rather, we chose several moments — "memory objects" — from the interviews we had conducted and edited them into short videos that we later located within an interactive model of the prison building. The interactive model thus became an archive in which testimonies were placed within the spaces they described. This archive will grow as more testimonies are collected.

During our work toward reconstructing something of the events, spaces, and incidents endured in Saydnaya, we realized that the building functioned not only as a space where incarceration, surveillance, and torture regularly take place, but that it is, itself, an architectural instrument of spatial and acoustic torture, and as such, one of the most extreme manifestations of architecture.

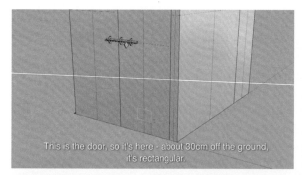

This is the door, so it's here - about 30cm off the ground, it's rectangular.

It's a bit longer than my face.

He said: "Put your head out".
I didn't understand.

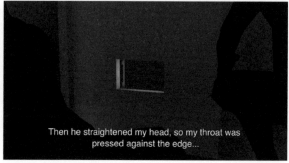

Then he straightened my head, so my throat was pressed against the edge...

MEMORY OBJECT 1: THE HATCH

After their arrival, prisoners spent the first period of their incarceration — between a week and five months — in small cells 2.35 meters by 1.65 meters — about 7.5 by 5.5 feet. These cells were built for solitary confinement, but are used to hold up to fifteen people at one time. Prisoners had to take turns sitting; there was no space to lie down. While modeling the solitary-confinement cell according to the descriptions of Samer Al-Ahmed, Hania Jamal asked about the door. Al-Ahmed told her that there was a small hatch in the bottom of it. She asked him for dimensions. He said that it was "a bit longer than my face ... and thirty centimeters [eight inches] up from the ground." The attempt to model the location and dimension of the hatch triggered a description of an incident: one day, a guard patrolling outside asked him to push his head out through the hatch. It was too narrow, but Al-Ahmed finally managed to squeeze his head through by turning it sideways and pushing through. The guard then turned and straightened his head, putting his throat against the edge, and started kicking it repeatedly.

TOP: Hania Jamal modelling the door to the solitary cell according to instructions by Samer Al-Ahmed. BOTTOM: Rendering according to Al-Ahmed's memory. When describing the hatch he recalled the way he was tortured with it. FORENSIC ARCHITECTURE AND AMNESTY INTERNATIONAL

Describe the corridor for us – this is your cell.

He slapped me and I opened my eyes accidentally.

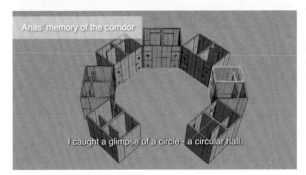

Anas' memory of the corridor

I caught a glimpse of a circle - a circular hall.

MEMORY OBJECT 2: THE HALL

Another of the detainees, Anas Hamado, has never seen the outside of his cell; when he was taken there, he was forced to press his hands firmly against his eyes. On one occasion, he was taken to the corridor outside his cell to be beaten. He had to keep his hands against his eyes and was not allowed to scream, even when the strikes landed. However, a strike aiming at his face caused his hands to slip away for a brief moment. In a flash, he caught a glimpse of the spaces he hadn't previously seen: "I caught a glimpse of a circle, a circular hall with lots of cells . . . a huge circle, like a cylinder." The instantaneous sight he gained was a momentary leak of vision into a spatial perception otherwise fully defined by sound.

We know from other witnesses and from our own analysis of the architecture of Saydnaya that the corridor outside his cell was straight. Rather than a precise architectural description, Hamado's description of a circular corridor is possibly the result of the beating and a sense of total incarceration. This lapse might thus testify to the violence of Saydnaya more precisely than any faithful architectural description.

LEFT: Anas Hamado models the corridor from memory as a spherical space. RIGHT: A rendering of the circular corridor according to Hamado's description. FORENSIC ARCHITECTURE AND AMNESTY INTERNATIONAL

Photographers, filmmakers, and artists have collaborated with human rights organizations since the birth of the human rights movement in the mid-1970s. Human rights groups made good use of the affective power of the arts in helping stir public compassion. And the emergence and development of a human rights sensibility and its attention to victims opened a new pathway for artists to engage with political issues. The compassionate sensibility that developed was different from the revolutionary aesthetics of the political art of the early twentieth century. It sometimes bypassed the desire for overarching historical and political narratives in favor of accounts of personal tragedies.[60] Registering this entangled development and the emergent sensibility that ensued, the office lobbies of human rights organizations were often dedicated to art and photography exhibitions of this kind. However, with several important exceptions, artists' work was kept external to, and merely illustrative of, the actual investigative work.

Forensic architecture seeks to shift away from this use of the arts and to employ aesthetic sensibilities as investigation resources. Forensics is an *aesthetic* practice because it depends on both the modes and the means by which reality is sensed and presented publicly. Investigative aesthetics slows down time and intensifies sensibility to space, matter, and image. It also seeks to devise new modes of narration and the articulation of truth claims.[61]

"Forensic aesthetics" is a term that Thomas Keenan and I proposed in our book *Mengele's Skull*. We used it to describe the way in which an affective image — a superimposition of Mengele's face and his skull produced as part of the scientific process — had acquired the potential of conviction (in both the sense of a legal verdict and that of the subjective sensation of confirmed belief — being convinced and getting convicted)[62] that was in excess of the protocols of both science and the law.

The use of aesthetics traverses the three sites of forensic operation, the field, the lab/studio and the forum, and refers to different things in each. Its first and basic level is that of "material aesthetics": the modes and means by which material objects — bones, ruins, or landscapes — function as sensors and register changes in their environment. Matter can be regarded as an aesthetic sensorium inasmuch as its mutations register minute transformations and differences within the force fields around it. Material aesthetics is both prior and primary to human perception, apprehension, and judgment. Aesthetics in this context is close to the ancient

Greek meaning of the term, in which to sense is to be aestheticized, just as, inversely, to be unaestheticized is to make oneself numb to perception. For Bruno Latour, aesthetics designates the ability to perceive and to be concerned, "to render oneself sensitive, a capacity that precedes any distinction between the instruments of science, of art and of politics."[63] While aesthetics is generally understood as what pertains to human senses and perception, "material aesthetics" instead captures the way in which matter absorbs or *prehends* (rather than apprehends or comprehends) its environment. Such "non-sensuous perception," proposed by the early twentieth-century English mathematician and philosopher Alfred North Whitehead, can help form the link between human sensing and material sensors. Matter prehends by absorbing environmental forces into its material organization. Aesthetics, conceived in this way, is the mode and means by which material things relate to and affect each other.[64]

Such an aesthetics of sentient materiality is familiar to the forensic anthropologist, who sees in the texture of bones a medium in which extended processes of life — habits, labor, nutrition patterns, as well as abrupt incidents — become texture and form. It is also a familiar concept to the building surveyor, who seeks to identify the processes that led to a structural crack. Bones and buildings could be said to be "aestheticized" because their deformations register variations and differences in the environment that surrounds them. Inversely, these formal mutations *image* (a verb) the

Images produced using photographs of Mengele and images of his skull in Richard Helmer's face-skull superimposition demonstration, Medico-Legal Institute labs, São Paulo, Brazil, June 1985. COURTESY OF MAJA HELMER

environment. Not everything gets registered in a similar fashion — some things get recorded, and others don't.

While in the nineteenth century, celluloid soaked in gelatin and silver salt particles was the means — through photography — to record its relation to other objects and the environment around it, today, some digital instruments are sensitive enough to help us read the way different surfaces that have not been designated as sensors may function as such. A table, for example, senses the room in which it is located, objects, hot or cold placed on top of it, as well as the heat and radiation of living matter in various degrees of proximity to it. Material aesthetics is the quality of relations between things — the being of matter in the world, its ability to absorb and the degree to which it might. This extends the principles of photography to the rest of the material world, breaking film's and digital photography's monopoly over visual representation. The inverse must also be true: as objects become images, images should be studied as things, parts of the material world.[65] Still, to be read as sensors, the transformations of material objects must be captured by other sensors, such as photographs, analog or digital, remote or proximate, single or hyperspectral, that translate the sensorial capacity of matter into data and help make sense of them.

On the next level, in the forum, the term "forensic aesthetics" refers to the mode by which things appear. It involves different techniques and technologies of demonstration, rhetoric, and performance — gestures, narrative and dramatization, image enhancement and projection. All this takes place in the media environment. International criminal courts and tribunals depend on video cameras to broadcast their proceedings to the public. Each participant in the trials of the ICC or ICTY sits in front of a screen. The legal teams watch these screens for the images, documents, or videos presented to all sides simultaneously in evidence. Face-to-face interaction has been superseded by face-to-screen or screen-to-screen communication, as Susan Schuppli and others have demonstrated.[66] This is very different from traditional courts, which are still largely allergic to the presence of media. But it has a precedent: in the Nuremberg trials, a screen was set at the apex of the courtroom's perspective, otherwise reserved for the judges. Now the space of international tribunals resembles more a film set or a live-broadcast studio, recording and archiving the processes that unfold in front of multiple cameras and screens. It is for this reason, perhaps, that the ICTY could be established in the anonymity of the rented floors of a former insurance building and the ICC could fit comfortably within the former headquarters of a mobile phone company.[67]

Contemporary conflicts include different optical regimes. Image-making capabilities are spread among all its participants. Militaries employ satellite and drone-mounted sensors, helmet-mounted cameras, as well as optical heads on guided munitions — kamikaze witnesses that crash into their subjects. Beyond their use as "operational images" — automatically produced by machines for machines transferable as data without ever being converted into anything recognizable by humans as a representation of the visual field — footage from optical heads on projectiles can also be used for propaganda purposes, when, for example, bits of warhead footage get publically circulated.[68]

Guided missiles make for the most immediate physical relation between cameras and subject — they hit it. The satellites on which their guidance depends are the farthest removed. Since the beginning of the new millennium, satellite imagery has become publically accessible and commercially available at ever-increasing resolutions. These images are shot from beyond the vertical extent of the state's sovereignty — national airspace is cupped by the lowest possible orbit along which a satellite can travel, an altitude that remains unspecified because the lowest orbit — that of spy satellites — is kept secret. When human rights organizations use satellite imagery to monitor violations of human rights, they continue a well-honed Cold War practice: information gathering about foreign states from beyond their national borders. This often accounts for their designation as spies. They also literally demonstrate the universal aspirations of the movement — human rights principals perceive themselves to be above state sovereignty.[69]

Before the 2000s, satellite imagery was exclusively a resource of governments, but in the late 1990s, the market was privatized, enabling non-governmental organizations to obtain satellite imagery from commercial providers. When a crisis occurs, commercial image satellite operators align the orbits of their satellites to cover "regions of interest," hoping to sell their images, as other photographic agencies would. The satellite continuously scans the globe into a digital archive. Only the metadata — where and when the satellite passed — is available upon first search. No one watches the images, indeed they are not images, before an analyst orders them from the archive. It is only at that point that data becomes an image. While the cost of a single satellite photograph, for just over a thousand US dollars, is generally affordable for most human rights groups, "tasking" a satellite, that is, paying for it to change orbit and pass over specific sites at specific times costs several tens of thousands of dollars and is affordable only by states and large corporations.

As previously noted, the photographic resolution at which satellite images are made publicly available is degraded, for both privacy and secrecy reasons, to a level that masks the human figure within the square of a single pixel. State agencies have access to the full optical resolution of these photographs, as well as to data from other sensors in them.[70] They can also limit the public availability of certain satellite images by purchasing them and "taking them off the shelf" for a specified amount of time.[71]

Image satellites take an average of ninety minutes to complete a full orbit around the earth. These satellites can potentially be over the same site only after twenty-four hours because by the time they have completed a full circle the earth has already rotated. Satellite photography is thus distinguished by two of its most pronounced limitations: it can capture neither people (because of the resolution) nor incidents (because of orbit time). They are thus the very opposite of the focused, time-bound incidents of spectacular violence scaled to the human body, the central trope of photojournalism. They are photographs in which the human event is replaced by the *event of architecture* — the changes and variations across the surface of the earth that become visible in a "before" and an "after" photograph.[72] Juxtapositions of buildings with ruins, icebergs with water, and tropical forests with monocrop fields present history as a series of radical breaks and catastrophes. Before-and-after photographs are thus the very embodiment of forensic time. The "before," often retrieved from the image archives of satellite companies, establishes the baseline, the supposedly normal state, against which the "after," often "tasked" to capture the same site, is studied for differences and deviations. Satellite image archives are thus depositories of potential "befores" to devastating "afters" yet to come. The juxtaposition of this and other such pairings of before-and-after images produces the fundamental element of what Sergei Eisenstein called "dialectic montage" — a juxtaposition in which the meaning lies not in the images, but in the tension or discord between them.

The gaps between the before-and-after images are filled by continuous aerial observation platforms such as drones and by user-generated media on the ground. Indeed, one of the most important forms of documentation emerging from the battlefields of Palestine, Iraq, Syria, Ukraine, and elsewhere is produced by the people living there and made available on social networks almost instantly. For human rights researchers, citizen-produced images are the complementary technology to satellite imagery.

The architectural image complex. Three-dimensional models allow us to locate multiple images in space and establish the relation between them. The image is from the investigation into Black Friday, Rafah, 2014 (image 2015). FORENSIC ARCHITECTURE AND AMNESTY INTERNATIONAL

These kinds of videos include testimony, as well, because the people recording them often speak as they record. But unlike those testimonies collected by professional human rights researchers well after the fact, these recorded video testimonies are delivered in real time, as things happen, on the terms of those collecting and distributing them. Photographs and video files are sent out like messages in a bottle in the hope that somebody will see them and offer some help. Often, this is too hopeful. [73] The Syrian citizen-witnesses of the early years of the revolution believed that the constant flow of videos that they risked their lives filming and uploading would shock the world's conscience enough to lead to action against the regime. They were wrong, of course, and their hopes were drowned by rivers of blood. Other images of decapitated heads, immolations, and the spectacular bombing of archaeological sites replaced them. As years of conflict ensued, media activist groups in Syria were formed to document and log events.

The increase in the number of primary sources has expanded the visual field, but this expansion has not always added clarity. While it has helped corroborate truths and dispel some lies, it sometimes facilitates the creation of new lies and the spread of propaganda. Images often become embroiled in a secondary conflict about authenticity, veracity, and interpretation.[74] The proliferation of photographic and video testimonies makes necessary a complementary practice of trawling through blogs and social media sites, collecting images and watching carefully.

While debates in the fields of photography and visual culture over the past decades were concerned with the spectators' relation to single images and photojournalistic trophy shots, with questions regarding the image's ability to capture "the pain of others,"[75] today, the sheer number of images and videos generated around incidents means that to view images requires understanding the relation between them. We look at photographs not only for details captured in their details but as doorways to other photographs; that is to say, we look at images through images.

Most videos that end up being broadcast or becoming viral on the Internet contain, in a single image frame, both perpetrator and victim. This has been the case in most videos of police brutality since the video recording of Rodney King, the black motorist beaten by the Los Angeles Police Department in 1991.[76] But for every shot that includes a beater and a beaten or a shooter and a victim, there are many more that include only one or the other, or just audio, or things that happened just before or after the incident. Their relation to other images and the main incident is not obvious. It is harder to view and understand incidents that slip between images. Images containing partial information are rarely broadcast and are often discarded as trash. Searching through this image flotsam, however, we can sometimes find, synchronize, and reassemble images to reenact incidents visually and virtually in space. Viewing in this context requires construction and composition — thus, architecture. Constructing virtual models from the spatial information harvested from images, we can locate cameras in time and space.[77] What we refer to as the *architectural image complex* is a method of assembling image evidence in a spatial environment. The architectural image complex can function as an optical device that allows the viewer to see the scene of the crime as a set of relations between images in time and space. It can also be used as a navigational device to help move between images, exploring a space that is at once virtual and photographic.[78] Essentially, it makes manifest the necessity for composing evidence that is simultaneously material, media-based, and testimonial. The architectural image complex thus replaces both the thematic classification system of archives and the linear transition between images in before-and-after montages. It is best demonstrated in relation to the two cases — the Nakba Day killing and Black Friday — presented in Part 2.

The exposure time of early nineteenth-century photographs was often too long to record moving figures and abrupt events, capturing only static elements. Louis Daguerre's image of the Boulevard du Temple in Paris, taken in 1838 or 1839, required ten to fifteen minutes of exposure and recorded only two human figures on an otherwise busy street — a customer having his shoes polished and the bootblack. Before-and-after images emerged out of such limitations to the photographic process. As Ines Weizman and I explained in a book on the subject,[79] two photographs were necessary to describe incidents.

Perhaps the earliest photographic representations of urban conflict was a pair of before-and-after daguerreotypes captured by Eugène Thibault from a hidden window in Paris, before and after a clash between workers and the National Guard that occurred on Sunday, June 25, 1848. The "before" image shows a sequence of three barricades that appear to have been assembled out of sandbags, cobblestones, and broken carriages. Only a few ghostly figures were stationary enough to be registered

Paris, June 25, 1848 and June 26, 1848. Eugène Thibault, the barricade in rue Saint-Maur-Popincourt before and after the attack by General Lamoricière's troops.
MUSÉE D'ORSAY/RÉUNION DES MUSÉES NATIONAUX. HERVÉ LEWANDOWSKI, 2002

on the photographic plate. The "after" image shows the state of the street after the battle. The barricades are broken, and the windows that were closed in anticipation of battle are now open. One can make out soldiers and a few horses. The workers were defeated. The pair of images was printed, two months after the battle, in the reactionary (and, later, collaborationist) Parisian weekly *L'Illustration*, to convey a warning to the workers. This short sequence of two images prefigured the possibility of the moving image, a decade before it was invented.[80]

One hundred and fifty years after the invention of photography, the problem of capturing the human figure and incidents persisted in what had become the most common form of before-and-after images — satellite imagery. Satellites impose a different set of limitations on photography. The human figure is erased, as we can see in the pair of images from Darfur below, because the resolution of satellite imagery is designed to mask it. Traces of violence are captured by spatial transformations between two points in time.

Further scaling up the pairs captured in *Before and After*, in January 1973, less than five months after Landsat 1 went into orbit, the first photographic survey of Cambodia was undertaken from outer space. That year saw the culmination of an escalating campaign of "secret" bombing unleashed by the Nixon administration. The satellite image captured a landscape transformed by close to three million tons of bombs dropped on Cambodia between 1965 and 1973, ravaging villages, fields, and forests. The image became known, however, not so much for the damage it showed, but rather for providing the "before" image — the supposedly normal baseline — against which another crime would be registered: the atrocities perpetrated by the Khmer Rouge regime a few years later on this very terrain. A satellite survey undertaken in 1985, six years after the Khmer Rouge regime was eliminated, shows a huge orthogonal grid — a vast canal system dug

Damage to a village to the east of Shangil Tobay, North Darfur, Sudan. March 10, 2003 and December 18, 2006. DIGITALGLOBE. ORIGINAL SOURCE: AAAS, HIGH-RESOLUTION SATELLITE IMAGERY AND THE CONFLICT IN CHAD AND SUDAN, WWW.AAAS.ORG/PAGE/ APPENDIX-DARFUR-SUDAN-AND-CHAD-IMAGERY-CHARACTERISTICS

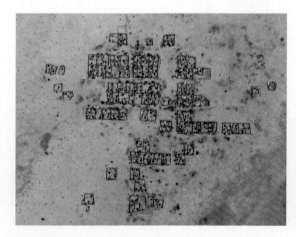
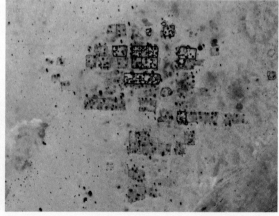

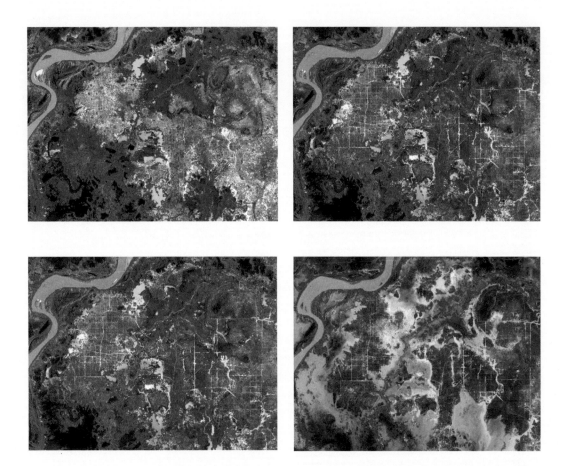

TOP ROW: Northeast of Phnom Penh, Cambodia. These are false color images in which red represents vegetation. Visible in the "after" image is an orthogonal grid of canals. January 3, 1973, Landsat 1 (path/row 135/52); and December 14, 1985, Landsat 5 (path/row 126/52). BOTTOM ROW: The area near Phnom Penh, Cambodia, before and after massive flooding. February 25, 1995 and January 14, 2009. Landsat 5 (path/row 126/52).
COURTESY OF US GEOLOGICAL SURVEY

by the Khmer Rouge along the one-square-kilometer gridlines on their maps. This irrigation system, whose construction was based on the slave labor of hundreds of thousands, was also the site of its killing fields. Of the two destructive periods in Cambodia's history, the US bombing is the less-represented episode, partially because although it was captured in the 1973 Landsat photograph, there was no "before" image to which it could be compared.[81]

The third major destruction to have befallen Cambodia in the last half century was the result of climate change. Although one of the countries contributing least to anthropogenic climate change, Cambodia is paying one of the highest prices for it in the increased frequency and severity of the monsoon floods. In 2011, the worst flood in Cambodia's recorded history saw three-quarters of its land area inundated and about 80 percent of the harvest destroyed. Climate change and its resultant ecocide now seems to have replaced genocide as the defining tragedy of our generation.

At different times throughout the Syrian conflict, Forensic Architecture was asked to locate air strikes based on images and clips posted on social media. Of all the strikes we worked on, I present here one likely undertaken by the US and one undertaken by the Russian and Syrian air force.

On March 8, 2015, three bombs were dropped on an area abutting the Turkish border, between the town of Atimah and a displaced-persons camp where more than thirty thousand civilians were sheltered. No military force has claimed responsibility for this attack, but it was likely a US strike on al-Qaeda militants who operated in the area.

Forensic Architecture was asked by the casualty-monitoring group Airwars to undertake an analysis that would confirm the exact strike location. People in the camp and in the town photographed the bomb clouds shortly after the strike and uploaded their images and videos on social media websites. We verified two sources to be of the same strike, taken from different perspectives — one from the town and the other from the displaced-persons camp. We reconstructed the cameras' locations and their cone of vision by identifying recognizable elements in the images. We intersected these perspectives to locate the strike. Comparing the size of the smoke plumes with those of other known bombs in our archive, we estimated that these were one-ton bombs.

The strikes targeted the eastern edge of the town of Atimah, close to homes and a public building, possibly an improvised hospital. The blasts were less than a kilometer away from the densely inhabited refugee camp. Six civilians were reportedly killed.[82]

LEFT: A photograph of bomb clouds rising next to the town of Atimah, Syria. The image was posted via Twitter by @Ahmadmuaffaq, March 8, 2015. RIGHT: A still image from a video clip of a bomb clouds rising next to the town of Atimah, Syria. The arrangement and shape of the bomb clouds is a mirror image of their arrangement in the previous image. It is taken from the opposite direction, March 8, 2015. SYRIAN OBSERVATORY FOR HUMAN RIGHTS

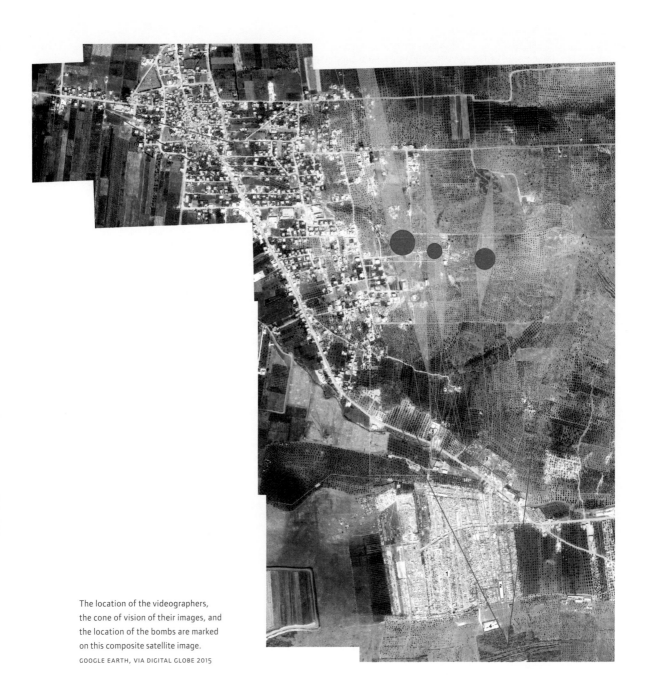

The location of the videographers,
the cone of vision of their images, and
the location of the bombs are marked
on this composite satellite image.
GOOGLE EARTH, VIA DIGITAL GLOBE 2015

On the morning of February 15, 2016, a hospital supported by Médicins Sans Fron-tières (MSF) in al-Hamidiah, a small village located south of Ma'arrat al-Numan, Idlib Province, Syria, was hit in two separate air strikes. This investigation was undertaken on behalf of MSF, as part of a project that seeks to investigate and publish informa-tion about every strike on their facilities. One strike completely destroyed the hos-pital. Twenty-five people died and eleven were wounded. Because the first attack occurred during the changeover from the night shift to the day shift, the patient count had not yet been carried out. This meant that in the early stages of the res-cue operations, first responders could not know the extent of the number of people trapped or crushed under the rubble.

A second attack occurred roughly two hours later. The town of Ma'arrat al-Numan and its outskirts were also attacked, with a strike later that day targeting the national hospital. Members of the opposition group, the Free Syrian Army's Observatory who operate like plane spotters, posted that on the morning of the attack Russian war-planes were spotted leaving Hamaymen airport, a Russian military base. These planes likely committed the first set of strikes. Later that same day, MiG-23 fighter jets belonging to the Syrian military were spotted leaving Hama airport and most likely took part in the later bombing raid.[83]

LEFT: A still frame from a video posted on JISRTV (the pro-opposition satellite channel Al Jisr TV) shows a bomb cloud seconds after a blast destroyed the MSF-supported hospital of al-Hamidiah, in Ma'arrat al-Numan, Syria, February 15, 2015. RIGHT: A still frame from a video found on Twitter shows the same bomb cloud from a slightly different angle, February 15, 2015. IMAGE ANALYSIS BY FORENSIC ARCHITECTURE

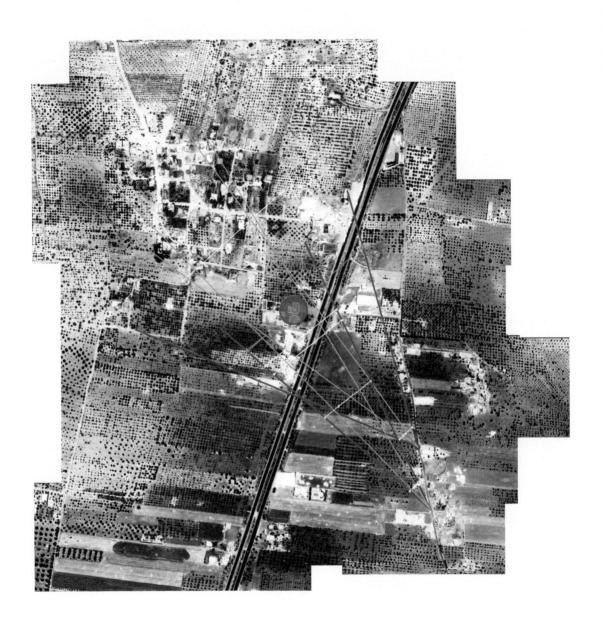

The location of the videographers,
the cone of vision of their images, and
the location of the bombs are marked
on this composite satellite image.
GOOGLE EARTH, VIA DIGITAL GLOBE 2015

On Friday, April 17, 2009, near the West Bank village of Bil'in, an unarmed demonstrator, Bassem Abu Rahma, was shot and killed by a tear-gas canister fired across
the fence of the separation barrier (wall) there. Four years previously, the military
had declared this protest area one of its "closed military zones," arresting and impris-
oning nonviolent activists. In the context of such encounters, open-fire instructions
allow soldiers to use only "nonlethal means," such as, ostensibly, tear gas and rubber-
coated steel bullets, unless their lives are in danger. But these can be used to kill and
have killed on dozens of occasions. It was the military's way to make such nonviolent
protests harder and to force events to escalate into armed encounters in which it has
the advantage. Where there were no activists' cameras around to record the incidents,
no police or military investigations were conducted. This was one of the reasons why
protestors started using cameras extensively.

Tear gas is considered a nonlethal munition, but it can kill when the hard alumi-
num canister, fired through a special gun, hits a human body directly. Soldiers are
supposed to shoot these munitions only upward, in a ballistic trajectory of 60 degrees.

The killing of Abu Rahma was recorded not by one, but by three video cameras
from different angles. However, the military had persisted in denying responsibility,
claiming that the soldiers did not fire the canister directly at Abu Rahma and that he
might have been hit by a deflection, and they closed the investigation. After the closing of the file, Forensic Architecture was commissioned to undertake a scene reconstruction at the request of Michael Sfard, who was acting for Abu Rahma's parents
and the Israeli human rights organization B'Tselem.[84] The legal team appealed to the
High Court to force the military to investigate the killing.

One of the three people filming that day was David Reeb, an Israeli artist/activist
who was standing right next to Abu Rahma when he was shot. His footage showed a
group of Israeli soldiers on the opposite side of the fencing system of the separation
barrier. A few seconds later, a single still frame captured a faint and blurry streak.
This was the projectile moving horizontally in midflight. Three frames later, the canister impacts. Abu Rahma is heard calling out in pain. Reeb quickly turns the camera
toward him.

Our report located the videos and the participants in a 3D model and demonstrated that the lethal strike was shot in direct aim, intentionally to kill or maim. The
report was signed February 22, 2010, and presented to the Israeli High Court on March
28, 2010, in a petition against the military's decision to close the case. The ruling

forced the Military Advocate General (MAG) to reopen the criminal investigation. The military thus had to engage our evidence and confront our analysis. On April 3, 2014, we received the military's "counter expert report," signed by Lieutenant Colonel Naftali XXXXX (his surname was crossed out), presented as the "Senior Deciphering Officer of the IDF Intelligence Corps." His report claimed that the streak we identified in the video "has not directly hit Abu Rahma" and provided drawings that attempted to explain his determination.

Our response was submitted on July 25, 2014: it was impossible to analyze the movement of a projectile in space based on two-dimensional images only. Photographs or video stills need to be located within three-dimensional models to determine relations between elements such as characters, objects, points of origin, and trajectories, otherwise flattened on a two-dimensional surface. We provided a set of models that constructed the scene in 3D and located the projectile in space. Our 3D model showed that it had to have passed only a few centimeters from the lens of the camera to be captured as a streak.

A wide panoramic collage of the still frames from Reeb's footage helped reconstruct more elements of the sequence of events in the incident: Reeb's camera is zooming in on the soldiers and holding on them for a few seconds; a soldier is seen looking directly

Video still from David Reeb's camera showing the faint trace of the path of the lethal projectile flying from left to right seemingly across the fencing system. FORENSIC ARCHITECTURE AND SITU RESEARCH

at the camera, then raising his gun. Reeb starts panning to the right while zooming out. While the camera moves across the fences, the sound of a shot is heard at the same time that the blurry streak appears in the aforementioned frame. Abu Rahma is seen falling to the ground. Looking at this sequence repeatedly, we started to suspect that the shot might have aimed at the very camera that recorded it. It was possible that the soldier aimed directly at Reeb's camera, missed it by a few centimeters, and hit Abu Rahma, who stood right next to him. It was the same incident documented in Emad Burnat and Guy Davidi's documentary *Five Broken Cameras*. The broken cameras in

A panoramic collage made out of footage captured in David Reeb's camera. The different sizes of frames are due to Reeb's zooming out. The image with the streak is marked in the red frame and was enlarged on page 109. FORENSIC ARCHITECTURE AND SITU RESEARCH

0:00:02,06

Bil'in demonstrated the degree to which the military perceives image making as a threat and also the risks involved in documenting soldiers in action.[85]

The case still drags on in the military courts without resolution. Lieutenant Colonel XXXXX, the military expert, now agrees with our analysis that the canister was fired directly, but now, incredibly, he claims that the military police do not know who the soldiers seen in our video analysis are, nor have they interviewed them since, despite a killing having occurred. Seven years after the incident, no one has been arrested or even interrogated in this case.

אירוע אבו רחמה 4/9/2009
ניתוח סרט של מערכת תצפית באלאדין

צילום מעמדת תצפית אלאדין - רגע הפגיעה. מיקום אבו רחמה ולידו הצלם ריב.
מסומן נתיב ירי ע"פ תניתוח תצלומי ריב.

מסקנה עיקרית - צילום הירי בפריים של ריב, בהנחה כי זהו האמצעי הפוגע - לא נורה ישירת לאבו רחמה אלא ניתז.

Lieutenant Colonel Naftali XXXXX's trajectory study in his counterforensic report on our first report. Abu Rahma is marked by the red circle, Reeb (Reev, in the report) is marked by the blue circle. The lines in yellow are Reeb's camera's cone of vision. The projectile trajectory, according to him, is marked by the dotted purple line. The Hebrew caption on the image reads: "Analysis of the Abu Rahma incident. April 9, 2009 [the incident took place on April 17]. Photograph from [military] observation post Aladin. The moment of impact. The position of Abu Rahma and near him Reeb, marking the trajectory of fire according to analysis of Reeb's footage. Main conclusion: the photograph of the trajectory in Reeb's frame, assuming it is the impacting measure—was not aimed directly at Abu Rahma, but was deflected." IDF INTELLIGENCE CORPS

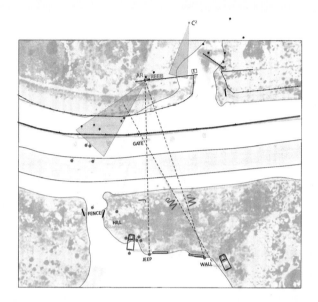

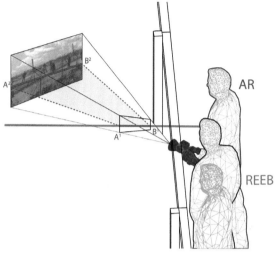

LEFT: A top view of a 3D model showing the location of Abu Rahma and Reeb in relation to the soldiers on the other side of the fence. J represents the trajectory of the canister as it would travel from the "Jeep Position" to strike Abu Rahma. W represents the trajectory that the military counterforensic expert proposed. It does not directly strike Abu Rahma. It is an impossible trajectory, according to our 3D model. W1 represents the trajectory of the canister as it would travel from the "wall" position to strike Abu Rahma, passing close to the camera. It is more likely the trajectory that was recorded as the streak. RIGHT: A model showing the trajectory of the projectile (the streak) in three dimensions. It passes very close to the camera lens, missing it by a few centimeters before striking Abu Rahma (AR). Positions A and B indicate the same endpoints of the trajectory that appear on the two-dimensional photographic plane in Reeb's footage. FORENSIC ARCHITECTURE AND SITU RESEARCH

113

PATTERNS

Violence unfolds on different scales, over different durations, and at different speeds: it manifests itself in the instantaneous, eruptive force of the incident, evolves in patterns and repetitions across built-up areas, and then manifests itself in the slower, incremental degradation of large territories along extended timescales. The different scales and speeds of violence are interrelated and convertible to one another. Incremental processes of environmental degradation build up tension that can then erupt with the kinetic force of armed conflict. But although the different scales, durations, and speeds of violence are entangled and codependent, seldom are they studied and presented together. Each becomes perceptible by different optics, is often engaged by different organizations, and relates to different juridical and political frameworks. The problem is similar to that of the figure-ground gestalt. An observer, at a given moment, can see either a figure or the ground.

At other times, such scalar arrangements can be wrongly interpreted as the structure of causality, but the large-scale political, strategic, or territorial conditions cannot be understood as a root cause of all local incidents. The connections between what historian Marc Bloch called "micro- and macro-history, between close-ups and extreme long shots," run along multiple threads and feedback loops in which local, sudden, unforeseen, eruptive incidents or accidents, the result of chance or of miscalculations, can reorient development in unexpected directions and trigger large-scale transformations.[86] Our investigations adopted a cross-scalar approach in which we might start with a shooting incident, then zoom out to map repeated patterns of such incidents in time and space, then open up further to study the area's long-term history and politics, and the transformation of its environment over time.

The individual is the molecular level of human rights analysis and the vanishing point of its optics. Small-incident analysis, whether evidenced in testimony of image/video material, seeks to connect individual perpetrators to individual victims. It could thus be tried in a criminal context, whether local or international. Foregrounding individual perpetrators might be legally effective, but such individuations can also mask the political reality and historical context. Although they are generally reluctant to do so, when put under pressure, states and militaries might single out and even indict individual soldiers who perpetrated violence and insist that it was in excess of orders and aberrations of standard operating procedures. Labeling such cases "abnormal" creates a threshold that helps present the rest as legitimate.[87] If evidence is to exceed the individual soldier's criminal liability and implicate the higher military and political levels, it is essential to demonstrate that an incident is part of a repetitive pattern of similar violations, that takes place in different parts of the battlefield by different units. Patterns allow lawyers to attribute violations to the military's mode of operation, rather than to individual decisions. Mapping such patterns can help establish what international lawyers call the "widespread and systemic" nature of the violations, which, alongside their "gravity," is an important condition for a war crime conviction.[88]

The larger the data set, the more reliable and coherent the time/space patterns that might emerge. Different algorithms can establish correlations, clusters, and associations between incidents that otherwise would have remained invisible.

Pattern analysis originated in the development of technologies of risk management by financial or security companies, and as previously noted, had been weaponized by the CIA in the preemptive drone strikes.[89] But like countermapping and counterforensics, pattern analysis can also be repurposed to be employed while investigating state violence.

In recent decades, human rights research was limited by the scarcity of sources and evidence; at present, there is such a large quantity of information that the problem becomes instead how to manage and generate insights from an overabundance of data. As the stack of hay is getting higher, human rights analysis must simultaneously both be looking for the needles (the incidents) and at the disposition of the stack (their patterns).

Employed in the analysis of state violence, patterns can reveal the modes and frequencies of attacks on specific target types, the modes of their destruction, casualties, and more. They can reveal trends, origins, and phase transitions. A shift in strike policy might be traced back to a preconceived plan, to an operational order, to a change in standard operating procedures, or to tacit political approval of certain violations. Patterns can reveal how peaks of violence and rapid escalation emerge in retaliation for military setbacks, for example. It can also capture more elusive processes of "cumulative radicalization," in which different military units of the same force might mimic or compete to outdo each other. Other types of pattern analysis can look at situations in which a particular type of information is being repeatedly withdrawn, erased, obfuscated, denied, or censored by military or other state agencies. Such patterns in the withdrawal of evidence can become evidence in their own right.

Starting in 2014, Forensic Architecture (in a project coordinated by Francesco Sebregondi) developed an open-source software called PATTRN, designed as a crowd-sourcing device that allows activists to upload information and then map relations between discrete events, identifying patterns and trends in time and space. PATTRN was conceived to enable citizen-driven participatory mapping. Our aim was to support the sharing and collation of first-hand reports of events on the ground by the very people who are subjected to violence, to assemble reports and produce analysis, and eventually to bypass the need for professional investigators. Crowd-sourcing needs to be able to safeguard the anonymity of users. Data protection is key, and the anonymization technologies that we employ are the basic condition of participation in situations where identification of researchers could be risky. Verification can be undertaken not by tracing the provenance of evidence back to the identity of users (which could be dangerous for them and would render the tool vulnerable in court), but by peer-to-peer correction with minimal editorial oversight.[90]

PATTRN is employed by several organizations. Some require pattern analysis for identifying trends in past data. The ICC in The Hague, which is considering opening proceedings against Israel for the 2014 Gaza war, needed to undertake pattern analysis to determine if violations were "widespread and systematic" and has been studying the database of Israeli attacks during this war processed by Forensic Architecture's software.

But pattern analysis also can be used to provide general predictions and indications of where and when vulnerabilities might be expected. Organizations working on risks to migrants in the Mediterranean used PATTRN to identify the convergence of categories that would help identify such emergent risks or where people might most likely be intercepted or left to die. The accuracy of prediction is based on the quality and quantity of data. Any result needs to be treated with caution, merely as an indicator of possibility. But pattern analysis in the human rights context might open the way for forensic techniques to be used not only for studying the past, but also, tactically, in predictive manner, oriented toward the future.

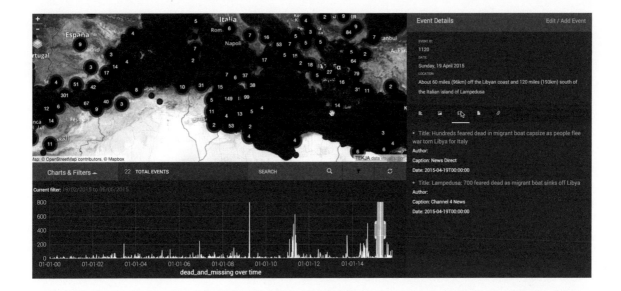

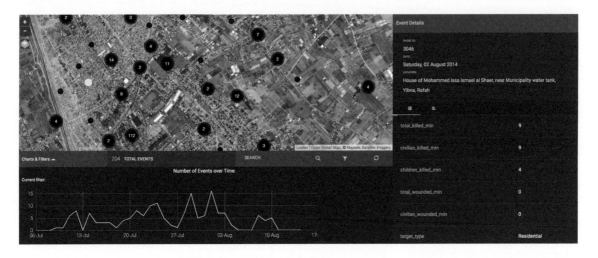

TOP: Events in which people died trying to reach Europe. Fortress Europe: Visualization of the Migrants' Files datasets. The Migrants' Files is a consortium of journalists from fifteen European countries that collect data on the number of people who die in their attempt to reach or stay in Europe. BOTTOM: The Gaza Platform: an interactive map of Israeli attacks during the 2014 Gaza conflict, which logged in and found patterns within more than twenty-three hundred incidents during that war. Data collected and shared by the Al-Mezan Center for Human Rights, the Palestinian Center for Human Rights, and Amnesty International.
FORENSIC ARCHITECTURE/PATTRN; AMNESTY INTERNATIONAL AND FORENSIC ARCHITECTURE/PATTRN

The environment, whether built, natural, or the entanglement of the two, is not a neutral background against which violence unfolds. Its destruction is also not always the unintended "collateral damage" of attacks aimed at other things. Rather, environmental destruction or degradation over an extended timescale can be the means by which belligerents pursue their aims. The targeting of life-sustaining resources such as fields, forests, and water sources or infrastructural systems such as roads and electricity networks can erode the conditions that sustain life. This is a form of environmental destruction that can be undertaken as a means of population control and ethnic cleansing. And the effects of environmental degradation can linger for years after the actual fighting has ceased. It can also become a contributing cause to the eruption of further conflicts or to the aggravation of existing ones. The environment thus belongs within the histories of violence, and to include it, we must engage the historical perspective of the *longue durée*, that is, to be both geographically broad and historically deep.[91]

Some forms of environmental violence[92] are largely invisible. "Slow violence," literary critic Rob Nixon has pointed out, "occurs gradually and out of sight, a violence of delayed destruction that is dispersed across time and space, an attritional violence that is typically not viewed as violence at all."[93] His examples include the aftereffects of the use of the defoliant Agent Orange in Cambodia and Vietnam and the toxic drift of oil spills. The slow violence of environmental degradation is lethal, and not only because it causes or aggravates armed conflict. Slow violence exacts its own victims who, in many cases, outnumber the direct casualties of war.[94] Mortality rates increase when water sources get contaminated or depleted, when fields or a forest on which a community depends are burned down, cut, or poisoned. While direct mortality—from trauma, bullets, or explosives—is visible and mappable, figures of indirect mortality, resulting from the destruction of life-sustaining environments or infrastructure, are more difficult to establish. This kind of environmental violence is slow, often formless, diffused, and continuous and thus largely imperceptible, unimageable, and unimaginable.[95] It is often not considered violence at all, thus demanding that we expand our definition of what might constitute violence, what might count as killing, and also what amounts to evidence. Indeed, evidence of this kind of violence is hard to establish because the consequences are spread across extended periods of time and large territories, and its perpetration involves the interaction of various agents and phenomena. When used as a weapon of war, environmental violence can become a subtle way of killing that masks perpetrators by distancing them from the victim. It also accounts for slow and painful ways of dying.

In generating evidence, we should look at the environment as a medium of inscription. Plants are useful sensors. The long-term biomonitoring of plants across extended territories and time spans is one of the ways in which the facts of environmental violence and other forms of environmental change can be established. Whether in agricultural environments, savannahs, or forests, plants are sentient, sensing bodies. Shifts in their year-to-year patterns of vigor and decay record long-term transformations in the environment — changes in the climate, but also political transformations, the result of conflicts, as well as combinations of all the above. An archive of plant transformations over extended regions and decades exists in the remote sensing data of earth-observation satellites such as Landsat, which go back to the start of the program in the early 1970s.

Using environmental data as evidence for armed conflict poses challenges that are not only scientific, but also representational, legal, and political. While criminal law seeks to establish a linear string of causal relations between intentions, actions, and victims or between, so to speak, the two ends of a smoking gun, the representation of the causes of environmental violence demands the establishment of more complex and diffused causal structures. I propose the term "field causality" to refer to indirect forms of causality, multidirectional and distributed over extended spaces and time durations. It is an inherently spatial form of causality whose employment seeks to reconnect the multiple threads that linear juridical protocols have torn apart.

Inversely, when presented in isolation, particularly in legal settings, field causality can also end up becoming the bastard's best line of defense. Often, perpetrators will attempt to use such explanatory structures to deflect accusations of their direct responsibility. It is indeed currently more common as a form of deflection than as an operative form of forensic analytics. Against a persistent defense in the context of a criminal trial, it is hard enough, chief forensic scientist of the ICC Eric Baccard sarcastically informed a group of us in a work meeting, to establish that a hole in a skull measuring 5.56 millimeters is the result of a 5.56-millimeter bullet, let alone to suggest complex and diffused field causalities.[96] Extending causal ecologies and pulling more actors and agents into them might result, in the eyes of the legal professionals, in the production of "dirty evidence." That is, an excess of information that lawyers often feel compelled to distill into a linear chain of distinct cascading actions—according to the mechanical or "billiard ball" model of criminal causality which finds it necessary to draw straight lines between perpetrators and victims. But whatever evidence is excessive in relation to the protocols and institutional needs of one forum might become important in another. And the "dirt" in one context might be exactly the operative element in another.

The necessary forums for dealing with field causalities are currently not juridical, but political. To establish field causalities for environmental violence is to articulate the material basis for the imperative to reconfigure the political field fundamentally, as opposed to the tendency of international justice to isolate and punish a few individuals and leave the social and economic structure intact.

GUATEMALA: ENVIRONMENTAL VIOLENCE

The violence inflicted by Guatemalan security forces—both the military and military-organized civil militias—on the Ixil Maya people in the El Quiché region of West Guatemala between 1978 and 1984 amounted, according to Guatemala's 1999 Comisión para el Esclarecimiento Histórico (CEH), to "acts of genocide."[97] Indigenous Maya, 60 percent of the population of Guatemala, accounted for some 83 percent of the victims of the civil war. Thousands of people were massacred and ninety villages were destroyed, along with large-scale deforestation, the latter purportedly to expose guerrilla hideouts, but in fact meant to render the area uninhabitable, which it did.

American historian Greg Grandin called these events "the last colonial massacre" and the culmination of a five-century-long process of colonization, land grabs, and massacres suffered by the indigenous people of Central America.[98] However, the CEH considered the events of the civil war to be an isolated historical incident, an aberration from the existent social order thereby ignoring the terror of the area's colonial history. This problem was nested in another: as substantive as the final report of Guatemala's CEH was, it was largely textual and was not furnished with extensive maps. Statistics about destruction and mortality were provided, along with the testimonies of survivors, but the civil war remained little understood as a process of physical transformations continuous with Guatemala's colonial history.

LEFT: The foundation of a house overgrown by vegetation near the village of Pexla Grande. RIGHT: A stone from the foundation of a house burnt to the ground during the massacre of the village of Pexla Grande in 1982.
FORENSIC ARCHITECTURE

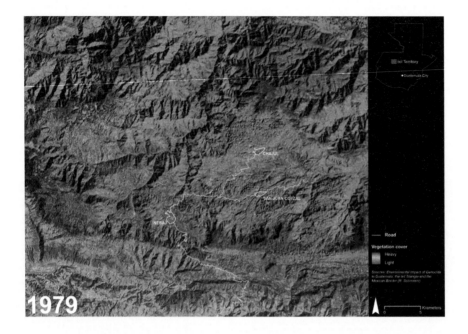

1979

Road

Vegetation cover
   Heavy
   Light

Sources: Environmental Impact of Genocide in Guatemala, the Ixil Triangle and the Mexican Border (R. Schreiner)

Forensic Architecture was commissioned to undertake spatial research in support of action promoted by an NGO, the Centro para la Acción Legal en Derechos Humanos (CALDH), which attempted to foreground such colonial continuities.[99] The research, undertaken with Paulo Tavares, was conducted on two distinct scales. On the architectural scale, we aimed to help locate remnants of destroyed buildings, mainly in and around the villages of Pexla Grande and Xolcuay, to help estimate their size and population. On the larger scale, we studied environmental transformations between 1978 and 1983, at the height of the repression, in the larger Quiché region of West Guatemala, where these villages were located. Besides CALDH, the research was also undertaken on behalf of the Oficina de Derechos Humanos del Arzobispado de Guatemala (ODHAG), and the exhumation teams of the Fundación de Antropología Forense de Guatemala (FAFG), introduced to us by Clyde Snow. The context included several legal processes. In 2012–2013, the trial of Efraín Ríos Montt, former military dictator of Guatemala between March 1982 and August 1983, took place in the National Court of Guatemala. After Montt's genocide conviction was overturned by the Guatemala Constitutional Court in 2013, our research was presented as part of a legal process pursued in the Inter-American Court of Human Rights, where the Ixil Community took its demands for justice.[100] The second trial concerned the period of General Lucas Romeo García, who ruled before Montt, between July 1978 and March 1982.

We examined vegetation change between a satellite image taken by NASA Landsat 3 in February 1979 and one taken by Landsat 5 in March 1986, the images most closely bracketing the period of the genocide. The resolution of these images — in the two images, a pixel is 30 and 60 meters square, respectively — is not sharp enough to capture individual villages, but sufficient to record territorial-scale vegetation change. Normalized difference vegetation index (NDVI) analysis visualizes the vigor of the earth's vegetation cover. Green indicates vegetation gain, while red/ pink shows vegetation loss during the period of the military campaign in the mountains. FORENSIC ARCHITETURE WITH THE COLLABORATION OF SITU RESEARCH

1986

Legend:

- ▪▪ Military base
- ▢ Community destroyed between 1980 and 1984
- ◁ Model village completed by 1986
  Total: 8 completed villages
- ▷ New settlement
  Total: 7 new settlements
- Road built within the development poles program
- Road built prior to development poles program

Vegetation cover
- Heavy
- Light

Sources: ODHAG, CEH, Refugees of a Hidden War (B. Manz, 1988), and Environmental Impact of Genocide in Guatemala (the Ixil Triangle and the Mexican Border (R. Schlosmer)

0   1 Kilometers   5

Our work was based on three periods of fieldwork in Guatemala, undertaken in December 2011, November 2012, and March 2013. Because the buildings of the Ixil were constructed of wood and adobe, once they were destroyed, the organic remains were quickly consumed by the cloud forest. To identify building remains we learned to follow the plants. Fruit trees such as avocados, papayas, or peaches signal the possible former presence of house and village sites.[101] Only the foundations were made of stone, but more than thirty years of overgrowth made it necessary to probe the ground with sticks to find their harder surfaces, then clear the shrubs with a machete to measure the extent of the ruin.

Like other Maya peoples across the mountains of Guatemala, the Ixil inhabited this area with dispersed homesteads surrounded by small subsistance gardens of beans and maize set in clearings within the otherwise dense cloud forest. The forest was considered a commons and was to some extent man-made, with cultural afforestation of medicinal plants and fruit trees existing in higher densities around inhabited areas.

The Ixil Mayas were refugees from the centuries-long process of colonization, gradually pushed from the fertile valleys and coastal plains up toward the harsher highlands and mountaintops. The military's repressions in the area that it referred to as the "Ixil Triangle" escalated between 1978 to 1983. The entire territory was occupied by the military, which considered the Ixil Maya people to be "subversives" and their villages to be

The natural environment registered this process in two distinct ways. In the south, where villages were destroyed and "poles of development" were erected, large parts of the forest were burned down. This is registered as vegetation loss in the southern areas. In the northern areas of this image, abandoned villages were taken over by the forest—shrubs and trees are more robust and durable than cultivated plants—and registered as a rebound in vegetation biomass. What otherwise could have been interpreted as a return to wilderness, as nature repairing itself, is in fact evidence for a process of ethnic cleansing. FORENSIC ARCHITECTURE WITH THE COLLABORATION OF SITU RESEARCH

the material base of an insurgency. Despite the insurgency being responsible for only some 3 percent of the acts of violence conducted during the conflict, according to the CEH (the rest was undertaken by government forces), it was characterized, in the contemporaneous language of the Cold War, as "infiltrating Communist cells" operating deep within the forests, an environment that, from Cuba through Peru to Colombia, eluded the US military and its proxies.

It was in fact the autonomy that the Ixil enjoyed in the high mountain areas — they were not citizens of the state and did not participate in the national economy — that was in itself perceived as a threat to national sovereignty. The campaign was about more than putting down an insurgency — it was about the "domestication" of these unruly areas and bringing them into the fold of the state. The logic was both strategic and political: the destruction of the environmental conditions upon which the ways of life of the Ixil Maya depended was meant to bring them under state control.

The Guatemalan military command marked many of the landlocked highlands as "red zones." In them, they explained the logic of the operation as "draining the water to kill the fish," an inversion of one of Mao's famous dictums, "the guerrilla must move among the people as a fish swims in the sea." This involved acts of both construction and destruction. Abut 80 percent of the Ixil villages were razed, and thousands of civilians were killed. Fields and forests were burned down. Alongside all this destruction, a major project of construction and territorial reorganization also took place. Survivors were resettled in "poles of development" — concentration towns surrounded by "model villages" — where they were educated in modern agricultural techniques and monocrop cultivation of modern seeds, a strategy similar to the methods of "territorial reduction" — the concentration of dispersed indigenous people to free up the land for development — used by Spanish colonizers.

Model village of Acul, ca. 1984.
MAGAZINE OF THE GUATEMALAN ARMY,
POLOS DE DESARROLO Y SERVICIOS, 1984

The case of the village of Beit Surik, north of Jerusalem, was the first petition brought against the separation barrier known as "the Wall" in the Israeli High Court, but typical of the rest to come. When a topographical model showing the path of the Wall was brought to court, at the request of the judges, the parties had to leave their designated places and assemble around it. The physical properties of the model interrupted the court's protocol and its formalities, and the legal process came to resemble a design session, with different proposals for the "best of all possible walls" debated by the parties. The result was a new route that was a little less invasive, but that also justified the presence of the Wall. Forensic Architecture participated in another case which attempted a different approach.

The Palestinian village of Battir is located south of Jerusalem, close to the 1949 Green Line that established the original borders of the state of Israel. Its farmers have long cultivated an ancient terraced landscape using a unique network of open irrigation channels dating to the Roman era. It is a small and jewel-like landscape, only a kilometer-and-a-half long, a fragile garden surrounded by an otherwise torn

Parties assemble around the model.
CHRISTINE CORNELL WITH EYAL WEIZMAN

landscape. In June 2014, UNESCO, the first UN body to have recognized Palestine as a member state, placed this landscape on its list of World Heritage Sites. The decision was implemented in an emergency process, after UNESCO found that "the landscape had become vulnerable under the impact of socio-cultural and geo-political transformations." UNESCO was referring to Israeli plans to erect the the Wall on this very site.

Forensic Architecture was approached by Michael Sfard, who in 2012 brought a petition against the construction of the Wall in Battir to the Israeli High Court on behalf of the Friends of the Earth Middle East. He commissioned us to undertake a survey of the area and to model the impact the Wall would have on the landscape.

The case provided a number of important lessons. It was the first petition against the Wall that was not pursued on the basis of human rights, which previously had resulted in negotiations between human rights lawyers and the military over the "least invasive" route of the Wall under the principle of proportionality, but rather on the basis of environmental rights. The claim we made for Battir was on behalf of the landscape, archaeology, and nature. Animated by the law, elements of this landscape assumed something of a nonhuman "legal personhood" in the same way that corporations receive the rights of persons in US law or ecosystems in the Ecuadorian or Bolivian constitutions.[102] The case might thus be aptly named *The Landscape of Battir v. the Government of Israel,* or simply, the landscape against the state.

This legal strategy allowed the formation of an odd coalition composed of Palestinian villagers, environmental NGOs, archaeologists, and even some Jewish settlers who supported UNESCO's determination regarding the site's heritage value and who objected to the Wall on the basis of this landscape being "biblical" — likely due to the nearby presence of an ancient ruin, Khirbet el-Yahud (the Jewish Ruin), the presumed site of Beitar, where a celebrated and partially successful Jewish revolt against the Roman Empire was believed to have taken place. The paradox of this case was that bypassing the frame of human rights and claiming the rights of the environment best served the human rights of the villagers and their political struggle against the Wall. On January 4, 2015, after a three-year battle, the high court ruled against the government, rejecting the plan to build the Wall anywhere within this landscape. Whereas all previous cases achieved mere improvements in the path of the Wall, this case achieved its cancellation entirely within the limited area of the petition. There will be a permanent gap in the Wall there. In legal terms, it was a small, but rather satisfying victory. Disrupting the politics of partition in one place might also help challenge it in other places. More generally, we used it to challenge the very principle of separation. If it is possible to avoid building the Wall on this site, why not everywhere? Is Palestine not in its entirety an environment endowed with cultural heritage and delicate fragile beauty? This case taught us that the common environment might be a good place to start building a politics of sharing.[103]

TOP: The landscape of Battir, 2009. At the lower right is the train line and the proposed path of the Wall. BOTTOM: Advocate Emily Schaeffer presents the Battir file with computer renderings by Forensic Architecture, 2014. TOP: SAMIR HARB; BOTTOM: FORENSIC ARCHITECTURE

We cannot know the past as a conclusive, transparent fact mechanically etched into matter or memory or perfectly captured in an image. Histories of violence will always have their lacunas and discontinuities. They are inherent in violence and trauma and to a certain extent evidence of them. When undertaking our investigations, we must take into account the difficulties and complexities of memory, just as we do with photography and other forms of material investigation. No evidence ever speaks for itself. It must always be presented and face cross-interrogation—nothing is guaranteed. In trying to interpret and present the evidence before us, we must continually try to steer between the two opposing tendencies into which all discussions of truth gravitate—a totalizing view of a single, privileged position, and a relativist, anti-universalist perspective that regards all truths as multiple, relative, or nonexistent. Access to truth can be obtained by local communities and groups rather than only by institutional science and law, but this "positional" truth has to be fought for.

The starting point for each of our investigations is the inherent contradiction in all accounts—not only between the claims of the state and its military and the accounts of its civilian victims, but also within each of these groups and sometimes within a single testimony or a single bit of material or media evidence. Sometimes from that great, messy flood of testimonies and pixels, from the contradictions and unknowables, it is possible to assemble, with some effort, a more or less coherent narrative (or a counternarrative) that is cognizant of the problem of truth-telling, and claim, "This is what happened here." But even in such cases, we record the situated perspectives and divergences and regard them not as falsehoods, but as information in their own right.

We do not have at our disposal the same access to technologies and information that rich states, corporations, and their militaries might be able to muster. We sometimes have only weak signals at the threshold of detectability with which to disrupt the flood of obfuscating messages and attempts at denial—a faint and blurry streak, identified in a single frame of a video shot by a videographer-activist, a few pixels, lighter than their surroundings, that indicate, in the absence of other photographic documentation, the likely place of impact of a drone-fired missile, changes in the vigor of vegetation that demonstrate the loss of biomass in the cloud forest and thus the displacement of the indigenous peoples who lived there.

It is precisely because of the potentially fragile nature of such evidence that political mobilization is necessary. Unlike law, politics does not seek to render judgment on past events from the vantage point of the present and its institutions. Rather, it is driven by a desire to change the way things are.

One of the most important insights from time spent in forensic work together with activist and human rights groups is that rather than numbing our perceptions of the pain of others, work on sensing, detecting, calculating, processing, and presenting the facts of violence and destruction has, in fact, further sensitized us to the world around us.

In achieving a heightened state of sensitivity to the actuality and material consequences of politics, we realized that we had grown to have something in common with the objects of our investigation. No matter if you are a building, a territory, a photograph, a pixel, or a person, to sense is to be imprinted by the world around you, to internalize its force fields, and to transform. And to transform is to feel pain.

Khirbat al-Adas

8.2

UNWRA

H

Najjar Hospital

al-Genenah District

supermarket

Al-ourouba st/ Uruba st./ Orooba st

Abu Shawara building

Salam District

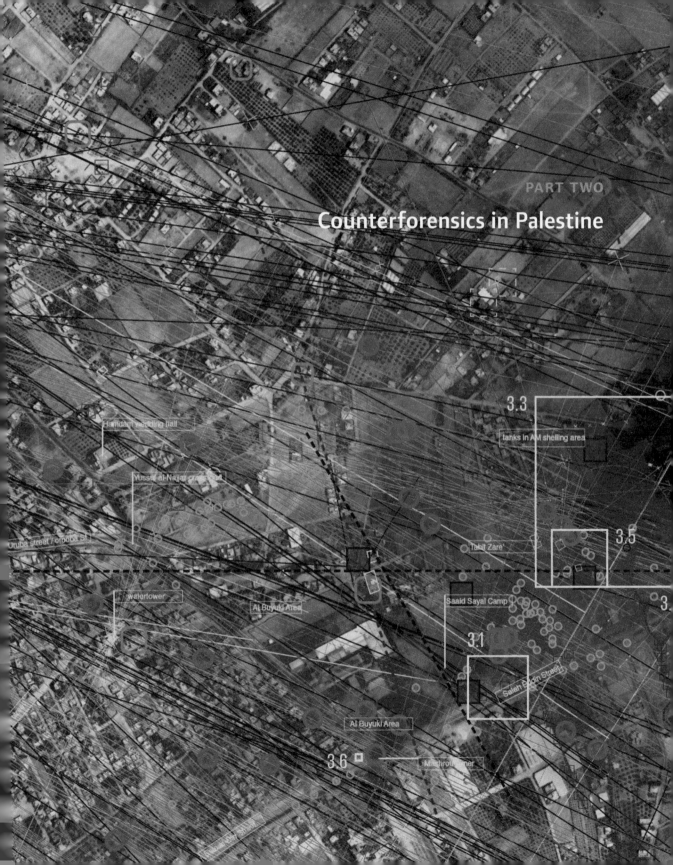

PART TWO

Counterforensics in Palestine

3.3

tanks in AM shelling area

Hamdam wedding hall

Yussif al-Najjar crossroad

3.5

Uruba street / orooba St

Tahit Zare'

3.

watertower

Al Buyuki Area

Saaid Sayal Camp

3.1

Salah al-Din Street

Al Buyuki Area

3.6

Mashrou Amer

The Forensic Dilemma

"TRAGEDY ENDEAVORS . . . to confine itself to a single revolution of the sun."[1] But to reconstruct the events of a single day, it is necessary, according to this schema in Aristotle's *Poetics*, to understand the sets of values and beliefs that drove them, that is, to pull out their historical threads and reconstruct the world of which that day is part. At the culmination of what follows is a reconstruction of the events of two days: the killing of two Palestinian teenagers on Nakba Day, May 15, 2014 — a tragedy that took place while commemorating another — in the town of Bituniya in the West Bank, and, a few months later, the events of August 1, 2014, in which the Israeli military manhunt of one of their own troops caused the deadliest incident in that year's Gaza war in the strip's southernmost city of Rafah.

To tell the story of these two separate, but related days requires movement between scales: it is in the details of those specific incidents that the longer shadows of the history of Palestine can be identified. Investigating specific incidents within a decade-long and ongoing history of colonization, domination, separation, and violence — a history so generously offered by the Palestine conflict — might otherwise seem futile: every day brings new violations and raises the pile of rubble even higher. Such outbreaks of violence are not interruptions of an existing peaceful order; they are endemic to Israel's system of domination and are essential to maintaining it. The two investigations are reproduced here in nearly complete detail, not because they are more detailed or complex than other investigations I presented in the previous part of the book, but in order to give more complete examples of how our investigations are conducted and how they might interact with the existing political reality.

Before starting to engage with the reconstruction of these two separate days, this chapter will present shorter accounts of other investigations Forensic Architecture has undertaken in Israel/Palestine in recent years. The reasons for presenting this material are both methodological and political. Methodologically, this material seeks to demonstrate a shift between two distinct architectural approaches. The first looks at architecture as an instrument of violation—of crimes committed on drawing boards and by buildings and infrastructure—a violence that is incremental, slow, and ever-present. The latter studies violent incidents—eruptive and kinetic events—in which the built environment has been a backdrop and a crime scene. While the former is concerned with the violence *of* architecture, the latter engages with violence that unfolds *within* it. In relation to the latter, such environments contain many eyewitnesses. They are saturated with both news media and media generated by those simply present at the events. Investigating events in such contexts involves cross-referencing multiple types of evidence: clips and images, material evidence and witness testimonies. We use architecture, or more precisely, virtual architectural models to create "evidence assemblages" that locate these elements in space and study the time/space relations between them.

Politically, this introductory material offers the possibility for reflection on the potentials, double binds, and limits of forensic architecture. Work in Palestine offers a good laboratory for such an undertaking. Indeed, as a political practice, forensic architecture seems to offer the kind of optimism expected of a pathologist. When we start our investigations, it is most often too late for many of those involved. The same applies to the practice's relation to the discipline of architecture: architects are trained to deliver new buildings; we get to study their last moments. Working in Palestine, we sometimes feel like coroners, investigators of a spatial murder—"spatiocide," in the words of Sari Hanafi, the murder of the landscapes of this country.[2] This might appear to be a cause of despair or even an allegory of the state of the Left (and of architecture) today. True enough, but this does not capture the entire picture.

This part of the book is being written at a time of great political impasse. Racist tendencies latent in Israeli society and its institutions are erupting, with bloody consequences. Looking at the ground, it is hard to imagine a future other than further dispossession, settlements, and violent repression. In such a context, examining the pathology of incidents will not right the wrong. Still, we document the precise form and measure of atrocities in their full and explicit horror because we are determined to set down the reality of what is taking place. Confronting denial, in our context is more than just a historical reckoning with the crimes of the past in the context of "transitional justice," that is, with efforts to redress the legacies of past human rights abuses. No such transition has yet occurred. Confronting denial is important because denial, in all its multiple forms, is the condition of possibility for violence to be perpetuated in the future. What has been denied will go on being perpetrated, and sometimes charting the architecture of hell is the only possible response.

The following investigations bear testimony to the contradictory, but always entangled modes of denial: negation and justification. Underscoring all instances of the denial of local incidents of Israeli violence against Palestinians is the negation of the Nakba that is at the foundation of the state. Israel's official history never acknowledged the ethnic cleansing of the areas of Palestine that became Israel in 1948, a crime that was always perceived to be too grave to be casually recognized as a historical fact. As historical documents made this denial harder to maintain, justification was called on to join an incoherent cacophony of official contradictions: the land was uninhabited; people ran away to join our enemies; the ethnic cleansing of Palestine was a horrible necessity without which Israel could not exist; allowing people to return would bring an end to the state; and so on. As in Freud's famous parable of a neighbor having to explain why the kettle s/he borrowed was returned broken,[3] arguments that "it never happened," "it didn't happen because of me," and "it had to happen" are employed simultaneously or in short succession, despite the contradictions involved.

The different ways in which Israel's legal system is part of the state's mechanism of domination and denial is something that others and I have written about at length.[4] There are two separate legal systems in existence in the area occupied and controlled by the state of Israel, one for Israelis and one for Palestinians. The mandate of the military legal system, inasmuch as it deals with Israeli military personnel, for example, assigns criminal responsibility via the most narrow of frames and is thus oriented exclusively toward low-ranking soldiers: it investigates only harm caused by a breach of commands, never the legality of these commands. Because the system is inaccessible to Palestinians, if they want to press charges against soldiers, they must rely on human rights organizations to file complaints on their behalf. Military investigators pursue cases primarily by taking soldiers' statements, "subcontracting" human rights groups to obtain Palestinian testimonies, which the military later most often dismisses as biased. That the military legal system draws legitimacy from the fact that it collaborates with human rights groups demonstrates the danger of collusion all such groups continuously face. In reality, less than a third of a single percent of complaints lead to charges being brought against implicated soldiers.[5] When it comes to Palestinians facing criminal charges in the military courts, the chances of conviction are mirror-inverted and have in recent years been 99.74 percent.[6]

Despite this structural inequality, Forensic Architecture has worked to provide evidence for human rights organizations that doggedly sought to document and make public the facts of military violence and violations. We undertook commissions from bereaved families to analyze acts of killing, and from residents fighting land expropriation who sought, often desperately, to protect what little land they had when we estimated our research could support a larger political initiative. We believed that we could make public, in multiple forums, the physical violence perpetrated by state agencies, and could expose and denounce the violence perpetrated by the law itself.

Official Israeli spokespersons use the existence of such a compromised legal system to claim that the state does everything in its power to investigate and charge the criminal offenses of soldiers. Thus, international humanitarian law is bound by the principle of "complementarity." The ICC, for example, is mandated to be a "court of last resort" that will step in only if states show themselves unable or unwilling to launch a process that addresses violations of international law.[7] Prosecuting a few single cases is thus a useful way to support the claim that the national legal system is competent and willing to examine itself and that therefore international action is redundant.

In 2014, despite several "successes,"[8] we at Forensic Architecture determined that withdrawal from the Israeli legal system is preferable to cooperating with it, that confronting Israel's regime of domination is better undertaken outside of the state's legal institutions, and that despite being compromised in other ways, international forums present a better chance for achieving accountability. We decided to no longer support legal cases or undertake forensic analysis on behalf of cases that are presented in Israeli legal forums except to deal with cases in the Israeli court system that we had already begun and remain committed to investigating to publicize Israel's violations and abuses in other forums.

Our forensics might be employed with a measure of hope, but certainly with no illusions: international courts, human rights reports, and UN commissions are not in themselves transformative platforms. They, too, need to be engaged with caution. We should be cautious that cases pursued in such contexts do not replace political and social processes with a stale, bureaucratized sense of justice. When we address such institutions, it is because this is part of a wider political strategy that includes other forms of civil action. Forensics, in this context, is only as good as the political process of which it is part.

ARCHITECTURE AGAINST ARCHITECTS

The practice of forensic architecture is not limited to the Palestine conflict, but its trajectory started there. Its origins are with a project that attempted to turn architecture against architects. In 2002, B'Tselem, the largest human rights group in Israel/Palestine, asked me—I was a recent architectural graduate at the time—to participate in the preparation of a report that would implicate the architects and planners involved in designing and building settlements in the West Bank as being in violation of human rights and international law. The preparation of the report necessitated a close reading of hundreds of urban and architectural plans, which were obtained from regional councils in the West Bank by logging freedom of information requests and through painstaking archival surveys in municipal planning offices. Although the settlements were present on the ground, their physical extent and form were not available from maps and drawings.

It was on the drawing boards, these plans demonstrated, that crimes were committed in the most basic gesture of architecture—lines drawn on paper. The violence performed on the drawing was later transferred to the ground. Such crimes against the landscape and people were intended to and succeeded in generating social and political harm—cutting apart communities, enveloping and isolating villages and neighborhoods, robbing cities of their open areas, landscapes, and water resources, limiting Palestinians' ability to use and enjoy space or to move through it. This was part of a general policy that sought to encourage people to move away, indeed, to force them to migrate—it was ethnic cleansing architecturally performed. I will not endeavor to tell the details of this story once more (it is available in *Land Grab*, the human rights report we published, as well as in *Hollow Land*, the book I wrote on its basis), but note that for reasons that are both technical and bureaucratic-judicial, our wish to see an architect in the dock of an international tribunal, alongside generals and politicians, has not yet been achieved.[9] Still, the architectural evidence produced in this process was presented in several other contexts, trials, UN commissions, and in a case pursued by the International Court of Justice (ICJ) in The Hague. It was also presented in various civil-society initiatives against the Israeli regime of domination and occupation, such as the publication of the Palestinian Civil Society Call for Boycott, Disinvestment, and Sanctions, which, when it emerged, relied on the ICJ ruling.[10] At the time, the project demonstrated both the violence perpetrated by architecture and the potential of architectural investigation and evidence to be used to confront it.

This image is a segment from a map of the West Bank produced as part of a human rights report entitled *Land Grab* that I coauthored with B'Tselem. In the blue spectrum are the Jewish settlements, areas of their planned extension, and larger areas under their jurisdiction; in the brown spectrum are Palestinian-built structures and their areas of limited jurisdiction, demonstrating the astounding interplay of political forms to which the conflict has given rise. This is an elastic, almost viscous process by which territories are continually transformed, made and remade in response to force fields around them. The map is nothing but a freeze-frame shot in a process of ongoing transformations. If we could press "play" on this map, we might see events unfolding at different speeds. At the speed of a day per second, we could see the displacement of people, uprooting of trees, and replanting of fields on their ruins. The speed of a month per second would show the way settlements expand to bisect and envelop Palestinian communities, and at the speed of a year per second, we could see, in a duration shorter than a minute, the complete physical and environmental transformation that the West Bank has undergone since its occupation, the way small outposts grow and connect, the way the roads are built to serve only those outposts, as well as the slow drying out of all Palestinian-held areas as water is diverted for the exclusive use of the colonies.[11] The fact that the map describes a complex interplay of material forms, rather than a homogenous blue (Israeli) surface, means that resistance does have effects on the ground. Hence the double premise of forensic architecture: if form is the product of forces, something of the history of those forces can be read in an analysis of form. Conversely, it demonstrates that architectural form is an active form, able to mobilize forces and violently snap back.

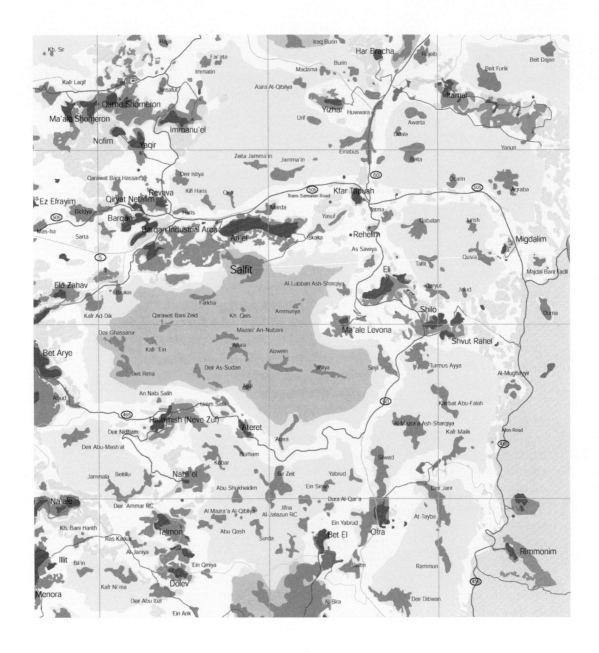

Map of the West Bank, 2002 (detail).

EYAL WEIZMAN AND B'TSELEM

Edward Said wrote critically about the imperial use of cartography: "In the history of colonial invasions maps are always first drawn by the victors, since maps are instruments of conquest." In addition he advocated for a form of "counter-cartography" able to confront the geographical violence of European imperialism: "Geography can also be the art of resistance if there is a counter-map." He posed counter-cartography as a critical practice that confronts the epistemic violence of imperial maps. The range of such a practice extends from the psychogeographical representation of the daily lives of the oppressed and the charting of its multiple modes of knowledge production to the exposure of the spatial logic of domination, the removal of the privilege of mapping from the state.

The latter approach was manifested in Said's own attempt to map the realities on the ground.[12] In December 2000, three months after the start of the bloody second Intifada, Said proposed that for too long the Palestinians had conceded the ability to map to the Israelis. "The Palestinians themselves have until recently been mapless. They had no detailed maps of their own."[13] He subsequently promoted a "spatial turn" that would break Israel's monopoly over the representation of the terrain. This gave birth to a multiplicity of cartographic practices and led to the production of the map mentioned in the frame above.

That one of the strongest critics of mapping would also propose cartography as a form of resistance was surprising, but not contradictory. Unlike the colonial projects of recent centuries, the mode of operation of contemporary colonialism is to erase and cover up the traces of its own violence, to become so invisible as to no longer appear as power at all. To remove traces is also to erase the traces of erasure. Mapping is not only about plotting a crime built into a material reality, but about uncovering such acts of double erasure.

Several years later, with the increased availability of satellite photographs and the online proliferation of user-generated images, mapping became an image practice, and counter-cartography grew to embrace image analysis. While maps are able to deal with the slow architectural violence of settlement planning and construction, architectural image analysis provides an accelerated and focused form of cartography that has helped us bring our analyses to bear upon eruptive, kinetic forms of urban violence and reconstruct incidents unfolding at much faster paces and on smaller scales. However, these forms of violence are related: the seemingly benign environmental violence of the settlements can at any time erupt into instantaneous and spectacular violence. The settlements demand other forms of violence: roadblocks, walls, night incursions into cities and neighborhoods, the beating and often shooting of demonstrators, targeted assassinations, and bombing.

PRECEDENTS

Increasingly, with the penetration of cameras into the conflict zone, video clips documenting the killing of Palestinians have emerged. But the fact that clips existed did not always make a clear-cut case and shed conclusive light on incidents. Images and their absence have themselves become controversial and contested material that has needed to be analyzed, presented, and contextualized.[14] I will recount two cases from a potentially very long list: in the first, the existence of video evidence was a contested feature, while in the second, the absence of video evidence was a determining factor.

The first major controversy was around filmed evidence surrounding the killing of Mohammed al-Dura, a twelve-year-old Palestinian boy shot in his father's arms near the Netzarim settlement junction in the Gaza Strip in September 2000 at the very start of the Second Intifada—he was later to become a symbol of Palestinian martyrdom. Al-Dura's killing was caught on camera and broadcast by a French television station with a voiceover suggesting the obvious—that he was shot by Israeli soldiers. Israeli officials disputed the report, some going so far as to say that it was staged and that al-Dura was still alive. A private French businessman undertook ballistic and video analysis, accusing French Channel 2 of using the footage in a manipulative manner, and dragged the case through the French legal system for years until finally losing it. In May 2013, not content with the end of the case in France, Prime Minister Netanyahu released a state-commissioned report suggesting that al-Dura had not been hit by Israeli fire and reiterated the claim that he may not have been shot at all.

The response to the killing of al-Dura demonstrated that without the independent ability to investigate, leaving the field of forensics to Israeli investigators reinforces their monopoly over the narrative of critical events in the same way that their control of cartography has reinforced their territorial rule. As the stronger side, with wide access to the terrain, to optics, and to the media, they will otherwise be able to determine the narrative, and given an opportunity to deny, they will always seize it.

The second of the two controversies concerns the killing of Jawaher Abu Rahma, Bassem Abu Rahma's sister, on the last day of 2011. (See "Abu

Rahma: From Video to Virtual Modeling," pp. 108–13.) She died in a demonstration in Bil'in after inhaling tear gas, almost at the same spot her brother was killed two-and-a-half years earlier. The military proposed an astonishing barrage of contradictory explanations in its attempt to argue that Jawaher Abu Rahma died by forces other than its own: she wasn't at the demonstration; she was stabbed in a family honor killing; she was diagnosed with leukemia, thus being abnormally susceptible to otherwise nonlethal tear gas. The fact that there was no video of her actually succumbing to and suffocating within a tear-gas cloud—because, as witnesses explained, those with cameras preferred to rush to her help—was used by the military to claim her killing was fabricated. In an era of omnipresent video, the absence of video can be used as "negative evidence"—helping to claim that the thing in question did not happen.

Both these killings were undertaken in the context of military action to protect settlements. Al-Dura was killed by fire originating from a military base established to guard the Netzarim settlement. Jawaher Abu Rahma was killed in a demonstration against the Wall, whose path on the land of her village was established to protect the Ultraorthodox settlement Modi'in Illit. The slow, architectural violence of the settlement project extracts constant sacrifices in fast, kinetic violence.

These killings and the controversies around them also echo violence unleashed by American police forces on black bodies. In recent years in such places as Cincinnati, Cleveland, Staten Island, Houston, San Antonio, North Charlotte, Chicago, and Baton Rouge, facts of such killings have been exposed by videos from security cameras, journalists, activists, passersby, or bystanders. In all these cases, it seems that today's compulsion to take pictures of everything and install CCTV camera everywhere has reached its paradoxical apex with "Big Brother's" tools turned around. Unlike the stylized violence of movies and computer games, these video clips are harrowing in the explicitness, ugliness, and sometimes clumsiness by which death is administered. They describe situations that are predictable but shocking nevertheless.

THE PYRAMIDS OF GAZA

The pyramids of Gaza, a forensic analyst once told me, occur as a result of an encounter between two elements common in the area: an armored Caterpillar D9 bulldozer and a three-story building, typical of refugee homes in Gaza. The bulldozer's short blade can topple only the peripheral columns. The internal columns are left intact, forming the peak of the pyramid. The floor slabs break at their approximate center, then fold down and outward to form the faces of the structure. The geometry of the pyramids of Gaza is not as ideal as that of the pyramids of Giza. Their irregularities register differences in the process of construction—the uneven spread of concrete, for example—or in the process of destruction, whether a firefight or a tank shell struck the building.

The pyramid is but one of several typologies of destruction that can be told apart. The ruins that result from engineers placing explosives next to all major columns might end up looking like a series of floors "pancaked" over each other. Large air-dropped bombs with delay fuses break through all the floors of a building and blow up under its foundations. The remnant is a large conic crater into which the building has disappeared. Sustained artillery fire turns buildings into piles of rubble. Poke holes around windows designate a firefight. A tank shell fired into a building opens large round holes in the façade.[15]

The first time I explicitly mentioned the term "forensic architecture" was in the context of critically engaged research into the potentially adverse effects of human rights and international law and their collusion with military and state power. An essay in the journal *Radical Philosophy* titled "Forensic Architecture: Only the Criminal Can Solve the Crime" recounted the strange case of Marc Garlasco, Human Rights Watch (HRW)'s munitions expert.[16] In 2003, as a Pentagon employee at the time of the invasion of Iraq, Garlasco was in charge of planning the targeted assassination of the state's Ba'ath leaders by bombing the multistory residential buildings in which they took shelter. Under the American interpretation of the legal principle of proportionality, he was tasked with limiting to twenty-nine the number of civilians expected to be killed in each of these strikes. The death of the thirtieth civilian would have been considered, by the standards of the Pentagon lawyers, the first one to be illegal or disproportional. But this calculation was about more than human lives. It needed to engage the structural characteristics of the buildings being bombed. To maintain "proportionality"—the acceptable number of casualties in relation to military objectives—the bombing needed to become an act of "design

Human Rights Watch's munitions expert Marc Garlasco presenting a photograph that he took in the aftermath of the 2008–2009 Gaza attack (Operation Cast Lead) at the Human Rights Project, Bard College, in April 2010. In the image, a woman stands admirably steadfast in front of the ruins of her house. This photograph demonstrates the shift in emphasis from victim testimony to forensic architecture and its problems. In narrating this image, Garlasco shifts his attention from human figure to ground, interrogating the rubble of the house behind the witness while masking her completely. HUMAN RIGHTS PROJECT, BARD COLLEGE, 2010

by destruction" in which only some building parts, a few stories here or a single side or wing there, could be removed and involved design calculations that combined blast analysis with structural engineering. After the war, Garlasco resigned from the Pentagon and was hired to work for HRW, where he was asked to undertake a similar, if reverse, kind of task—reconstructing, by studying the shape of ruins, the events that led to their destruction.

Garlasco's evolution from an agent of targeted assassination to a human rights advocate is a warning about the growing proximity between the human rights movement—its principles, and the organizations advocating them—and the militaries they purportedly oppose and a reminder of the dark origins of some of our techniques and technologies of evidence gathering. The problem for Garlasco, however, lay elsewhere. After Israel's 2008–2009 attack on Gaza, he visited Gaza in the context of HRW's war-crime investigations and assembled important and effective evidence for Israeli war crimes there. He was forced to resign from HRW when pro-Israeli bloggers "discovered" (though Garlasco never hid that fact) to great media fanfare that he was a collector of Nazi memorabilia and thus allegedly a Nazi sympathizer unsuited to investigating the Israeli military impartially. The fact of his less-than-ordinary (for a human rights person) hobby I thought to be irrelevant—there is something of a fetishist in every forensic analyst seeking to read history from objects. He was certainly no Nazi, nor was he at all "anti-Israeli"—quite the contrary. This fact was merely used in order to attack his work on Israel.

LAWFARE

The significance of Garlasco's story is that in its extreme way, it offers an allegory to the paradox of forensics in a human rights context. On the one hand, it outlines the potential dangers of proximity and collusion between human rights analysis and the military that it seeks to oppose, while on the other hand, the fierceness of the antagonism he aroused due to his investigative work is testimony to the effectiveness of his forensic techniques.

The master's tools might not by themselves bring down the master's house, but taking them over surely had the potential to make him run mad. Perhaps the paradox describes two conditions that are not only related, but in fact interdependent and, as the subtitle for my essay on Garlasco in *Radical Philosophy* suggested, "only the criminal can solve the crime." Indeed,

Garlasco's suspension from HRW was one of the first shots in an all-out war that the Israeli government and its surrogates started waging against human rights groups.

Those completely dismissive of the potentials of legal activism should take into account the extent to which Western states perceive themselves vulnerable to such actions and the resources they invest in countering them. Israel went so far as to define international human rights, humanitarian, and legal action against it as a "third strategic threat," a close third after nuclear Iran and Hezbollah and on par with the BDS movement. Similar actions have been referred to by Western militaries and security think tanks as "lawfare," as discussed in Part 1.[17]

When international law protecting civilians stands in the way of state militaries, it is easy to see why military lawyers would also adopt the attitude of critical legal-studies scholars seeking to challenge "law's normative status" and to offer insights into its "indeterminacies and internal contradictions."[18] This once led Michael Sfard to play on the name of the group Anarchists Against the Wall to describe Israeli military lawyers as "anarchists against the law," reflecting the ironic position by which activists on the Left now insist on the dry letter of the law.

In 2010, Danny Ayalon, then Israel's deputy foreign minister, argued that legal activism was one of the biggest challenges Israel would face in the years ahead: "Today the trenches are in Geneva in the Council of Human Rights, or in New York in the General Assembly, or in the Security Council, or in The Hague, the ICJ."[19] That year, a report by the Ministry of Foreign Affairs took the accusation against legal activists a step further: "just as Carl von Clausewitz stated that 'war is…a continuation of political activity by other means,' so too lawfare is a continuation of terrorist activity by other means."[20] The paranoid comparison of human rights groups to terrorists, a comparison that sometimes leads to violence against activists, was made because Israel perceives international legitimacy to be essential for its perceived necessity to bomb in civilian areas.[21] This is the reason why Israel severely restricts the entry of human rights groups and UN commissions into Gaza.

In recent years, the function of lawfare has been further complicated, with Jewish settler groups and other extreme-right nationalists adopting it themselves, mirroring the strategies of the very human rights groups they oppose. As Nicola Perugini and Neve Gordon have shown, these groups have taken on the mantle of human rights and started using techniques and vocabularies similar to those of activist NGOs in documenting, making claims, and arranging legal action against "Palestinian land invasion," "illegal construction," and "violence against settlers," and this in order to rationalize dispossession and justify violence.[22]

These groups, together with members of the Israeli government and parliament, the police, and various semiautonomous right-wing groups, as well as most Israeli media, condoned campaigns on Left human rights groups and sent people to spy on, digitally surveil, infiltrate, incite, smear, harass, and arrest human rights and legal activists. The nonviolent civil action of boycotting Israel was made illegal, and a new law forced Israeli human rights activists to identify themselves as paid agents of foreign governments.

Living outside Israel, I was spared the worst of this treatment, but when Forensic Architecture's reports were published, they were attacked by such groups as the products of "a long-time anti-Israel and pro-BDS activist," and the British government, our partners and funders, as well as my university, have been reproached for helping me "advance my objectives" and "hire a number of fellow long-standing and obsessive anti-Israel activists."[23] Members of our groups have been detained upon landing at Tel Aviv airport, only to be sent back after a day or two of interrogations. Sfard has been spied upon by private detectives commissioned by a state-sponsored association. The detectives tried to gather information on cases, some of which we worked on, by going through Sfard's office trash. "I knew when it was cleaned, when the trash was taken out. I would argue with the guys on the garbage truck before they took away the trash," a detective was forced to tell the police when they finally investigated. "From the trash, on more than one occasion we managed to rescue documents and torn pages and even shredded pages," he said.[24]

Still, out of all those born in that land, Jewish Israelis like me are those most privileged by the regime. Unlike most Palestinians, we are able to travel through Palestine and outside it and are afforded greater latitude of expression and access to information. Being Israeli in this space, we cannot avoid a degree of collusion, even when we confront the regime, even when we migrate away, as I did. Unable to escape our privileges, we choose to use them against the regime that granted them to us and ultimately in order to undo them.

For Palestinians, the risks are far more acute. Palestinian journalists and citizen-journalists taking photographs of Israeli soldiers are arrested, beaten, and threatened, and their equipment is confiscated. Palestinian bloggers and even ordinary social-media users have been arrested for as little as posting their status on social media when expressing support for boycotting Israel.[25] In August 2016, Amira Hass reported about "Black Ops" being used against Palestinian legal NGOs. Nada Kiswanson, a Palestinian human rights lawyer working with the Palestinian human rights organization Al-Haq received anonymous murder threats over the phone for presenting evidence on the 2014 Gaza war to the ICC in The Hague.[26] When, together with Amnesty International, a group from Forensic Architecture presented our own findings on the 2014 Gaza war at a press conference in East Jerusalem, we received unspecified death threats, including the following message: "I plan on visiting you with an M-16 very soon. Consider yourselves warned."[27] We changed hotels at the last minute and hired a private Palestinian security company, but nothing transpired.

When soldiers invade Gaza, using cameras becomes extremely precarious—soldiers will shoot to kill anyone pointing a camera at them. The level of contestation and risk in the use of evidence makes us sometimes refer to such acts as "forensic warfare." This might demonstrate how contested the fields of human rights and legal activism have become, but can also invigorate them with a sense of renewed agency. The threats are proof that the public and legal actions that activists bring before international forums might be worrying those who should be worried.

Investigating incidents demands calm and systematic work that slows down time to examine minute details. It is hard to seek verbal and visual eloquence when shock, rage, grief, and disbelief make one speechless, when the heart aches and the blood boils. People who risk their lives to take images and post them outside the space in which they are held under siege—as if they were messages in a bottle, without knowing if, who, and when their messages might be looked at—demand such attention, the closest attention we can muster. We must attend to these messages as carefully as we can, despite and perhaps because the content is hard to watch.

The Nakba Day Killing

In 2014, on Nakba Day, May 15, two Palestinian teenagers, Nadeem Nawara and Mohammad Abu Daher, were shot and killed in the town of Bituniya, near Ramallah in the West Bank, after a protest marking the sixty-sixth anniversary of the establishment of Israel. Forensic Architecture's investigation of the Nakba Day killing was undertaken on behalf of a Palestinian NGO, DCI–Palestine, and the parents of the teenagers.[28] It started with an attempt to identify the perpetrators of a double murder, but evolved to include an investigation into different modes of denial.

Significantly, because the events took place on May 15, the annual commemoration of the Nakba, the story is also haunted by that historical event—the Palestinian exodus of 1948. The "Nakba Law" that the Israeli parliament passed in 2011 imposed harsh fines on public organizations that refer to Israel's "Independence Day as a day of mourning."[29] Every May 15, however, the Nakba is marked by protests throughout Palestine, from the Galilee to Gaza, the Naqab, the West Bank, and also abroad in Syria, Lebanon, Jordan, and other Palestinian diasporas. These protests often lead to clashes with Israeli security forces.

On the morning of Nakba Day in 2014, one of the flash points of protest was close to the Ofer military prison. After the main part of the protest was aggressively dispersed, witnesses heard three distinct gunshots roughly an hour apart. The first, at around 12:20 p.m., wounded Muhammad 'Azzah, fifteen, with a shot to the chest. The second, at 1:45 p.m., killed Nawara, seventeen, with another shot to the chest. The third, at 2:58 p.m., killed Abu Daher, sixteen, with a single gunshot to the back. All three teenagers were hit along the same patch of pavement, right in front of a small carpentry workshop.

Dozens of Palestinian teenagers have been killed or wounded by Israeli soldiers and other security personnel in the West Bank in recent years. Most of those killings took place off camera, responsibility was always denied, and a very small minority of them were even investigated. The bodies of Palestinian victims are buried hastily, often before nightfall, according to

Islamic laws and almost never with pathological investigation being undertaken. Children leave the house in the morning and disappear into the ground before sunset.

Unlike many other instances, on Nakba Day 2014, the killings were captured on multiple cameras. Footage relevant to the fatal shootings of both Nawara and Abu Daher was recorded by security cameras, by local and international media crews that came to cover the clashes, and by Israeli security personnel. The scene, unfolding in a confined space of several hundred square meters, resembled a film studio with multiple cameras, but no single director.

That the incident was most clearly captured by security cameras was not immediately appreciated by those reporting on the incidents. On May 19, four days after the shooting, while surveying the site for physical evidence, DCI researchers noticed CCTV cameras outside the carpentry workshop of Fakher Zayed and asked him for the footage. Zayed was hesitant about passing it on, fearing military retaliation. Finally, though reluctantly, he allowed DCI to examine the files. Going through hours of material, DCI's researchers identified the relevant footage in four of Zayed's eight cameras. After receiving both Nadeem's and Muhammad's parents' permission, DCI posted short segments of this material online.[30] The security camera footage is chilling. It shows both Nawara and Abu Daher walking casually and alone, uninvolved in any activity, when they are shown suddenly collapsing. The silent video makes the fall appear soft. For several seconds, the video shows the bodies remaining motionless, face down, then other people are seen rushing into the frame, evacuating the teenagers outside of it. The footage was picked up almost instantly and went viral on social media, gathering more than seven hundred thousand viewings. This resulted in condemnation of Israel from many states, from the UN, and from human rights groups. Even the Obama administration expressed its "concern."[31]

There was another crucial bit of evidence available. After the funeral, Siam Nawara, Nadeem's father, received his son's backpack and other belongings. In the bag he found a 5.56-caliber bullet, the standard ammunition used by Israeli security forces. In a rare decision, given that Islamic law forbids such acts, Siam Nawara gave permission for the exhumation of Nadeem's body. The autopsy, conducted by Palestinian doctors and attended by Israeli and international pathologists, confirmed that it was the bullet that killed Nadeem and then left his body.[32] In the meantime the indefatigable B'Tselem researcher/spokesperson Sarit Michaeli was

The position of the CCTV camera on a parapet on one end of Fakher Zayed's carpentry workshop.
FORENSIC ARCHITECTURE

prominently working alongside DCI–Palestine to investigate elements of this narrative and to keep the story in the news.[33]

In response, Israeli spokespeople stated that their "preliminary report concluded that there had been no live fire" and that the forces on site deployed only what they referred to as "non-lethal means," namely, rubber-coated steel bullets and tear gas, and further suggested that "the chances of fabrication were high."[34] The minister of defense, Moshe Ya'alon, pursued the usual contradictory lines of explanation. In remarks delivered at an event in a West Bank settlement, he started by claiming that the Bituniya killings were the result of a violent encounter in which the teenagers killed were engaged in throwing Molotov cocktails at the soldiers, who felt at risk for their lives and acted appropriately. Referring to the videos showing that the youths were shot while uninvolved in any activity, he sarcastically added that he was "familiar with the ways such videos are edited," referring to them as malicious and fictional constructions of the growing cottage industry of "Pallywood" — a derogatory term by which Israeli spokesperson refer to "pro-Palestinian" user-generated evidence of killing as Palestinian Hollywood: the soldiers had to do it and they didn't do it, all claimed in one single breath. Israeli spokespersons

05-15-2014 Thu 13:45:11 (S)

Closed-circuit TV (CCTV) camera footage showing Nadeem Nawara falling after being hit by live fire.

explained that the CCTV videos showing the boys collapsing were "tendentiously edited." A senior officer briefing journalists cast doubt on the fact that the two were even dead. Michael Oren, former Israeli ambassador to the United States, offered a live analysis in the CNN studio of the manner in which the boys were seen falling—Nawara had his hands stretched forward to soften his fall forward—claiming this was inconsistent with a frontal shooting, which usually causes the body to drop backward. If he was shot dead, he would also not have been able to stretch his hands forward, Oren explained. In reality, Nawara died of his wounds in the hospital a few hours later. Other spokespersons claimed that the youth seen in the videos were not the same as the two boys whose deaths were registered. A post by Danny Ayalon, another former Israeli ambassador to Washington, called for DCI–Palestine's tax-exempt status in the United States to be revoked because it was fabricating the truth. What was the truth? Israeli security forces were seen filming the clashes, but all requests to examine their footage were denied.[35]

The CNN footage at the moment of shooting.

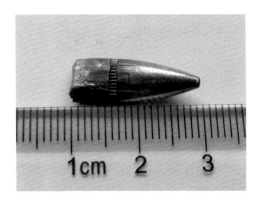

The bullet head found in Nawara's
bag measured to confirm it is
the standard IDF ammunition.
COURTESY OF DCI–PAELSTINE

Synchronization. We started by synchronizing the relevant bits of footage from CNN and the CCTV cameras by identifying the same visual markers in both sources. The videos both ran at twenty-four frames a second. To find the overlapping frame, it was necessary to look for distinct shifts in the direction of movement of different characters. In both sequences, a man in a white shirt is seen running toward the ambulance. He makes two distinct turns. The first turning point allowed us to synchronize the videos and the second to confirm that we had done so correctly. The CCTV image on the left is magnified fivefold from the original.

INTERSECTIONS

In the Bituniya killings, the media attention and persistent Israeli denials led CNN producer Kareem Khadder, who was filming on site that day, to reexamine the footage he had shot. He realized that his camera had captured the moment of the shooting of Nawara from a crucial, different angle. On May 22, 2014, a week after the killings, CNN released the video.[36] It showed a group of Israeli border policemen (an enlisted unit under police command, rather than military command, recognizable by their darker uniforms) and a single Israeli soldier aiming their rifles toward the place where Nawara fell. A border policeman and the soldier are seen shooting their guns toward the demonstrators. After recording the shooters, the camera pans to the right to show the evacuation of Nadeem Nawara. The sequence ends when an ambulance arrives at the scene.

Earlier that same day, May 22, three days after DCI–Palestine had obtained the security-camera footage from Zayed, Israeli forces raided his wood workshop and confiscated the security cameras and the computer hard disk on which the video files were stored. Two weeks later, on June 13, as the story gathered momentum, Israeli forces returned to confiscate all other CCTV cameras installed in the area, as well as the computer hard drives of their owners, returning them a few days later after copying all the footage on them. On June 17, Fakher was arrested, exactly as he had

The moment of impact. Rewinding both videos at the same speed, we can see the moment when the CCTV footage shows Nawara starting to fall. There is also a faint smoke plume rising next to the border police-man behind a small bush, marked in the red frame. At that moment, the CNN footage captures the sound of a gunshot.

feared, and was taken to a nearby military base for interrogation, where other officers screamed at him for sharing the security videos with human rights groups and for "lying" and "fabricating evidence," and threatened that if he did not remove the security cameras himself permanently and within twenty-four hours, they would "crush him" and unleash dogs on his children. "They told me that the video I gave to the press was fabricated, that everything I said and all my testimonies are a lie, that this is a seri-ous violation of the law, and that I made the IDF look bad and caused a lot of problems."[37]

On June 6, 2014, three weeks after the incident, DCI–Palestine, working for the parents, commissioned Forensic Architecture to investigate the inci-dent, which was still being denied. The main element in our investigation, which was coordinated by Nick Axel and included sound artist and investi-gator Lawrence Alan Hamdan, was to generate a virtual, architectural model of the site in which we could intersect and cross-reference all the videos and images, together with material and testimonial evidence, to help estab-lish who shot Nawara and Abu-Daher. The result of our investigation, we insisted, should not be provided to the Israeli police, which was the same body that had perpetrated this act. DCI–Palestine would publically release our findings in response to developments on the ground in order to intervene in the process from the outside, with the aim of exposing both the crime and the shortcomings of the legal process.

Rubber-coated steel bullet. When the CNN camera (right) captured the second shot, fired by a soldier marked in red frame B, the CCTV footage shows Nawara is already being evacuated. At the same moment, the CCTV footage (left) shows a cameraman, marked in red frame A next to the helpers who carry Nawara to the ambulance.

Incidentally, another photojournalist, Samer Nazzal, took a high-speed, high-resolution photograph at that very moment from a different direction. His photograph shows the same cameraman at the same position and at the same moment as seen both in the CCTV and the CNN footage, marked in red frame A, allowing for nearly perfect synchronization of the three images above. Nazzal's photograph also captured an object in midflight before it hit and wounded the head of the Palestinian paramedic seen wearing a bright orange vest. It can only be a rubber-coated steel bullet — live munitions travel too fast to be captured on regular cameras. It is marked with red frame C and enlarged on the facing page. This allowed us to identify the sound signature of a rubber-coated steel bullet (FACING PAGE).

Every gunshot makes its own kind of sound. Knowing the second shot (right) was the sound made by a rubber-coated steel bullet, rather than live fire, allowed us to compare the sound signatures of both shots. Lawrence Abu Hamdan, a sound specialist on Forensic Architecture's team, processed the sound of these two shots through software that created spectrograms to identify their distinct visual signatures. The visual signature of the sound of live fire is distinct: it is louder than the sound of a rubber-coated steel bullet in the higher frequencies and softer in the lower frequencies.

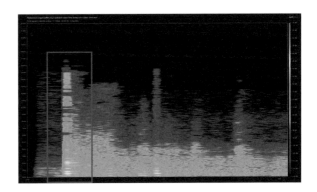

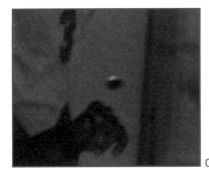

C

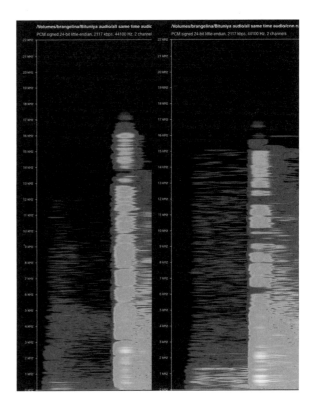

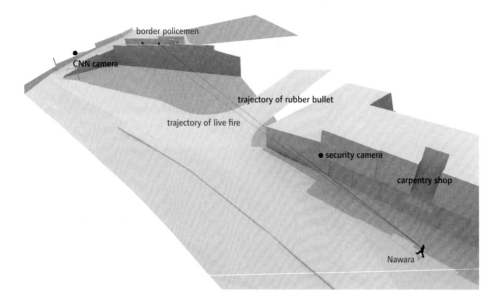

border policemen

CNN camera

trajectory of rubber bullet

trajectory of live fire

security camera

carpentry shop

Nawara

Israeli sources claimed that there was no sight line and thus no fire trajectory between the border police-man and Nawara when he was shot. We undertook a ground survey of the site and constructed a virtual model based on all available sources. On the model, we marked the location of both the CCTV and the CNN cameras and modeled the trajectories from each of the shooters to Nawara. A direct line of sight and fire to Nawara did exist from the border policeman, whom we identified as shooting at the moment when Nawara was seen falling. The line of fire passes close to the corner of the building. Nawara's direction of movement confirms that he had just entered into the border policeman's line of sight when he was shot and thus that the shooting could not have been a response to any activity Nawara was said to have been participating in prior to being shot.

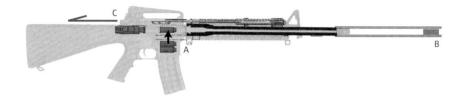

M16 rifle in operation. To determine whether the soldier had actually fired live ammunition through the rubber-bullet extension, it was necessary to examine the way an M16 rifle works. When live ammunition is fired, it creates pressure high enough for the gun to eject the spent cartridge from the chamber automatically and reload. ABOVE: M16 rifle with extension. To fire a rubber-coated steel bullet, a blank cartridge is loaded into the rifle's chamber, marked A. The rubber bullet is manually inserted into the end of a special extension, marked B. The explosive power pushes the rubber bullet out, but because there is not the same amount of fire power in the blank cartridge as in a live round, there is not enough pressure for the gun to eject the blank cartridge automatically and reload. Reloading has to be done manually by cocking the gun in the area marked C.

An Israeli "firearms ballistic expert" pointing to the enlargement of the CNN footage showing the rubber bullet extension on a gun. This "expert," interviewed by Israeli TV Channel 2, claimed that the extension cannot be used to fire live ammunition. "The thickening that we can see here around the barrel is not intended for firing live ammunition, only for firing rubber [-coated steel] bullets."[38] The catalog for the rubber bullet extension's manufacturer, Israel Military Industries, disproves this statement. It advertises the possibility of shooting immediate live fire through it.[39]

Spent cartridge ejected. Looking repeatedly at the footage, we could identify in three light-colored pixels — an object flying out of the gun, here marked in a red frame. This is the spent cartridge, automatically ejected, indicating that a live round was fired, not a rubber-coated steel bullet. If a live round were fired accidentally into a rubber-coated steel bullet loaded into the end of the extension, the gun could explode. The sequence of actions thus had to have been carefully planned: both replacing the blanks with live ammunition and not loading the rubber bullet at the end of the extension. CNN

The shooter is seen cocking the gun. This could be consistent with the firing of a rubber-coated steel bullet, but given that the spent cartridge has already been ejected, the border policeman's previous actions are possibly an attempt to conceal from the CNN camera crew standing nearby or from anyone else watching that he previously shot a live round. Marked by a red frame is the unspent bullet dropping from the gun as a result of its cocking. CNN

מאת עדו:

24 באפריל 2012 בשעה 7:52

אגב, עוד דבר לא חדש הוא השימוש במטול רימונים. כשהייתי בעזה פגשתי איש יחידת שמשון שסיפר
לי על הטריק הקבוע: לירות את הרימון (נשאר המטול הריק מולבש על הרובה) ואז לירות אש חיה
כשהקצין שלידך חושב שאתה יורה רימון גומי. במילא – כך הוא אמר – הם חוטפים את הגופה ואין
חקירה, אז למי אכפת?

מאת ש.ב.:

24 באפריל 2012 בשעה 12:57

אתה מדבר על "טמפון" לירי כדורי גומי. גם אני שמעתי את זה מחיילים. שמלבישים את המתקן,
אבל שמים מחסנית עם כדורים חיים. הם, אגב, סיפרו את זה כמשהו טוב ומשעשע.

Soldiers' blog. An online post in a forum used by former soldiers describes a similar practice. This and another frame in the blog read: "When I was in Gaza, I met somebody that told me about a common trick... you shoot the rubber bullet and then you are left with the empty extension on the rifle. Then you shoot live rounds through the extension." In any case, "the Palestinians take the body, and there is no investigation, so who cares."

CCTV. At 2:58 p.m., about an hour and a half after Nawara was shot, Abu Daher was shot and killed while passing the same stretch of pavement. The still is from footage recorded by another CCTV camera installed at the same carpentry workshop. The shadow line has since moved and now covers the body of Abu Daher.

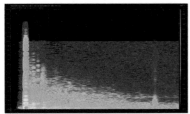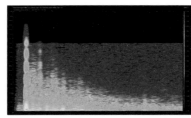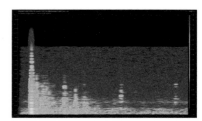

Spectrograms of gunshots captured by the Palestine TV camera. After the CNN camera crew left, another film crew from Palestine TV arrived on site. They were there when Abu Daher was shot. The camera did not aim at Abu Daher or at the border policeman. But it did capture the sound of the lethal gunshot. To help verify the source of this shot, we collected available sounds of gunshots captured by the same Palestinian TV camera throughout the day. Lawrence Abu Hamdan's spectrograms were used to compare their visual signatures. Clip 4, fourth from the left and marked with a red frame, captures the sound of the lethal shot that killed Abu Daher. The difference between it and all other shots—rubber-coated steel bullets—is clear: as in the gunshot that killed Nawara, the sound of the gunshot that killed Abu Daher is louder than rubber-coated steel bullets in higher frequencies and softer in lower frequencies, suggesting Abu Daher was killed in a similar fashion: by live fire shot through a rubber bullet extension. The still frame from the moment when Abu Daher is shot shows the protesters ducking for cover. Ramallah-based journalist Samer Hisham Nazzal from Raya News who was at the scene, wrote that most participants in demonstrations can hear the difference between rubber bullets and live fire.[40] Abu Hamdan explained: "these Palestinian teenagers can exactly identify a tiny distinction in the frequencies and react accordingly. Those are the real acute listeners in this case."[41] PALESTINE TV

We kept working on this investigation all throughout the 2014 Gaza war. It felt odd to investigate the killing of two teenagers when more than five hundred Palestinian children were being killed, but it was our way to respect every young life lost. The first part of our analysis was delivered to DCI–Palestine in September, soon after the end of the war. The organizations used it in their approach to the UN and the US Congress, which lead US Congresswoman Betty McCollum to call upon, unsuccessfully, the State Department to investigate whether this killing amounts to the violation of the "Leahy Law" that prohibits the United States from providing military assistance to

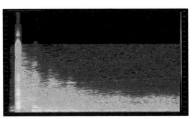
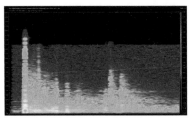

foreign military units that violate human rights with impunity.[42] It was a symbolic gesture, using the harshest language a US congressperson has used so far. No ban on weapons exports has, of course, been imposed.

On November 11, 2014, the police arrested a border policeman and identified him as Ben Deri. The bullet found in Nawara's bag was traced back to his gun.[43] On November 23, 2014, Deri was indicted for the manslaughter of Nadeem Nawara and placed on house arrest. His home immediately became a site of pilgrimage for politicians and cultural figures. Demonstrations and social-media campaigners called for his immediate release, and demanded the government "unties the hands of the military." The indictment was rare — almost all other police and military killings of Palestinians are written off as self-defence — but the charge of manslaughter was insufficient.[44]

We joined Siam Nawara, Nadeem's father, in claiming that his was a deliberate act of killing, a murder. A day after the charge was announced, we released a video refuting the terms of the indictment. Explaining the reduced charge, the police claimed that four minutes before he was shot, Nawara was throwing stones at the policemen. Our video showed that Nawara had just entered Deri's line of sight when shot. Deri could not have responded to anything Nawara was previously involved in. We also showed that negligence was extremely unlikely. For Deri, to unintentionally shoot a live bullet, a sequence of two distinct and rare errors would have to have taken place consecutively. A live round would need to have mysteriously found its way into a special magazine reserved for the blanks he used to propel the rubber-coated munitions. Then, precisely when that bullet came to be fired, Deri would have also to forget to place the rubber-coated ammunition at the end of his barrel extension. Firing a live round at an object stuck within the barrel could make the gun explode. Further reducing the probability that this was an error, the sequence these two rare coincidences would have had to be repeated twice more: Muhammad 'Azzah was wounded an hour and twenty-five minutes before Nawara and Mohammad Abu Daher was killed an hour and thirteen minutes after him in a similar manner at the same location.

The trial in the Jerusalem District Court was continuously delayed by the defence while pressure was building up on the witnesses and on Nawara's family. In January 2017, Siam Nawara wrote us to say that: "the defence and a representative of the Israeli government are putting pressure on me to sign a deal." The deal, as we have shown, described an impossible situation: Deri agreed to admit to negligence and be convicted of a wrongful killing for unintentionally firing a live round "which accidentally fell into his magazine." "Your case is not famous anymore," Siam Nawara was told, "it is not in the international media, nobody cares." The plea was accepted by the prosecution without Nawara's consent.

We have also released a video investigation about the killing of Mohammad Abu-Daher, which the media and the police have previously ignored. His family did not allow for an exhumation and there was no TV footage of the shooting to link them with the victim. It was only the sound of the shots that connected the two acts of murder: just like Nawara's the shot that killed Abu Daher had the sound signature of a bullet fired through a rubber bullet extension. The police, predictably, claimed that there was not enough evidence on go on and closed the case.[45]

Investigating individual violations is a problematic matter politically: state representatives always start by denying all allegations. Whenever denial could no longer be maintained, they privatize the violation, place it in the hands of individual soldiers and render the state's own violence legitimate and legal. Even in these rare cases, light punishment is the norm. It communicates to Palestinians that their arbitrary killing is acceptable and possible at any time. From our perspective, investigating the split seconds of single incidents must always seek to show how they might be embedded with the longer duration of the state's systemic violence and include attempts to expose the state's attempts at denial.[46]

Hannibal in Rafah

In the weeks following the fatal shootings in Bituniya, violence escalated throughout the West Bank. Israeli forces kept on firing live ammunition and rubber-coated steel bullets at youths, resulting in injuries to over a dozen other children. A reprisal for the killings was not long in waiting. Less than a month later, on June 12, 2014, three Israeli teenagers were abducted by Hamas operatives near a West Bank settlement. Israel launched a large-scale crackdown on Hamas infrastructure and personnel, killing eleven Palestinians and arresting more than one thousand, including many who had only recently been freed under the terms of a prisoner exchange deal in which a captive Israeli soldier in Gaza, Gilad Shalit, was released three years earlier.[47] This deal had been controversial with settlers, and the massive arrest operation sought to placate them. The Israeli Air Force also conducted air strikes against "Hamas facilities" in the Gaza Strip. On June 30, the bodies of the three missing teenagers were found near Hebron. They had been murdered. The following day, a Palestinian teenager from Jerusalem was burnt alive as the cycle of revenge spiraled on. His killing sparked Arab protests throughout the West Bank. Rocket fire from Gaza continued. Israel escalated its bombing of the strip. Hamas sent an armed group into Israel through a tunnel. The group was intercepted, but the Israeli military decided to start an operation to destroy all the other known tunnels. On July 17, 2014, the Israeli military invaded Gaza.

In early August, as the war was still being waged, Amnesty International commissioned Forensic Architecture (the investigation was subsequently coordinated by Christina Varvia) to undertake a large-scale investigation of architectural destruction in Gaza.[48] Five years after Marc Garlasco had undertaken the architectural analysis of war damage, we found ourselves in his shoes, but sought and, in fact, were compelled to do things differently. The conditions of investigation were indeed different. During and after the conflict, both Israel and the Egyptian authorities denied entry into Gaza to Amnesty International and our team, along with all other human rights groups and many journalists.

When the war ended, the scale of destruction became clear — the results were more devastating than previous rounds of conflict in Gaza. According to the Gaza-based Ministry of Public Works, twenty thousand tons of explosives killed 2,251 people, 1,462 of whom were civilians, destroyed 23,500 homes, damaged a further 150,000 — almost a third of all homes in Gaza and three times the level of destruction caused by Israel's previous invasion in 2008–2009 — and generated roughly 2.5 millions tons of rubble.[49]

If that was an extreme, yet familiar enough type of result, the difference was that the 2014 Gaza conflict took place in a different juridical, technological, and political reality from previous rounds. A mere three months earlier, in April 2014, the Palestinian Authority reluctantly conceded to Palestinian popular pressure and ratified the Rome Statute extending the jurisdiction of the ICC in The Hague over the occupied Palestinian territories, this in spite of Israeli warnings that joining the ICC "would be viewed as an act of war," the United States and the European Union threatening to cut aid, and also the risk to Palestinian leaders from counterpetitions.[50] That the 2014 war unfolded under the shadow of the court, as faint and blurry as this shadow was, given that the people of Gaza had few illusions about the way the ICC bureaucratic process makes it prone to geopolitical pressures, still energized the gathering of evidence. It also led to the formation of the Joint Documentation Unit, a coalition of Palestinians and NGOs whose aim was to prepare a joint submission to the ICC.[51] The conflict also took place in a different technological space, with more widespread availability of smartphone cameras and access to the Internet in Gaza changing the nature of evidence and of the investigation.

After the 2008–2009 Israeli bombing there was little user-generated content online, and evidence had to be collected on the ground, well after the war, in 2014, one of the most important sources for understanding the unfolding events was material produced by the people living in Gaza on their own terms and made available on social networks almost instantly.[52] As bombs and artillery started raining on the city, some of its inhabitants, as well as journalists and members of various organizations, took their cameras and started recording the events around them, often risking their lives in the process. They photographed from the streets, from windows, roofs, and balconies, sometimes before or instead of escaping, despite knowing that the Israeli military's open-fire instruction is to shoot to kill anyone directing a camera at soldiers. More than producing evidence, they wanted to document and set the record straight regarding events around them. They wanted to believe somebody would look at the images. These were extremely

Rafah, Gaza, August 1, 2014.
Photographs and stills from various
social and mainstream media sources.

Images provided to Breaking the Silence by testifiers who served in the Gaza War of 2014. The bottom right image shows an Israeli machine gun placed in a home. The organization does not reveal the names of the photographers or the time and the location in which these images where taken. It also blurs the faces of the soldiers. BREAKING THE SILENCE

valuable documents, but each was only a partial view of a complex and multiparticipant event and had to be combined and cross-referenced with others to create the photographic space of the battle.

There was also a different kind of testimony that prominently emerged during this conflict. It was delivered by soldiers, members of an Israeli NGO called Breaking the Silence, which was founded in 2004 but became prominent around this war.[53] Besides participating in the fighting, its testifiers/soldiers also see themselves as first-hand witnesses and speak out about human rights violations that were undertaken by them and by other soldiers next to them. Sometimes they make available photographs and videos recordings on their own smartphones, or from small video cameras embedded in their helmets.

Breaking the Silence testifiers are both participants and witnesses, perpetrators and human rights activists (the organization defines itself as a human rights group). Their testimonies are ethically and politically distinct from the testimonies of the victims, not least because the organization leaves out crucial details about the context of the events described and submits the testimonies to the review of the military censor before publishing them. However, because they make claims against the military of which they are part, these witnesses gain much prominence and notoriety and provoke enormous contestation and vilification from the Israeli media, government, and general public. Together with the citizen witnesses of Gaza, the soldier witnesses have taken over the task of reporting on events from professional, sometimes embedded, journalists and human rights researchers.

RAFAH, BLACK FRIDAY, AUGUST 1, 2014

Given the volume of evidence, to undertake an analysis that synthesized all these sources and testimonies, we had to focus on one day. If a tragedy in the Gaza war extended across a single day, Friday, August 1, 2014, was certainly it. It was the deadliest in the 2014 Gaza conflict. What took the Israeli military a day to destroy (and will take the Palestinians a decade to rebuild, based on current pace and subject to current restrictions imposed on the importing of building materials) took our team a year to research—the time ratio of a day to a year demonstrates the duration and labor necessary in forensic work—though we managed to reconstruct only a little of what happened in the southeastern outskirts of Rafah, the southernmost city in the Gaza Strip, during these twenty-four hours.[54]

The tragedy of August 1 has to do not only with the exceptional death toll, but also with the logic of fratricide—the Israeli military manhunting to kill one of their own, lest he fall prisoner in the enemy's hands—that determined the turn of events.

The contested territory that day was the subsoil. The city of Rafah is jammed between two borders: Israel's and Egypt's. Across and between these borders runs an extensive network of tunnels. It was for the purpose of destroying these tunnels that the Israeli military had invaded Gaza in the first place. On August 1, Hamas fighters captured an Israeli officer and dragged him into one of the last remaining tunnels, hoping to remove him from the battlefield and later exchange him for many of their own prisoners, as they had done with Gilad Shalit and in defiance of the fact that most of those whom Israel had released had been rearrested after the events that spring.

Determined to avoid negotiations, the implicit recognition that goes with them, and the potential release of prisoners, the military unleashed a secret command—the Hannibal Directive—that called for concentrating massive fire on the entire area in which the soldier was suspected to be. The events of August 1 thus involved an attempted fratricide by which Israeli soldiers tried to kill one of their own. The military denied this, claiming they did all they could to save the soldier. However, as the investigation we pursued showed, the events of that day added up to a manhunt. Even though the contested territory that day was the subsoil and the tunnels, the unleashed violence was mainly from the air. Nonetheless it was the surface of the earth, the layer where civilians struggle to live, that bore the brunt of the destruction.

On August 1, the fate of the soldier and of the civilians killed in Rafah were entangled. We concentrated on the events of that day because it described a unique situation—a world upside down, in which Hamas was trying to save the life of a soldier that his own military was trying to kill, an inversion that had the potential to depart from the mode of accounting incidents in Gaza and unsettle common binaries.

We collected close to seven-thousand photographs and video clips extracted from Arab, English, and Hebrew mainstream and social-media websites such as Twitter, Facebook, and YouTube. Many images were sent directly from people in Gaza, as well as from Amnesty International and other human rights groups such as Al Mezan. The images showed different instances of carnage—civilians under attack, families escaping along the roadways holding white flags, bombs blowing up, tanks raising dust, artillery barrages, smoke plumes, bomb clouds, burned-out ambulances, and more. Our task was to piece these sources together with other testimonies, bits of evidence such as hospital logs, ambulance data, and news reports, in order to assemble a narrative. We used spatial models to compose assemblages of evidence. Architecture here was not only the object of analysis, but an optical device with which to view separate elements of evidence and the relations between them. Our report, with Amnesty International, was submitted to the ICC, and we sat with the investigative team there for a day-long session to go through our evidence and methods.

THE TIMELINE

The day that was later to be known as Black Friday started rather well. Slightly more than an hour into August 1, at 1:18 a.m., an agreement, negotiated by US Secretary of State John Kerry and UN Secretary General Ban Ki-Moon, regarding a "72-hour humanitarian ceasefire" was reached. "This humanitarian ceasefire will commence at 8:00 a.m. local time on Friday, August 1, 2014. It will last for a period of 72 hours unless extended. During this time, the forces on the ground will remain in place," the resolution read.[55] Israel consented because the military understood its mission in Gaza to be close to complete—all the tunnels that it knew of but one had been found and destroyed, and the top command sought to withdraw in order to reduce further risks.

It was supposed to be the beginning of the end of that war. But different interpretations—or, better, willing misinterpretations—of the ceasefire agreement were about to doom it and the lives of so many in Rafah. The Israeli Army claimed that during the ceasefire it would still continue to search for and demolish tunnels within the area it held, a strip of about two kilometers west of the border. Hamas said it had agreed to stop its cross-border rocket fire only "against Zionist cities and settlements" and did not agree to hold its fire against the Israeli military in Gaza. It later explained that it "cannot operationally cease fire against troops inside the Gaza Strip that conduct operations and move continuously. These enemy forces could easily come in contact with our deployed ambushes, which will lead to a clash."[56] That is indeed what took place.

On the night of August 1—following the announcement of the approaching ceasefire—Ofer Winter, the commander of the Givati Brigade, in charge of military operations in the area, ordered his troops to find and destroy the last known tunnel that still eluded the army, southeast of Rafah, about two kilometers on the Gaza side of the border, before the ceasefire went into

effect. They frantically searched for it in an agricultural area of fields and small plantations. A few homesteads and greenhouses were scattered across the area, which was beyond the lines that the Israeli Army held at the time. In a testimony delivered to Breaking the Silence, a "junior infantry field officer in Rafah" described the following events:

> The incursion occurred the night before the ceasefire. The entrance happened at midnight, and everyone knew that at 8.00 a.m. the next morning it would be over, apparently.... We entered the area in order to destroy the entire tunneling infrastructure that still remains there. If you think about it, that really means every house and agricultural structure in the area. There was pressure to go in and finish the job very quickly.... Just to purposelessly destroy stuff, to finish the job.[57]

Nabil Sha'ath, the former Palestinian prime minister, explained that "destroying tunnels is destroying houses" and claimed that about nineteen houses were destroyed during that night's incursion alone.[58] Heavy fire and bombing continued through the night. Medical staff in the Najjar Hospital, the hospital closest to the area, reported that civilian casualties began arriving before dawn.[59] Rockets and mortars fired out of Gaza were intercepted in Ashdod, with a few landing in or near the settlements across the border. Despite an aggressive search, the Givati forces did not find the tunnel before the ceasefire went into effect at 8:00 a.m. Shortly after that time, Palestinian civilians started returning to their homes in areas from which they had been

The scene of the firefight and the capture, Pléiades satellite photo, July 30, 2014. The photograph was taken a day before the incident and describes the state of the site at the start of the encounter. Yellow arrows mark the movement of the Israeli soldiers. The circle marks the cinder block structure over the tunnel mouth.

forcefully evicted.[60] In previous weeks, the military had warned people to leave every neighborhood in which it operated. This was not only because of humanitarian considerations—it made it easier for the military to operate in deurbanized areas and to consider every person who remained to be a combatant by definition. Moving people around was also part of Israel's war strategy, a point of leverage over the population and its leadership.

Slightly before the ceasefire came into effect, at 7:30 a.m., according to Hamas' version of events,[61] or just over an hour after the start of the ceasefire, at 9:06 a.m., according to the Israeli military's, a group of Israeli commandos patrolling on foot in search for a tunnel beyond military lines[62] fell upon the hideout of a group of Hamas fighters. A short exchange of fire ensued, at the end of which two Israeli soldiers and one Palestinian fighter were dead. Another Israeli soldier, an officer, Hadar Goldin, was captured and taken into a tunnel. This was a local, tactical ingression that the Israelis feared could develop into a system-wide crisis with strategic repercussions that could change the outcome of the war. The capture of an Israeli soldier for the purpose of forcing prisoners' exchange was long declared as the aim of "the resistance."[63]

Much of the military narrative of the day was provided by the Givati Brigade's debriefings (the "Givati enquiry"), a forum set up to draw operational lessons.[64] The firefight, they said, occurred near a slender two-story-high cinder-block structure.[65] The Israeli force divided into two groups of three fighters each. The commander, his radioman, and another officer, Lieutenant Hadar Goldin, approached the structure directly, walking across a field of watermelons that would have been harvested if the war had not begun. The second group of three soldiers outflanked the building from

The cinder block structure above the mouth of the tunnel. The photograph is attributed to an unnamed Israeli soldier.
ILANA DAYAN, "FROM DEEP UNDER," *UVDA* (A DOCUMENTARY SERIES ACCESSED THROUGH MAKO.CO.IL, APRIL 19, 2015)

behind a large greenhouse slightly to the east. Just as the two groups were separated by the greenhouse, the command group was heard shouting for help. This was quickly followed by a blast and two sequences of fire. The Givati enquiry timed the firefight at 9:06 a.m. From bullet casings found on site, it concluded that the Hamas unit was composed of five or six members.[66] When the outflanking unit arrived at the scene, they found three bodies on the ground and initially believed them to be the bodies of the three soldiers. Hamas confirmed that its fighters were wearing Israeli uniforms and explained — in support of its claim that the firefight took place at 7:33 a.m. — and that it must have taken the Israelis two hours to realize that the Hamas fighter wearing a military uniform was not a soldier.[67] Indeed, there was much confusion, and it was only at 9:36 a.m., according to the military, that the army realized that one of the bodies they had found was that of a Hamas fighter and that Goldin was missing. Winter screamed "Hannibal" over the radio,[68] possessed by the realization that what he feared most had indeed taken place, thus unleashing the operational directive that would set in motion the events of the day.

The difference in the time lines can be understood as each of the parties' eagerness to cast blame for the collapse of the ceasefire on the other. Because Hamas fired the first shot, it wanted to claim that the firefight took place before the ceasefire. Israel was naturally eager to show that it was Hamas that violated the ceasefire. Palestinian witnesses had different versions: many claimed that the massive strike initiated by the invocation of the Hannibal Directive started shortly after 8:00 a.m., while others timed it after 9:30 a.m. Such diverging versions are common in war. We were unable to establish the time of the firefight independently, but our attempts to do so helped us develop the techniques of shadow and plume analysis that were important in reconstructing the events later that day. The parties might argue about who violated the ceasefire in time, but we could show, at least, that the violation took place in space: an Israeli unit proceeded into an area controlled by Hamas during a time when they claimed there was a ceasefire. This fact was also complicated by the three-dimensional architecture of tunnel warfare, which renders unclear the meaning of "front lines": Palestinian fighters could be under Israeli ones, and a tunnel mouth harboring some of them could exist within an area surrounded by the Israeli military during the ceasefire. Be the differences in accounts around the timing of the firefight what they may, shortly before 10:00 a.m., the time lines of both Hamas and the Israeli military coincided. Both sides agreed it was then that the massive attack on the city of Rafah had begun.

THE PRISONER'S DILEMMA

The Hannibal Directive is a secret IDF operational order designed to deal with the event of a capture of an Israeli soldier by an irregular armed force. Although the military has denied this interpretation, it is understood by Israeli soldiers and commanders that they are asked to kill a comrade during the process of capture before he can become a prisoner in the enemy's hands. The issuing of the command must be understood in relation to the central function that capturing Israelis had played in the Palestinian armed struggle since the late 1960s. By hijacking planes or obtaining hostages by other means, Palestinian groups were attempting to force Israel into implicit recognition where none existed, into negotiations, although often indirect, and into the release of prisoners, most often hundreds for every captured Israeli.

At the time, Israel denied that there even was a Palestinian people. Out of this denial came others: it did not recognize the Palestinian Liberation Organization and other Palestinian groups as legitimate representatives of the Palestinian people. The armed wings of these groups were thus also not recognized as legitimate military forces. Captured Palestinian fighters were not granted prisoner of war status in line with the Geneva Conventions and were sentenced according to Israel's criminal law. (After 9/11 and following the US example, some Palestinian prisoners—admittedly, only a few—were held in the limbo zone of contemporary warfare as "unlawful combatants.")[69] Capturing Israelis entangled both sides in a knot that forced them to communicate and was often the only possible way by which Palestinian political prisoners could be released.

Whereas it was primarily civilians who were captured in the infamous hijackings of the 1960s and 1970s, starting with the 1982 Israeli invasion of Lebanon, soldiers were closer at hand, outside their fully controlled zones, and could be captured and taken away from the battlefield. In June 1982, three Israeli soldiers were captured by the Popular Front for the Liberation of Palestine-General Command (PFLP-GC), a splinter group of the PLO headed by Ahmed Jibril. In May 1985, after indirect negotiations, Israel and the PFLP arrived at a prisoner-exchange deal. In exchange for the soldiers, 1,150 Palestinian prisoners were released. Leading the civil campaign against the deal and the release was the national religious settler movement Gush Emunim, which saw it as a proof of the weakness of "secular-liberal" Israeli society and demonstrated publically and vigorously, sometimes violently, against it.[70] The deal was also controversial with many in the military, who feared it would encourage further attempts at taking hostages and that Israeli civil society was too weak to resist the pressure of captured soldiers' families.[71]

In 1986, when the Hannibal Directive was issued, the military was occupying the border region in southern Lebanon and engaged in a guerrilla war with Hezbollah and other armed groups, which also experimented, after the success of the Jibril deal, with the tactics of capture. Rumors that an Israeli command directive called for the killing of captured Israeli soldiers circulated from the start, but parts of the directive were not made public until 1995, and it was only in 2003 that the military censors permitted revealing its very existence.[72] Its content is still classified, but the following formulation, at the top of the directive, was made public: "the kidnapping must be stopped by all means, even at the price of striking and harming our own forces."[73] This confirmed that the military allowed striking their own, but it was unclear whether the captured soldier was being identified as the actual target or as acceptable collateral damage in vigorous rescue attempts. It is of course illegal both in Israeli law and under international law for a military intentionally to kill its own captive soldiers, because captive soldiers are not part of a fighting force that constitutes a direct threat — the only category that justifies killing in battle — regardless of how they might be instrumentalized by their captors.[74] In 1988, when an Israeli officer was recorded briefing his soldiers, he could not be more explicit about the meaning: "We no longer have in our language 'an IDF soldier was kidnapped.' We stop the kidnapping at any price, even if it means to target our soldier, we prefer our soldier to be harmed rather than in their hands."[75] In 1999, with the IDF still in Lebanon, Shaul Mofaz, then chief of staff, explained why: "With all the pain that saying this entails, an abducted soldier, in contrast to a soldier who has been killed, is a national problem."[76]

The terms "kidnapping," and in other places "hostage," in the language of the command, are used in order to delegitimize an otherwise legitimate military tactic on the part of the Palestinians. The use of these terms might also suggest that Israelis understand the capture of soldiers on a continuum with civilian hijackings.

After the controversy that followed the command's exposure, its language was softened. It clarified the principle that the killing of the soldiers can be only a "collateral effect" of attempts to stop the capture. However, all along, an "oral tradition" — common military parlance for commands whose practices are too controversial to be written down, but that represent a prevailing systemic practice — was maintained by which the captured soldier was in fact the target of the operation.[77] Given that rescue was unlikely, the killing of captured soldiers, whether they were the target or collateral damage, was always the preferable outcome of the Hannibal Directive.

Although the military claimed that the Directive's name was randomly selected by a computer program, it is an apt one for a command that involves the killing of a captive. Hannibal Barca, the Punic-Carthaginian military commander, killed himself in 181 BC in order not to fall captive to Rome. "Let us relieve the Romans from the anxiety they have so long experienced, since they think it tries their patience too much to wait for an old man's death."[78] But thirty years earlier, the Punic Wars also saw a moment of Roman resolve: when Hannibal sent representatives of the captured Roman survivors of his victory at Cannae to try to convince the senate to pay ransom for their lives, the senate, after a heated debate, decided to refuse, leaving the prisoners to their fate.

Different states deal with the capture of their citizens and soldiers in different ways. The Europeans and Japanese usually engage in secret prisoner exchanges or negotiate ransoms. The United Kingdom and the United States have publically declared that they will not negotiate or comply with captors' demands, and although they have not always strictly held to their declared policy, they have favored inaction and noncommunication when a rescue operation seemed impossible. "Hannibalism," in this context, is the most extreme action on the spectrum of options facing states after an act of capture. Its logic is to preempt any deal by actualizing the worst an enemy can do, thus undoing the logic of the threat. This demonstration of military resolve mirrors that of its enemies, who see themselves as invincible because they do not fear death.

The Hannibal Directive must also be understood in relation to the existence of an economy of exchange and not in situations when prisoners are taken for the purpose of the videographic spectacles of their executions. Regardless of the fact that such ritualized killings were never part of the vocabulary of the Palestine conflict, and were performed elsewhere, they were useful in order to make Israeli soldiers accept that their killing by their comrades is a lesser evil, a form of euthanasia, perhaps, in the same way that members of colonial expeditions preferred death to being captured by people they called savages and cannibals.[79]

French Philosopher Gregoire Chamayou has proposed that in recent decades, conventional warfare, with its "fronts, linear battles and face-to-face opposition," has been replaced by the tactics of the manhunt. "The structure does not involve two fighters facing off, but something else: a hunter who advances and a prey who flees or who hides."[80] Chamayou is mainly referring to the counterterroristic tactics of assassinating suspects by drone strikes. Hannibalism, in which the military hunts one of its own, is at once a radicalization and reorientation of this doctrine. The hunted is not an enemy but a friend.

The logic involves what military game theorists call a "repeat game" — every action is evaluated in relation to long-term possibilities. The employment of actual violence in the present (killing a single soldier) is evaluated in relation to the potential violence it might prevent in the future by deterring further attempts, leading, theoretically, to less violence in the long run.

The death of the soldier, however, is not the only one anticipated by the Hannibal Directive. "The massive fire strike over the entire area of capture," in the words of the command, is expected to kill civilians. Military lawyers justify civilian deaths by determining that they were "proportional" to military aims. But high levels of civilian deaths and destruction are in fact essential for the maintenance of military deterrence. It is hard to deter a committed guerrilla force, but harming civilians, as Israel has done in Gaza and Lebanon in recent years and has threatened to continue, has been used as a leverage against the civilian base of popular resistance. Such deterrence is of course the hallmark of state terror. Ofer Winter, who unleashed the Hannibal Directive on the morning of August 1, explained the massive use of fire that killed about one hundred and twenty civilians as a kind of tutorial in fire: "They simply messed with the wrong brigade."[81]

Proportionality is a legal instrument used to measure the level of civilian casualties that the operation might legitimately bring about. It is a controversial category in international law because it makes legitimate anticipated damage to civilian life and property by balancing it against military objectives. The principle, formally codified in international law only in 1977, prohibits "an attack which may be expected to cause incidental loss of civilian life, injury to civilians, damage to civilian objects, or a combination thereof, which would be *excessive* in relation to the concrete and direct military advantage anticipated."[82] Proportionality is not about clear lines of prohibition, but rather about calculating and determining balances and degrees. The more the military task can be presented as crucial, the more civilian casualties the principle is willing to tolerate.

In the case of Hannibalism, the logic of proportionality took on an extraordinary form. Against the conventional understanding of the principle,[83] Israeli military lawyers put forward the argument that the level of civilian damage — that is, the number of dead civilians that military planners could find acceptable—should be measured against the danger of a possible release of prisoners. In other words, the military measures the carnage and destruction it allows itself to produce against risk that would come from its own actions—from the release of prisoners, not the capture of its soldiers.

Hannibalism thus mobilized different economies, or better, necroeconomies, of calculation, the currency being death, each with different mechanisms to measure the changing values of life and risk. One calculated the cost of the life of the captured in relation to that of the prisoners, while the other calculated the cost of the lives of "enemy civilians" in relation to the projected risks of releasing prisoners. The existence of such economies inevitably bring to mind the history of human trading, of slavery and colonialism, with the paradox being that by establishing the "exchange rate," the captors reinforce the perception that a life of one of the dominating is worth as much as many of the lives of the dominated. There is a crucial difference, though: in colonial history, similar exchange rates were indeed imposed, but significantly, they were imposed by the dominators. From the perspective of the Palestinian armed groups, the demand for an unequal exchange takes place in a situation that is asymmetrical to start with and on terms least convenient for their dominators. Thus, in 2011, when Shalit was exchanged for 1,027 Palestinian prisoners, it was the Palestinian armed groups that established a benchmark exchange rate for future deals.

Furthermore, the preemptive power of the Hannibal Directive is not aimed at the enemy alone—after all, they could have been left to do with the captives as they wish—but rather at Israeli society, which the military always saw as too weak to withstand the pressure to release prisoners. Indeed, whenever an Israeli soldier was captured, his family, friends, and supporters took to the streets and started campaigning for their release, until, most often, the government acquiesced.[84]

It was the settlers and the national-religious movements that were the most adamant critics of such deals, including the deal for the exchange of Gilad Shalit. On August 1, 2014, it would be the Givati Brigade, the unit most closely associated with the national-religious and settler movement, that had a chance to demonstrate a decisive alternative to such exchanges. Givati infused its soldiers with a religious consciousness that promotes self-sacrifice. At the beginning of the war, the brigade's commander, Ofer Winter, called the invasion a religious war "on the Gaza enemy who blasphemes against the Lord"—a kind of Jewish jihad.[85] In recent years, such religious sentiments have become manifest throughout the military, affecting military decisions and actions on the battlefields. It is a useful framework for the military because it allows it to steel soldiers' resolve to engage in ongoing occupation and domination without the self-questioning that human rights frames could otherwise encourage.

HANNIBAL UNLEASHED

Although the military acknowledged that Hannibal was invoked over the radio, in the months following the war, it denied that the Hannibal Directive was put into effect, and more so that the military tried to kill the captured soldier. Contrary to those claims, the account that follows demonstrates that what took place on August 1, 2014, was in fact a manhunt in which the military sought to resolve its "prisoner dilemma" by killing the prisoner and that this resulted in death and destruction brought on civilians in Rafah.

An "infantry officer" described to Breaking the Silence the events that unfolded after the invocation of the Hannibal Directive was heard over the radio:

> The minute "Hannibal Directive" is called on the radio, there are consequences. There's a fire procedure called the "Hannibal fire procedure"—you fire at every suspicious place that merges with a central route. You don't spare any means. A thousand shells were fired that Friday morning, at all the central intersections.... After the area was hit by 1,000 shells that Friday morning, I saw Tancher [military code for the main north-south Gaza artery—Salah al-Eddin Street] in ruins. Everything totally wrecked.[86]

An "artillery soldier" testified that his battery was "firing at a maximum fire rate" right into inhabited areas.[87] The Givati enquiry confirmed that more than two thousand bombs, rockets, and shells were fired during the day, one thousand in the massive fire strike in the three hours following the announcement of Hannibal.[88]

Invoking Hannibal is a way to bypass the military hierarchy. The commander on the ground—in this case Winter—was able to call in artillery and airstrikes without the necessity for authorizing strikes being slowed down by having to pass through the hierarchy of central command. The fire strike caught thousands of disoriented civilians in the open along the routes of eastern Rafah. Some were returning home because of the ceasefire, while others were escaping from the strikes now being unleashed. It was hard to know where to go for safety. One of the survivors of this strike, Saleh Abu Mohsen, described it thus: "People were running away

Abdul Rahim Lafi returned to his home in the neighborhood of Al Tanur with his two sons shortly after 8:00 a.m.[89] "My son Yehia and I left the house. We reached the Abu Youssef al Najjar roundabout when the first rocket fell ahead of us by about 13 meters. I fell and was injured in my right leg. When I looked next to me I found my son. He looked up at me for seconds and died immediately after. When the first missile fell, two women to the right on the road toward Abu Youssef al-Najjar round-about died." LEFT: Abdul Rahim Lafi points out the location of the strike to an Amnesty International researcher. RIGHT: Traces of a missile on the pavement of the route traversed by Lafi. KENT KLICH/FORENSIC ARCHITECTURE AND AMNESTY INTERNATIONAL

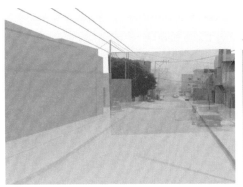

The first video we obtained was taken outside the Al Najjar Hospital looking south along the Al Najjar road. The metadata puts it at 10:22 a.m. The clip shows columns of dust raised by artillery fire a few hundred meters away, near the Al Najjar roundabout. This video was taken at the approximate time that Lafi was making his way to the hospital with his dead son. Both images contain stills from the video placed within a 3D model in order to establish their exact location.

from their homes in terror. It was a scene reminiscent of 1948, which we had only seen on TV. People were barefoot, women were running with their heads uncovered—it was a very difficult scene."[90] Other witnesses described the sky full of jets, drones, and helicopters. The Israeli military, suspecting the captured soldier might be among these people or in cars or ambulances that took the wounded away, declared a large area of eastern Rafah a "closed military zone."[91] Israeli helicopters were hovering over the main intersections like aerial checkpoints, reinforcing the siege by continuous fire aimed at anything on the roads. Cars, ambulances, trucks, and motorbikes were torched by missiles; pedestrians were torn by artillery.

Assuming that the captured soldier was wounded, the military suspected that he would have been taken to the Youssef al-Najjar Hospital, the one closest to the area of capture. This small hospital was also the main destination for the dozens of wounded and dead and their families. Shortly after the fire strike began, the hospital had reached a breaking point. The morgue was overflowing, and some bodies had to be sent to a vegetable wholesaler's refrigerator for storage. Dr. Ashraf Hijazi, head of the hospital's surgery department, recalled that "an officer from the Israeli intelligence services called a nurse at the hospital, said that the missing Israeli soldier was in the hospital and that we wouldn't be allowed to leave the hospital until we released the soldier. This was absurd." Rockets started

A residential building bearing the marks of military fire or tank shells. The large holes were made by rockets. There are traces of gunfire on all of the interior walls.

ALA'A HAMMOUDA AND SHOURIDEH MOLAVI FOR FORENSIC ARCHITECTURE AND AMNESTY INTERNATIONAL, 2015; ANALYSIS BY FORENSIC ARCHITECTURE

falling near the doors of the hospital. At 3:30 p.m., the patients started fleeing the hospital. Another doctor recalled: "some had plaster casts, with drips in their chests and stomachs. I saw a young boy in a plaster cast crawling trying to flee by dragging himself along."[92]

Shorty before 11:00 a.m., several columns of tanks, armored personnel carriers, and D9 bulldozers started charging toward the areas they suspected to harbor the tunnel, about two kilometers north of the point of capture. It was an area of low-density housing and some agricultural installations, just north of Salah al-Eddin Street. In the area was also the Sa'ad Sayel military base, a Hamas training facility that was evacuated throughout the war.

Dolev Ohayon, a Givati soldier who participated in the ground assault, describes the situation in an entry in a diary he kept throughout the war: "The air force, tanks, artillery, engineering, machine guns, all the IDF fire power was there."[93] The D9 bulldozers moved at the head of the columns, uprooting trees, demolishing buildings in their path, and piling up earth mounds to mask the movement of the infantry that followed them. Another soldier recalled: "a crazy amount of artillery was fired, armored D9 bulldozers plowed the entire area. After them the tanks moved in two lines, continuously shooting at houses as they moved along."[94] The tank crews were ordered to shoot at any building, car, or structure along the path of movement, as well as at any structure overlooking their route. Massive fire aimed to reduce the risk to the soldiers at the expense of civilians who were still present across the battlefield. The armored vehicle in which Ohayon rode stopped for a long pause just south of Salah al-Eddin Street (the "Tancher route") while the D9 bulldozers and deminers were blasting new routes through previously built fabric and flattening buildings. Ohayon noted in his diary the unbearable heat: "it was 99 percent humidity inside the vehicle... fire burning everywhere outside." It was also the first day of a desperately hot August, the hottest recorded to date. His comrades in the armored vehicles were shooting nervously in all directions.

When the D9s completed their work, the infantry was ordered to charge into the burned and almost completely destroyed neighborhood. Ohayon described the scene: "everything was completely on fire, I never saw such complete destruction, almost every building in this neighborhood was hit."[95] In all, 2,201 houses were destroyed completely or partially that day, 42 percent of them homes.[96]

When approaching a house, a tank would first fire shells at the building. Then, covered by the tank's continuous heavy machine-gun fire, soldiers would approach and fire a portable antitank rocket at a ground-level wall to produce a large hole. They then would enter the house through this hole, avoiding the doors and windows, where they could be expected. Before entering individual rooms, they would throw in grenades, regardless of there being civilians inside.

A military officer explained that "the motto guiding lots of people was, 'Let's show them.'"[97] Other soldiers reportedly said that they came "to settle scores," to "extract a price," or to "let out steam."[98] The soldiers wrought so much destruction that Eli Gino, Givati's deputy commander, was heard screaming over the radio: "Stop shooting! Stop shooting! You are shooting like morons, you will kill each other, STOP!"[99] There was hardly any return fire. Winter later said: "I hoped they [Hamas] would come face to face with us, but they chickened out.... That's not combat. There were very few places where there were fighting retreats. They left everything and escaped."[100] If there was no resistance, what could justify the level of fire the military used?

Twenty-year-old Mohammed Abu Duba's describes what happened as seen from his home, one of the houses in the area. He heard the

> sounds of tanks clearly as if they were next to our home. From far away, approaching. They struck the house and I no longer saw what was happening as we hid under the stairs.... The tanks were right next to our demolished house, one side of the tank touching the fallen masonry of our home, and continuing to bombard. And another in our street, one behind and one in front of the Mashrou' Amer [roundabouts].
>
> Munir went up to the roof—without of course our father knowing—and he began to count the flags on top of the tanks. They numbered about thirty-seven and more just in...our area. Sometimes they fly above the roof. They were just the ones we managed to count before fleeing. We counted and came straight back down. We weren't going to stay up there. He told me and my father and we went up to the roof. And sure enough. There were so many tanks. For every street, at least four or five tanks. And each one was bombarding the homes and people—wherever there were people.... The tanks were coming from everywhere, from every street as if in shifts: five would leave and another five would take their place going round and round.... We went up to the rooftop and saw the bulldozers from far away demolishing buildings one by one. And one of them was coming toward us. The tanks had [begun to move] but the bulldozer was coming toward us. My father said we're going to die. If we die, we die.... So we all got into the car. All of the window glass was smashed. We all got in with our belongings....

We went toward the area around the municipality building. I can't describe what we saw. It was as unrecognizable as our area. They weren't our streets. The cemetery is better by a million times than those streets. There were bodies... on the street and there was not enough room in our car to carry them. The municipality building was burnt and shattered glass was all around. There was not a single undamaged building....

I looked and saw three trucks drawn across to block the street; their windows covered in bullet holes and the tyres punctured. There were bodies in there. They [Israeli army] had killed the drivers....

I looked out left and right and saw bodies every three or four metres. Every three or four metres a child, a woman, a young boy, a young girl. All dead. We were looking to see if there was anybody moving. But they were all dead. None of the bodies was intact.[101]

The single deadliest aerial strike of August 1 took place in the Tanur neighborhood of eastern Rafah. It killed sixteen people and wounded many others. The bombing was captured on multiple videos. The closest was a hand-held video shot from a nearby rooftop. The clip is watermarked with the words "Resistance Press" — the media channel associated with Hamas in Gaza. The clip was posted without the metadata. Toward the end of the sequence, a second before shutting off the camera, the videographer zoomed out and captured two short upright extensions of the building columns casting a clear shadow on the flat roof, about a dozen meters away from the videographer. These were useful sun dials. We built a detailed model of the rooftop and the area around it and ran a shadow simulation on it. Using the columns as the arms of the sun dials, we were able to determine that a strike took place at 10:53 a.m., with a five-minute margin of error.
RESISTANCE PRESS, 2014; ANALYSIS BY FORENSIC ARCHITECTURE

IMAGE SPACE

To reconstruct the events of the day, we needed to study the relation between the close to seven-thousand photographs and video clips that we had collected and received. When extracted from social media websites such as Twitter, Facebook, and YouTube, the metadata that could have helped us establish the time and location of these sources was no longer available. In the absence of digital time markers, we searched the images for analog time indicators—things we referred to as "physical clocks." The most common of those were shadows. Shadows contain information about the location, orientation, and time at which an image was taken. We thus tried to match the shadows visible in images with simulated shadows that we generated in our modeling software. We used the three-dimensional model of the city as a virtual sundial to match the shadows found in images.[102]

Locating the images in space was most often undertaken by finding recognizable features in the image. After locating an image in space, we would orient the camera's point of view by matching its cone of vision with simulations of eye-level perspectives extracted from the model of the city that we constructed.

Placing all images and clips within the model one by one, we gradually turned an image archive into an architectural-image complex—a space-time relation between multiple sources. The relations between a large multiplicity of images made viewing spatial. Navigation between one image and the next takes place by moving through this image space, a space that is both virtual and photographic. The model, in turn, became an optical device to establish and view images and the relations between them.

The margin of error in determining time by undertaking shadow analysis depends on proximity. If the shadows in the image are relatively close to the photographer, the margin of error in determining the time can be as small as five minutes. We referred to this margin of error as "time resolution"—as if the time line would be composed of time units five minutes in size that are analogous to the pixilation of images. Whenever the shadows captured in the image were farther away from the photographer or when, as happened closer to noon, with the sun high in the sky, they were considerably shorter, the time resolution increased to half an hour—sometimes even an hour, a time span no longer useful for our purposes.

RIGHT: At 11.39 a.m., a European Pléiades image satellite passed over Rafah, capturing a multispectral photograph of the city before continuing over the Mediterranean at a ground speed of ten kilometers a second. It would return over the same spot only on August 14, ten days after the Israeli military retreated from the Gaza Strip. The image provided a rare snapshot of the battle at a resolution of 50 centimeter per pixel. Operated by a European consortium and available since 2012, the Pléiades satellite is not bound by the same restrictions as US image satellites—which otherwise hold a near monopoly on the satellite image market—on providing high-resolution images of Israel and the Occupied Territories. In the Pléiades images, buildings and landscape features come into focus, although people remain below the threshold of detectability. The Pléiades photograph provides a rare snapshot of a city under attack, capturing multiple simultaneous incidents. On top of this image we located incidents, cameras, and the cones of vision of their photographs and videos, smoke plumes, bomb clouds, and the location of witnesses and incidents.

1. Israeli tanks and D9 bulldozers along Salah al-Eddin Street. The smoke plume of burned trailers at the Mashrou' Amer roundabout confirms Moshen's testimony. About an hour after the ceasefire came into effect, he returned home with his three daughters. They found it partially destroyed and started to clear up the rubble.[103] At 11:00 a.m., shortly after hearing a massive explosion, they decided to leave. They ran toward Salah al-Eddin Street, a few minutes away (their path is marked in blue). When he got there he was surprised to find a trailer on fire: "I found tanks in front of the Sa'ad Sayel barracks. The tanks fired at us.... I took two of my daughters and my third daughter stayed with the wife of a neighbour. [When crossing the Mashrou' Amer intersection], I looked behind me and did not see my daughter [Aseel]." He found the body of Aseel next to the roundabout four days later.[104] The satellite photograph was taken about half an hour after the incidents but it is likely to be the same tanks that killed his daughter.

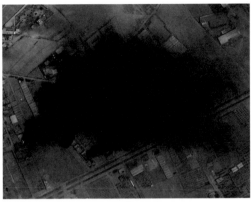

2. At precisely the same time, a bomb cloud rises over a neighborhood north east of there. Because the metadata on the satellite image is precise and available, we could establish the time of all photographs (whose metadata was not available) that captured the same cloud from the ground.

3. Fire and a thick smoke plume from a bombing raid that took place about an hour before the photograph was taken. The area, as I will later show, was suspected to contain the mouth of the tunnel into which Lieutenant Goldin was taken, and this fire is the result of attempts to collapse it.

4. The impact craters from artillery shells and air strikes are recorded as vegetation loss by studying vegetation vigor (NDVI). A bomb destroys all organic life next to it, including small plants not always visible to the naked eye. Such craters and burn marks can be seen all along the roadways and around the major intersections in eastern Rafah.

5. The location, according to Saleh Abu Mohsen, of the body of Aseel Abu Mohsen, his daughter. At a resolution of 0.5 meters per pixel, her body cannot be within any two pixels. This image shows the limit of detectability from space.

6. Identification of tank tracks. Comparing the Pléiades satellite images of August 1 and 14 shows clear changes in the condition of vegetation. Tanks crush the vegetation under their tracks.[105] There are five tanks along the route at the top left part of the image. Tanks tend to avoid roadways, where they might be expected. They usually maneuver off-road, where they crush vegetation. A "tank commander" quoted by Breaking the Silence explained: "I assigned one of my company commanders to document the maneuver by video, so we could illustrate it in training . . . because in training we don't have planted grove areas we can keep running over or a variety of 'live' houses to shoot at."[106]

ANALYSIS BY JAMON VAN DEN HOEK AND FORENSIC ARCHITECTURE

The tank paths are recorded along most of their length because of the semi-agrarian nature of the frontier zone. The choreography of the war could thus be recorded by its effect on vegetation. Following the crushed vegetation of tank paths backward leads to staging areas next to Israeli agrarian settlements (marked in white circles) that surround the Gaza Strip. The use of civilian settlements for envelopment, surveillance, and military supply is significant, given that Israel claims that Hamas is endangering its civilian population by locating its installations in inhabited areas. This image shows Israel does the same, though it has enough space to choose not to.

AIR: NEPHANALYSIS OF BOMB CLOUDS

After several weeks of unsuccessful attempts to improve the time resolution in the images and videos in which the visible shadows were more than several hundred meters away from the photographer, we realized that we were looking for physical clocks, analogue time indicators, in the wrong part of the image. Almost every image had some sky in it. August 1 was a cloudless day, but because of the massive bombardment, almost every piece of sky caught on camera contained one or several bomb clouds. These bomb clouds, columns of dust hundreds of meters high, could be seen from everywhere in the strip and even from Israeli cities, where people reportedly saw giant columns of dust from forty kilometers away or more.[107] Their monstrous size made photographers tilt their cameras upward to include their full extent and captured more sky in the frame at the expense of the earth. The constant transformation of these bomb clouds and their unique form in doing so meant they could function as a form of metadata — indicators of an image's time/space coordinates — with which we could synchronize and sequence many of the images of the day as we built a narrative.

Unlike meteorological clouds, bomb clouds are anchored to the ground. Still, like weather clouds, they undergo constant transformations and metamorphoses. Each has a unique signature at any given moment. We started by forming an archive of bomb clouds, dividing them by shape, type, and stage of transformation. It was perhaps a contemporary version of a nineteenth-century cloud atlas. We consulted our colleagues in art history.

According to art historian Hubert Damisch's book *A Theory of /Cloud/: Toward a History of Painting*, when in sixteenth-century painting the territorial part of landscape painting started to be organized according to the rules of perspective, the sky part of the image still belonged to an older symbolic order, referring to spirituality or sacredness.[108] That clouds are undergoing constant metamorphosis, that they move, change, and transform from one form to another, dissipate, or gather out of nowhere posed an ongoing problem for their classification and pictorial representation. The problem persisted in the early years of photography: the long exposure time wiped the clouds away from the sky in the same way that it wiped people away from a Paris street. (See "Before and After" in Part 1.) Clouds simply changed their form faster than a painter's hand or the exposure time of daguerreotypes could capture.

Different techniques and technologies had to be conceived to capture clouds as static objects in measurable skies. These extended from the cloud contraptions developed by the fourteenth-century architect Filippo Brunelleschi to project the geometries of the sky onto the inner surface of a dome through the rectilinear and curvilinear perspectival grids proposed by Victorian art and architecture historian John Ruskin.

Beginning in the early nineteenth century, amateur meteorologists started engaging in the morphological science of cloud study. Luke Howard, a British chemist who observed the skies from his house in Tottenham, North London, classified clouds by their visible characteristics, harnessing their infinite variation by genus and type—cirrus ("a curl of hair"), cumulus ("a heap"), and stratus ("layer")—as if they were singular objects, plants, or animals.[109] The nascent science of "nephanalysis"—the study of cloud form, types, and movement—influenced artists such as John Constable and J. M. W. Turner, who focused their meteorological attention on the dynamic texture and shapes that had started to be named by science.

The clouds we were looking at in Rafah were of course not caused by the weather, although they interacted with it. The relevant expertise was not meteorology, but blast engineering and fluid dynamics. The unique fingerprint of a constantly transforming bomb cloud depends on the materiality of the target and the ammunition used to destroy it, as well as on microatmospheric conditions such as humidity, variations in temperature, wind direction, and speed at different altitudes.[110]

Regardless of these variations, bomb clouds go through several distinct phases. The blast generates a zone of low pressure that sucks in all aggregate substance that the bomb had just pulverized, including recoil from the earth, and debris dust from the building. These tiny particles of aerosol rubble then mix with smoke and gather water vapor around them. The heat generated by the blast pushes this aerosol mixture rapidly upward. The column rises in turbulent, gyrating verticals until its temperature and pressure even out with that of the surrounding air. At this altitude, the rising vapor and dust column start pouring sideways as if hitting a glass ceiling, and the cloud opens up like an umbrella or a mushroom. Moments later, the debris starts raining down onto the shadow of the cloud, which starts slowly dissipating. The entire process lasts for about ten minutes.

In his essay "The Storm-Cloud of the Nineteenth-Century," John Ruskin, who was also the patron saint of the Cloud Appreciation Society, lamented the loss of the skies to a new form of cloud—the formless smog of the Industrial Revolution. He thought of these clouds not as natural phenomena, subject to meteorological study, but as technology, human products, the atmospheric materialization of human labor and mechanization.

The material composition of bomb clouds is even more devilish than those two-centuries-old products of exploitation. They include everything that a building pulverized by a bomb once was — sand and soil from under their foundations, the concrete of their structure, the crushed plaster of their interior, the plastic, fabric, wood, glass, paperwork, utensils, and furniture in them, as well as, sometimes horrifyingly, remnants of human bodies.[111] These clouds are airborne cemeteries of architecture and flesh. A resident of Gaza to whom I spoke during the bombing of 2008–2009 told me about neighborhoods "turning from solid structures to dust, and the dust of homes filling the air," about survivors breathing in pulverized life.

The soft, temporary, and ever-changing architecture of bomb clouds contrasts with the solid, hard architecture of buildings on the ground, but it is architecture nevertheless, a temporary, gaseous architecture with a life span of seven to ten minutes. In its extreme form, it demonstrates a truth about all buildings. I started Part 1 of this book with a description of a surveyor studying building transformations as the proper condition of all architecture. A bomb cloud in this context is the extreme condition of architecture, its cycle of emergence and decay played in fast-forward mode.

Bomb cloud atlas, Rafah, August 1, 2014.

MULTIPLE SOURCES; ANALYSIS BY FORENSIC ARCHITECTURE

Our cloud atlas included all bomb clouds captured on the images we had of August 1 in Rafah. We carefully classified and grouped each cloud by stage—blasts, upward moving columns, mushrooms, dissipations. This allowed us to estimate how long after the explosion each photograph was taken. Particular formal irregularities distinct to each bomb cloud allowed us to find the same clouds in other images. When we managed to identify the same cloud from two or more perspectives, we could determine that the images were synchronous. We modeled some of the clouds volumetrically, as architectural forms, to establish the angle from which they were captured. We could thus establish the location of the bomb by plotting and intersecting the camera perspectives on the satellite image. When we managed to establish the time/space coordinates of one bomb cloud, we looked for all other images that had that same cloud plus another, thus determining the time of the other bomb and then triangulating further.

After locating the time and space of the images of clouds in the sky, we turned our attention back to the ground parts of these images and to events unfolding there. The bomb clouds helped anchor media with testimonial evidence. Many testimonies were organized around the bombing incidents that people recalled—could not forget—because of what happened to their homes or families. They often described their own movement through the city as a sequence of events punctured by bombing incidents. The bomb clouds could thus function as anchors for the events of the day, grounding testimony and evidence, meteorology, buildings, and ruins in a forensic assemblage was at once the product of media, memory, and material reality.

SUBSOIL: THE UNDERGROUND MANHUNT

The two one-ton bombs that were dropped on the Tanur neighborhood landed atop a small, single-story, corrugated tin structure that stood empty between several buildings. The small structure was completely devoured by a crater fifteen meters wide and ten meters deep. That such a structure was targeted by two of the largest bombs in the Israeli arsenal suggested that the air force was likely aiming at something else. We believe this might have been a tunnel that they suspected ran underneath the little shed. The shed could have been an entrance or a shaft.

From the shape of the crater, it became apparent to our munitions adviser, Chris Cobb-Smith that the bombs employed in this strike were ground-penetrating bombs. Such bombs do not explode upon impact. The milliseconds of delay between impact and detonation allow them to bore into the subsoil and explode underneath the surface. The pressure caused by the shock waves is designed to collapse any tunnel in the vicinity. Because the tunnel is the only source of oxygen underground, a fireball could form there and storm along its length. Sometimes, as reported by a Breaking the Silence witness, "When one side of a tunnel is bombed, a kilometer away, on the other side, you see the tunnel's other shaft fly up in the air."[112]

To verify whether the military bombed the tunnels, knowing their captive was within, under the terms of the Hannibal Directive, we needed to shift our attention to the subsoil and try to map the tunnel network there.

During the war, the military started to realize that its most vulnerable borders were not the airspace, where its "iron dome" antimissile system proved quite effective, or the fences and walls it erects around the Gaza Strip, but the crust of the earth separating the subsoil from the ground's surface. It was a space into which it had no effective means to survey. The Israeli ground incursion, which began July 17, aimed to destroy the network of tunnels without being able to see them, a fact that contributed to the massive destruction of entire neighborhoods that ensued.

The city of Rafah is where the tunnel project in Gaza began, where it grew, and where it became increasingly sophisticated. The city has more tunnels than anywhere else in the strip for geopolitical, geological, and socioeconomic reasons. Geopolitically, it is located between two sealed borders, to Israel and to Egypt. Geologically, it is in a more arid area, and the water table under the southern end of the Gaza strip is lower; the soil there is compacted sandstone, lighter, drier, and thus easier to dig through than elsewhere in the strip.[113] Consequently, several families from Rafah hold a near monopoly on the "market" for tunneling work throughout the rest of the Gaza Strip.

Rafah's first underground tunnels were dug across the short border to Egypt following Israel's 1982 retreat from Sinai. The Egypt-Israel agreement led to the partition of the city between the sides. Soon enough, tunnels became the only way for goods and weapons to be brought into the strip outside Israel's control. A decade later, starting in 1992, with the launch of the Israeli-Palestinian Oslo process, Israel started gradually isolating Gaza and fencing in its population. Throughout the years of the second Intifada, starting in 2000, and to a greater extent following Hamas's takeover of power over the strip in 2007, the closure of Gaza tightened, and the tunnel system connecting it to Egypt was expanded to maintain an essential inward flow of goods, food, and other provisions, as well as weapons. While most tunnels ran across the border to Egypt, some also started to be

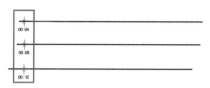

These three video clips capture the same bomb cloud. We synchronized the clips by matching details in the form of the cloud. Next, we established the location of each camera and its cone of vision. Then we triangulated the three perspectives. Their intersection led us to the Tanur neighborhood in eastern Rafah. LEFT: RESISTANCE PRESS; CENTER: CBS; RIGHT: ABDEL RA'OUF SHA'TH AND AHMED ABU SAUD; ANALYSIS BY FORENSIC ARCHITECTURE

dug across the border to Israel. In 2006, it was through such a tunnel coming out in Rafah that Gilad Shalit was captured.

Until Israel's retreat from Gaza in 2005, military attempts to destroy the tunnel network connecting the Egyptian and Israeli parts of Rafah led to the destruction of eighteen hundred homes in the border area.[114] As long as Egyptian president Hosni Mubarak and his elected successor Mohammed Morsi were in power, the tunneling business prospered. Following the 2013 coup in Egypt, the Egyptian military, under the self proclaimed president Abdel Fattah el-Sisi started demolishing Hamas's tunnel network—it perceived Hamas as its enemy—on their side of the border, destroying all buildings in the Egyptian part of Rafah that were within a two-kilometer strip from the border—almost the entire extent of the Egyptian town.[115] The direction of Palestinian tunneling was then reoriented toward the Israeli border though there were tunnels going toward the border before. Unlike the wide "smuggling tunnels" to Egypt, the "attack tunnels" to Israel were only as wide as was necessary for the movement of combatants walking single file—about a meter in width—though these channels were also quite well supplied with electric generators, living quarters, food, ammunition, and sometimes even small command centers. With spades, buckets, and increasingly with pneumatic drills, teams of diggers working

3.6M±0.3M

0.6M±0.3M

3.6M±0.3M

0.6M±0.3M

When closely studying the changing morphology of these bomb clouds, we noticed an additional detail. Two single still frames captured bombs in midfall, fractions of a second before impact (ABOVE). In order to identify these bombs, we needed to measure their size. We placed the photographic surface at the location of the bombs into the 3D model (BELOW). RESISTANCE PRESS, 2014; ANALYSIS BY FORENSIC ARCHITECTURE, 2015

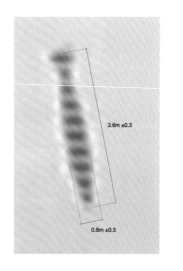

MK-84, GBU-31 Specifications

Class:	2,000 lb.
	General Purpose Bomb/Fragmer
Guidance:	Ballistic
Weigh:	2039 lbs / 925 kg
Length:	3.28m
Diameter:	0.45m
Explosive:	945 lbs. H-6 or Tritonal
Unit cost	$3,100
Source:	FAS Military Analysis Network

Because we were able to measure the image plane—it was 150 meters long at the distance intersecting the bomb—we could determine the dimensions of the bombs. An online catalogue helped us identify them as US-manufactured MK-84/GBU-31 JDAMs. These bombs are packed with one ton of explosives and are among the biggest and most destructive in the air force's arsenal. A one-ton bomb dropped on an inhabited civilian neighborhood is possibly a war crime.

round the clock in two twelve-hour shifts can dig and reinforce an average of ten to fifteen meters of tunnel a day. Hamas spends a large part of its budget making and maintaining these tunnels. The more complete Israel's control from the air became, the deeper and the more fortified the underground tunnels were made.

The creation of an extensive and deep tunneling network by different digging groups necessitated the establishment of something resembling underground traffic regulations to avoid collisions. Underground traffic control is similar to air traffic control in that both regulate movements within three-dimensional volumes that start and end at the surface, only they go in opposite directions. Israel's exposure of these underground traffic regulations allowed its military to estimate the paths of tunnels after identifying an entry or an exit point. Tunnels mostly progress along one of two possible directions: east-west, for smuggling tunnels to Egypt, or perpendicular to the direction of the Israeli border, from northwest to southeast, for attack tunnels. Keeping to these basic directions requires the use of GPS, compasses, and satellite images. Each grid of tunnels leads to a number of exits or mouths, usually hidden within buildings, greenhouses, or workshops.[116]

As the bombardment began, two photographers—Abdel Ra'ouf Sha'th and Ahmed Abu Saud—ran up to the eighth-floor offices of the Smart Media Center in the Masri Towers and started taking photographs. The images they sent us after the war showed a wide panorama of a city under fire. The frame, horizontally divided between the cityscape and the sky, linked by bomb clouds, recalls all-too-common representations of the cities of the Arab world: Baghdad, Beirut, Gaza, Damascus, and Sana'a. The metadata on the images was intact, but the clocks were wrongly set—the photos registered a time close to midnight, while it is obvious from the photographs that we thought they were taken during the day. However, the time gaps between the photographs were consistent throughout the sequence.

11:39 AM

In a rare coincidence, the Pléiades satellite photograph of August 1 captured a bomb cloud closely after detonation. Satellites have their metadata available; it was taken at 11:39 a.m. local time. We matched the bomb cloud view from the top with a view of the same cloud from the ground, which we found among the photographs of Sha'th and Abu Saud. We were thus able to synchronize their entire sequence of photographs (PREVIOUS PAGE) determining the time in each and matching this time to a cloud form. Then, whenever we found the same clouds in other photographs, we were able to determine the time in them, also.

We superimposed the location of the strikes which we previously established through the triangulation of the bomb clouds in the air, on top of the assumed paths of tunnels underground. The materiality of these media each described another limit to architectural investigation: in the air, it was the fast metamorphosis of soft elements, while underground, it was the invisibility of the negative spaces of tunnels that posed a challenge for us. However, if the location of the strikes overlapped with the location of the tunnels, and if the timing of the bombing coincided with the time the military believed the captured soldier was in them, we could support claims that a manhunt aimed at the captive might have taken place.

We were careful not to collect information or map more of the location of the tunnels than was necessary for us to make our point. It was not safe for our partners and for us to collect and exchange information about their locations, and despite not being supporters of Hamas, we also did not intend to do the Israeli military's work for them. Inasmuch as we inadvertently received information about their paths, we removed it from our files. We mapped only those parts of the tunnel networks that were already exposed or dug up by the military, that is, only those places where the military already knew or believed tunnels to be. The traces of deep mechanical digging were visible in ground-level photographs taken by our team members Ala'a Hammouda, Nael Mosallam, Shourideh Molavi, and Kent Klich. These locations were corroborated by studying satellite photographs from August 14, the next time after the battle that a high-resolution satellite survey was undertaken. In them we could identify deep traces of excavations.

Other useful sources for determining the path of the tunnels were accounts made public by the military. The most comprehensive of these sources was the first-hand account of Lieutenant Eitan Fund, an officer in the Givati reconnaissance unit and a personal friend of Lieutenant Goldin. On the morning of August 1, Fund led a small team of soldiers into the tunnel in pursuit of Goldin. Half a year later, in February 2015, Fund received the highest military decoration given to any Israeli soldier during this war. On that occasion, his account of moving through the tunnel was extensively reported in the media, which needed a hero in a war that was otherwise seen by many as a military failure. Inadvertently, it provided much of the missing information.

At 9:54 a.m., slightly less than an hour after the firefight in which Goldin was captured, Lieutenant Eitan Fund, after repeated requests, received Ofer Winter's permission to enter the tunnel.[117] Fund stormed in, pistol in

The architectural image complex. The three-dimensional model provided us with a means of composing the relations between multiple images and clips and an optical device to navigate between them. The smoke clouds were used as the anchors that connect the multiple sources.

In'am Ouda Ayed bin Hammad was knocked unconscious by the Tanur bombing. She described the
scene: About sixty people poured onto the streets
after an artillery barrage hit the neighborhood. Then
a bomb fell. "Suddenly there was smoke, dust, rubble, and shrapnel flying above us." Hers is a description of the Tanur bomb cloud from below: "A column
from a wall fell, protecting my daughter Remas and
me from the shrapnel. I lost consciousness for a few
minutes, and when I recovered, I felt a pain in my
leg. I got up from under the rubble, took my daughter and stepped out."[118] Twelve out of the sixteen
people killed in this bombing were her relatives and
included her five-year-old son, Anas Bin Hammad.
Because of the curfew and the ongoing fire,
ambulances could not come near, and the wounded
and dying were left for long hours on the road.

hand, with three other soldiers behind him. He described the tunnel as pitch dark, head high, concrete cladded, and with electrical wires running its length. The soldiers used flashlights and shot forward continuously as they pushed forward. Fund has almost lost his hearing from the reverberations. When asked if such shooting would not have killed Goldin, Fund explained: "I instructed the soldier next to me to open fire if he identified any figures — even if it meant killing or wounding Hadar (Goldin). Painful as it is, it is better that way."[119] Fund seemingly understood Goldin's death to be preferable to him being taken alive, in line with the manhunt logic of the Hannibal Directive. That he received a decoration shows that his actions were not only condoned, but rewarded. After "three to four hundred meters," Fund recalled, he reached a T junction. Next to it, the soldiers found blood traces, along with some of Goldin's clothing and personal equipment. Two hours later, Fund reentered the tunnel to retrieve them. The right turn of the T, leading toward the Israeli border, was blocked off with a blanket. Behind it, he said, was a pile of military bags with battle-ready equipment, food, and water. Fund ordered two of the soldiers to stay at the junction. Together with another soldier, he started running into the left branch of the intersection leading toward Rafah. He noticed another bifurcation. After a few minutes, another group of soldiers entered the tunnel to shout to them (the radio didn't work underground) to get out immediately. Fund then turned around and started running back. According to Fund, the incursion into the tunnel lasted slightly over thirty minutes. He could not have covered a third of a twenty-five-hundred-meter-long tunnel when ordered out. Goldin and his captors were likely still in the tunnel, only farther on.

The soldiers left the tunnel at about 10:30 a.m. At 10:47, according to the military's own description of events, the air force bombing began. We were able to locate and time to 10:52 a number of massive bomb clouds from one-ton bombs dropping in the area north of Salah al-Eddin Street. (This is the area marked 3 in the satellite image on page 187.) At 10:53, as previously shown, the Tanur neighborhood was bombed with another pair of one-ton bombs. The fact that these strikes took place just over fifteen minutes after the soldiers left the tunnel points to a temporal correlation: it is consistent with the military ordering the soldiers out of the tunnel in order to start bombing it.

The location of several of the bomb clouds overlaps with the location of the excavation made by the military in its search for tunnels. The timeline of these bomb strikes coincides with the time immediately after the search was aborted and the tunnel was evacuated by Lieutenant Fund and his soldiers.

LOCATION 7
(SEE PAGE 187)

The red square marks the cinder block structure, over the tunnel mouth where the firefight took place.

A moonlike landscape—the search for the tunnel involved the destruction of every building and agricultural installation in the area. The depression of the tunnel mouth can be seen in the area marked by a red square.

LOCATION 8

A small shed, marked in red square, can be seen within the Sa'ad Sayel military base.

The shed has been removed and traces of deep mechanical digging can be seen in its place.

LOCATION 9

Fields and greenhouses.

The greenhouses are destroyed, and heavy mechanical digging can be identified in the area marked by a red rectangle.

Military excavations in search
of the tunnel mouth.
KENT KLICH FOR FORENSIC ARCHITECTURE
AND AMNESTY INTERNATIONAL, 2014

An excavation site for tunnels
secured by a fence.
NAEL MOSALLAM AND SHOURIDEH
MOLAVI FOR FORENSIC ARCHITECTURE
AND AMNESTY INTERNATIONAL, 2015

It was not any single incident, testimony, image, or clip that helped suggest the logic of this manhunt, but a time-space puzzle of relations between a large multiplicity of incidents captured by different classes of evidence in hundreds of images from the air and ground, and dozens of testimonies, both civilian and military.

"It was likely," the Givati enquiry admitted in retrospect, "that the Hamas unit and Goldin never left the tunnel."[120] Ohayon's diary noted that after August 1, his unit was told that Goldin "was buried in the collapsed tunnel."[121] Hamas' statement seems to concur: "We have lost contact with the mujahedeen unit that was in that ambush, and we think that all the fighters in this unit were killed by Zionist shelling along with the soldier."[122] "The bottom-line," another Givati commander said of Goldin's captors, weeks after the end of the war, "is Goldin is not with them and the Hamas unit is probably exterminated."[123] The passive voice hides the fact that killing Lieutenant Hadar Goldin was what the military intended to do and likely did.

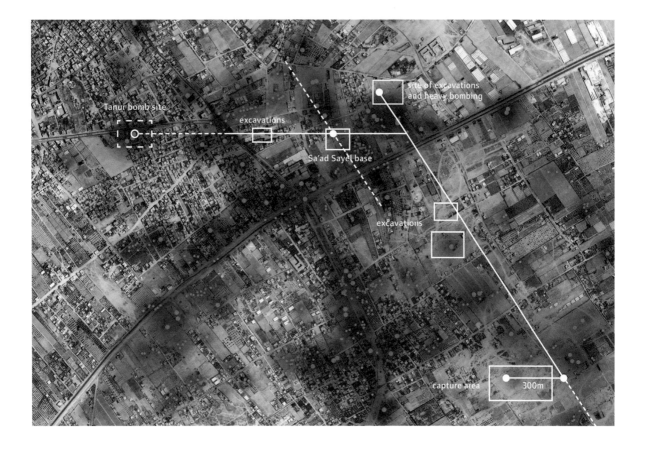

Identifiable locations of about fifty air strikes (large circles, with the gradient being their "kill area") and artillery craters (smaller dots) are marked. Places where excavations were undertaken, derived from ground and satellite research, are marked with white frames. The presumed tunnel path is marked out in white lines and presumed tunnel mouths in circles. There is an overlap between the presumed architecture of the tunnel network and the known pattern of bomb strikes. At the extremities of the tunnels, in dotted lines, are the possible extensions of the tunnel. In the top left, the extension could lead to the Tanur neighborhood, site of the deadliest bombing that day. It is thus possible that this strike aimed at the tunnels.

PLÉIADES SATELLITE, CNES, DISTRIBUTION AIRBUS DS; ANALYSIS BY FORENSIC ARCHITECTURE

Lieutenant Goldin's personal items retrieved by Lieutenant Fund on his second incursion into the tunnel were helicoptered to the military forensics lab in Tel Aviv in order for his condition to be assessed. DNA analysis confirmed that the blood was his. It also reportedly demonstrated that vital organs were hit: "it was concluded," military sources were quoted as saying, "that even if Goldin had been taken alive, there was no possibility a Hamas doctor could have kept him alive."[124] The original statement was potentially controversial: if Goldin was taken alive and survived for two hours in the tunnel, he could possibly have been killed in the air force bombings at about 10:53 a.m. The statement was later amended: the military confirmed, without acknowledging the retraction or making the forensic report public, that Lieutenant Goldin was killed in the initial firefight, at about 9:06 a.m.

The following evening, Saturday, August 2, after the end of the Shabbat, Minister of Defense Moshe Ya'alon, incidentally a relative of the Goldin family, arrived at their family home to share the results of the medical-forensic report and personally break the most terrible of news to the family. The family had only been previously informed that their son had been made captive. In the meantime, a rabbinical court (Beth-Din) was hurriedly assembled to issue a death certificate.[125] In the absence of a body, the level of proof required by the religious authorities to pronounce death is higher than that required by the legal system. In previous years, in response to lessons drawn from captures where the military had no certainty regarding the state of the soldiers, the rabbinate acquired new forensic technologies meant to help establish death remotely, without the necessity of examining the body. Forensics thus has become a strategic parameter on the battlefield. Identification could be based on "fingerprints, X-rays, dental records and DNA" and "cameras could beam evidence from the field in a very short time to the chief rabbi's desk."[126] The necessity for fast identification and assessment is part of the logic of the Hannibal Directive, because it likewise seeks to take away the enemy's asset. According to the military, Hamas, aware of these forensic capabilities, tried to hide evidence of Goldin's condition in order to increase uncertainty.

At 11:25 p.m. on August 2, the rabbinical court established Goldin's death, and his death certificate was signed by Chief Military Rabbi Raffi Peretz. The military confirmed that in declaring Goldin's death, it took into account both the forensic finds and "other relevant considerations." Peretz later explained what these other considerations could be: "the rabbinate was part of the combat theatre, and in a combat theatre, commanders take responsibility...our contribution to the fighting was certainty."[127] Peretz ruled that the bodily fluids retrieved were enough to conduct a funeral. What remained in Gaza was now body parts, and although Hamas later claimed to have retrieved the body, for the time being, the Israeli government has not been willing to enter into negotiations about it.[128] The death certificate and the funeral thus completed the task of the Hannibal Directive. The pronouncement that Goldin died in the firefight was also convenient for another reason. The military could now conveniently claim that they had not killed him when they collapsed the tunnel: you can't kill a dead man.

MEANWHILE...

The bombing of Rafah continued as this medico-theological drama was unfolding. About an hour after the death certificate was signed, a young medic in Rafah named Yasser Wahhab called his wife, Nehay. She and their children had taken refuge at her brother's house while he was on ambulance duty.

> My wife had left me a message, so I returned her call at 1 am and we chatted for a while about normal things—whether the children had gone to bed, whether they had eaten. She said not to worry about them; they were all fine where they were. All of a sudden, a missile landed on their house and the mobile went dead. I tried calling her back but it did not connect."[129]

Nehay was killed, along with four of their children, while their father was on the phone with them.[130]

The next morning, the young Mohammed Abu Duba, the first part of whose testimony was reproduced earlier, managed to find the bodies of his father and brother Munir. He went to search after they did not return from a trip to salvage belongings from their home close to the battlefield.

> I rang Munir's phone and heard it ringing. I said "thank God." It was the ring tone I recognized ringing around me. I looked and saw...he had been thrown onto high voltage wire....If it hadn't been for his shirt, I wouldn't have recognized him. I ran to him and pulled him off the wire. He and I both fell to the ground. I looked at him. His face and left hand were all burnt and all his fingers were cut off except for one: his forefinger. I embraced him. I turned off his mobile phone. And carried on holding him.

I wondered where my father was. I looked around and found him strewn about six metres away without a head. I ran to my father but before I got to him I fell, fainted. I tried to reach him but I couldn't. I called for help but nobody was around. Every time I tried to carry him I fell over. I fell to the floor and lost consciousness. Every time I woke up I saw him and so fainted again.... I thought I was dreaming and that none of this had happened.[131]

All this killing, including that of an Israeli officer, is heartbreaking. Analyzing and recounting the events of August 1, is hard to get through. It was Goldin's funeral, taking place at 5:30 p.m., August 3, 2014, that gave the signal for the Israeli withdrawal from the Gaza Strip. Aerial bombings lasted until August 26, after which the level of fire went down and the situation returned to the status quo—the state of strangulation, isolation, deprivation, siege, and unemployment that defines life in Gaza.

POSTSCRIPT: TRIAL AS DENIAL

In the aftermath of the Gaza war, the two cases, that of Hannibal in Rafah and that of the Nakba Day killings, got entangled. In September 2014 the ICC announced its intention to open a "preliminary investigation" into Israeli war crimes (Amnesty International and Forensic Architecture submitted the above report in evidence, and were invited to meet the prosecutors to provide clarifications). Slightly more than a month later, in November 2014, the arrest of Ben Deri for the Bituniya killing seemed like a strategic move. Minister of Defense Ya'alon used the indictment (for the same killings he had previously denounced as fabrication) to argue that the state's legal system was capable and willing to investigate the 2014 Gaza War, and even to charge its own personnel, thus rendering international process redundant under the principle of "complementarity" previously mentioned. Behind the trial of Deri could thus have been an attempt to silence the investigation into the carnage of Gaza. When used in this way, a trial might itself be used as a means of denial.

The relation between the two cases got further complicated when another incident was made public. On March 24, 2016, in the Jewish settlement of Hebron, an Israeli soldier, Elor Azaria, was caught on camera executing a wounded Palestinian assailant, Abdel Fattah al-Sharif. Al-Sharif was first shot when stabbing a soldier, but was lying severely wounded on the ground when executed a few minutes later. The video, recorded by a resident of Hebron, was posted online by B'tselem and from there made it to the front page of most international news. Azaria was arrested and charged with manslaughter. Because the killing could not be denied, the case revolved around the interpretation of its context. The defence referred, as it often does in such cases, to the duration of a "split second" in which a soldier must decide how to act. Azaria claimed he feared al-Sharif had a suicide belt (there was none). But the prosecution ruptured the "split second" argument by showing Azaria casually handed his helmet to another soldier before the shooting, and told another after it that al-Sharif "deserved to die." This, however, resonated well with the Israeli public. Polls showed that sixty per cent supported Azaria. Netanyahu spoke to and comforted his parents and publically advised the judges to keep the larger context in mind.[132] Of the government ministers, Ya'alon was alone in taking public position against the killing in the name of "military ethics" and in recognition of the implications that failure to prosecute might have in the forums of international law, but he quickly lost public support. In May 2016, Netanyahu fired and replaced him with extreme right politician Avigdor Lieberman, who had vigorously campaigned for Azaria. When on January 4, 2017, Azaria was convicted, and more demonstrations erupted, the entire government called for his immediate pardon. The vigorous public calls for pardon have in turn put pressure on the prosecution in the Deri/Nawara case. It was a few days after Azaria's conviction that attempts to force the negligence plea mentioned earlier were made.

In May 2016, shortly before Ya'alon was sacked, the defence establishment decided to cancel the Hannibal Directive. Israeli legal experts cited its application on August 1 as the prime example for the command's incompatibility with international law.[133] It is unclear what will replace Hannibalism and whether the cancelation of the command will help stop a full criminal investigation into the incidents of August 1 by the ICC. Considering the death and destruction that the directive has brought, its cancellation might save some lives. If our investigation had a part in this, it might seem satisfying, but in the complex politics of counterforensics in Palestine, any partial success could also be abused, and the line between winning and losing is often unclear. We will keep on investigating and making public Israeli violations and brace ourselves for a political struggle in the long haul.

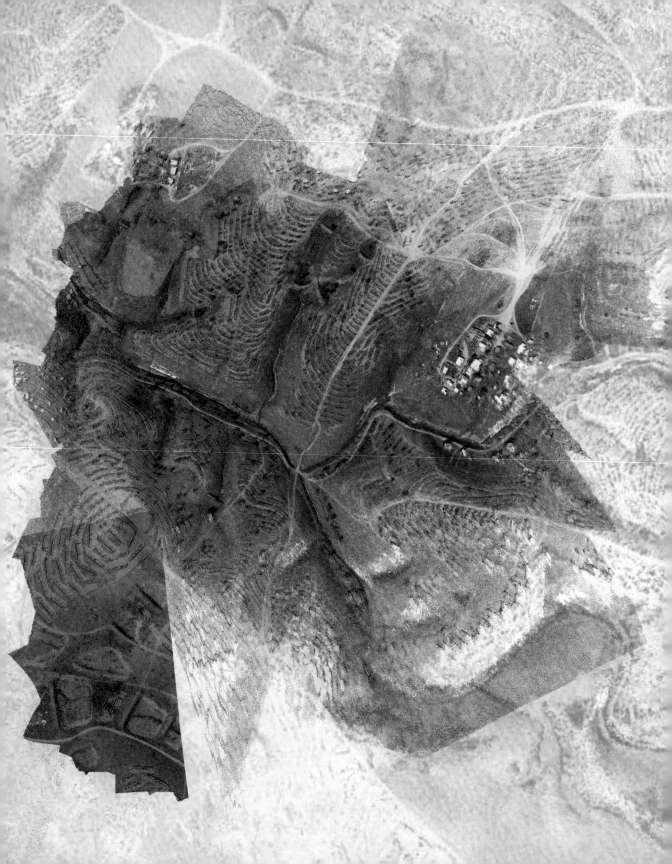

PART THREE

Ground Truths

BY THE TIME THIS TEXT IS PRINTED, the residents of the Bedouin village of al-'Araqīb, a dozen or so kilometers north of Beersheba on the northern threshold of the Naqab/Negev Desert, will have recorded the village's 103rd demolition. The largest of these demolitions, in 2010, involved almost a thousand Israeli policemen riding fleets of trucks and bulldozers, using clubs, tear gas, and rubber bullets to drive the residents forcefully out of their improvised ramshackle structures. Most were smaller affairs involving the visit of a single tractor quickly squashing several empty tents on the way elsewhere in the desert after a policeman pinned a photocopy of a court order onto a structure or small tree. It becomes increasingly hard for the police to find anything on which to pin the court orders.

At its most populous, the village numbered about four hundred people, mostly from the extended al-Tūri family. Now only a small core of a dozen or so inhabitants remains, within the grounds of the old al-Tūri cemetery, right next to the graves. The current demolition count started only in the early 2000s, but the first expulsions had already begun in 1951, three years after the end of the 1948 war, when the Israeli military turned its attention to the Bedouins and started expelling them, as it did with other Palestinians. Almost ninety thousand Bedouins, some 90 percent of their population in the Naqab, were pushed over the Egyptian and Jordanian borders. The rest were scattered internally and concentrated in a limited area in the more arid parts of the desert. In 1953, the military ordered several of the families inhabiting the al-'Araqīb, including the al-'Uqbis and al-Tūris, to evacuate their land temporarily, for six months, and move some fifteen kilometers southeast, purportedly to allow for a military exercise.[1] In 1954, after their requests to return were repeatedly denied, Sheikh Suleiman Muhammad al-'Uqbi took his family back to al-'Araqīb in the first effort to return. The structures he set up were swiftly destroyed and the inhabitants roughly handled and expelled. Since then, at irregular intervals that sometimes lasted months, other times decades, the original inhabitants of al-'Araqīb and their decedents have exercised their "right of return,"

Al-'Araqīb Destruction Diary. MARIM ABU MAD'IM, SALIM AL-TŪRI, OREN ZIV / ACTIVE STILLS

physically, persistently, continuously, on the ground, rebuilding after every cycle of demolitions. Traces on the ground — wells, structures, ruins, and, most importantly, the cemetery — keep that possibility of return alive. Returns are followed by expulsions, but the Bedouin Nakba continue.

"A TRIBE AGAINST A STATE"

From 1973 onward, the returns to al-'Araqīb were led by Nūri al-'Uqbi, Sheikh Suleiman's son, who had since founded the Association for the Defense of Bedouin Rights, a small (often one-man) NGO, the first of its kind committed to the Bedouin land struggle. The cycle of returns, demolitions, and confrontations escalated in the early 2000s after the al-Tūris returned to build their village next to their ancestral cemetery. In these years, Nūri al-'Uqbi set up a protest tent a kilometer or so west, next to the ruins of his father's house. By then, the area had been radically transformed. Al-'Araqīb was no longer part of the open frontier of the desert's edge, but had become a small landlocked "island" surrounded on all sides by Jewish agricultural settlements, forests, military bases, a highway, a railway, and a major waste-disposal facility.

The recent cycle of demolitions, like those of other illegalized Bedouin settlements, form the most recent chapter in what the Israeli establishment and the media now calls "the battle over the Negev": a systematic state campaign meant to uproot the Bedouins, concentrate them in purpose-built towns located mostly in the desert's more arid parts, and hand over their lands for the purpose of Jewish settlement.

In 2009, Nūri al-'Uqbi filed a claim for his lands in the district court in Beersheba.[2] He was ambivalent about engaging the Israeli legal system. He had already experienced the way Israeli courts had refused to protect his and other Bedouin claimants. In all previous cases, the courts had ruled against the Bedouin plaintiffs and had upheld state policy. Al-'Uqbi was also aware that appealing to the court's arbitration would give it and the Israeli state an aura of legitimacy. But he had gathered much evidence for his family's ownership of his land — aerial photographs, land-sale documents, tax receipts, correspondence with Ottoman, British, and Israeli officials, and military orders testifying to his family's and other Bedouin tribes' settlement and cultivation practices in the northern threshold of the Negev over the past 150 years that he believed no one could contest. Al-'Uqbi hoped that he would be able not only to reverse the dispossession of his family, but also to confront the very foundations of the legal regime that enabled the dispossession of

earthworks for afforestation
(Ambassadors Forest)

subsistance garden

destroyed goat pen

dam

bulldozer shovels

al-Tūri cemetery

tent over the traces of
the demolished mosque

traces of repeated demolitions

funeral tent

traces of demolitions

The al-Tūri village and cemetery in al-'Araqīb. This collage is made of forty images taken by a kite-mounted camera. The collage is superimposed over a 2015 Digital Globe satellite image of al-'Araqīb found on Google Earth. The village is invisible and unmarked on the satellite image.

HAGIT KEYSAR/PUBLIC LAB, FORENSIC ARCHITECTURE, ARIEL CAINE, ZOCHROT, AL-'ARAQĪB VILLAGE

other Bedouins in the area.[3] The case, one among dozens of others unfolding in these parts, was at the center of a public campaign of protests and demonstrations and was supported by a small, but committed group of activists from Israel and abroad. Nūri al-'Uqbi said the struggle was that of "a tribe against a state,"[4] but this tribe seemed not only one of blood relations, but of a small political community that formed around this issue.

His belief in the law was misguided, and his hopes were crushed under the bulldozers' chains. *Al-'Uqbi v. the State of Israel* was heard in 2009. On March 15, 2010, the court ruled against his petition. Still hopeful, al-'Uqbi filed an appeal. On May 14, 2015 — incidentally, the eve of Nakba Day — the appeal was dismissed and the legal avenue was closed. During that entire month of May, now known among Bedouins and activists as Black May, the state escalated its raids and demolitions of Bedouin villages in Israel and the West Bank.[5] The struggle now continues outside the Israeli court system. Popular committees of Bedouin, Israeli, and international activists now scramble to protect forty-six other villages facing demolition, including, next, Umm al-Ḥīrān and Atir.

In Part 2, I mentioned that to understand an incident, it is necessary to locate it in the world of which it is a part. In the case of the village of al-'Araqīb, the meaning is quite literal: it includes the environment and its transformations, the climate and climate change. Indeed, central to the land struggle is the unique climatic condition at the threshold of the desert, which the state mobilized against its Bedouin inhabitants. Eviction and displacement are based on a legal doctrine, codified in 1975 by a team of experts at the Israeli Ministry of Justice, that combined the mid-nineteenth-century Ottoman land code — to which Israel is committed by the principle of legal continuity — with meteorological data, both contemporary and historical.

The operative principle of the Ottoman Land Law instituted in 1858 is a distinction between cultivated and uncultivated land. Seeking to expand cultivation after a cycle of devastating droughts that threatened to bankrupt the empire, the Ottomans incentivized agricultural production by granting a form of private ownership to those who cultivated land and took that land away from those who didn't. Uncultivated land, referred to as *mawāt* — literally, "dead" land — rocky mountaintops, swamps, and deserts, areas untouched by or orphaned from human husbandry, came under the ownership and control of the sovereign, then the sultan, now the state of Israel.[6]

The Israeli interpretation of the Ottoman code is tautological, self-serving, and goes against all contrary evidence.[7] In the desert, it postulates, the possibility for agricultural cultivation of cereal crops did not exist—this is the scientific definition of "desert," as we will see. Because cereal cultivation was supposedly impossible, there could never have been permanent settlements in this area. Consequently, the Bedouins there must have been nomads—a common perception that is largely wrong—and nomads possess no land rights.

Resting on a simplified spatial and conceptual distinction between nature and culture, barren and cultivated lands, what critical geographer Oren Yiftachel called the "dead Negev doctrine"[8] mobilized the threshold of the desert to mark a border beyond which lies a vast zone, half of Israel's total land area, within which no land rights exist.

Israel went on to register all lands in the desert as "state lands" and declared the Bedouins living there to be squatters. Those Bedouins who were expelled during and after 1948, according to this doctrine, were banished from lands that did not belong to them in the first place. Inasmuch as their presence was tolerated, it was only as a matter of charity.

Not only did the threshold of the desert mark the border of a zone of dispossession, but it also gave shape to denials that such dispossession has taken place. The doctrine also reflected a core element of Zionist ideology—one that imagined Jews as having returned to a desolate, neglected "dead land," a land belonging to no one, and having revived it.

Over the years, during a number of Bedouin land-rights trials, this legal doctrine kept on revolving around the same elliptical groove it had carved within the law: if the border of the desert marks the limit beyond which no cultivation can take place, there could be no permanent settlements and property rights beyond it. Because it allows no private land rights, state control over the territory is unrestricted, and it can do in this space as it wishes.

On the ground, however, there is of course never a clear borderline that defines the beginning of the desert. Rather, there is a gradient of slowly changing environmental and botanical conditions that throughout the generations gave rise to slowly shifting agricultural practices. The Bedouin inhabitants of the northern threshold of the desert, like previous civilizations, have developed ways to use much smaller quantities of rainwater to cultivate cereal crops, as well as a host of other species of plants. The threshold of the desert is a thick frontier in which aridity and cultivation exist side by side and its location widely fluctuates between drought years and rainy years. There is plenty of evidence for the permanent settlement and cultivation of Bedouins deeper within the more arid parts of the desert during Ottoman, British, and Israeli rule. This evidence is important, because it can be mobilized not only within the Israeli legal context, but to demonstrate the fallacy on which Israeli law stands and the climatic imagination that guides it.

In January 2016, together with the al-'Araqīb Popular Committee, other Bedouin organizations and the anticolonial organization Zochrot, Forensic Architecture took part in building and assembling an alternative civil forum entitled Ground Truth, curated by Debby Farber with Aziz al-Tūri and Nūri al-'Uqbi.[9] It was an improvised institution in a temporary structure we built outside the al-Tūri cemetery. It involved testimonies and the collection of documents, and it also included the closing session of the Truth Commission on Nakba in the Naqab, a long-term project by Zochrot.[10]

The term "truth commission" might be misleading. Those truth commissions instituted in South America or in South Africa were instruments of "transitional justice," conceived to help societies engage the wounds of periods of state terror and move on. A truth commission undertaken in situations of ongoing conflict and colonization, however, is a tactical, political act which forms part of the struggle itself. Ground Truth was a forum for the gathering and presentation of testimony and evidence that was denied in court for reasons and under pretexts that we will see later. It thus also had to engage with the very conditions by which historical and legal evidence can be gathered, presented, seen, and heard. In addition, it examined the environment and the climate as subjects of history and law. This in itself required a radical shift between scales and several acts of translation: the nature of testimony and evidence of environmental violence is different from those pertaining to incidents of fast, eruptive violence. The temporality of the climate is long, and its physical extent could be vast. Environmental violence is slow and is produced by multiple lines of causality, both proximate and remote. Furthermore, such environmental transformations and land conflicts are entangled with human-induced climate change.[11]

Ground Truth was scheduled for January 1 and 2, 2016, because we hoped the new year would give us a little breathing space, a stay on the forum's inevitable demolition. On January 3, the structure was dismantled by its users, shortly before the bulldozers arrived to demolish it. The salvaged raw material has been used for the construction of several other structures in the area of the desert threshold.

The temporary forum of Ground Truth on January 1,
2016. Designed and built with Aziz al-Tūri and
Sharon Rotbard, the al-ʿAraqīb village council,
Forensic Architecture, and Zochrot.
ALINA SCHMUCH, JAN KIESSWETTER

Speakers at the Ground Truth/Truth Commission on Nakba in the Naqab forum. FROM TOP LEFT: Sayāh al-Tūri, Nūri al-'Uqbi, Aziz al-Tūri, Dr. Safa Abu-Rabia, Nūri al-'Uqbi, Ranad Shaqirat (RIWAQ) and Umar al-Ghubari, Debby Farber, Nura Resh and Erella Shadmi. ALINA SCHMUCH, JAN KIESSWETTER

Collection and photography of documents,
and the creation of an online archive
(forthcoming), Ground Truth, January 1–2,
2016. ALINA SCHMUCH, JAN KIESSWETTER

Traces of Ground Truth after its
destruction, January 3, 2016.
ALINA SCHMUCH, JAN KIESSWETTER

Although one of the most contested frontiers in Palestine, the threshold of the desert is not demarcated by fences and walls, but rather by a line that exists only on meteorological maps. It stretches continuously for more than seventy-five hundred kilometers and separates the subtropical Mediterranean climate zone from the Sahara and the Arabian deserts. The long history of the village of al-'Araqīb has unfolded in relation to other historical-climatic transformations along this vast and shifting environmental threshold. When the desert line ebbs or flows, due to natural cycles, human processes, or their combination, it does so along its entire length.

The threshold of the desert is an elusive category. Botanists define it according to changes in plant type, geologists by studying soil formations, and geographers by studying the density and form of human inhabitation. However, the desert edge is most commonly defined in meteorological terms, by the distribution of rainfall. As fleeting as this threshold is, maps demand decisive demarcations. Because the zone of dispossession in the Negev is coextensive with the meteorological definition of the "desert," it was necessary to establish a clear definition of what constitutes the desert's threshold. When a fleeting meteorological threshold is drawn on maps and coded into laws, it starts affecting the territory itself.

To set climatic areas apart, meteorologists draw what they call "isohyets" — lines that connect all points with the same average amount of annual rainfall. The 200-millimeter isohyet is the one most commonly considered to be the "aridity line" — that is, the beginning of the desert. Across this line a narrowing gradient of thinning blue bands in which each lighter shade represents an area of less rain in iterations of 25, 50, or 100 millimeters per annum flips over to gradually more saturated bands in the spectrum of yellow and orange as the rain is gradually phased out.[12]

The 200-millimeter limit as the threshold of the desert was first suggested in 1918 by a German-Russian climatologist and botanist named Wladimir Köppen as a part of his climate classification system, the basis for contemporary meteorology.[13] Köppen was one of the pioneers in developing atmospheric measurement with balloons, and he also published one of the first cloud atlases. His long-term research, which involved calculating average temperature and evaporation, was published at the end of World War I, when Europeans started ruling vast tracts of the Middle East after their defeat of the Ottoman Empire. Climate mapping was then a largely colonial and imperial science. Köppen tried to settle the differences

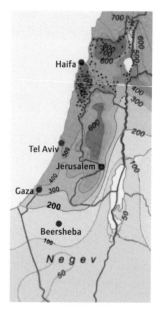

Mean annual rainfall in 100-millimeter annual precipitation isohyets, September 1931 – September 1976.
ATLAS OF ISRAEL

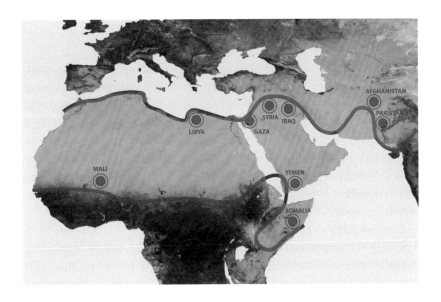

between the various accounts of travelers and cartographers who had attempted, since the nineteenth century, to determine environmental thresholds. Orientalist travelers employed mainly visual observations to identify the last line of cultivation, but things were not so easily defined on the ground, because topography, politics, and different cultural habits fragmented the position of the desert edge. Furthermore, the European travelers could identify only the kinds of cultivation they were familiar with and often missed the variety and subtlety of different agricultural practices in more arid zones, a mixture of wilderness and cultivation.

The reason that Köppen proposed the 200-millimeter isohyet as the aridity line was that, as his botanical experiments confirmed, it was the minimum amount of water necessary to cultivate cereal crops without artificial irrigation on a flat surface. Wheat grows best in warm climates, never too far from arid areas. The species originated in today's northern Syria and southern Turkey, a few dozen kilometers from the Syrian Desert. The plant will also sprout with less annual water and produce edible wheat, but it needs at least 200 millimeters to create grains large enough for the cultivation to be economically viable and, more importantly, firm enough to be stored without disintegrating. The threshold of the desert was thus not an observable border, but a calculated one. The calculation involved an interplay between several factors: meteorological data (rainfall), patterns of human use (agriculture, economy), and plant species (the "einkorn" wheat on which Köppen experimented).

The definition of desert in relation to a single class of grassy grain crops registered for Köppen the centrality that such plants had in the formation of human culture. The organized cultivation of an otherwise marginal reed originating near the deserts of the Fertile Crescent led hunter-gatherers to settle some eight to ten thousand years ago. As historian Yuval Noah Harrari puts it, wheat was not domesticated by humans, but rather domesticated them—literally so: it made our species settle, build homes, silos, and roads, and live in villages, cities, states, and empires, those "great heaps of people and grain," as political scientist James Scott calls them.[15] The role of wheat was so decisive in human history not only because of its nutritional value, but also because of the unique capacity for its surplus grains to be stored for years without crumbling or losing their nutritional value and thus for them to be circulated as a currency. It was wheat's function as money that made it one of the most biologically successful substances on earth, to the extent that it now occupies more than two million square kilometers of the earth, more of its dry surface than any other plant. It is easy to see that the opposite would also appear reasonable to ancient and contemporary men—if cereal crops led to the development of economy, culture, the state system, and law along the threshold of the desert, past the line of their cultivation no economy or culture or state could exist. That the desert was seen as the primary extraterritorial zone is a fact that still casts a shadow on contemporary politics.

The problem of defining, delineating, and mapping the threshold of the desert was thus never only an environmental question, but one that bore upon historical, political, and juridical considerations. For the Ottoman Empire as well as for the British Empire that ruled after it, the desert marked the limit beyond which their effective sovereignty waned. It was the end of economically productive territory, of the area that was governed because it could be taxed. Both empires governed little beyond the desert threshold, and the Bedouin tribes that were living there were granted or effectively enjoyed degrees of de facto autonomy to run their own affairs according to their customary law and traditional land system.[16]

In 1921, as a secretary of state for the colonies, Winston Churchill promised the Bedouins that the empire would respect their traditional customs and law, in effect recognizing their degree of autonomy and their system of land titles.[17] But such autonomy beyond desert lines had also another side to it. A year earlier, in 1920, while still acting as the secretary of state

A demolished Bedouin settlement near 'Arab al-Rashayida, a Bedouin village on the aridity line, south east of Bethlehem. The traces on the ground are the shovel marks of a single bulldozer driving back and forth to demolish the homes. The "civil administration" run by the Israeli military demolished this community as part of its attempts to force the Bedouins of the West Bank to accept resettlement near Jericho.

for air, Churchill proposed a solution to governing these sparsely inhabited zones across the empire: to use the nascent air force to punish rebels. Indeed, after the end of World War I, the history of the aircraft and that of the desert became entangled. The British in Iraq, Afghanistan, Egypt, Somalia, Darfur, Palestine, and the tribal areas of Waziristan, the French in Algiers, and the Italians in Libya and Ethiopia preferred not to send their policemen, cartographers, tax collectors, and troops beyond the threshold of the desert and left this task to their nascent air forces.[18] What the British called "aerially enforced colonization" was based on the ability of the aircraft to bomb rebels into submission as an economically efficient alternative to the otherwise onerous and expensive tasks of colonial control on the sparsely populated and arid frontiers of the empire.[19] To that extent, the threshold of the desert became the end of a certain kind of manifestation of imperial violence and the beginning of another. It is thus hardly a coincidence that the combination of partial autonomy and violence imposed from the air is still enacted along these same frontiers.

However, beginning in the second half of the nineteenth century, another process became evident. The desert line was not only established as a fixed cartographic object, but was seen as an elastic entity that could be continually pushed against in order to extend, through economic incentives, irrigation projects, and new seed types, the areas of agricultural cultivation into arid areas. Pushing at the desert line enlarged the zone of economy, of law, and of state control and reduced the extent of the extraterritoriality. Around the turn of the twentieth century, the Ottomans built a string

LEFT: Aerial view of colonial farmhouses on the northern threshold of the Sahara, Libya, 1939. RIGHT: Aerial view of the Olivetti Project, by the Italian architect Florestano Di Fausto, built to the west of Tripoli, Libya, from 1935 to 1938. PHOTOGRAPHER(S) UNKNOWN; COURTESY OF PIER GIORGIO MASSARETTI

of new garrison towns and administrative centers a few dozen kilometers into the desert as it crossed their empire, from Egypt through the areas that are now Palestine/Israel, Jordan, the Syrian Desert, and Iraq.[20] Many of these towns are now abandoned, because the high-tide line of the desert has overflowed them. One survived: the town of Bir al-Saba', later British-ruled Beersheba, is now the Israeli metropolitan city of Beersheba.

The French, Spanish, and Italians who colonized North Africa improved the use of artesian wells and artificial irrigation gradually to push their line of cultivation, which previously ran closely parallel to the southern Mediterranean coastline, farther south into the Sahara. In the process, they also massacred Bedouins and other seminomadic people and expelled the rest deeper into the desert. In the post–World War II era, the Arab national governments likewise employed artificial irrigation to cultivate the lands at the desert's edge and expel or control the Bedouins by concentrating them in towns.[21]

Of all the colonial projects in North Africa, the Italians, who colonized Libya beginning in 1910 (and as Fascists beginning in 1922) were the most similar to the Zionists, similarly arguing their colonization as a form of "return" to a Roman patrimony. A string of agrarian settlements was built along the edge of the Libyan steppe, and forests were planted to stabilize the Saharan sand dunes. Almost half the Cyrenaican Bedouin population was displaced into concentration camps deeper in the desert. When they rebelled, starting in 1930, the Italians bombed them with mustard gas. In late 1932, while these "pacification wars" were drawing to a close, an enthusiastic American journalist reported from Libya under the headline of "Will the Libyan Desert Bloom Again?" The journalist wrote: "The far-seeing eyes of Mussolini looked way beyond the wastelands that had been abandoned for more than a thousand years by all but fighting Arabs when he made a triumphal journey through the colony…the frontier of cultivation moved thirty-five miles from the coast…acreage of barley has been quadrupled, hundreds of thousands of new olive trees have been set out, bringing the total to about a million."[22] This could have been a Zionist text about the Negev.

THE CONFLICT SHORELINE

The longest continuous aridity line on metrological world maps begins in West Africa, just north of the Morocco/Western Sahara border. This is the conflict shoreline—the shifting threshold of the desert, which connects local histories and is currently the site of conflicts all along it.

This aridity shoreline passes through Algeria, Tunisia, Libya, and northern Egypt. It enters Palestine in an area of sand dunes on the southern shores of the Gaza Strip, north of the city of Rafah. This area is inhabited by the poor Bedouin fishing community of the al-Musawi. It was on the ruins of their homes that the largest Israeli settlement block of Katif was established in the early 1970s (and destroyed in the summer of 2005).[23] The meteorological threshold then passes by the neighborhoods, refugee camps, and greenhouses of eastern Rafah, the site of some of the bloodiest battles of the 2014 Gaza war, including that of Black Friday, August 1, 2014. One of the reasons for the fierceness of the battles in southern Gaza is that, as I noted in Part 2, the earth there is dryer and the water table is lower, conditions more conducive to military tunneling. The line then moves across the rubble piled everywhere along the Gaza side of the border zone and then crosses the mighty fences that enclose the Gaza Strip. (It is possible to do so because we are moving with the weather.) On the Israeli side of the fences, the landscape immediately becomes lusher. The line moves through miles of field crops — strawberries, melons, herbs, and cabbages — irrigated by state-of-the-art watering systems. The line then crosses a number of towns and settlements, including Ariel Sharon's Sycamore Ranch, his home and burial place. After that, it cuts across the al-'Araqīb stream and the gentle hills around it, moving right over the old cemetery and the ruined homes of the al-Tūri. It is here and on the hills farther to the east that "the battle for the Negev" is waged, where the ramshackle homes and animal pens of the illegalized Bedouin villages are bulldozed time and again. Moving north and eastward, the topography gently rises and the desert line enters the large pine forest of Yatir. The forest ends abruptly at the high barbed-wire fences that mark the length of the West Bank wall in these parts. On the other side of the fences, the landscape immediately falls barren. It is on these hills that the military and "independent" settler groups carry out the destruction of homes, the blocking of wells, and the displacing of Bedouin communities, and this with no pretense of following the due legal processes required within Israel. The aridity line then crawls up the interspersed soft and hard limestone of the Hebron Mountains. East of the city of Hebron, it passes through the militant-religious-nationalist Jewish settlement of Kiryat Arba, whose inhabitants put the Palestinian families at the center of the city under permanent siege.[24] North of the city, the hills rise like broken teeth made up of sharp cliffs and canyons that drain rapidly into the Dead Sea. Keeping to a more or less constant altitude of about three hundred meters above sea level, it passes by several other settlements.

A dozen or so kilometers east of Jerusalem is Ma'ale Adumim, one of the biggest settlements in the West Bank, built on top of a hill on the lands of the Jahalin Bedouins, who still struggle to hold onto the outskirts of this green suburb. Several years ago, the settlement authorities attempted to displace the Jahalin Bedouins by releasing raw sewage downhill directly onto their homes.[25] Now, the military simply sends its bulldozers to do the job.

Following the aridity line, we descend several hundred meters and move along the western slopes of the Jordan Valley at an altitude close to universal sea level. A few dozen kilometers later, we dive three hundred meters under this altitude. Many of the eight thousand Bedouins in this area are refugees displaced from the Negev during and after the 1948 war. Israel designates most of the area as either "nature reserves," "closed military zones," or agricultural fields and orchards belonging to the thirty-seven Jewish settlements of the Jordan Valley. The military, trying to keep the area bordering Jordan "sterile," sends the Bedouins away by shooting at herders and herds.[26] Several dozen kilometers north of the Dead Sea, it is a relief to see the tail of the environmental monster of the aridity line sliding past the border fences into Jordan and disappearing behind the western slopes of Jabal Amman.

But the line continues its course, connecting histories otherwise defined by and confined to national borders. Following it forces us to think about history beyond the frame of the state. In Jordan, the aridity line moves north and east, crossing into Syria precisely at the border city of Daraa. It was into this city that the drought of 2006–2010 displaced one-hundred thousand farmers impoverished by crop failures. Almost 1.5 million farmers across Syria shared a similar fate. In 2011, this contributed to the protests that marked the beginning of the Syrian civil war. The line continues from the eastern outskirts of Damascus, through Homs, then eastwards toward al-Raqqah, declared by Daesh as its capital. Many of the battlefields in the civil war are strung along the threshold of the great Syrian Desert.

From Syria, the desert line crosses into Iraq, where the out-of-use channels, dams, and water pipes of previous decades' agricultural push into the desert are now the backdrop to spectacular fighting.[27] The aridity line then crosses Iran to the frontier desert provinces of Afghanistan and Pakistan near the shallow Hāmūn basin lakes now almost entirely dry and moves up along the Helmand river—where some of the fiercest fighting in the ongoing insurgency took place, as well as some of the most robust opium cultivation and persistent Western aerial bombing campaigns.[28]

There are other continuous aridity lines. The Sahel, the southern threshold of the Sahara, is a belt of desert threshold that runs across the entire African land mass. It was there that the consequences of desertification were first measured in the late 1960s, following repeated cycles of drought and famine and the eventual introduction of instrument measurements. It was one of the last parts of the world that had previously not been meteorologically measured. The word *Sahel* is Arabic for "shoreline"—but recently, this shoreline seems to be only receding as the desert advances. Temperature and evaporation are on the rise, and millions of square kilometers of steppe and former arable land are turning brown, leaving miles of baked plant remains where the sparse green pastures and fragile agriculture of the savannah once were. Droughts often lead to increased competition over shrinking resources, aggravating the consequences of civil strife. In turn, continued conflicts in these areas have caused the destruction of vegetation and agriculture and have accelerated the processes of desertification.[29] Like the northern Saharan conflict shoreline along the Sahel, existing tensions have been aggravated by climate-related shifts of the aridity line. In past decades, conflicts have broken out in most countries all along the aridity line: Senegal, Mauritania, Mali, Niger, Chad, Sudan, Somalia, Ethiopia, and Eritrea. Capturing the tension between desertification, conflict, and planting, the London *Sunday Times* recently reported on a European-funded five-thousand-mile-long wall made of millions of trees across the Sahel, meant to slow down desertification and to do nothing less than "hold back Saharan terror."[30]

METEOROLOGICAL TRACES

Developing a more nuanced understanding of the desert climate—the long-term history of its weather, variation, steady change, and interaction with notions of law, territory, and extraterritoriality—is thus an essential task in the Naqab/Negev and elsewhere. Evidence for varying climatic conditions for periods prior to the institution of the meteorological record in the area under the British mandate in 1931 (Ottoman rain measurements, starting at the second part of the nineteenth century, did not include the Naqab), can be found in documents and material records that were not intended to be meteorological: oral traditions of the indigenous people living there, travel literature, diaries, cultivation logbooks, and governors' correspondence written by Orientalist cartographers, soldiers, and spies who were roaming through Palestine at the time. Land-transfer documents and tax records contain information about declared volumes of cultivation. Sections cut through stalactites found in caves tell us something about quantities and patterns of rainfall as annual rings in a way analogous to tree trunks. Archaeological remains, wells, dams, farms, fossilized seeds, and plants testify to continuity and change in agricultural patterns. Interpretation of early twentieth-century aerial photographs confirms settlement and cultivation patterns in these parts. In addition, sometimes the film's very blurriness can indicate the moisture content of the atmosphere — the thickness of the air between the lens and the surface of the earth — at the time the photograph was taken. These records allow us to understand the ways in which climatic shifts over time and space interacted with political processes. Looking at these records, we can see how much conditions of aridity fluctuated over the centuries.[31] Remains of some Nabataean and later Byzantine towns, cereal fields, grape vines, and olive orchards could be found some fifty kilometers south of today's average aridity line, within otherwise dry and desolate lands. On the other hand, beginning in the late nineteenth century, cartographers such as the German-American Gottlieb Schumacher and the British colonial administrator Herbert Kitchener drew the threshold of the desert a few dozen kilometers north of where it is marked today, roughly along where the 300-millimeter isohyet is now drawn on contemporary maps, right through acres of orchards and fields.[32]

Reading the history of the climate from such nonmeteorological records can provide only general indications.[33] But because climatic fluctuations along the threshold of the desert are not registered simply by variations in crop productivity —which depend on many different factors, but more often on crop failures, in the sharp differences between life and death, which are more likely to affect human culture and thus be reported — it is among the clearest environmental sensors for registering shifting historical climate patterns.

The movement of the line of the desert has been understood since antiquity in theological terms. Divine retribution was exercised by turning fertile lands to desert ("the cities of the Negev shall be shut up"[34]) or, conversely, biblical prophesies promised that, given good conduct, adequate sacrifices, and some prayer, the desert will be made to flourish (turning "the desert into pools of water, and the parched ground into springs"[35]). These biblical passages are the source for the colonial and Zionist messianic meteorology of "making the desert bloom."

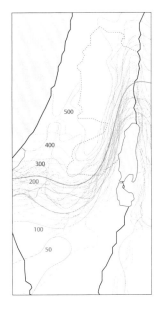

Map of fluctuating isohyets on the aridity line, 1931–2010.

SOURCE: *ATLAS OF ISRAEL*; DRAWING: FORENSIC ARCHITECTURE

NEGEV SETTLEMENTS, VEGETATION, AND PRECIPITATION

In 1947, Bedouin tents were densest in the northwestern part of the Negev and existed on both sides of the aridity line as seen in the map on the right. The NDVI map on the left shows Bedouin villages (black squares against yellow/orange background) concentrated in the more arid eastern parts of the northern Negev, almost entirely south of the 200-millimeter isohyet. Jewish settlements are now located in the area previously most densely settled by the Bedouins (white squares against green background). They are surrounded by robust vegetation — fields and gardens — supported by artificial irrigation. The juxtaposition of these two maps tells the story of the displacement of Bedouins in relation to meteorological conditions and the uneven distribution of land and water.

LEFT: Agrarian settlements and annual precipitation markers on top of an NDVI map prepared by Jamon Van Den Hoek. (For an explanation of the NDVI process, see "Plant Vigor as a Political Sensor," p. 250.) RIGHT: A British survey of Palestine map from 1947 marking the distribution of Bedouin tents (black dots) in the Negev. FRANCESCO SEBREGONDI/FORENSIC ARCHITECTURE

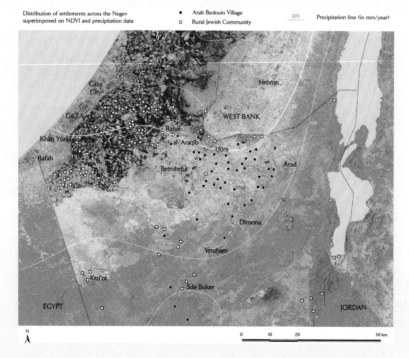

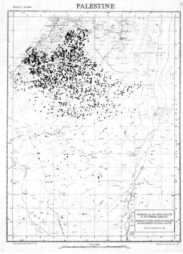

"Making the desert bloom" requires obtaining land. When the land is already occupied, it requires purchase or the displacement of its inhabitants. Zionists did both. In the decades preceding the state's establishment, they bought land from the Tarabīn, al-'Azāzme, al-Jubarāt, and Tiyāha tribes in the northern Naqab.[36] This was a clear recognition of the Bedouins' land ownership, an ownership the forthcoming state later ignored. In this period, Zionist settlers tended to see the Bedouins not as dangerous competitors possessed with a strong national identity, but as "orientalised biblical figures embodying the way of life of their forebears," as historian Meron Benvenisti has put it.[37] A Zionist leader proposed that the Bedouins were "the type closest to that of ancient Semitic population…and thus blood relations of the Jews." David Ben-Gurion toyed with an idea of converting them back to Judaism.[38] What Zionists could not see was that, at the turn of the twentieth century, the Bedouins were undergoing a rapid process of social and political transformation.[39] Toward the end of the Ottoman period, the pressure on land grew, and Bedouin tribes were expelled from northern Palestine and moved south. The Bedouins of the Naqab started to adopt a more settled pattern of life. "Migration" occurred along short routes between fixed summer and winter accommodations, primarily from the higher to the lower slopes of the same hill and within well-defined territories of tribal control, or *dira*. The process of sedentarization led to the "closure of the frontier" (around the same time it closed in the American West), and nomadic life effectively ceased.[40] The settling of Bedouin tribes was apparent in the proliferation of hard structures, or *bāyka*, structures built of adobe and stone as anchors at the center of tribal lands.

Since 1931, when the Zionists, under the British Mandate, instituted systematic meteorological measurements, the location of the aridity line has been a product of monitoring, calculation, averaging, and adjustment. Like a shoreline, it ebbs in drought years and washes past its cartographic delineation in rainy ones. The line drawn on the official maps in the *Atlas of Israel* officially constituting the border of the Negev is the average between all the years since records began to be kept. Annual fluctuations are generally of the range of twenty kilometers on either side, but the line was also known to have shifted some one hundred kilometers in each direction.[41]

The northern threshold of the Negev is where the conception of a Jewish return to a "dead area to be revived" was most clearly manifested. The colonization of the desert was not concerned only with territorial expansion, but also with the transformation of the figure of the Jew from one associated with cosmopolitan, wandering nomads into a native, setting down roots again while expelling the area's inhabitants, themselves now perceived to be nomads, as if expelling or exorcising its own past identity. It also involved, quite literally, an attempt at changing the climate. Indeed, the introduction of artificial irrigation, new seed types, technologies of intensive farming, synthetic fertilizers, pesticides, and large-scale afforestation—the secular vocabulary of the worldwide "green revolution"—forced the desert into a gradual retreat, together with its original inhabitants, and made, at least temporarily, the desert bloom.

Most Palestinian urban or farming communities were expelled from the areas that became Israel in 1948, but the Israeli military turned to deal with the Bedouins only after the end of the 1948 war. Between 1948 and 1953, the Israeli military expelled almost 90 percent of the one-hundred thousand Bedouins of the Negev to the West Bank, Gaza, and farther into Jordan and Egypt.[42] These displacements involved massacres of people and livestock, the burning of tents, the destruction of *bāykas*, and the sealing of wells, as well as, on some occasions, strafing from light planes. On the eve of the 1948 war the area most densely settled by Bedouins was northwest of the 200-millimeter isohyet. Afterwards, the twelve-and-a-half thousand Bedouins who remained were displaced southeast into a one-thousand-square-kilometer saline area known as the *siyag*, Arabic for "enclosure" or "fence," in which the average precipitation was about 150 to 100 millimeters per year, an area which Israeli agronomists determined is not suitable even for intensively irrigated agriculture. Bedouin displacement in the Negev was not only a matter of territory, but also of climate. The *siyag* operated, as political scientist Neve Gordon has suggested, like a Native American reservation of the nineteenth century.[43]

When the Bedouin villages of the northern Naqab were removed, also erased were the names of the hills, rivers, and archaeological sites by which the desert was known for hundreds of years. A new Hebrew map was drawn up, and new road signs were installed. Zalman Lifshitz, head of the Negev Names Committee established by David Ben-Gurion in the late 1950s to take charge of this process, declared: "the whole question of Arabic place-names in the Negev has become irrelevant since there are almost no Bedouin there."[44] The Naqab had fully turned into the Negev. Between and sometimes within settlements, fields, and forests, some physical traces of Bedouin life remained, but the empty cemeteries, wells, water holes, and ruins of stone houses were publically attributed by state-sponsored tours or signs to ancient cultures. Such remnants, of which the cemetery in al-'Araqīb is but one example, became the anchors to which Bedouin communities would try to return some sixty years later.

To settle the Negev, the paramount Zionist challenge involved the trafficking of water. Even before the state's establishment, water was channeled from the coastal plains. It was the ability of the national water company (Mekorot) to undertake large-scale water engineering projects that enabled the establishment — during a single day in 1946 — of eleven settlement points in the northern Negev. The Yarkon-Negev water link was constructed in the 1950s — after the displacement of the Bedouins and to irrigate their seized land — with recycled firefighter pipes imported from London, where they had been used during the Blitz.[45] The pumping stations and pipelines were built underground for "security reasons" and in order to avoid water theft.

THE POLITICS OF DROUGHT

In a response to the presentation of this study in the Ground Truth forum, historian and land rights activist Gadi Algazi and Bedouin scholar Awad Abu-Freih suggested that the cycle of drought interacted with the history of Bedouin land struggle, with alternating acts of displacement and return.[46] I will try to trace this process.

The first years after the establishment of Israel in 1948 were plentiful with rain. This enabled the expansion of Zionist agricultural cultivation into the desert. During the first decade of the state, some 30 percent of all cereal cultivation in Israel came from the northern Negev. In 1950, Yosef Weitz, who since 1932 had been the force behind afforestation and was then head of the Jewish National Fund (JNF) Lands and Forests Department (also, not unrelatedly, one of the leading forces behind the expulsion of Palestinians in 1948), reported back to Ben-Gurion about the planting of a million eucalyptus and tamarisk seedlings. Weitz saw forests as "a biological declaration of Jewish sovereignty," a means of erasing Bedouin settlements and of preventing their return.[47] Weitz thought the forests would combine ecological and security logic in "rolling back the desert with trees, creating a security zone for the people of Israel."[48] The relation between afforestation and Judaization of the landscape was not confined to the Negev. Shortly after Israel's establishment in 1948, the JNF, under Weitz, also planted millions of conifers in different parts of the country, covering up the remains of Palestinian villages that had been destroyed during or after 1948, preempting any claim or possibility of return. This practice still takes place in the Negev, where afforestation is used as a means of erasing former Bedouin settlements and of preventing their resettlement.

The plentiful early years of the state led to the displacement of even the last remnants of Bedouin inhabitation still left in the northwest part of the desert, close to both sides of the aridity line, the part somewhat suitable for cultivation. The agrarian settlements of the Kibbutz and Moshav movements fought each other for the spoil of Bedouin lands.

During these years the emptied lands of the northern Negev were also handed over for the construction of several "development towns"—Ofakim, Yeruham Arad, Dimona, and Mitzpe Ramon—in which the state settled mainly North African Jews in public housing blocks built around state-subsidized industries (the European elite believed that these Arab Jews would be better accustomed to the desert edge than migrants arriving from Central and Eastern Europe).[49] One of the largest "state factories" constructed in 1958 on Bedouin lands just outside the borders of the *siyag* was the Negev Nuclear Research Center near Dimona, where Israel produces, without acknowledging it, its nuclear warheads. Bedouin tribes are ordered to keep fifteen to twenty kilometers away from its fence.[50]

Drought hit hard in 1956, lasting for five years, until the autumn of 1962. It was the longest drought of the twentieth century. Field crops failed, and so did newly planted tree saplings in the JNF's afforestation of the desert threshold. Seeing their investment in mechanization, agricultural infrastructure, and irrigation going to waste, farmers and private investors started abandoning their projects, retreating northward from the Negev. It was in response to this drought that a state-run agricultural firm was established to insure farmers from natural disasters. It decided to use the aridity line as an instrument of redlining and did not provide drought compensation to farmers cultivating south of it. This led to further agricultural abandonments in areas just south of the 200-millimeter line.[51] The drought affected the remaining Bedouin communities, too. In some places, it led to severe malnutrition and even hunger. However, unlike the commercial farmers, the Bedouins were able to adapt, shifting from agriculture to grazing, and they held on to the area.

The climate played a complex and dialectical role in the land struggle. Droughts were used politically by both sides in opposite ways. Moshe Dayan, who during most of the drought years was Ben-Gurion's minister of agriculture (1959–1964), attempted to use the Bedouins' hunger to push tens of thousands of them outside the Negev. Writing in *Haaretz* in 1963, Dayan explained:

The Bedouin must become urban laborers—in industry, service, construction, and agriculture. Eighty-eight percent of Israel's residents are not farmers. The Bedouin will become part of that majority. While it is a sharp transition, it means the Bedouin will not live on his land with his flock, but rather will be part of the urban class that comes in the afternoon and puts on his slippers. His children will become accustomed to a father who wears pants, who doesn't carry around a dagger nor is pulling lice out in public. They will go to school with their hair combed and parted. It will be a revolution, but it can be done over two generations. Not forcefully, but directed by the government. The reality known as "Bedouin" will disappear.[52]

This is a kind of racism, Algazi commented, that is different in kind from the racism that seeks to displace, expel, and exclude. Rather, it seeks to erase a culture by its forced incorporation into the dominant group.

Dayan's policy led to the establishment of Bedouin settlements near Arab towns in northern and central Palestine, as well as to informal settlements on the outskirts of Jewish cities. As a child growing up in Israel in the 1970s, I can still remember Bedouin villages with some envy, children on horses or herding goats, and even a few camels that we could see while driving just outside the suburbs that ringed the metropolitan centers. After a few years, they were evicted from these sites, too, mostly displaced into a number of desolate towns—known by Bedouins as "concentration towns."

Although in the drought years of the late 1950s and early 1960s it was possible to expel some of the Negev Bedouins and to harass the others, it was not possible for the state to settle the northern Negev effectively. The abandonment of Zionist agriculture in the south and the Bedouins' relative advantage in dealing with drought opened a space for the first wave of Bedouins to return and gave the land struggle a small breathing space.

In the mid-1960s, the plentiful years returned and violence escalated. The return of the rain allowed the Zionist line of afforestation and cultivation to push south beyond and over Bedouin settlements. In 1966, afforestation began in earnest again with Yatir, the largest forest in Israel. It was planted on Bedouin lands and was meant to separate the Bedouins of Israel and 1948 Palestine from those of the West Bank, many of whom were refugees from the Naqab.

During these years, the National Water Carrier, designed and built during the drought years, one of the largest of its kind worldwide, gave another boost to Zionist colonization. It started channeling an annual quantity of 100 million cubic meters of water from the Jordan Valley basin

to the Negev settlements, which could expand their cultivation southward regardless of annual fluctuations in rain totals.[53] The Bedouins traditionally had cultivated along the streams and tributaries, but now it was the entire surface of the northern desert, including the shallow hill slopes, that was put to agricultural use.

The Zionist transformation of the desert's edge had an ecological footprint that reached far beyond the region and that has contributed, since the 1960s, to a drop of about one meter a year in the level of the Dead Sea, because most of its incoming waters are being diverted through the National Water Carrier. Thus, the farther south the cultivation line was pushed, the lower the lowest point on earth has become.[54]

Until 1966, the Bedouin enclosure or *siyag* was placed under a military regime. In 1966, after the termination of the military rule, the *siyag* was replaced by another well-tested colonial strategy: the concentration of indigenous populations in higher densities to reduce the extent of the land they possess and free up land for state exploitation. Seven "concentration townships" were built between 1968 and 1989 and are now home to one-hundred-and-thirty-five thousand people. Forced urbanization severed Bedouins from their pastoral and agrarian lives and facilitated their proletarianization in industrial and agricultural projects, as well as their incorporation as salaried soldiers into the Israeli military, where they are

The Yatir Forest, planted over lands previously inhabited by Bedouins. The forest abruptly ends at the border of the West Bank (the hill on the right), where the Jewish National Fund no longer has authority to plant.
ALINA SCHMUCH, JAN KIESSWETTER

Earthworks and plantation work organized by the Jewish National Fund south of Yatir. The method of "savannization" used is a mix of sparsely scattered acacia or eucalyptus trees with bushes and grass between. Long terraces collect rainwater. Although the average annual rainfall is around 200 millimeters, the saplings absorb between 500 and 1,000 millimeters during the rainy season, which dries out the valley downstream. These sparse forests claim land for the state that was inhabited by Bedouins for years. ALINA SCHMUCH, JAN KIESSWETTER

employed mainly as trackers or as an interface with the civilian populations of Gaza and the West Bank.

Many Bedouins refused resettlement, their population expanded, too, and today they number about eighty thousand. Their villages had been declared illegal, and the state considered them trespassers or squatters, refusing to mark them on maps or to provide them with basic infrastructure and municipal services, even medical ones.[55] Without ownership of the land, Bedouin settlements were continually uprooted as state priorities in the Negev shifted. In the early 1980s, many Bedouin settlements were displaced when the military transferred its major air force bases to the Negev following Israel's withdrawal from the Sinai as part of the peace agreement with Egypt.[56] More recently, Bedouins were displaced to make space for the construction of the Ariel Sharon City of Training Bases—with accommodation for one hundred thousand military personnel—south of Beersheba.[57] The irony is that while the state claims it is trying to settle the Bedouins by changing their traditional nomadic life (which has not been their life for more than a hundred years) to an urban existence (the concentration towns might be dense, but they have none of the qualities that make them urban), it has repeatedly moved them around in the desert, leading to what Palestinian legal activist and planner Hana Hamdan has called "a condition of forced nomadism."[58] Recent government plans have sought to contain the escalating conflict with new proposals. But these plans have merely tried to solve the problem with more of the very thing—concentration towns—that had aggravated it in the first place.[59] As Nūri al-'Uqbi explained to me: "The Bedouin Nakba was not to be expelled outside the country; our catastrophe was to be concentrated."[60]

There were other institutions set up for the task of displacing Bedouins. An organization called the Green Patrol was established in 1977 to deal with Bedouins' return to the land at the threshold of the desert. Its name was yet another manifestation of the strategic importance that ecology plays as a political tool on the desert threshold. It had a seemingly benign task, the ecological preservation of the threshold of the desert, but was in fact tasked with policing the expansion of the illegalized Bedouin villages.[61] The quest for "nature preservation" put the Green Patrol into direct conflict with indigenous culture and Bedouin land ownership claims. "They would attach a jeep to a tent and just drive off. They would poke holes in our jerry cans so that we'd run out of water," a former Bedouin soldier in the Israeli military and a resident of one of the illegalized villages recounted. "Imagine how a man felt when he returned from the army to find his tent destroyed and his wife beaten."[62]

The official understanding that areas where unrecognized Bedouin villages are located are considered "empty" had tragic consequences during the 2014 Gaza war. The "iron dome," the missile-interception system installed by Israel to protect them from rockets fired from Gaza and elsewhere, is designed to calculate the rockets' approximate landing spot. If they are predicted to fall in an "open area," the system doesn't fire one of its $20,000 interceptors. On July 19, 2014, two days after the Israeli invasion of the strip, a rocket fired from southern Gaza, aimed, most likely at the nuclear reactor, was projected to land in an "open area." It did so indeed, except that in this open area, as marked on maps, was the unrecognized village of Jaraabah. Thirty-two-year-old Auda al-Wadj was killed, and four of his family members were wounded.[63] Still, the state has not installed shelters in these villages, as it does in all other civilian communities, and has advised the Bedouins simply to lie on the ground with their hands protecting their heads when they hear a rocket about to land.

The drought years of 1999 to 2001 further interrupted the afforestation efforts and led to water shortages, the failing of saplings, and bush fires. The interruption contributed to the return and resettlement of al-'Araqīb on an area the state had reserved for a forest. Plantation around al-'Araqīb resumed in the plentiful year of 2002. By this period, the methods of plantation started to shift to the so-called "savannization" method — planting lower-density forests of species more suitable to aridity, such as acacia or eucalyptus, behind long earthen dams that pooled and collected between 500 and 1,000 millimeters of water for the saplings out of the 100 to 200 millimeters available on average annually, thus drying up much of everything else downstream.[64] These forests were the tools with which forced evictions were then undertaken.

In the early 2000s, when international attention was captured by the Second Intifada, attacks on the Bedouins came from the air, as well as from the ground. In February 2002, crop dusters, to be seen everywhere spraying pesticides over the intensely irrigated fields of the Jewish settlements, started spraying toxic herbicides on the small sustenance fields of illegalized Bedouin settlements, acting now, literally, as agents of desertification.[65] On March 4, 2003, almost four hundred acres of cultivation were destroyed by crop dusters flying over the unrecognized village of Abda. The matter was debated in the Knesset, where it was defended by Avigdor Lieberman, then minister for national infrastructure and responsible for land management. Other state representatives explained that because "the act of invasion is manifesting itself in the seeding of state lands," the state was justified in acting directly against these biological "invaders."[66] The session, as Algazi reported, turned into a discussion of scale: "What is the right dose of herbicides to be used to minimize health risks?"[67] The villagers and rights groups appealed to the Supreme Court, demonstrating the effects of the chemical

A crop duster spraying herbicides on the land of Abu Kaff, next to Hūra, ʻali Abu Shkhēta, March 10, 2004. The writing on the photograph reads: "Yet, we will stay despite what you have burned."

Roundup, produced by the multinational agrochemical corporation Monsanto, on a person's skin.[68] After the court forbade the practice, old habits resumed, and the crops were simply crushed under the wheels of the Green Patrol's road vehicles or uprooted by the blades of their bulldozers.

During the recent decade, on the lands in and around al-'Araqīb, the JNF has overseen the planting of three forests. The Ambassador Forest, inaugurated in 2005, had diplomats from forty-nine nations planting trees on behalf of their countries. Only the South African ambassador was wise enough to decline the honor.[69] The God TV Forest was planted in 2008 as a gift from an organization that propagates the millenarian view that ultimately all Jews must convert to Christianity or face an "everlasting lake of fire." The Nuremberg Forest was paid for by that German city. It had a dedication sign reading: "Lest We Forget." This combination of selective commemoration and erasure is a common practice. In the Jerusalem corridor tens of millions of conifers were planted by the JNF on top of the ruins of dozens of Palestinian villages destroyed in 1948. Some of these forests are holocaust memorials. On its website, the JNF claimed that it has planted 250 million trees in Israel since 1901. It is also the largest landowner in Israel, and, despite a number of complicated legal challenges, it still refuses to lease or sell land to non-Jews.

These days, the most common justification for planting forests is that they are responses to desertification. Recognition of year-to-year patterns of desertification (as opposed to cyclical droughts) in the Negev started in the early 1970s and went hand in hand with increased global attention to the consequences of human-induced climate change. The JNF used the alarm about the consequences of climate change and desertification to promote its own agenda of Bedouin displacement, suggesting that in the Negev, "desertification could be stopped by large-scale afforestation" and by "restrictions imposed on livestock grazing."[70] Both methods are directly mobilized against the Bedouins: the former by planting forests over and around their settlements and the latter by further restricting their pastoralism.[71]

Environmentalists continually protested, in vain, that JNF afforestation damages the ecosystem. Earthworks, piled high by heavy machinery to create dams to irrigate forest saplings, destroy surface soil composition, and stop rainwater from reaching the valleys below, increasing their salinity. The area is also made toxic with herbicides used to eradicate local vegetation prior to planting the saplings.[72] Trees do cool the areas around them, but only because they remove precious water from the soil and release it

into the atmosphere. Although carbon sequestration (the absorption of CO_2) has a positive effect on climate change, afforestations in desert areas might actually contribute to global warming because of the increased heat absorption due to their darker color, compared with the light-colored steppe, which better reflects heat. The desert's light yellow areas, rather than the thicker greens of the forest, protect it from overheating.[73]

The gift that Ben-Gurion thought Zionism was to nature has seemingly been rejected.[74] Pushing the line of cultivation south contributed to the northward shift of the average aridity line. Although the attempt was to make the desert green, in many places, the green has yellowed. The Bedouins, like other people all along the edges of the desert, now felt themselves squeezed between two major forces pushing in opposite directions — Israeli colonization pushed the desert edge south, while desertification pushed it north.

The next cycle of droughts, culminating in 2010 and 2011, affected the entire region. It also tied together the fate of people living on the opposite shores of the Sahara. Sudanese and Eritreans escaping war and famine along the southern shores of the Sahara—the drying Sahel—were compelled to make the journey north across the desert and ended up incarcerated in prisons in Israel, on the northern shore of the great desert, prisons built in places from which Bedouins were displaced.[75]

Earthwork mounds raised in preparation for planting an extension of the Ambassador Forest (savannization) where the village of al-'Araqīb used to be. EYAL WEIZMAN

PLANT VIGOR AS A POLITICAL SENSOR

The Normalized Difference Vegetation Index (NDVI) is a graphic indicator that measures the coverage and robustness of vegetation. One of its indicators is photosynthesis. This study, undertaken with Jamon Van Den Hoek, then at NASA, was a by-product of our study of the Gaza/Israel frontier during the 2014 war (see Part 2). It shows that the border of the arid area, now generated by artificial irrigation, no longer overlaps the 200-millimeter isohyet.

NDVI MAP BY JAMON VAN DEN HOEK; ANALYSIS BY JAMON VAN DEN HOEK AND FORENSIC ARCHITECTURE, 2014. IMAGE COURTESY OF LANDSAT 8, NASA; CAPTIONS BY JAMON VAN DEN HOEK AND EYAL WEIZMAN

1 The border between the Negev (Israel) and Sinai (Egypt) is distinguished by the heavy grazing of goats and camels on the Egyptian side. On the Israeli side of the border, the exclusion of Bedouin shepherds is indicated by the moderate, but consistent vegetative cover. The presence of vegetation is evidence of the expulsion of the Bedouins from this area. At the bottom of the frame are a number of agrarian settlements established to "fortify the border." Ktzi'ot was abandoned because of the harsh climatic conditions and subsequently converted into a detention camp, initially for Palestinians and then for illegalized African migrants. Israel's later "prison archipelago," developed around it, is made visible here by small gardens within the prison walls.

2 The cultivation border between a number of Israeli agrarian settlements and the dunes of Nitzana. This is where some of the Jewish settlers who were evacuated from Gaza in 2005 were relocated.

3 The border with Gaza is apparent in the differing agricultural patterns and levels of vigor in the vegetation. On the Israeli side are large, well-irrigated fields; on the Gaza side, small fields are cultivated with less available water. This border area was the site of the 2014 Israel-Gaza conflict.

4 The development town of Ofakim, nested between the fields of the neighboring agrarian settlements, has a cluster of small urban gardens within it.

5 A group of artificially irrigated agrarian settlements, Revivim, Mash'abei Sadeh, and Ashalim.

6 Sde Boker, a kibbutz practicing experimental desert agriculture and a college specializing in solar research. This is where Ben-Gurion lived at the end of his life and where he is buried.

7 The Avdat experimental desert farm, where traditional irrigation methods are used to support cultivation for scientific purposes.

8 Rahat, the largest Bedouin town in the Negev, is an arid island surrounded by the well-irrigated fields of the Jewish settlements nearby. Its urban center and adjacent lands are much drier than the nearby Jewish development town of Ofakim.

9 Al-'Araqīb. See "The Area of al-'Araqīb in 1998, 2002, 2008, and 2014" below.

10 Area within the former siyag, the Bedouin enclosure of 1948–1966, where many of the illegalized Bedouin villages are located. The former siyag area is made distinct by the low vegetative vigor associated with its small subsistence fields.

11 The Otni'el settlement in the West Bank, distinguished by the clear vigor of its vegetation—well-irrigated domestic gardens.

12 The forest of Yatir, where planting started in 1966 and has been ongoing ever since. Its northern edge abuts the border of the West Bank, seen clearly in the immediate reduction of vegetative cover and vigor. (See the image of the Yatir Forest, above, p. 244.)

13 The air force base of Nevatim is located in the middle of an area dense with Bedouin villages (legal and illegalized) within the former siyag. Note how the runways are visible as strips without vegetation, but how the gardens in the residential part of the base are better irrigated than the surrounding Bedouin settlements.

14 The city of Hebron. East of the city, where the settlement of Kiryat Arba is located, vegetation levels increase due to greater water allocation to the Jewish settlers.

15 The Negev Nuclear Research Center near Dimona. The small spots of vegetation here are the gardens within the secret reactor laboratories where Israel is reportedly constructing its nuclear weapons.

16 The settlement block of Nokdim (home to Israeli politician Avigdor Lieberman), Tekoa, and Kfar Eldad is distinguished by high vegetative vigor at the edge of the desert.

17 Afforestation within the Jerusalem corridor on both sides of the Tel Aviv–Jerusalem highway (Road No. 1).

18 The settlement of Ma'ale Adumim, conspicuous by the vigor of its vegetation at the edge of the desert.

19 The Palestinian city of Jericho, a desert oasis nourished by springs from underground aquifers.

20 An Israeli agricultural settlement block and agricultural fields. The surrounding arid areas are where the Bedouin communities of the Jordan Valley are located.

THE AREA OF AL-'ARAQĪB IN 1998, 2002, 2008, AND 2014

This series shows the decline of agriculture in the area of the cemetery (marked by a red square) of al-'Araqīb from 1998 to 2014. The thinner tree plantation beginning in the early 2000s dissolves farm-plot boundaries as planted trees encroach upon and eventually dominate agricultural fields.

NDVI READING BY JAMON VAN DEN HOEK
AND FORENSIC ARCHITECTURE

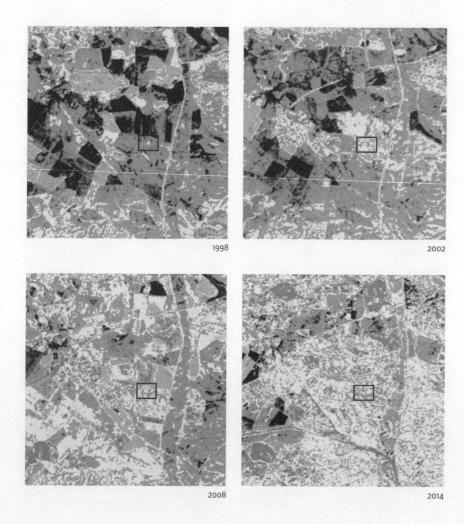

1998

2002

2008

2014

Reading the history of the interaction between climate change and conflict requires a constant navigation between scales: from a close reading of small-scale evidence, local conditions, incidents, and cultivation techniques to examination of environmental conditions that are geographically vast and historically deep. Environmental violence brings together different types of sources and frameworks to analyze them — literature, geology, archaeology, and photography, to name but a few. The shift between these different scales and frameworks reflect the equally complex structure of environmental causation.

Historical change results from the coming together of long-term structural processes as well as from contingent, eruptive, and unpredictable developments. When dealing with the relation between history and climate change, we must be wary of the essentialist approach of "geographic determinism" that seeks to explain conflict and revolts as the inevitable consequence of environmental conditions and their transformations.[76] Different locations, cultures, or states dealt with the challenges of desertification, for example, in different ways. Some areas succumbed catastrophically, while others found ways to mitigate environmental change. At other times, technological inventions, catastrophic defeats, or the introduction of a new plant species led to political and cultural transformations.

Fernand Braudel, the great French historian of the mid-twentieth-century Annales School, proposed to extend the frame of historical investigation to include the environment, topography, climate, and wind over centuries, a historical perspective he has called the *longue durée*. He pays considerable attention to the thresholds of the deserts around the Mediterranean. But over sixty years ago, Braudel thought of the climate as governed by a cyclical pattern. The history of "man's relationship to the environment," he wrote, has been so slow that it is "almost timeless."[77] But in the era of rapid human-induced climate change, the climate can no longer be considered as shifting along constant cyclical patterns. It is changing at the same speed as human history, racing alongside it, getting entangled and interacting with it in an ever-aggravated feedback loop of cause and effect, with consequences that have spiraled out of control.[78]

Debates about the origins of climate change tend to foreground the adverse effects of industrialization and the excessive atmospheric accumulation of greenhouse gases produced mainly by the burning of fossil fuels. This was the reason that when ecologist Eugene F. Stoermer and atmospheric chemist Paul Crutzen introduced the concept of the Anthropocene to name a new geological epoch in which humans are considered as climatic and geological forces akin to earthquakes and ocean currents, they initially proposed dating its beginning to the invention of the steam engine.[79] Climate change in this scenario is the accidental and indirect consequence of industrial development, demographic growth, trade, and transport triggered by the Industrial Revolution in Europe and North America. Even if these consequences were predictable, no one actually wanted the climate to change. Things just happened.

It is surprising that even the most militant environmentalists repeat the structure of this argument and regard climate change as something akin to the collateral damage of history. The collateral argument is familiar to human rights researchers. We have grown to be extremely wary when Western militaries claim, as they often do, that the large civilian death toll in recent wars is a "collateral effect" of their attempt to target armed groups, of the violent but necessary process of protecting or exporting democracy. Human rights activists learned, perhaps too slowly, not to accept the argument for collateral damage, especially when the killing of civilians is predictable, predicted, and even legally tolerated under such principles as that of proportionality. As I noted in Part 2, sometimes civilian casualties, argued as collateral, are a way for militaries to generate deterrence and govern populations through fear.[80] Perhaps climate activists have something to learn from human rights activists. Accepting the argument for collateral damage necessarily forced human right activists to enter into the economic logic of negotiations about the correct proportions between military necessity and civilian casualties (recall Garlasco's proportionality limit of twenty-nine civilian victims) at a time when a fundamental rejection of that logic was necessary. Posing global warming only as the collateral damage of history enables the entire debate to be framed in an analogous form of cost-benefit calculations, the distribution of a global "carbon budget," and degrees of acceptable global warming. (The debate in the climate talks in Paris was locked between 2°C and 1.5°C.) This makes a convenient assumption under which we are all perpetrators of climate change as well as its victims.[81]

Seen from the point of view of colonial history, however, climate change is no longer the collateral of history that we have made it out to be. Since the late eighteenth century, colonial settlers, officials, and *hommes des lettres* have debated the relationship between human-induced transformations across the expanding frontiers of colonialism—by such actions as deforestation, afforestation, species introductions, irrigation, and agricultural cultivation—and measurable, year-to-year changes in temperature and precipitation.[82] The term "climate change" was born in late eighteenth-century debates between figures such as Hugh Williamson, David Hume, Thomas Jefferson, and Noah Webster who held opposing views about human capacity to affect the climate and the relative advantages of doing so.[83] However, once climate change was articulated as a possible result of human action, it also began to be considered as a potentially beneficial form of control over nature and man, indeed, as a possible tool in the arsenal of colonization. Pushing beyond existing frontiers and taking over harsher, unfamiliar land also required their climatization so as to make them more inhabitable and productive for Europeans. The concept of climate change thus existed in the historical imaginary of the frontier as a project well before it was considered as an adverse, collateral, or unintentional side effect of industrialization. Climate change thus could be thought of as a form of government over both nature and man.

Many of the projects that sought to change the regional climate across colonial frontiers were proven scientifically false. "The rain follows the plow" was the guiding myth of American westward expansion in the nineteenth century, but it had no scientific basis. Amateur meteorologist James Espy—known as "the Storm King"—proposed that the burning of forests in the Appalachians could help precipitate rain clouds that would be carried westward to irrigate the desert frontiers.[84] The transformation of the landscape across the surface of the earth not only had local effects on temperature and precipitation, but is also recognized as having contributed to climate change on the global scale. Environmental scientists today accept that ongoing environmental destruction and monocrop cultivation have significantly contributed to planetary climate change and global warming. Fossil-fuel-enhanced industrialization and urbanization thus are not the sole drivers of climate change, though they are currently the biggest.[85]

The desert thresholds were not the only environmental limit that eighteenth-century and nineteenth-century colonial climate changers had in mind to eliminate or push against. While deserts had to be cooled down and irrigated, the tropics had to be made drier and safer from disease. From the late eighteenth century on, using logging and fires, the thresholds of the tropical forests were driven in the opposite direction from that of the deserts (in the same hemisphere, that is) as means of extending agricultural lands and of bringing tropical diseases under control.[86] Like deserts, rain forests have been extraterritorial to the states or empires in which they were located. Forests, since Roman times were perceived as the condition against which human culture, law, and sovereignty were defined. Their human inhabitants were regarded as primitive and animal-like. It is interesting that a recurrent metaphor describing the shift of both environmental thresholds is "savannization"—in the desert, it is used to describe techniques of planting to buttress against desertification, while along the edge of the rain forests, it refers to the slash-and-burn agriculture that creates desertlike conditions.[87]

In the European imagination, the line between fields and forests is sharp, holding apart two simplified conditions: a systematized monocrop agriculture and an extraterritorial one yet to be cultivated.[88] For indigenous people, the transition zones between fields and forests and between fields and deserts are deep frontiers where a liminal kind of agriculture slowly gives way to areas that are not cultivated or that are cultivated very little. Even the so-called extraterritorial zones were not completely untouched by humans—indigenous cultures knew how to encourage useful plants to grow in small pockets of the rain forest or how to channel the momentary gush of floodwaters deep in arid deserts to cultivate a few plant types.[89]

As already discussed in Part 1, one of the most recent colonial massacres took place in Guatemala some thirty-five years ago (see pp. 121–24). The indigenous Ixil Mayas inhabited the highland cloud forests, an extraterritorial zone that was beyond the last line of plantation and also beyond state control.

Deforestation in Kalimantan, Indonesia. WALHI

The genocidal campaign of the early 1980s broke through this environmental line, destroyed large tracts of forest, and pushed the line of agricultural cultivation deeper into the forest environment. Like the Bedouins along desert lines, the Ixils were massacred and expelled, and the survivors were concentrated in new towns, reducing the extent of territory they occupied and freeing up agricultural land to the exploitation of large plantations. Similar processes took place elsewhere along the edges of tropical forests. From the cloud forests of Central and South America to the forests of Central Africa, from the Democratic Republic of the Congo to Rwanda, and to those of East Asia — Malaysia, Indonesia, Singapore, and Papua — the conflict shoreline of the ebbing forest edge was a site where lines of fire and savannization pushed back the forest to make way for monocrop plantations, cattle farms, and mining and oil extraction projects.[90] Indigenous people, who were seen as part of the *terra nullius* of the natural environment, were displaced along with the climate, pushed beyond all these conflict shorelines into harsher climates — deserts and forests, but also, in the north, across the lines of frozen tundra.

In Palestine, the environmental and climatic results of colonialism were referred to by the biblical phrase "making the desert bloom," just as it was by farmers on the American frontier and Italians in Libya. But in the early twentieth century, Otto Warburg, a German professor of botany and an expert in colonial agriculture (and in 1911, the third president of the Zionist Organization), attempted to give the biblical language explicit scientific

The last line of fields in the American desert. SEAN ANDERSON

backing by arguing that afforestation should be considered as a mode of climate change. Forests, he suggested, would reduce year-to-year temperatures and increase rainfall across Palestine.[91] In stating this, he was simply using similar concepts and knowledge gathered from his research and commercial activities in Germany's African colonies.

THE CLIMATE OF THE NAQAB'S HISTORY

The Naqab/Negev is governed by violent shifts in climate. Beginning in late October, meteorological depressions heavy with moisture start rolling eastward from the Mediterranean. Rain falls on the coastal plains and northern mountains. But south of Gaza, the coastline makes a sharp turn, its orientation changing from north–south to east–west. South of this turn, the west wind arrives not pregnant with rain from over the Mediterranean sea, but dry from the hot North African coastal area. Annual rainfall in the desert decreases by a staggering annual four millimeters for every kilometer south of this coastal turn.

Slight changes in wind direction, however, will carry the rain clouds southward toward and past the desert's edge. When these clouds meet hot air rising up from the surface, they break into sudden storms. The dry, crusty earth cannot absorb the quantities of water falling all at once, and floods begin to rush down thousands of gullies that are dry for the rest of the year. This is a dangerous period. The Bedouins know how to gauge their distance from the gushing streams, but for generations, foreign travelers and adventurers have been overtaken by flash floods, their bodies found kilometers downstream. Like the ancient farmers of the Naqab, the Bedouins have learned to make dams and channels to control the runoff from the hillsides and to collect it in order to irrigate their fields within or close to the beds of these seasonal streams.

I know the area well. Driving south past the clutter of the peripheral ring of logistical infrastructural and industrial zones that surrounds Israel's metropolitan center, the vista slowly opens up into a hilly landscape of fields and forests. Paradoxically, most of the year, the threshold of the desert is greener than the center of the country. Farther south, this landscape abruptly splinters. The gradient of cultivation that for generations has been incrementally shifting from arable to barren lands has been replaced by a fragmented territory of microclimatic conditions with interspersed patches of dry and artificially and intensively irrigated lands, the latter roughly coextensive with Jewish Israeli and Bedouin inhabited and cultivated areas.

Farther south still, any trace of green slowly thins out, with the yellow of dry reeds shading away into the brown and orange spectrum of the mineral geology of the desert, here and there augmented by the florescent blue patches of toxins from industrial zones and the burned sand of military training and testing grounds. Roughly past the 100-millimeter annual precipitation marker, the fields die out. The area is the dumping ground for everything Israel's economy needs, but that the state wants to keep far away and out of sight. It was there that the state located its most polluting industries, garbage dumps, and radioactive storage sites around the concentrations of illegalized Bedouin habitations. In 1979 when Israel's largest toxic-waste disposal facility—the Ramat Hovav Industrial Complex—was constructed south of Beersheba, its planners argued that its location was suitable because "no one lived there," disregarding the Bedouin settlements.[92] Farther south still, Bedouin settlements thin out, and the area is dedicated to military live-fire training zones, as well as serving as the site of a remote archipelago of prisons and detention camps in an area that is often referred to as "desert Siberia." In it, the military runs a number of little-regulated, out-of-sight detention camps for Palestinian prisoners from the West Bank and Gaza in conditions defined by human rights groups as "illegal and inhuman."[93] The use of incarceration has recently been expanded into the world's largest constellation of detention centers for sub-Saharan asylum seekers.[94] Because these refugees cannot be deported back to war zones, they are held in these camps in violation of international conventions on refugees.[95]

Driving between these military live-fire fields, one passes by a series of archaeological sites—ruins of agricultural towns strung along the Nabataean Incense Route. Nothing contributed to Zionism's self-perception as a climatic force—to the association of the national project with that of intentional climate change—more than the presence of archaeological ruins of these large abandoned cities in the arid part of the Naqab/Negev—Haluza, Memphis, Avdat, Ruheiba, and Shivta. They were built by the Nabataeans around the second century BC, fell to the Romans, and were subsequently expanded by the Byzantines, who turned them into self-sufficient agricultural settlements. Seeds of wheat, barley, and olives and the bones of salted Red Sea fish testify to a rich diet. In the valleys around these ruins there are thousands of ancient terraces, flour mills, cisterns, and wine and olive presses, as well as a strange feature made of repetitive piles of rocks known in Arabic as *tuleilat al-'ēnab*, or grapevine mounds. These cities and farms were abandoned during the early Arab period, between the seventh

TOP: "Fossilized grapevines" The small mounds of earth are ancient grapevine mounds referred to in Arabic as *tuleilat al-'ēnab*. BOTTOM: Agricultural terraces within the bed of a seasonal stream. Ancient agriculture in the Negev and in Bedouin agriculture that evolved from it are based on the principle of "runoff irrigation." Small terraces act as dams that collect floodwater into irrigation basins. In an area with less than 100 millimeters of annual rain such irrigation systems could collect annually up to 400 millimeters and support cereal cultivation. Both sites are located north of the Nabataean city of Avdat/Abdah, in an area with less than 100 millimeters of annual rainfall.

YEHUDA KEDAR, *ANCIENT AGRICULTURE IN THE HIGHER NEGEV* (JERUSALEM: BIALIK INSTITUTE, 1959); THANKS TO HADAS KEDAR

and tenth centuries. The retreat was gradual: in Shivta, for example, from 170 buildings at its peak, only 20 to 25 remained occupied in the years prior to its abandonment. The doors of the last homes were sealed. Their dwellers believed that they would return one day. These settlements and agricultural installations have posed a scientific mystery during the past two centuries, given the area's aridity.

The scientific debate about the abandonment of the desert cities of the Al Naqab/Negev is somewhat ideologically colored. There are two main schools of thought: one long-held explanation suggests that the desertification of the Naqab — a northward shift in the aridity line — was the consequence of the climate cycles of the earth. This theory was recently supported by geologists and paleoclimate historians who found organic substances — remnants of

TOP: The Avdat Farm. It was reconstructed in the 1950s and repurposed by a team of botanists and archaeologists led by Michael Evenari. It is currently maintained by the Desert Research Institute of Ben-Gurion University in Sde Boker.
BOTTOM: The archaeological remains of the Nabataean city of Avdat/Abdah. Avdat was the most important Nabataean city on the Incense Route after Petra. It is now located on a main road to the border with Egypt and is encircled by military live-fire training zones. The image was taken before parts of the city were reconstructed.
MICHAEL EVENARI, LESLIE SHANAN, AND NAPHTALI TADMOR, *THE NEGEV: THE CHALLENGE OF A DESERT* (CAMBRIDGE, MA: HARVARD UNIVERSITY PRESS, 1971)

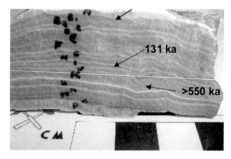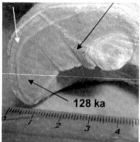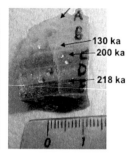

The paleoclimate of the Negev, reconstructed from sections of speleothems — stalactites and other mineral deposits found in caves in different locations in the Negev. On the left is a stalagmite from the border to the southern Negev, at the center is a stalactite from the northern Negev, on the right is a flowstone from the central Negev. The rings on the speleothems are a geological record of rainfall over the last five-hundred thousand years. By dating the different colored rings (the KA unit is per thousand years), it is possible to tell at which points in history the Negev has been wetter and when the sequence of speleothems is narrower, we know this indicates less rain. Testing the carbon samples dating to the numerous wetter periods (thicker rings), Dr. Anton Vaks, a research fellow at Oxford, found Mediterranean vegetation species, which helped to calculate that the border between the Mediterranean climate and the semi-desert (the aridity line) was twenty to twenty-five kilometers farther south that it is today. ANTON VAKS

grasses, scrubs, and trees — in rock formations in the arid parts of the Negev. There were not only cyclical fluctuations of the aridity line, but importantly, a consistent northward crawl over the past two millennia: climate change, they concluded, is what affected life patterns in the area, leading to the shift of the historical last line of systematic cultivation.[96]

Another school has favored a political scenario. Starting in the mid-1950s, Israeli scientists, led by the botanist Michael Evenari, established several experimental desert farms in the Negev and tried to cultivate them using the agricultural technologies available to the ancients. They have repaired or reconstructed some of the ancient terraces and dams that channeled floodwater into special irrigation basins. Using this method, Evenari and his colleagues managed to collect some 400 millimeters from about 100 millimeters of available annual rainwater.[97] Successfully raising their the first crops of wheat, the scientists could argue that the climate in the region must not have necessarily been wetter in antiquity. The ancient agrarian settlements, they proposed, were a result of concentrated hard work and were subsidized by the Byzantines in order to fortify the frontier. This explanation sat well with the Zionist narrative, which employed similar territorial strategies. But there was also an ideological point folded into this narrative. Because the abandonment of the Negev cities took place after the Arab conquest, the scientists proposed, it must have happened due to Arab neglect. In support of that claim, Evenari quoted the English Orientalist traveler Edward Henry Palmer who, while crossing the Negev in 1869, suggested of the Bedouin:

> [he] brings with him ruin, violence and neglect. To call him a "son of the desert" is a misnomer, half the desert owes its existence to him, and many fertile plains from which he has driven its useful and industrious inhabitants become, in his hand, like the "South Country," a parched and barren wilderness.[98]

The Arabs, in this text, not only inhabit the desert or adapt to it, but are considered to be themselves the agents of desertification — climate changers in their own right — pushing the environmental frontier in the opposite direction from that of the European colonizers, whose labor would always seek to make the desert bloom.

This scenario does not tally, however, with more recent archaeological evidence, which suggests that soon after the Arab conquest in 640 AD, during the early Umayyad period and up until the mid-eighth century, the cities of the Naqab were expanding and proliferating, and improved techniques of irrigation were being introduced.[99] The Israeli scientists who engaged in the desert farming experiments could have also avoided much of their trouble had they carefully studied techniques of Bedouin cultivation, which were directly continuous with those of the ancients. But after the establishment of Israel, most of the Bedouin tribes were forcefully displaced. When Evenari's scientists complained that the labor force assigned to them was composed of "new immigrants from Morocco, Tunis, India, or Pakistan" who "proved rather difficult to manage" and did not allow them to complete their job, it was a neighboring Bedouin tribe, one spared the fate of transfer experienced by so many others, that sent "twenty-one men and their camels and plows" to plow the fields skillfully on behalf of the Israeli scientists.[100] Rather than neglecting the Naqab, the Bedouins were the only people to have actually maintained its ancient knowledge and to have further developed the existing infrastructure of runoff farming, using terraces, dams, canals, wells, and cisterns and often repairing existing ones. Many of these elements could be seen in and around al-'Araqīb as historical evidence not only of ongoing use, but of a historical continuity with all previous cultures of the area.

THE TESTIMONY OF THE WEATHER

On December 7, 2009, Nūri al-'Uqbi was called to deliver testimony in the trial adjudicating his land claims. The first of his attorneys, Shay Gabso, aimed to establish that the al-'Uqbi settlement in al-'Araqīb was permanent and that it engaged in agricultural processes of cultivation. Al-'Uqbi testified that he was born in 1942 in al-'Araqīb. His father and grandfathers were born there, too. The al-'Uqbi tribe had arrived in the Negev in the eighteenth century and settled on these lands. Gradually, they learned to cultivate. They repaired the dams (*asada*), traces of which they found within the seasonal streams, and planted small orchards of figs, pomegranates, vines, melons, watermelons, and prickly pears. The British and the Ottomans collected taxes, and later the Israeli authorities did the same. Al-'Uqbi's family did not register its land because neither the Ottomans nor the British had ever threatened to take it from them.[101] They simply relied on their traditional land-tenure system.

GABSO   I want to bring you back to your childhood, before 1948. What did the area look like in this period, as far as you remember?

AL-'UQBI   There were houses dispersed through the area—each family had a house on its plot. Each family plowed and seeded its land. There were stone houses, but also tents. And there were fences around each plot. There were also enclosures for sheep and goats. There were cows, but very few, because cows need much water. Camels were used for plowing. There was a large distance between the houses. My father's house was 400 meters away from the next houses on both sides—his brothers' houses, my uncles'.

DOVRAT   [the presiding judge] What else can you remember?

AL-'UQBI   My father cultivated the land. Sometimes he hired people to help him. They plowed with camels. My grandfather had twelve camels that were used in plowing and seeding. This took three months: October, November, December. We finished around January fifth. In 1948, my father bought a tractor. I remember it well. It was red…. We cultivated chili peppers, Arab cucumbers, pumpkins, those with a neck, pumpkins of the kind you can empty and dry.

GABSO   There were stone houses? What kind of stone?

AL-'UQBI   Yes, we wetted the loess earth [sandy clay] and dried it in the sun—you can make very good thick walls…. The house was not only residential, it was also a courthouse, the tribal court. Until 1948, the tribal court was in Beersheba. In 1948, they transferred it into my father's house. The house had the Israeli flag and the sign with the menorah and Herzl's photograph [Theodor Herzl, founder of the World Zionist Organization]. I remember that as a child I was impressed with his beard.[102]

Al-'Uqbi's testimony was corroborated by seven other witnesses who testified in Arabic via an interpreter on October 26, 2009.[103] The state lawyers constantly interjected, objecting to their testimonies as "hearsay." Judge Dovrat reminded the witnesses that they could testify only to what they had experienced first-hand. The childhood memories of witnesses almost sixty years after they were displaced she also considered as "hearsay." Al-'Uqbi's team countered that the state had damaged such evidence by not doing anything about this case previously and now contending that they became invalid. This was rejected. Also dismissed was an entire tradition of oral history, one of the important modes by which the history of indigenous peoples is recorded, presently accepted as evidence in former colonial states such as Canada and Australia.[104]

For processes and events not experienced firsthand, Dovrat was willing to allow only the testimony of scientific experts. The trial thereafter pitted the expert for the state, Ruth Kark, a professor in the Geography Department of the Hebrew University, against Oren Yiftachel, acting for the al-'Uqbis. While the oral tradition of those native to the land was largely discredited, the written accounts, often in narrative form, of occasional European travelers, cartographers, priests, spies, and amateur biblical archaeologists who had passed through the Negev in the nineteenth and early twentieth centuries were admitted. Ruth Kark, whose earlier work on the Negev was scientifically sound and made mention of Bedouin agriculture and their process of sedentarization,[105] provided the court with an expert report that was unequivocal in its negation of Bedouin rights. Her report included only documents, maps, and quotes in which the Negev was described as desolate, devoid of settlement and agriculture. On May 13, 2010, the human rights lawyer and our frequent collaborator, Michael Sfard, who replaced Gabso leading the case, cross-examined Professor Kark on her report.

SFARD   On page four of your report, in the middle of the page, you refer to the American missionary Dr. William Thompson. [Thompson traveled through the Negev in 1856, two years before the enactment of the Ottoman land law, and passed fifteen kilometers north of al-'Araqīb.]

KARK   Yes.

LEFT: A three-year lease for a land plot in al-'Araqīb between Salam al-Marabi from the Albidaniyat family and Ibrahim Abu-Hassan and Salman Abu-Zayed from the Abu-Jafim family. The contract defines the boundaries of the land by noting all surrounding owners. The Hebrew stamp at the bottom left reads: "Beersheba District Court, Examined: January 17, 2006." The document demonstrates the existence of an effective land-tenure system and the density of inhabitation in the area. RIGHT: Tithe tax, 1942. A receipt addressed to Suleiman Abu-Mad'im from the British Mandatory Government of Palestine for the payment of tithe tax. It demonstrates the existence of cultivation before the transition to Israeli rule. AL-TŪRI FAMILY ARCHIVE

LEFT: A land-sale agreement between al-Tūri and al-'Uqbi families in the al-'Araqīb area, 1905, confirms the purchase of the area in which the al-Tūri cemetery was established. RIGHT: The renewal of contract between the al-Tūri and al-'Uqbi families from 1929. AL-TŪRI FAMILY ARCHIVE

SFARD   Now pay attention. In the third line of your quote, you put three dots. Now, the following is what is written within these three dots: "neither is the country what we refer to in the US as virgin land. It was plowed throughout thousands of years in the same way that it is plowed at present."[106] This is what you turned into three dots.

Sfard kept up the pressure. He went on to present Kark with her previous academic work, where she did mention Bedouin cultivation. Kark continually reverted to the meteorological logic of the "dead Negev doctrine."

KARK   So let me put it to you this way: there is very limited possibility to cultivate in the Negev because of the natural conditions. I brought here maps from the *Atlas of Israel* that show the isohyets, that is, the rain lines.... It is clear that agricultural cultivation is dependent on the level of rainfall, so it's clear that there is a very limited possibility to cultivate there.[107]

In her March 15, 2010, verdict against the plaintiffs, Judge Dovrat claimed that the petitioners were not able to show that "the area was used for agriculture or residence."[108] She went on to quote Kark: "There was no agriculture and no remnants until the end of WWI, none, none, none,"[109] as if shouting Bedouin agriculture away would make it disappear as a historical fact.

ORIENTALIST METEOROLOGY

The reason that some texts and maps from the nineteenth century did not record agriculture and settlements, Yiftachel explained, was due to "cognitive and cultural filters" that made Western travelers see this area from a narrow European and Christian perspective. "Sparse tent settlements with few stone houses," Yiftachel explains, "did not seem to these travelers to be settlements as they knew them to be from Europe."[110] In the trial, Sfard explained that not mentioning something is not proof that it was not there: people might not notice something, not understand what they see, or decide it was not important enough to note.[111] However, for those willing to read carefully, the accounts of nineteenth-century travelers contained evidence for Bedouin settlement and cultivation and for far more nuanced climatic conditions in the northern Negev than those claimed by the state.

In considering these accounts, we need to develop a form of reading that is both close and distant—close reading in the sense of being tuned to nuanced descriptions of the fragile and shifting environment of the desert's threshold, "distant reading" as understood by literary critic Franco Moretti for analyzing recurrent descriptions of the environment from within larger collections of travelers' texts.[112] In this form of reading it is the patterns that count.

We must also pay attention to the locations traversed, to the season, and to information, if any existed, concerning drought and plentiful years. Indeed, different travelers described the same hills alternately as arid or fertile, desert or sown, dead or alive. State lawyers used the summer travelers and those who passed through during drought years. In the al-'Uqbi trial, Yiftachel presented the accounts of winter travelers. These included the famous priest, botanist, and ornithologist Henry Baker Tristram, who wrote about the area round Beersheba, a dozen or so kilometers south of the al-'Araqīb hills, in late January and early February 1858, noting "cultivation of large portions of unfenced land for corn by the Arabs.... The rich low-lying flats by the Wadi Seba are plowed, or rather scratched, for wheat and barley." Similarly, Edward Hull, head of a British geological expedition who traveled through the Negev in the winter of 1883–1884, reported on what he saw fifteen kilometers west of al-'Araqīb: "the district is extensively cultivated by the Terabin Arabs.... The extent of the ground here cultivated, as well as all the way to Gaza, is immense, and the crops are wheat, barley, and maize must vastly exceed the requirements of the population." The area reminded him of southern Italy.[113]

One of the accounts on which the Israeli courts liked to rely, and repeatedly did, when contesting Bedouin land claims with descriptions of deserted aridity was that of Edward Palmer. We have already encountered Palmer as the Orientalist traveler who claimed that the Arabs were the "fathers" rather than "the sons" of the desert. He must have struck a bizarre figure when crossing the area in 1869–1870 wearing Bedouin dress and presenting himself as "Abdallah Effendi." In *Orientalism*, Edward Said described Palmer's biblical-archaeological survey of the Negev as suffering from the same Romantic attitude that haunted most contemporary travelers to the Orient, one that masked all differences, pluralities, internal dynamics, and historical complexities of the Arab people that they saw but didn't notice. Said was too kind. Palmer was also possessed by a genocidal hatred of the Bedouins and proposed all sorts of ways to destroy them by unleashing regional wars or starving them out of existence so that "this terrible scourge might be removed." Then, trying to temper what he had written, Palmer embarked on a fantasy by negation: "I do not advocate a war of extermination against the Bedawin…and I have still, even in the days of *mitrailleuses* [an early machine gun] some old fashioned notions about the sacredness of human life, but I would put an end to their existence qua Bedawin."[114]

Palmer's diary was published in 1871 as *Desert of the Exodus: Journeys on Foot in the Wilderness of the Forty Years' Wanderings*. He was killed by Bedouins when he returned to the region ten years later, "the most unsuccessful of the many who performed similar services for the Empire," as Said curtly sums it up.[115]

However, it is not enough to read in Palmer only his racist prejudice. We need to sieve out his writings, reading through them or in spite of them, for some account of the environment and the weather. It is important to confront Palmer's text in this way precisely because the desolation and ruins it describes have become, for the Israeli legal system, a benchmark

Edward Henry Palmer, *The Desert of the Exodus: Journeys on Foot in the Wilderness of the Forty Years' Wanderings* (Cambridge: Deighton, Bell and Co., 1871), vol. 2, pp. 389 and 393.

description for the state of the Naqab in the nineteenth century. At the al-'Uqbi trial, Judge Dovrat quoted a previous ruling handed down by the Israeli Supreme Court.[116] "The condition of the Negev in 1870 was researched by the scholar Palmer who traveled in that area and closely studied the Negev. He found wilderness, ancient ruins, and nomad Bedouins, who did not particularly cultivate the land, did not plow the land, and did not engage in agriculture at all." The ruling thus repeated the "dead land" justification for the displacement of the Bedouins, citing "this, in conjunction with [Palmer's] observation regarding the nomadic characteristics of the Bedouin tribes, and the fact that the region is usually dry and without rain most days of the year."[117]

Still, there is some important information to be gleaned from this text if we read it not against or with, but *for* the grain—that is, for traces of cultivation. This is important also because Kark, too, presented Palmer's account in support of her position that the area was desolate. The following paragraph is the one to which they referred. In this paragraph, after a day that saw some wandering and a close brush with armed people, Palmer lets loose with a biblical fantasy:

> Long ages ago, the Word of God had declared that the land of the Canaanites, and the Amalekites, and the Amorites should become a desolate waste; that "The cities of the Negev shall be shut up, and none shall open them" (*Jeremiah xiii. 19*)—and here around us we saw the literal fulfillment of the dreadful curse. Wells of solid masonry, fields and gardens compassed round about with goodly walls, every sign of human industry, was there; but only the empty names and stony skeleton of civilization remained to tell of what the country once had been.[118]

"Stony skeleton of civilization" sounds conclusive, and, as Kark said, Palmer did describe "ruins, and remnants from ancient settlements." However, two pages on, it seems that it wasn't *only* the fulfillment of a biblical curse that made the area arid and desolate, but rather something more common in these areas—a severe drought that had struck the region in the very year of his visit.

Today, we can try to reconstruct Palmer's whereabouts by locating places described in his book. On page 390, we read that Palmer had started the previous day in Beersheba rather late: "At one o'clock we left Beersheba, and...proceeded the ruins of El Haurá, where we were to have encamped."[119] This is easily reconstructed: moving northeast of the old city of Bir el Saba, we drive along the Wadi Khalil (Nahal Hevron, in Hebrew),

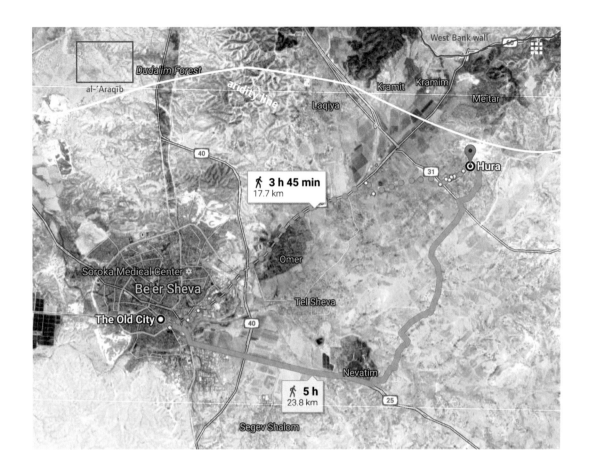

Palmer's likely route from Beersheba to Haura
marked on Google Maps. Al-'Araqīb is marked
in red frame on the top left and the West Bank wall
on the top right. The aridity line is marked in white.

GOOGLE MAPS; ANALYSIS BY FORENSIC ARCHITECTURE

or the ancient "way of the Patriarchs"—today, more simply, Route no. 60—that connects Beersheba through Hebron to Jerusalem and Nazareth. After a three-hour camel ride and a diversion to the wrong site—fifteen to twenty kilometers, say—Palmer's expedition reaches "Haurá" at sunset and sets camp near some ancient ruins. It is there that he has his biblical vision regarding the destruction of the cities of the Negev. On today's map, he is likely a little west of the Bedouin town of Hura to which the al-'Uqbis were displaced in 1951. In 2014, an archaeological excavation conducted on site unearthed a Byzantine monastery with wells, a church, and small gardens from the sixth century. Some of its ruins could have certainly been seen by Palmer, but they were certainly not "biblical ruins."[120] The place is precisely twelve kilometers east of al-'Araqīb. A couple of pages on, we read: "The next day we entered Palestine and left the desert region of the South Country."[121] Palmer is crossing what he identifies as the threshold of the desert—then understood as the southern border of Palestine. Walking north of Hura, along the ancient route, Palmer has just passed the location where, 130 years later, the Wall separating the northern Negev from the West Bank would be built. In meteorological terms, Palmer's route tracks the contemporary 200-millimeter isohyet, which curves up the Hebron hills at that location. This means that he is on the same isohyet as al-'Araqīb, and the meteorological conditions described should be roughly similar. On the same page, we read: "the brown mould beneath our feet was hard with the fibre of dried vegetation."[122]

"Brown mould" is interesting. Timeless desolation does not leave "fibres of dried vegetation" on the ground. What happened that year? A search of the historical record reveals that Palmer's travel during the agricultural year of 1869–1870 coincided with a tenfold increase in the price of grain. The export of grain throughout Palestine and Syria was prohibited—a clear indication of failed crops and severe drought.[123] The climatic conditions and barren state of the area on which Palmer reported and that the Israeli court took for permanent facts—"dry and without rain…wilderness, ancient ruins and nomad Bedouins"—were likely the temporary result of a severe drought that struck the area that year. The following year, the rain returned, and the export of grain was again permitted. Rather than describing timeless desolation, Palmer's book in fact confirms Nūri al-'Uqbi's testimony about the presence of agriculture in this area—"brown mould…of dried vegetation"[124]—as well as the pulsating character of the desert threshold, where in a good year, one could see "miles around with grass, flowers, and herbage" and in another the desolate wilderness.

THE EARTH PHOTOGRAPH

While it is on the surface of the earth that the entanglement of land use, politics, conflicts, and climate change is played out, it is from the aerial perspective that it most clearly comes into view.[125] The surface of the desert appears to be different, depending on the season when the photographs were taken. In late summer, the vegetation is closely shaven off the surface, and the territory appears translucent, revealing features on and under it that would otherwise be obscured by the light plume of seasonal weeds. The enhanced shadows of early mornings or late evenings can reveal subtle undulations in the topographical surface, traces of erasure that would not be visible from the ground. The relative dryness of the terrain conserves traces better than any other environment. The surface of the desert thus resembles a photographic inscription, exposed to the direct and indirect contacts of human and climatic forces in a way similar to how film is exposed to light. This makes aerial images artifacts of double exposure: they are photographs of photographs.[126] For those willing and able to read its surface closely, the desert can reveal not only what is present, but also the subtle traces of what has been erased: traces of ruined homes and small agricultural installations, of fields and wells that can sometimes be noticed under the grid of newly planted forests, as well as the dark stains of long-removed livestock pens.

Beyond the threshold of the desert, climate and photography interact in other ways, too. There is an inverse relation between humidity and visibility: the farther south one flies, the drier the air and the thinner and more conducive to vision and photography it becomes.[127] It is for this reason that the only star observatory in Israel is located in the arid part of the Negev. Its telescopes traverse the same medium of desert air, but in the opposite direction. From 15,000 feet, it is not only the surface of the earth that is being photographed, but also the air that is between it and the lens. The thicker and more humid the air, the less focused the rendering of the surface becomes. Atmospheric blur and distortion are not only reductions in information that make interpretation necessary, but, inversely, a source of information themselves — an indication of humidity.

But reading aerial photography must not only concern itself with reading the surface captured digitally or on film, but also with the technology and politics that placed the camera up in the air in the first place, and it is often the military or other state agencies that have generated these images. The Negev desert is currently the largest and busiest training area for the

Different writings on the surface of the earth: The long mounds on the left are preparations for the planting of tree seedlings by the JNF. The small mounds in the middle of the image have been dug out by a bulldozer. Note how regular patterns of the mounds made in preparation for plantation are replaced by the irregular patterns meant for demolition (the remnants of a tent are visible in the bottom), demonstrating the entanglement of plantation and displacement. The three larger mounds on the top right are ground preparations by the al-Tūris for small subsistence gardens. They were made by damming the path of a small tributary to the al-'Araqīb stream. There are traces of the destruction of a small structure for storage on their right. The close lines at the bottom left indicate plowing by the al-Tūris in preparation for seeding for vegetables. The earth work is visible because this image was taken shortly before the rainy season when there is no vegetation cover. The area of close lines at the bottom left have also been made by the al-Tūris in preparation for planting vegetables. ARIEL CAINE/FORENSIC ARCHITECTURE

Israeli Air Force and has one of the most cluttered airspaces in the world. This airspace is partitioned into a complex stratigraphy of layers, air boxes, loops, and corridors dedicated to different military platforms: from bomber jets to helicopters to drones. This complex volume is an integral part of the architecture of the Negev.

But it was not only the Israeli Air Force that has taken aerial photographs there. Two sets of aerial photographs are important in relation to Bedouin land claims. The first was captured during the summer of 1918, at the end of World War I, by the German Imperial Air Force, and the second by the British Royal Air Force in the winter of 1945, toward the end of World War II. The reason that the area had been overflown by both militaries is that during World War I, the threshold of the desert was a military frontier and a battle zone. In World War II, it was expected to be one. The black-and-white military sequences did not aim to record Bedouin life, agriculture, and cultivation, but did so inadvertently, mainly at the edges of military sites, in the margins of the photographs, always slightly out of focus. These two sources document the state of the Negev during two different periods and in opposite seasons, capturing the threshold of the desert in each of its alternate states, arid (summer 1918) and in cultivation (winter 1945), and are thus important resources in confirming Bedouin presence and land use across time and different seasons.

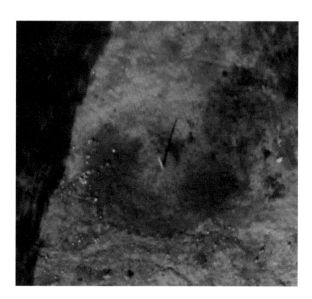

A darker circular stain indicates the earlier presence of a livestock pen (*sire*) in al-'Araqīb, 2016. The stain is the result of the body fluids (urine and excrement) from a goat tied to the central pole. The level of dark saturation is usually an indication of how long ago the pen was removed. This *sire* seems to have been destroyed more than a year previously, washed out by several periods of rain. The stains can remain in the earth for several years and when found can be seen as some of the clearest indications that Bedouins have lived on site. This crop is extracted from the kite image on page 220.

To understand what is made visible within them, the photographs need to be put in context and compared with contemporary aerial images, as well as with images from the ground. These days, one can easily access satellite images of the area. But as I mentioned in the Introduction, the publically available satellite images of Israel are degraded, as a result of Israel's lobbying with the US administration, to the coarse resolution of one meter per pixel, one in which Bedouin villages lie under the threshold of visibility. However, this does not mean that they are invisible to the state agencies that undertake continuous high-resolution aerial surveys of these sites, closely monitoring their expansion, but that the aerial perspective is not available to the inhabitants of the villages. Google Earth and other mapping software, in line with the policy of the Israeli state and its cartographers since 1948, does not mark the illegalized villages or their access roads. They have also been written off all travel maps, to the extent that travelers, guided by GPS navigators, often encounter these communities unprepared.

Aerial photographs would have provided useful maps to help plan and counter state claims for land. But taking aerial photographs requires the resources to rent an aircraft and specialized photographic and navigational equipment. These were in place for Fazal Sheikh when he took the aerial images for his "Desert Bloom" series in 2010.[128] However, such an endeavor is too complicated and pricy to repeat, and Bedouins have little trust in photographs from airplanes, which they associate with the military and the police.

Instead, a collaboration between the al-'Araqīb village council, Forensic Architecture, Zochrot, and Public Lab took aerial images using kites. Public Laboratory for Open Technology and Science is an organization that seeks to promote community-based environmental monitoring from the air. It was founded in the wake of the 2010 BP oil spill disaster to break the information blackout that was imposed by the oil giant and US federal authorities on photographing the spill from the air. Public Lab works to empower communities to undertake their own aerial photography using improvised "community satellites" made of standard digital cameras tied to kites or small helium balloons.[129] In al-'Araqīb, together with Public Lab, we arranged a number of photographic workshops and worked with the community, mainly children, on undertaking kite surveys of this and other illegalized villages.

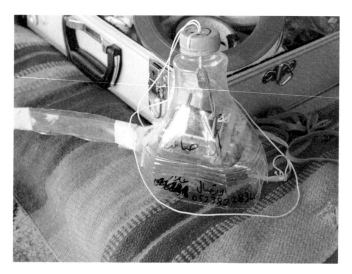

Kite kit. The camera is attached by rubber bands that keep pressing the photo button. The water bottle protects the camera at landing or if it falls. The telephone number is provided in case the camera gets lost. ALINA SCHMUCH, JAN KIESSWETTER

The GPS data available in the standard camera or smart phones attached to the kites facilitated the extrusion of these images into 3D models using photogrammetry. This facilitated their analysis and interpretation. Al-'Araqīb, 2016. ARIEL CAINE WITH HAGIT KEYSAR/PUBLIC LAB, FORENSIC ARCHITECTURE, ZOCHROT, AL-'ARAQĪB VILLAGE

Nūri al-'Uqbi undertaking a survey with a helium balloon, used as an alternative to a kite when there is less wind, in al-'Araqīb, 2016. EYAL WEIZMAN

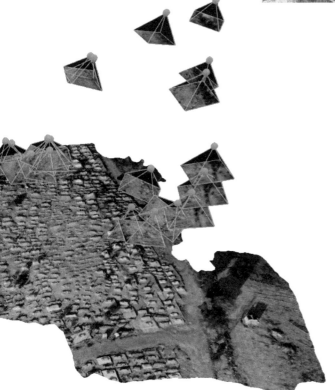

Kite survey in al-ʿAraqīb, 2016.
RAJAL KHATEEB

Kite survey in al-'Araqīb, 2016.
EYAL WEIZMAN

TOP: Wheat cultivated by Bedouins near al-ʿAraqīb.
BOTTOM: Common Whitlow, otherwise indigenous
to more rainy areas, blossoming in al-ʿAraqīb,
spring 2016. EYAL WEIZMAN

MILITARY ARCHAEOLOGY

The contemporary kite survey not only provided a precious record of al-ʻAraqīb just before the last of its remnants — stone houses, dams, wells — are buried under the afforestation earthworks; it also helped us read the older set of aerial images. The Bavarian state archive in Munich contains 2,872 glass plates of aerial photographs of Palestine dating from 1918. Most were taken by the Bavarian Squadron 304 (Königlich Bayerisches Fliegerbataillon 304) which, together with five other German squadrons (about eighty-five aircraft in total), was part of the army of imperial Germany that flew in support of the Ottoman military. These were the early days of aerial reconnaissance, a technology that became operational only toward the end of the war.

The context was the British invasion of the Ottoman Empire. In 1917, as the imperial British Egypt Expeditionary Force (EEF) progressed north from Sinai, the Ottoman armies fortified along the line they perceived to be the threshold of the desert — from Gaza through Beersheba to Hebron, about fifteen to twenty kilometers of today's 200-millimeter isohyet. Their calculation was simple: attrition along the desert edge would keep the European soldiers in the arid part, with less water and pasture to irrigate and feed the tens of thousands of horses and mules on which their military campaign depended. The strategy was successful, and the EEF got bogged down south of Gaza. But the British forces finally broke through Beersheba, taking the town in a massive charge on the last day of October 1917. Some of the Ottoman units managed to escape and retreated a few kilometers north, stabilizing a second line of defense right through the hills of al-ʻAraqīb. From November 1 to November 6, the armies fought "several sharp little actions,"[130] and the EEF managed to withstand an Ottoman counterattack along the al-ʻAraqīb stream. The battle incidentally coincided with another major political development. The Balfour Declaration — promising a national home for the Jews in Palestine — was signed on November 2 and published on November 9, while the imperial armies were clashing along the aridity line in al-ʻAraqīb.

The Bavarian aviators of Squadron 304 joined the retreat of the Ottoman military. Understanding they were fighting a lost war, the pilots also took to photographing archaeological and religious sites with no strategic importance. This made them among the first to use aerial imagery for archaeological purposes.[131] Their last task in the summer of 1918, a year of constant defeats and retreats, was to return and overfly British military

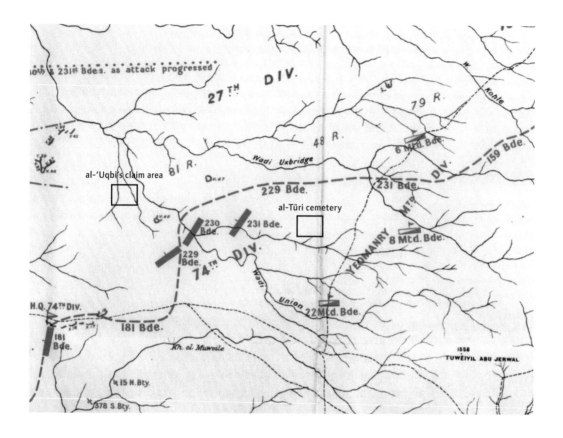

positions in the Negev. Most of their photographs are oblique shots taken from hand-held cameras as the airplane tilted its wings. On September 20, 1918, a few days after the last documented photograph was taken, they surrendered to the British at the Afule airstrip in the northern valley. Surprisingly—perhaps because the significance of aerial imagery was not fully understood by all ranks of the British military at the time—they were allowed to keep their glass prints and brought them back with them to Munich, where they are now archived.[132]

Despite exhausting the archive and its archivists, the closest photographs to the al-'Araqīb hills I could find were about one kilometer away in each direction. Because the surface of the desert appears barren in these photographs, the Bavarian images were presented by state lawyers seeking to demonstrate that Bedouins never settled in these parts.[133] Like Palmer's

Map of the front line between the British-led Egypt Expeditionary Force (EEF; in red) and the Ottoman forces in al-'Araqīb (in green) before the EEF attack on November 6, 1917, drawn by Cyril Falls and A. F. Beck, 1930. This map reconstructs the battle lines on land around al-'Araqīb. I have marked the location of the al-'Araqīb cemetery. (In 1917, it had been in existence for merely three years.) The front line closely overlaps the contemporary aridity line and the al-Uqbi's claim area.

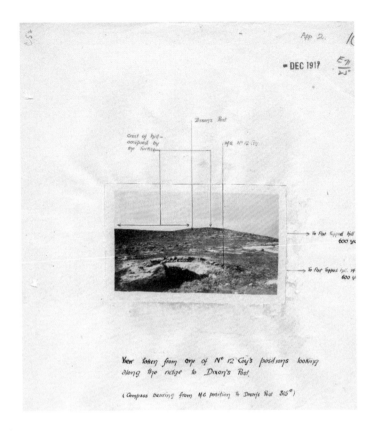

View of Tall al-Khuwēlfa (today the kibbutz Lahav), December 1917. Courtesy of the Australian State Archives. This page is organized around a photograph of the hilltop of Tall al-Khuwēlfa, where a battle took place between the EEF and a dug-in unit of the Ottoman Army in early November 1917. Officers drew battle plans directly onto photographic prints. Military photographers included objects in the foreground of their photographs for orientation. Here, the photographer positioned a water hole in the foreground, inadvertently confirming the presence of Bedouins in the area.

testimony from the drought year of 1869, this, too, is misleading. The photographs were taken in the summer months at the end of the war. The Bedouin tribes had been expelled from the area by the Ottomans because, after the fall of Aqaba to Bedouin forces led by Auda ibu Tayi and T. E. Lawrence "of Arabia" in July 1917, the Ottomans believed, not without reason, that the Negev Bedouins harbored animosity toward their empire and sympathies toward the British.

Reading these images requires a careful study of their surface at the highest possible magnification. It is then that these photographs start to reveal elements that are typical of Bedouin life at the threshold of the desert. These include structures and ruins, fields of cultivation next to the streams, and, significantly, the same indicative sign of round livestock pens of the kind still found today.

Tall al-Sharī'a, Bavarian Squadron 304, August 24, 1918. This site is about one thousand meters northwest of al-'Araqīb. Although identified as Tall al-Sharī'a in the German title, the site photographed is a few kilometers to the east of it, along Wādi al-Sharī'a. Today, within the area of the photograph's frame, there is the Bedouin town of Rahat, established in 1972, and Kibbutz Mishmar Hanegev, established in 1946. The 1918 image contains traces of abandoned Ottoman trenches and fortifications. Marked within the white frames and reproduced in the enlargements opposite are possible traces of Bedouin settlements consistent with Bedouin land use at the threshold of the desert.

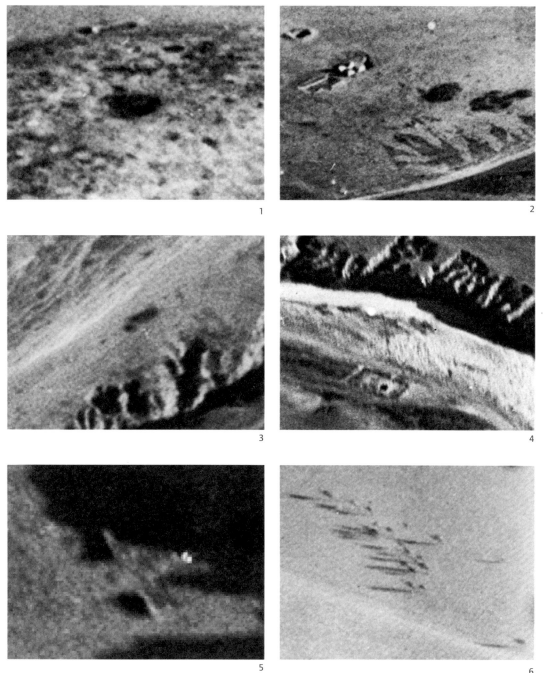

A systematic air survey of Palestine was conducted only toward the end of World War II, when the techniques and technologies for producing photographic series that could be tiled into a cartographic grid were developed as part of the war effort. The PS series (named after Port Said, the airport at the north of the Suez Canal from which the aerial flights took off, but often mistakenly referred to as the Palestine Survey) was produced between December 1944 and May 1945 by RAF squadrons transferred from the European front.[134] During World War II, reconnaissance planes could fly longer and higher, and the cameras were now integrated into the aircraft's structure.

The photographic mission progressed from south to north. The reconnaissance pilots overflew al-'Araqīb on January 5, 1945.[135] After the survey was completed, the Haganah, the largest Zionist paramilitary force, managed to convince a sympathetic archivist to smuggle some of the negatives of the aerial photographs out of RAF archives. They printed and returned the originals before their absence was noticed. A number of these reproductions were included in the "Arab Village Files" — intelligence documents on Arab localities that were used by the Haganah in 1948 to occupy and ultimately expel the villagers[136] and that are now available in Israel's cadastral center in Tel Aviv — providing a benchmark record for the condition of Palestine before the establishment of Israel and, ironically, evidence for the existence of these villages.

January is the peak of the rainy season. The black-and-white photographs captured the northern threshold of the Negev in a state of cultivation, almost completely covered with a patchwork of small agricultural fields. The photographs were submitted in the al-'Uqbi case on September 15, 2009, as a part of an expert report prepared by Shlomo Ben Yosef, a former aerial photography interpreter for the Israeli intelligence who was hired by the al-'Uqbi legal team.[137] In his report, Ben Yosef confirmed "continuous agricultural settlement in the area of the land claim" and identified tents, hard structures, and roads, but Judge Dovrat accepted the state claims that the photographs were inconclusive.[138] Mobilized against the claimants was the fact that Bedouin life leaves only gentle marks on the land and the inability of film to render these marks clearly, in the way that Western agricultural settlements would render.

Analysis of aerial images also requires some understanding of the material properties of negatives. From a cruising altitude of 15,000 feet, each of the nine-inch (twenty-three-centimeter) square films used by the RAF captured an area of about three-and-a-half kilometers square. The resolution of analog aerial photographs is measured by a unit called "line-pairs per millimeter" (lp/mm). It designates the number of pairs of white and black lines that could be captured within every millimeter of film. The Kodak Aerocon High Altitude panchromatic negative film used for aerial photography in full sunlight conditions at the end of World War II had a fine-grain resolution of thirty-five lp/mm — that is, it could potentially show seventy lines (half black, half white) within every millimeter of the negative. The width of a grain — the narrowest that a line could possibly be — is approximately 1/70 millimeters on the negative, which translates to 214 millimeters — roughly 20 centimeters, or 0.2 meters, on the ground.[139] However, the 15,000 feet of atmosphere between the ground surface and the film surface reduced the *effective* resolution of the film to 50 centimeters, which means that the grain represents an area of half a meter in diameter on average on the ground.[140]

The images were taken at the beginning of January 1945, at the same time that the Allies were preparing to charge across the borders into the territory of the German Reich. This was barely three months after the aerial photographs of Auschwitz, described in the Introduction, were taken. Both sets of photographs were shot from the same altitude of 15,000 feet with similar optics and using similar film.

The effective resolution of the aerial images of the Negev and those of Auschwitz were considered by aerial image analysts to be the same, and so was the problem of identifying those elements close to the "threshold of detectability."[141] I began this book with the problem of confirming holes in the roof of a concrete structure. In the RAF photographs of the Negev, the holes of wells and the gentle mounds of graves were the crucial elements to identify, close to the size of the grain in the images. Here, too, it was necessary to consider both the materiality of the objects represented, a well or a hole, and the materiality of the surface representing it, the photographic negative.

The translation from the surface of the terrain to the surface of the film is referred to as "ground truth" — a process used by meteorologists, remote sensing, or aerial interpreters, to calibrate the analysis of images because there is never a one-to-one relation between aerial photographs — indeed between any photographs — and the reality they capture.

To arrive at ground truth, an aerial image interpreter must measure and compare the ground elements with the elements that compose the image. Kite photography lends itself to establishing ground truth because the

The area of al-ʿAraqīb, image 5033 and 5034,
RAF, January 5, 1945. Red frames mark
elements compared with the contemporary
kite photography. SURVEY OF ISRAEL

unrecognized village:
Tarābīn as-Sāni (ext.)

well

☐ 5

JNF forest

☐ 1

unrecognized village:
Tarābīn as-Sāni (ext.)

JNF forest

☐ 4

The al-Tūri village and cemetery in al-'Araqīb:
kite imagery superimposed over RAF photograph (image 5033 and 5034) from 1945.
The kite image is composed of photographs
taken in two seasons, when the threshold of
the desert is alternatedly arid or green.
HAGIT KEYSAR/PUBLIC LAB, ARIEL CAINE, ZOCHROT,
FORENSIC ARCHITECTURE, AL-'ARAQĪB VILLAGE, 2016

cemetery

beika/remnants

destruction/
forest preparation

tents

ground truth forum

garden

cemetery

dam

funeral tent

JNF forest

bulldozer traces

3

water hole

beika/remnants

2

beika/remnants

beika/remnants

The framed areas in the RAF photo (1945; see pages 290–91), the kite image (2016; previous spread), and ground images (2014–16).

1   The stone house (bāyka) of Salam Salim al-'Sbihat al-'Uqbah, Nūri al-'Uqbi's maternal grandfather.
2   The stone house (bāyka) of Abu Zheiri (Ibn Beri) from the al-Tūri family.
3   The al-Tūri cemetery.
4   The house of Suleiman Muhammad al-'Uqbah in al-'Araqīb. The stone in the image below reads: "This is the house of Suleiman Muhammad al-'Uqbah (1914–1993). The house was built in 1936 and demolished after he and his clan were expelled in 1951. The house had hosted the tribal court in the first years of the Israeli state until the expulsion." In the background of the image is the recently planted God TV Forest.
5   The well of Suleiman Muhammad al-'Uqbah, Nūri al-'Uqbi's paternal grandfather.

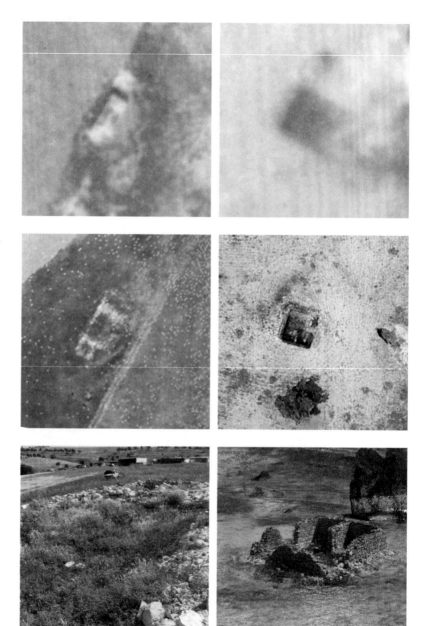

1   2

3 4 5

aerial survey is undertaken while the feet of those taking the images are firmly on the ground. Every element captured in the aerial image can be simultaneously experienced on the ground.

Aerial images, such as the RAF photographs from 1945, are not unmediated copies of the world, but products of material relations between objects: one composed of celluloid plastic coated with gelatin emulsion with silver halide crystals, the other of stone, earth, and vegetation, a relation mediated by the prevailing conditions of the climate between them.

The process of establishing ground truth thus combines an archaeology of material traces on the ground with an archaeology of the material properties of the photograph.

Undertaking this combined analysis, it becomes evident that the 1945 photograph brings together three distinct, but interrelated threshold conditions. The first is the threshold of the desert — beyond which lies uninhabitable aridity. The second is the threshold of the law — the line beyond which lies an extraterritorial zone where land rights no longer apply. And the third is the threshold of visibility — beyond which people, agriculture and political cultures can be rendered unseen and where dispossession is fuelled by denial.

Three years after Nūri al-ʿUqbi lost the trial, the 1945 RAF aerial photograph of al-ʿAraqīb surfaced in a different context. A reading of it was used as justification for the eviction and continuous demolition of the remaining al-Tūri settlement from the cemetery. The claim that the al-Tūri cemetery did not exist on the 1945 photographs was made in a report by an Israeli organization called Regavim, funded by government bodies to "establish state sovereignty and government control over state land and act against 'illegal land grabs' by Palestinians." In the Negev, it concentrates on "Bedouin trespassers."[142] To achieve this aim, it spies not only on Bedouin construction, but on anyone acting in solidarity with the other side. It was this organization, mentioned in Part 2, that paid for private detectives to go through Michael Sfard's office trash while he was working on the al-ʿAraqīb case as well as other land claims.

In December 2013, the group published a report that used a series of aerial and satellite photographs, the oldest being the aforementioned January 5, 1945, RAF image, to claim that the al-Tūri cemetery was not present on the site before the establishment of the state and that therefore burying the dead there was itself an act of invasion of state land. The report demanded that the state immediately evict the remaining members of the al-Tūri family still living there.[143]

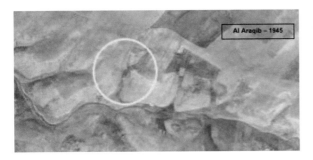
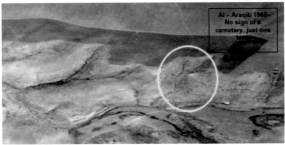
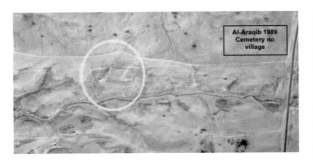

Aerial and satellite images of al-'Araqīb (1945, 1965, 1989, 2010), marked and annotated by Regavim, 2013. The captions on the images read: "1945: no cemetery and no village; 1965: no sign of a cemetery, just one tent; 1989: a cemetery but no village; 2010: a settlement and a cemetery." It is only in the 1989 photograph, and from that date on, the report claims, "that it is possible to notice the cemetery in its early stages."

I ordered the relevant 1945 photographs from the Israeli cadastral center and received them as high-resolution scans. Overlaying the twists and turns on the al-'Araqīb stream—the only identifiable feature on the site after almost seventy years of development and transformation—I was able to locate the present extent of the cemetery within the 1945 photograph. The reading of the 1945 photograph was undertaken while walking the ground of al-'Araqīb by continuously comparing it with the kite photography produced with Public Lab. In a small part of where the al-Tūri cemetery can be found on the ground today, in the 1945 photograph there is a small bounded area of lighter ground that stands out in contrast to its surroundings. Well-trodden paths appear lighter in aerial photography; planted areas darker. The extent of the lighter surface is smaller than the contemporary extent of the cemetery, but in 1945, the cemetery obviously would have been smaller.

Al-Tūri cemetery, al-'Araqīb. The white frame
marks the approximate location and size of the
cemetery in 1945. HAGIT KEYSAR/PUBLIC LAB, FORENSIC
ARCHITECTURE, ARIEL CAINE, ZOCHROT, AL-'ARAQĪB VILLAGE

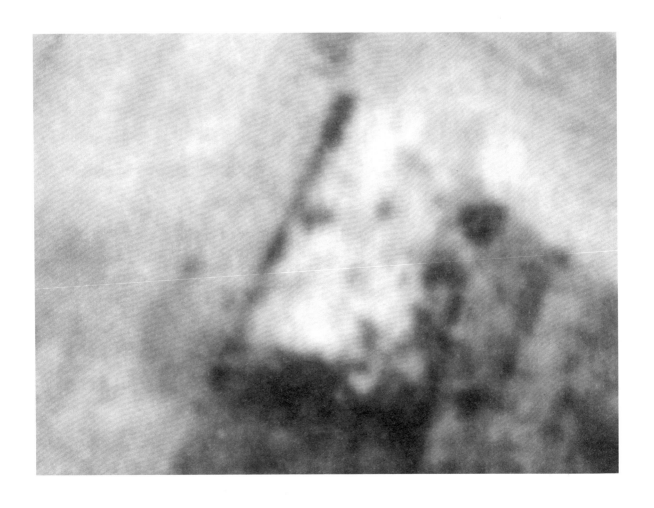

Al-Tūri cemetery, al-'Araqīb. IMAGE 5033,
RAF PORT SAID SURVEY SERIES, JANUARY 5, 1945

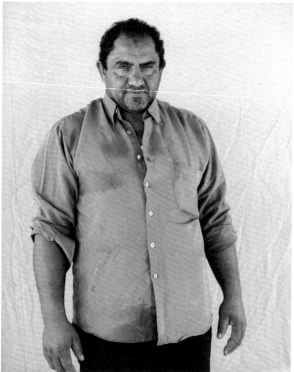

In order to understand what the film recorded within this piece of ground, we need to go back to the cemetery and study the graves carefully. Paradoxically, the place of the dead held the proof that this was not "dead land." Most graves that could be seen on site nowadays are made of horizontal and vertical stone or concrete slabs, but in a visit to the site in September 2014, Sayāh al-Tūri led me to the oldest part of the cemetery, where the graves were marked only by small piles of stones. It was only several decades ago that the Bedouins started using the hard concrete or stone gravestones. One of these piles was the first grave on site, dated, he said, to 1914.[144]

By the time the 1945 photograph was taken, al-Tūri explained, there were already about fifteen or twenty graves similarly marked with piles of stones. The piles of stone I could see on site were between a meter and a meter and a half long, between a half and one meter in width, and up to half a meter in height.

The current generation of struggle. Miriam Abu Mad'im and Salim al-Tūri, al-'Araqīb, 2010. MIKI KRATZMAN

On the 1945 photograph, these would occupy the size of a single grain, or at most, two silver halide grains side by side. The fact that the graves attributed to the period before the establishment of the state were unmarked and undated was used by all those state agencies that tried to deny the al-Tūris' claims. But in the lighter, distinctly bounded area there are a number of darker grains likely indicating the shadow of distinct objects. The process of establishing ground truth allows us to read the graves back into the grain. On the other hand, it also suggests that the authors of the Regavim report and the state that supports them — like many colonial travelers and cartographers — exercised an active form of "not seeing," of visual denial undertaken simultaneously both in the image and on the ground.

The white spots left on colonial maps of the seventeenth and eighteenth centuries were means of erasure: acts of "whiting-out" that led to the wiping out of entire native cultures. Those promoting aerial and satellite photographs over cartography tend to argue that the former are objective and neutral renderings of the surface that capture all things without the cultural prejudice of cartography. But photographs, whether from the air or from the ground, require close reading and interpretative labor, which can be politically and culturally conditioned. Reading the climate and its history requires putting into relation information of different kinds and a form of reading that is closely tuned to grain: in its cultivation, in texts, and in the materiality of photographic negatives.

The 1945 photograph of al-'Araqīb is a still frame in a process of continuous transformations. With every tidal cycle of the desert's ebb and flow, another image is created. When the desert ebbs and the green rolls south, we can measure the extent to which the line of colonial afforestation and cultivation has been expanded; every summer, yellow tones flood slightly farther north, revealing new traces of eviction on the bare surface of the earth.

Shortly before dawn on January 18 2017, a large police force raided the illegalized Bedouin village of Umm al-Ḥīrān in the northern threshold of the Naqab/Negev in order to demolish several houses. This raid was part of an ongoing attempt to remove the entire village, clear the area, and build a new community settlement for ortho-dox Jews. Two people were killed during the operation: a villager, Yaqub Musa Abu al-Qi'an, and a policeman, Erez Levi. The latter was part of the force that came to demolish the house of the former.

Shortly after the incident, Israel's Public Security Minister referred to it as a "ter-ror attack" claiming Abu al-Qi'an intended to murder as many policemen as possible. The chief of police further suggested he had "links to ISIS."[145] But local residents and activists who were on site when the incident took place claimed that the police-men shot Abu al-Qi'an, a local teacher, without provocation. Following this shooting, Abu al-Qi'an lost control of his vehicle, which accelerated down the slope toward the policemen, running a group of them over, killing Levi, and possibly wounding another.

Forensic Architecture collaborated with Activestills, a collective of documentary photographers, to undertake an emergency investigation in order to challenge the police version and open the case up to further investigation.[146]

We started by synchronizing two videos shot on the ground by a member of Activestills with a thermal imaging video of the incident shot by a police helicopter. The aerial video was released by the police to support their version of the events. The videos shot on the ground did not visually record the incident but did capture the sound of the first burst of gunshots. We synchronized and overlaid their sound track onto the silent aerial footage. The metadata on the ground–videos helped precisely time the incident.

Our analysis showed that Abu al-Qi'an's vehicle was proceeding slowly in the general direction of the policemen when it was shot three times. The video deter-mined that the shots were fired in the direction of the vehicle by examining the form of the heat clouds that were seen exiting the policeman's gun (image 1). The initial three shots were followed by a burst of four more gunshots. Four seconds after the first shot was fired, Abu al-Qi'an's vehicle changed course and gained speed toward a group of policemen. We established that the angle of the slope in the direction of movement was about ten degrees. The steepness of the slope might have helped the vehicle gain speed. Six seconds after the first shot, Abu al-Qi'an's vehicle is seen hitting a group of policemen (image 2). This was immediately followed by another

A video shot at the site did not visually capture the event but recorded the sound of the first burst of gunshots.

KEREN MANOR/ACTIVESTILLS

IMAGE 1: The still frame from a thermal imaging video shot from a police helicopter, time marked 05:36:02 a.m., shows Abu al-Qi'an's vehicle proceeding toward the police when they fired the first shot.

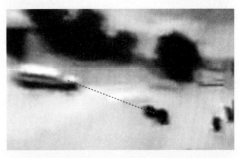

IMAGE 2: At 05:36:08 a.m., Abu al-Qi'an's vehicle loses control, changes course, and gains speed down the slope hitting a group of policemen.

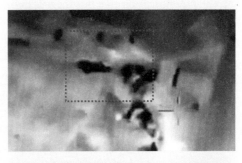

IMAGE 3: At 05:36:49 a.m., a shot is heard as policemen are seen surrounding Abu al-Qi'an's vehicle.

ISRAEL POLICE FORCE; ANALYSIS: FORENSIC ARCHITECTURE

long burst of gunfire. Thirteen seconds after the first shot Abu al-Qi'an's vehicle was brought to a standstill. During the last seven seconds of his drive, Abu al-Qi'an's vehicle horn is continuously sounding, suggesting he might be lying against the steering wheel, unconscious. After the car was brought to a standstill five or six policemen are seen surrounding it. Thirty-five seconds later we identified the sound of a single gunshot. This last shot could have occurred somewhere else but it is consistent with what Israeli security agencies call "verification shot"—the shooting of already incapacitated assailants. At this early stage of this investigation, it was too early to know. We suggested further investigation was necessary and demanded that the report on the postmortem autopsy be made public.

We released our analysis on January 19, a day after the incident. The police responded by saying that the first three shots were fired in the air. They also tweeted about our analysis:

> Tendentious editing will not rewrite reality. The documentation of the incident proved intention to murder policemen. This has one name: terror. No clips that distort data can change that.

Later the police admitted that the first three shots might not have been fired in the air but at "the wheels" of the car. Leaked results of the autopsy undertaken the following day revealed that Abu al-Qi'an was shot in the right knee. This might support a scenario in which Abu al-Qi'an lost control of his vehicle. The autopsy also showed Abu al-Qi'an died after bleeding for twenty minutes without medical care, despite the three ambulances present in the area.[147] In late February, based on our and others' analyses, the police finally retracted their version that it was a terrorist attack at all. We are now seeking a moratorium on all demolitions in the Negev.

I added a description of this ongoing investigation at the end of the book, well after it was already sealed (thanks to the committed Zone team), in order to demonstrate an important point about counterforensics: the slow violence of environmental transformation is convertible to, and can always flare up in, kinetic violence.

In justifying the shooting of Abu al-Qi'an, the police will no doubt revert to their duration of convenience—"the split second"—the time in which a policeman must decide how to act in view of the perceived threat of a car approaching. The unspecified duration of the "split second" is also the common temporality of forensics. The question must, however, always be: what ideology, politics, and "common sense" is already programmed or naturalized into the "split second." In this case, it seems to be preconditioned by a conception of the Bedouins as squatters, as threats and enemies to the state. Refracted within the "split second" of the decision to shoot at a slow moving vehible is therefore the long duration, now generations long, of the violence of colonization and environmental transformation.

Acknowledgments

My book acknowledgements are becoming longer, perhaps because the infrastructure involved in their production has become increasingly complex. This book relied upon a particularly long process and the participation of many people. Despite my immense gratitude to those whose collaboration taught me so much, I will attempt to keep it as short as possible (but not shorter).

Forensic Architecture was set up in 2010. In 2011, it gained support from a four-year European Research Council (ERC) grant. Susan Schuppli and Paulo Tavares helped write the application for it. Susan became the first project coordinator and senior research fellow on it. In the latter role, she undertook research on media forensics. The other research fellows were Anselm Franke, who cocurated with me the exhibition *Forensis*, Thomas Keenan, with whom I coauthored the book *Mengele's Skull: The Advent of Forensic Aesthetics* (Berlin: Sternberg Press, 2012), Adrian Lahoud, Alessandro Petti, Ann-Sofi Rönnskog, and John Palmesino (Territorial Agency), and Srdjan Jovanovic Weiss. Francesco Sebregondi, a young graduate from our MA in Research Architecture Program, was hired as an administrator, but soon became an integral part of the research team and the project coordinator after Susan. In 2014, he helped secure another ERC grant to develop PATTRN, crowd-sourcing, data-aggregation, and visualisation software for conflict mapping, and was in charge of the project until its successful release as open-source software. Christina Varvia, who oversaw the video analysis in our Black Friday investigation of the Gaza war of 2014, became the project coordinator after Francesco. Further financial support for Forensic Architecture came from additional ERC grants (a Proof of Concept Grant in 2014–2015 and a Consolidator Grant in 2016–2021), the Potter Foundation, the Sigrid Rausing Trust, and the Oak Foundation.

Some readers will recognize elements of this book from previous publications or exhibitions. The extensive reframing of these was essential in order to outline the methodological and political proposition that forensic architecture has become. Forensic Architecture still operates as an agency, and we are busy with a great number of new challenges that will be published in the future.

Many of our other researchers were graduates and students at the Centre for Research Architecture, University of London. Lawrence Abu Hamdan developed the new investigative field of audio forensics, Nabil Ahmed undertook investigations in Bangladesh and West Papua, Maayan Amir developed image analysis under the term of "extraterritorial images," and Ayesha Hameed worked on the history (and future) of fingerprints. Charles Heller and Lorenzo Pezzani inaugurated the critical field of research and activism that is forensic oceanography. Paulo Tavares developed the notion of environmental violence in relation to his work in Amazonia, Hannah Meszaros Martin in relation to her work on Colombia, and Godofredo Pereira in relation to the mining frontier in northern Chile. Nick Axel coordinated a few projects on video and data analysis. Helene Kazan's research on risk and the destruction of homes in Lebanon drew from and further contributed to this project. The work of Ġerald Nestler, Füsun Türetken, and Emanuel Licha intersected with the notion of forensics in different ways. Jacob Burns was an extremely committed researcher and assistant and partook in most investigations. Ariel Caine developed our ability to interrogate space through images, especially with the use of photogrammetry. Samaneh Moafi coordinated the environmental violence department and Stefan Laxness coordinated our Mexico investigation. Nico Czyz, Hana Rizvanolli, Dorette Panagiotopoulou, Gustav A. Toftgaard, Vere Van Gool, Sophie Dyer, Daniel Fernández Pascual, Andrea Bagnato, Blake Fisher, Hania Halabi, Samir Harb, Zahra Hussain, Steffen Krämer, Stefanos Levidis, Jason Men, Alon Schwabe, Camila E. Sotomayor, Solveig Suess, and others researched different elements of the project.

Shela Shiekh was the managing editor for *Forensis: The Architecture of Public Truth* (Berlin: Sternberg Press, 2014), where she was also a member of the editorial board, and for *The Conflict Shoreline: Colonization as Climate Change in the Negev Desert* (Göttingen: Steidl and Cabinet, 2015). The latter was a book written around the aerial photographs of Fazal Shiekh and started the research that lead to Part 3 in this book. Rosario Güiraldes cocurated (with Anselm Franke and me) the PROA/Buenos Aires, MACBA/Barcelona, and MUAC/Mexico City versions of our exhibition at the invitations of Adriana Rosenberg, Ferran Barenblit, and Cuauhtémoc Medina, respectively. Alejandro Aravena invited us to exhibit in the 2016 Venice Biennale of Architecture. Eitan Diamond and Shourideh C. Molavi, both international lawyers, were our legal researchers. David Kuper, legal advisor for Goldsmiths, has given us close legal advice and supervision throughout. Ana Naomi de Souza has prepared a documentary film, *The Architecture of Violence*, for Al Jazeera that included a section on Forensic Architecture and later worked on several investigations, especially on our collaboration with Amnesty International on the Saydnaya prison in Syria. Jamon Van Den Hoek offered continuous assistance with remote sensing. Chris Woods is still a close collaborator, initially through the Bureau of Investigative Journalism (BIJ) and later at the Airwars project. Together with the Centre for Investigative Journalism (CIJ), of which I am now one of the directors, we have inaugurated the Gavin MacFadyen investigation in memory of our beloved founding director and friend, who has recently passed away. Chris Cobb Smith offered expert analysis on weapons and munitions. Mohammed Abdullah, Mahmoud Abu Rahma, and Angela Gaff from al-Mezan closely collaborated on investigations in Gaza.

Organizations that were part of the first ERC-funded research project included DAAR (an architectural studio and residency I established together with Sandi Hilal and Alessandro Petti in Beit Sahour/Palestine), the Human Rights Project at Bard College, Grupa Spomenik from Belgrade, Situ Research from New York City, and Caroline Sturdy Colls from the Centre of Archaeology at Staffordshire University.

Groups for whom we undertook research included the Michael Sfard Law Office in Tel Aviv, B'tselem, Amnesty International, Airwars, Médecins Sans Frontières (MSF), the International Commission of the Red Cross (ICRC), the Argentinian Forensic Anthropology Team (EAAF), Centro Prodh in Mexico City, Centro Para la Acción Legal en Derechos Humanos, ODHAG, the Oficina de Derechos Humanos del Arzobispado de Guatemala, Working Group Four Faces of Omarska, Human Rights Watch, Migreurop, the Fédération Internationale des Ligues des Droits de l'Homme, the UN Office of the Special Rapporteur on Counter-Terrorism (UNSRCT), the Bureau of Investigative Journalism (BIJ), the Al Mezan Center for Human Rights/Gaza, the Palestinian Commission on Human Rights (PCHR), Yesh Din, Zochrot, the Public Laboratory for Open Technology and Science, the Foundation for Fundamental Rights Islamabad, Pakistan, the European Center for Constitutional and Human Rights in Berlin (ECCHR), Al Jazeera English, Reprieve, One World Research, and Witness.

I would like to thank Irit Rogoff, Jorella Andrews, Gavin Butt, and Astrid Schmetterling, who at different times were helpful heads of the Department of Visual Cultures at Goldsmiths, University of London, where the Forensic

Architecture project was housed, and the departmental manager, Tom Chivers, as well as other Goldsmiths colleagues such as Matt Fuller, Patrick Loughrey, our warden, and his deputies at the time, Roger Burrows and Jane Powell, who supported it. Thanks also go to Graham D. Burnett, Eduardo Cadava, Beatriz Colomina, Hal Foster, and Alejandro Zaera Polo for sponsoring my Global Scholar position to introduce forensic architecture at Princeton University.

I also would like to express my gratitude to the team at Zone Books: Michel Feher and Ramona Naddaff for commissioning, editing, and publishing this book; Bud Bynack for making sense of this text; Meighan Gale for making this complex book possible; Andrew Kiddie, Michael Newton, and Chloé Truong-Jones for the proofreading; and Julie Fry for giving it such a rich form. Finally, again, many thanks to my friends Sandi Hilal, Nikolaus Hirsch, Nina Katchadourian, Thomas Keenan, Laura Kurgan, Shourideh Molavi, Sina Najafi, Alessandro Petti, Bernd Scherer, and Susan Schuppli, as well as, as always, of course, my dear Ines.

Notes

PREFACE

1   Carlo Ginzburg in *Microhistories,* eds. Magnus Bärtås and Andrej Slávik (Stockholm: Konstfack, 2016), p. 37. In this quote, Ginzburg refers to history, but we find that it is relevant to architecture, too.

INTRODUCTION: VIOLENCE AT THE THRESHOLD OF DETECTABILITY

An earlier version of this essay was published as an introduction to *Forensis: The Architecture of Public Truth*, ed. Forensic Architecture (Berlin: Sternberg Press, 2014), and was the basis for a film that Harun Farocki planned to make using other elements from *Forensis* shortly before his death. This essay is thus dedicated to his memory.

1   Deborah E. Lipstadt, *Denying the Holocaust: The Growing Assault on Truth and Memory* (New York: Free Press, 1993), p. 181.

2   A precedent from the early 1970s in which architectural drawings were presented as evidence was the trial in Vienna of two of the architects who designed Auschwitz, Walter Dejaco and Fritz Ertl. Both architects were acquitted. Eyal Weizman, "The Architecture of Negation: An Interview with Robert Jan van Pelt," in *Forensis*, p. 149.

3   Errol Morris, *Mr. Death: The Rise and Fall of Fred A. Leuchter, Jr.,* 1999.

4   An extended version of van Pelt's expert report was republished as Robert Jan van Pelt, *The Case for Auschwitz: Evidence from the Irving Trial* (Bloomington: Indiana University Press, 2002).

5   David Irving v. Penguin Books Ltd. and Deborah Lipstadt, trial transcript, day 11 (January 27, 2000), p. 129, http://www.fpp.co.uk/Legal/Penguin/transcripts/day011.htm.

6   Van Pelt, *The Case for Auschwitz*, pp. 2–3; Daniel Keren, Jamie McCarthy, and Harry W. Mazal, "The Ruins of the Gas Chambers: A Forensic Investigation of Crematoriums at Auschwitz I and Auschwitz-Birkenau," *Holocaust and Genocide Studies* 18.1 (Spring 2004), http://www.holocaust-history.org/auschwitz/holes-report/holes.shtml. The team was able to show a construction detail necessary for the creation of a hole in a slab: rebar that was deliberately cut, with the ends turned upward.

7   David Irving v. Penguin Books Ltd. and Deborah Lipstadt, trial transcript, day 10 (January 26, 2000), p. 20.

8   *Ibid*. Day 11, p. 150.

9   *Ibid*. Day 10, p. 145.

10   Van Pelt, *The Case for Auschwitz*, pp. 3, 24, 458.

11   The argument went on to present the Holocaust as the ethical basis for American domination, perceived, in its own eyes, as the bulwark against an "evil" modeled on the Nazis. Instead of confronting the way in which the use of the Holocaust shaped the politics of the present as that

of the "lesser evil," these groups sought to reinvent history. Van Pelt, *The Case for Auschwitz*, pp. 3, 24, 458. One of the proponents of this approach was a Paris-based bookshop and publishing house called La Vieille Taupe, which became renowned in the 1980s for publishing anti-Semitic and Holocaust-denial literature.

12   Faurisson read the testimonies of survivors and Nazis alike for their contradictions. The testimonies of survivors were records of traumatic experiences and contained many lacunas. This he used as an excuse to declare all testimonies biased and flawed. The next step was to shift his focus to material evidence, including the debris of the crematoriums. In 1978, Faurisson traveled to Auschwitz to study the plans of the crematoriums. Robert Faurisson, "A Challenge to David Irving," *Institute for Historical Review* 5.2–4 (Winter 1984), http://www.ihr.org/jhr/v05/v05p289_Faurisson.html. It was not only the concrete roof that lacked the holes. Irving claimed that none of the surviving representations of the roof — drawings or photographs — showed them. He challenged Irving, by then only a Nazi sympathizer, not a Holocaust denier, to join his campaign of denial.

13   Weizman, *Forensis*, p. 152.

14   This occurred on April 25, 1983. *Stern*'s largest competitor, the *Bild Zeitung*, smuggled Irving into *Stern*'s press conference to announce the discovery. Irving later changed his mind and claimed that the diaries were authentic. He might have been the first to call them fake, but also the last to call them authentic. Van Pelt, *The Case for Auschwitz*, pp. 21–22.

15   A hole is more, not less, information than the matter that surrounds it, be that reinforced concrete or an ozone-rich atmosphere. It contains information in regard to both the materiality that it perforates and the form of the interruption. "There would be no void, no nought, even relative or partial, no possible negation without affirmation of materiality." Henri Bergson, *Creative Evolution*, trans. Arthur Mitchell (New York: Henry Holt, 1911), p. 294. Thanks to Susan Schuppli for this point.

16   Van Pelt explained that none of the drawings of the gas chamber showed the holes because the architects were not allowed to draw in these pieces of incriminating evidence. Van Pelt, *The Case for Auschwitz*, p. 458.

17   Dino A. Brugioni and Robert G. Poirier, "The Holocaust Revisited: A Retrospective Analysis of the Auschwitz-Birkenau Extermination Complex," February 1979, available at GlobalSecurity.org, http://www.globalsecurity.org/intell/library/imint/holocaust.htm.

18   The pattern interruption on these images of the vents is a result of the printing. The image has been filmed from a print. For the photographic interference pattern, see the next images.

19   Irving was referring to a 1992 study by John C. Ball. See van Pelt, *The Case for Auschwitz*, p. 56.

20   David Irving v. Penguin Books Ltd. and Deborah Lipstadt, day 10, p. 30.

21   *Ibid.* Day 11, p. 114. This was paraphrased by van Pelt in *The Case for Auschwitz*, pp. 84 and 353.

22   This is similar to what Alfred North Whitehead called "nonsensuous perception," with which matter has a direct, nonsensuous sense of duration in form. Alfred North Whitehead, *Adventures of Ideas* (New York: Macmillan, 1933), pp. 233–34.

23   One of the last of the Srebrenica cases at the International Criminal Tribunal for the former Yugoslavia (the Zdravko Tolimir case, decided in 2012) produced the following exchange in regard to an aerial image of the Nova Kasaba soccer field: "The Trial Chamber accepted the explanation of the witness on identifying darker pixels as people rather than shadows as claimed by the accused. THE WITNESS: I have spent numerous and numerous hours analysing all these pictures and identifying what reference they can have on the ground.... It's a football field. There are no bushes in the middle. So these grey zones are not shadows. Though, indeed, a shadow has the same pixel than [sic] a group of people on the picture, but if you compare what is officially said on the photograph and the corroboration (934) you can make of what a man represents in terms of a pixel

on such a photo, this is why I allow myself to say that the dots that I have marked previously are people." International Criminal Tribunal for the former Yugoslavia, trial transcript, March 29, 2010, pp. 933–34, http://www.icty.org/x/cases/tolimir/trans/en/100329IT.htm. Thanks to Patrick Korker for this point.

24 His evidence also included the interpretation of architectural plans drawn from the archive of Auschwitz Central Construction Office. In addition to *The Case for Auschwitz*, see also Debórah Dwork and Robert Jan van Pelt, *Auschwitz, 1270 to the Present: A History* (New York: W. W. Norton, 2002); Robert Jan van Pelt and Carroll William Westfall, *Architectural Principles in the Age of Historicism* (New Haven: Yale University Press, 1993); and many other articles and essays by van Pelt.

25 The project was coordinated by Susan Schuppli.

26 For Forensic Architecture: Eyal Weizman, Susan Schuppli, Jacob Burns, Steffen Krämer, Reiner Beelitz, Samir Harb, Zahra Hussain, Francesco Sebregondi, and Blake Fisher. Some cases were undertaken in collaboration with Situ Research. Other partner organizations included the European Center for Constitutional and Human Rights (Andreas Schüller), One World Research (Bridget Prince, Nasser Arrabyee, Anis Mansour), Al Jazeera English (Ana Naomi de Sousa), Chris Woods (freelance journalist), Edmund Clark (photographer), Chris Cobb-Smith (munitions expert and consultant), and Myra MacDonald (freelance journalist).

27 Forensic Architecture and the Bureau of Investigative Journalism, in collaboration with Situ Research, "Drone Strikes in Pakistan," http://wherethedronesstrike.com. The shift occurred in 2005–2006. Almost two-thirds of the strikes were directed at homes. Houses were twice as likely to be attacked at night. Strikes that took place in the evening, when families were likely to be home and gathered together, were particularly deadly. Alice K. Ross and Jack Serle, "Most US Drone Strikes in Pakistan Attack Houses," Bureau of Investigative Journalism, May 23, 2014, https://www.thebureauinvestigates.com/2014/05/23/most-us-drone-strikes-in-pakistan-attack-houses/.

28 Anti-tank missiles employ what is referred to as a "hollow charge" in which a compressed, molten-metal liner is shot forward to pierce armor. About fifteen-hundred Hellfire missiles were fired between 2002 and 2014 in Pakistan, Yemen, and Somalia. See Chris Woods, *Sudden Justice: America's Secret Drone Wars* (London: Hurst, 2015), p. 291 n.3.

29 Bill Sweetman, "Fighters without Pilots," *Popular Science*, November 1997; Avery Plaw, "Drone Strikes Save Lives, American and Other," *New York Times*, November 14, 2012, quoted in Grégoire Chamayou, *Drone Theory*, trans. Janet Lloyd (London: Penguin, 2015), p. 135.

30 Derek Gregory, "Theory of the Drone 12: 'Killing Well'?," *Geographical Imaginations: War, Space and Security*, December 8, 2013, http://geographicalimaginations.com/2013/12/08/theory-of-the-drone-12-killing-well/.

31 Ross and Serle, "Most US Drone Strikes in Pakistan Attack Houses."

32 Laura Kurgan, *Close Up at a Distance: Mapping, Technology, and Politics* (New York: Zone Books, 2013). Kurgan's book on satellite imagery is an excellent source for understanding the history of resolution.

33 The modulor originated in Leonardo's *Vitruvian Man* and in the attempts by Leon Battista Alberti and others to generate designs according to human proportions. Le Corbusier, *The Modulor: A Harmonious Measure to the Human Scale Universally Applicable to Architecture and to Mechanical Things* (Cambridge, MA: MIT Press, 1971).

34 Ma'ayan Amir, "The Extra Territorial Image," PhD diss., Goldsmiths Centre for Research Architecture, 2015; William Fenton, "Why Google Earth Pixelates Israel," *PC Magazine*, June 14, 2011, http://www.pcmag.com/article2/0,2817,2386907,00.asp.

35   At a resolution of 1.0 meters, an average residential building would take up about twelve pixels, making a bomb-damaged building look not very different from a building that is intact. On
the Kyl-Bingaman Amendment, titled "Prohibition on Collection and Release of Detailed Satellite Imagery Relating to Israel," see http://www.nesdis.noaa.gov/CRSRA/files/Imager%20
Restriction%20over%20Israel.pdf; Stefan Geens, "Whither High-Resolution Satellite Imagery of
Israel?," *Ogle Earth*, June 15, 2011, http://ogleearth.com/2011/06 /whither-high-resolution
-satellite-imagery-of-israel/; The US 1998 Land Remote Sensing Policy Act, http://geo.arc.nasa
.gov/sge/landsat/15USCch82.html; BBC, "US Lifts Restrictions on More Detailed Satellite Images,"
June 16, 2014, http://www.bbc.co.uk/news/technology-27868703. Since the end of 2011, the European satellite Pléiades, unaffected by the American restrictions, provided 0.5-meter-resolution
images of Palestine/Israel. See also Hito Steyerl, *How Not To Be Seen: A Fucking Didactic Educa-
tional .MOV File*, 2013. The size of the pixel in relation to the size of the body makes camouflage
unnecessary.

36   Duncan Campbell, "US Buys Up All Satellite War Images," *Guardian*, October 17, 2001, https://
www.theguardian.com/world/2001/oct/17/physicalsciences.afghanistan.

37   Heather Linebaugh, "I Worked on the US Drone Program. The Public Should Know What Really
Goes On," *Guardian*, December 29, 2013, https://www.theguardian.com/commentisfree/2013
/dec/29/drones-us-military.

38   Robert Mackey, "What Italian Drone Pilots See as They Scan Iraq for Militants," *New York Times*,
December 11, 2015, http://www.nytimes.com/2015/12/12/world/middleeast/what-italian-drone-
pilots-see-as-they-scan-iraq-for-militants.html.

39   In 1878, Lombroso published '*L'uomo delinquente*' (Criminal man), in which he measured the faces
of 383 lawbreakers to create an exhaustive record of criminal types. Beginning in 1911, Reiss published a series of volumes under the general title *Manuel de police scientifique*, and Alphonse Bertillon, while working for the Paris police force in 1879, also developed an anthropometric system
with particular focus on the measurements of the face and head.

40   Umar Farooq, "Rock and a Hard Place: The Neglect and Abuse of Pakistan's Tribal Areas," *Boston
Review*, December 9, 2015; Derek Gregory, "The Scene of the Crime: Customary Law and Forensic Architecture," *Geographical Imaginations: War, Space and Security*, March 15, 2014, http://
geographicalimaginations.com/tag/customary-law.

41   The operative concept in regulating this temporal inversion, "imminence," means "instant, overwhelming, leaving no choice and no moment for deliberation." However, the temporality of imminence has been made elastic, gradually pushed back by a series of qualifying formulations such as
"the risk of imminent harm," "imminent threat of violent attack," and "continuing and imminent
threat." Imminence, as Jameel Jaffer from the ACLU puts it, "is no longer a concept that implies
the coming of a specific event — instead . . . it is now more equivalent to menace: amorphous and
undefined." Jameel Jaffer, "The Justice Department's White Paper on Targeted Killing," *ACLU
Blog of Rights*, February 2013, https://www.aclu.org/blog/national-security/justice-departments
-white-paper-targeted-killing. In Israel, threats are often presented as "ticking bombs" but as
Israeli human rights lawyers have sarcastically commented regarding an analogous context,
such "bombs," can go on ticking for a long time. John Brennan has put it in this way: "We're
not carrying out these actions to retaliate for past transgressions. We are not a court, we're not
trying to determine guilt or innocence, and then carry out a strike in retaliation." John Brennan, *The Efficacy and Ethics of U.S. Counterterrorism Strategy*, The Wilson Center, International
Security Studies, April 30, 2012, http://www.wilsoncenter.org/event/the-efficacy-and-ethics-us
-counterterrorism-strategy.

42 Grounded on principles of insurance and risk management, the predictive technique in use in today's battlefields have their origins in the "predictive policing" that emerged in the United States and the United Kingdom as a consequence of the introduction of managerial approaches in the 1980s. Older roots could even be found in the Victorian era's "Suspect or Suspects Laws," a controversial policing technique that condoned arresting people for "intent to commit an arrestable offence." *Policing the Crisis: Mugging, the State, and Law and Order*, Stuart Hall et al. eds. (London: Palgrave Macmillan, 1978); Malcom Feeley and Jonathan Simon, "Actuarial Justice: The Emerging New 'Criminal Law,'" in *The Futures of Criminology*, ed. David Nelken (London: Sage, 1994), pp. 173–201. On ungoverned territories as an "analytical *terra incognita*," see Angel Rabasa et al., *Ungoverned Territories: Understanding and Reducing Terrorism Risks* (Santa Monica: Rand Corporation, 2007), http://www.rand.org/content/dam/rand/pubs/monographs/2007/RAND _MG561.pdf. On the history of the algorithm employed see Dan McQuillan, "Algorithmic States of Exception," *European Journal of Cultural Studies* 18.4–5 (August–October 2015), pp. 564–76.

43 The use of these scans in FATA were due to the fact that the CIA was often unable to recognize individuals or interpret the meaning of distinct actions: "enemy combatants look like everyone else; enemy vehicles look like civilian vehicles; enemy installations look like civilian installations." American Defense Science Board, quoted in Chamayou, *Drone Theory*, p. 46; Human Rights Clinic at Columbia Law School, quoted in Chamayou, *Drone Theory*, p. 236.

44 Jacob Burns, "Persistent Exception: Pakistani Law and the Drone War," in *Forensis*, pp. 400–407.

45 I am grateful to Grégoire Chamayou for directing my attention to this idea in my work. Grégoire Chamayou, in conversation with the author, Paris, July 3, 2015.

46 Forensic Architecture and the Bureau of Investigative Journalism, in collaboration with Situ Research, "Drone Strikes in Pakistan."

47 Louise Amoore, *The Politics of Possibility: Risk and Security Beyond Probability* (Durham: Duke University Press, 2013), p. 44.

48 Ross and Serle, "Most US Drone Strikes in Pakistan Attack Houses." The analysis also revealed that the time of the attack affected the number of civilian casualties. Homes are twice as likely to be attacked at night, when civilians tend to be present. These strikes are particularly deadly to women and children. Likewise, the analysis demonstrated that roughly half of all drone strikes hit targets in the Tochi Valley, the most densely populated area of North Waziristan, connecting three major towns — Datta Khel, Miranshah, and Mir Ali — with a continuous fabric of agricultural villages, nothing like the "remote tribal region" to which US spokespersons refer in the media.

49 Michel Foucault, *Fearless Speech*, trans. Joseph Pearson (New York: Semiotext(e), 2001), pp. 15–16. *Parrhesia*, Foucault explains, is a form of criticism articulated "in a situation where the speaker or confessor is in a position of inferiority with respect to the interlocutor. The *parrhesiastes* is always less powerful than the one with whom he or she speaks. The parrhesia comes from 'below,' as it were, and is directed toward 'above.'" *Ibid.*, p. 18. See also Michel Foucault, *The Courage of Truth*, trans. Graham Burchell (New York: Palgrave Macmillan, 2011).

50 Rachel Maddow, "Victims of Secretive US Drone Strikes Gain Voice in Pakistani Lawyer," MSNBC, June 29, 2012, http://video.msnbc.msn.com/rachel-maddow/48022434#48022434. See also Rabih Mroué, *The Pixelated Revolution*, performed at Documenta 13, 2012, https://vimeo.com/119433287.

51 See Ariella Azoulay, *The Civil Contract of Photography* (New York: Zone Books, 2008).

52 This situation recalls the photographs secretly taken by Auschwitz prisoners in 1944 from inside one of Auschwitz-Birkenau's gas chambers. In one, a large part of the image is a thick black frame — in fact, the room in the dark — because the light is calibrated to the outside. Beyond the door of the gas chamber, dead bodies are seen being burned. Often, when the image is used in

books and articles about the Holocaust, the dark frame is cropped off. In his seminal reading of these images, Georges Didi-Huberman objects to this cropping because for him, the frame is a crucial part of the image: not only is it the only documentation of the interior of a gas chamber, but it testifies to the mortal danger in taking this image. Georges Didi-Huberman, *Images in Spite of All: Four Photographs from Auschwitz* (Chicago: University of Chicago Press, 2012).

53 Shoshana Felman and Dori Laub, *Testimony: Crises of Witnessing in Literature, Psychoanalysis, and History* (London: Routledge, 1992); Shoshana Felman, *The Juridical Unconscious: Trials and Traumas in the Twentieth Century* (Cambridge, MA: Harvard University Press, 2002), p. 134.

54 Harun Farocki presented a similar experiment in embodied mediation in *Immersion*, a video work that dealt with a therapy session for soldiers suffering from posttraumatic stress disorder. An instructor, demonstrating this technique, wears a headset and replays a combat experience in a simulated environment that appears like a video game. The soldier moves through a virtual reconstruction of the scene in which he got wounded. Harun Farocki, *Ernste Spiele/Serious Games III: Immersion*, video installation, 2009. Working with the witness from the Mir Ali strike, our technique was related, but also different. The witness was building a model of the environment because, unlike the US military, we did not have an existing information about this environment, certainly not about the intimate spaces of the interior of victims' houses. Unlike the battle experience of a soldier, who can move around the battlefield and see space from different perspectives, our witness was spatially constrained, confined to a small space that was separated from the main part of the house, which was reserved for the men.

55 Frances Yates, *The Art of Memory* (London: Pimlico, 1992). The invention of the art of memory was attributed by Cicero and others to the Greek poet Simonides, he had just walked out of a banquet hall full of people when the roof collapsed, killing everyone inside. The bodies could not be identified, but Simonides was able to reconstruct the flow of conversation between the guests around the table and thus remember where each guest had been sitting and identify the bodies, which could then be returned to their families for burial.

56 However, Yates does not discuss the ghosting capacity of memory. According to the French poet Jacques Roubaud, even once removed, these memory objects tend to leave remainders in the rooms in which they were placed. The trace of their presence cannot be fully erased, however many times they are removed, and they repeatedly appear in the wrong speech, haunting the building in question. When this happens, the building has to be abandoned and burned to the ground and a new one mentally built in its stead. Roubaud's insight highlights the importance of forgetting, a task considerably more difficult than that of remembering, but nevertheless one on which memory depends. Jacques Roubaud, "Mnenomic Hand," presentation at *Memory Marathon*, The Serpentine Gallery, October 12–14, 2012, http://vimeo.com/61611210.

PART ONE: WHAT IS FORENSIC ARCHITECTURE?

1 Dale Paegelow, *Forensic Architecture, An Introduction* (Patterson, NY: Cromlech Architect, 2001), http://cromlech-architect.com/forensic-architecture.

2 Nelson Forensics+Consulting, advertising their forensic architecture service, http://www.nelson forensics.com/Architecture.html.

3 "A forensic architect is essentially a professional architect who applies the art and science of the profession to various aspects of architecture, construction, and legal issues. Activities associated with architectural forensics include the investigation, determination and causes for deterioration, deficiencies, and failures, in addition to the preparation of reports, and testimony under oath, or

offer advisory opinions that assist in resolution of related disputes. The forensic architect may also be asked to render a professional opinion in regarding responsibility for failure or deficiency. In the author's opinion, the forensic architect's job description should also include: failure and deficiency prevention and cure." Sam Kubba, *Architectural Forensics* (New York: McGraw-Hill Professional, 2008), p. 1.

4   "Architects who have given their practice over full time to forensic investigations and report writing are few and far between. If I had to hazard a guess, I would say less than 5 thousand across America. I believe that firms who employ architects for forensic investigation have been around for about 10 to 15 years." Paegelow, *Forensic Architecture, An Introduction*, unpaginated.

5   Other examples of firms offering architectural forensics include Berman and Wright Architecture, Engineering and Planning; the Diehl Group Architects, MKA Forensic Architecture and Engineering; KPA Associates, Inc.; Perkowitz+Ruth Architects; and Erwin and Bielinski (ELB Forensics). On the latter firm, see Edward Keegan, "The Building Sleuths: Inside a Forensic Architecture Firm," *Architect Magazine*, July 23, 2009. On risk, see Helene Kazan, "What the War Will Look Like," in *Forensis: The Architecture of Public Truth*, ed. Forensic Architecture (Berlin: Sternberg Press, 2014), pp. 157–65.

6   Jorge Otero-Pailos is a pioneer in this field. On his work, see, for example, Laura Raskin, "Jorge Otero-Pailos and the Ethics of Preservation," *Places Journal* (January 2011), https://placesjournal .org/article/jorge-otero-pailos-and-the-ethics-of-preservation.

7   Alfred North Whitehead discusses this principle in regard to all matter. Alfred North Whitehead, *Process and Reality: An Essay in Cosmology*, eds. Donald W. Sherburne and David Ray Griffin (New York: Free Press, 1985), p. 249.

8   Leonardo da Vinci thought that cracks are endemic to all structures. "Parallel cracks are constantly appearing in buildings erected in mountainous places where the rocks are stratified and the stratification runs obliquely, for, in these oblique seams, water and other moisture often penetrates, bearing with it a quantity of greasy and slimy earth; and since this stratification does not continue down to the bottom of the valleys the rocks go slipping down their slope, and never end their movement until they have descended to the bottom of the valley, carrying with them after the manner of a boat such part of the building as they have severed from the rest." Leonardo da Vinci, "Of Cracks in Walls Wide at the Base and Narrow at the Top and Their Cause," *The Notebooks of Leonardo Da Vinci*, vol. 2, chap. 38, in *Architecture*, ed. and trans. Edward Maccurdy (New York: George Braziller, 1958), no. 1048, https://archive.org/stream/notebooksofleona027479mbp /notebooksofleona027479mbp_djvu.txt; Peter Galison, in Carolyn Y. Johnson, "What the Rohrschach Tells Us: To Harvard's Peter Galison, the Inkblot Test Looks a Lot Like a Turning Point for Society," *Boston Globe*, June 10, 2012, https://www.bostonglobe.com/ideas/2012/06/09/what-rorschach -test-really-shows/06Fky1ZiXe26WF9DvxqvuL/story.html.

9   John Ruskin, the Victorian art and architecture historian, recommended examining buildings from a distance of one foot away. In the preface to *The Stones of Venice*, he wrote: "Every date in question was determinable only by internal evidence, and it became necessary for me to examine not only every one of the older palaces, stone by stone, but every fragment throughout the city which afforded any clue to the formation of its styles." Consequently, "my account of every building is based on personal examination and measurement of it," and "how much greater becomes the likelihood of error in the description of things which must be in many parts observed from a distance." John Ruskin, "Preface to the First Edition" (1851), in *The Works of John Ruskin*, vol. 9, *The Stones of Venice*, eds. Edward Tyas Cook and Alexander D. O. Wedderburn (New York: Longmans, Green, 1903–1912), pp. 4–5.

10   Bruno Latour, "Do Scientific Objects Have a History?: Pasteur and Whitehead in a Bath of Lactic Acid," *Common Knowledge* 5.1 (Spring 1996), pp. 76–91.

11   Thanks to our research fellow, Nabil Ahmed, who reported on this from Bangladesh. Sujaul Khan, "Never Again," *The Daily Star*, April 30, 2013, http://www.thedailystar.net/news/never-again-2; Sarah Butler and Saad Hammadi, "Rana Plaza Factory Disaster: Victims Still Waiting for Compensation," *Guardian*, October 23, 2013, https://www.theguardian.com/world/2013/oct/23/rana-plaza-factory-disaster-compensation-bangladesh.

12   Dana Behrman, "Born Again Landscape: The Politicisation of Archaeology and Architecture, the Case of Wadi Hilwa / City of David, East Jerusalem," master's thesis in research architecture, Centre for Research Architecture, Goldsmiths, University of London, 2010; Salim Siam et al. v. Municipality of Jerusalem et al. HCJ8938/08, in Hebrew, http://www.acri.org.il/pdf/petitions/hit8938.pdf; The Hashemite Kingdom of Jordan and the State of Palestine, "Status Report on the State of Conservation of the Old City of Jerusalem and Its Walls," presented to the UNESCO World Heritage Center, January 30, 2014.

13   Nir Hasson, "In a Tunnel Beneath Jerusalem, Israel's Culture Minister Gives Obama a Lesson on History," *Haaretz*, December 31, 2016, http://www.haaretz.com/israel-news/.premium=1.761757.

14   This expansion recalls the work of Leonard Horner — the nineteenth-century factory inspector for Lancashire (and an amateur geologist) who, by exposing poor working conditions in the garment industries (how little has changed!), according to Karl Marx, "rendered an undying service to the English working class…that should never be forgotten." Karl Marx, "Condition of Factory Labourers," April 7, 1857 (first published in *New York Daily Tribune*, no. 4994, April 22, 1857), http://marxengels.public-archive.net/en/ME1006en.html. See http://hutnyk.wordpress.com/2012/01/27/leonard-horner-hall.

15   See Eyal Weizman, *The Least of All Possible Evils: Humanitarian Violence from Arendt to Gaza* (London: Verso, 2011), pp. 131–32.

16   Forensic Architecture has confirmed this in relation to two conflicts: Israel's attack on Gaza in 2008–2009 and in relation to drone warfare in Pakistan's Federally Administered Tribal Area. The Gaza casualties assessment was presented in my introduction to "Forensic Epidemiology: Mortality Research in the Field and Forums of Contemporary Conflict," a workshop organized by CRASH/MSF and the Centre for Research Architecture / Goldsmiths, December 7–8, 2012, http://www.forensic-architecture.org/seminar/forensic-epidemiology. Our data related to Pakistan were presented in Alice K. Ross and Jack Serle, "Most US Drone Strikes in Pakistan Attack Houses," Bureau of Investigative Journalism, May 23, 2014, https://www.thebureauinvestigates.com/2014/05/23/most-us-drone-strikes-in-pakistan-attack-houses.

17   See Forensic Architecture, "Living Death Camps: Staro Sajmište/Omarska, Former Yugoslavia," http://www.forensic-architecture.org/case/living-death-camps. For Forensic Architecture: Eyal Weizman, Susan Schuppli, Francesco Sebregondi, Srdjan Jovanovic Weiss. In partnership with Grupa Spomenik of the Monument Group, Caroline Sturdy Colls of the Centre of Archaeology at Staffordshire University, and Matthew Shaw and William Trossell from ScanLAB Projects. For the archaeological report, see Caroline Sturdy Colls, "An Archaeological Assessment of the Area of the Former Judenlager and Anhaltlager at Staro Sajmište, Belgrade, Serbia," paper presented at the Fifty-Fourth October Salon, Belgrade, Serbia, October 2013. A summary exists in Caroline Sturdy Colls, *Holocaust Archaeologies: Approaches and Future Directions* (Cham: Springer, 2015), pp. 98–101. For the Stockholm Declaration, see International Holocaust Remembrance Alliance, "Declaration of the Stockholm International Forum on the Holocaust of 2000," https://www.holocaustremembrance.com/about-us/stockholm-declaration.

18   The Forensic Architecture home page is http://www.forensic-architecture.org. See also our book, *Forensic: The Architecture of Public Truth*.

19   Thomas Keenan, "Counter-forensics and Photography," *Grey Room* 55 (Spring 2014), pp. 58–77. The term first appeared in Allan Sekula, "Photography and the Limits of National Identity," *Culturefront* 2.3 (Fall 1993), pp. 54–55. Keenan explicates the notion: counterforensics "is employed by human rights investigators and their colleagues (including forensic anthropologists, photographers, and psychotherapists) in order to challenge oppressive regimes or respond to their aftermath." Sekula writes, referring principally to the work of Clyde Snow and Susan Meiselas in Kurdistan after the first Gulf War: "Counter forensics, the exhumation and identification of the anonymized ('disappeared') bodies of the oppressor state's victims, becomes the key to a process of political resistance and mourning." See Forensic Architecture, "Lexicon: Counter-Forensics," http://www.forensic-architecture.org/lexicon/counter-forensics.

20   The forum was a busy place: among other things, a market, a meeting place, the place where the courts convened. Cicero used the adjective *forensis* in a number of his speeches, and while this was often meant in the broader sense, as the general art of the forum, he seems at times to have used it in the more narrow, legal sense. In the Middle Ages, the Flemish translator Willem van Moerbeke used *forensis* to translate the Greek adjective *dikanikos*, which appears in Aristotle's *Rhetoric* and which literally means "judicial." This was an unambiguously legal use of *forensis*, though restricted to the way lawyers plead. The English language absorbed the Latin term in the form "forensic" only in the seventeenth century. The original meaning — pertaining to the forum or the courts — persisted into the early nineteenth century, when Thomas Carlyle spoke of "forensic eloquence." Only in the mid-nineteenth century, during a time of great scientific development, did the term "forensic" become used to denote a legal-scientific investigation.

21   Thomas Keenan and Eyal Weizman, *Mengele's Skull: The Advent of a Forensic Aesthetics* (Berlin: Sternberg Press, 2012), p. 28; Thomas Keenan, "Getting the Dead to Tell Me What Happened: Justice, Prosopopoeia, and Forensic Afterlives," in *Forensis*, p. 38. Quintilian discusses prosopopoeia in *Institutes of Oratory; or, Education of an Orator*, trans. John Selby Watson (London: G. Bell and Sons, 1903), bk. 9, chap. 2. See also Carlo Ginzburg, *Threads and Traces: True False Fictive*, trans. Anne C. Tedeschi and John Tedeschi (Berkeley: University of California Press, 2012).

22   Quintilian, *Institutes of Oratory*, bk. 9, chap. 2.

23   *Ibid.*, bk. 4, chap. 2.

24   Allen Feldman, "Securocratic Wars of Public Safety: Globalized Policing as Scopic Regime," *Interventions: International Journal of Postcolonial Studies* 6.3 (November 2004), p. 332.

25   Weizman, *The Least of All Possible Evils*, pp. 105–106.

26   Matthew Fuller and Nikita Mazurov, "How to Construct a Counter-Forensic Audit Trail: Disassembling the Case of The H8ful (CM)8," in "Posthumanities," *Theory, Culture and Society*, ed. Matt Fuller, special issue, forthcoming.

27   See Weizman, *The Least of All Possible Evils*.

28   Sometimes international forums emerge around the evidence. The International Criminal Tribunal for former Yugoslavia (ICTY) was established by the UN in 1993 soon after the beginning of the Bosnian war and the discovery of evidence of extreme violence there. The International Criminal Tribunal for Rwanda (ICTR) emerged after the massacres in Rwanda. See UN Security Council Resolution 808, adopted by the Security Council at its 3175th meeting, February 22, 1993, S/RES/808 and UN Security Council, *Report of the Committee of French Jurists on the Establishment of an International Criminal Tribunal to Judge the Crimes Committed in the Former Yugoslavia*, February 10, 1993, S/25266. The establishment of the court was seen by many as a way of intervening in

what was then a still ongoing conflict, while others thought it was established, alongside a strategy of sending humanitarian assistance, precisely in order *not* to intervene militarily in the conflict. Allison Marston Danner and Jenny S. Martinez, "Guilty Associations: Joint Criminal Enterprise, Command Responsibility, and the Development of International Criminal Law," *California Law Review* 93.1 (2005), pp. 75–169.

29 David Kretzmer, *The Occupation of Justice: The Supreme Court of Israel and the Occupied Territories* (Albany: State University of New York University Press, 2002); Weizman, *The Least of All Possible Evils*, especially the section "A Legislative Attack" in chapter 3. David Kennedy, *Of War and Law* (Princeton: Princeton University Press, 2006), p. 6.

30 Department of Defense, *Law of War Manual*, June 2015, http://www.dod.mil/dodgc/images/law_war_manual15.pdf.

31 Charles J. Dunlap, "Lawfare: A Decisive Element of 21st-Century Conflicts?," *Joint Force Quarterly* 3 (2009), p. 39, http://scholarship.law.duke.edu/cgi/viewcontent.cgi?article=6034&context=faculty_scholarship; Charles J. Dunlap, "Law and Military Interventions: Preserving Humanitarian Values in 21st-Century Conflicts," paper delivered at the conference Humanitarian Challenges in Military Intervention, Carr Center for Human Rights Policy in the Kennedy School of Government, Harvard University, November 29, 2001, http://people.duke.edu/~pfeaver/dunlap.pdf. See also Charles Dunlap, "Lawfare Amid Warfare," *Washington Times*, August 3, 2007.

32 Forensic Architecture, "Drone Strikes: Investigating Covert Operations through Spatial Media, Case no. 4: Gaza," http://www.forensic-architecture.org/case/drone-strikes; Breaking the Silence, "This Is How We Fought in Gaza: Soldiers' Testimonies and Photographs from 'Operation Protective Edge' (2014)," May 2015, p. 18, http://www.breakingthesilence.org.il/pdf/Protective Edge.pdf; United Nations Human Rights Council, *Report of the Special Rapporteur on the Promotion and Protection of Human Rights and Fundamental Freedoms While Countering Terrorism* (March 2014), p. 17, http://www.ohchr.org/EN/HRBodies/HRC/RegularSessions/Session25/Documents/A-HRC-25-59.doc; Protocol Additional to the Geneva Conventions of 12 August 1949 and relating to the Protection of Victims of International Armed Conflicts, article 57, paragraph 3, https://treaties.un.org/doc/Publication/UNTS/Volume%201125/volume-1125-I-17512-English.pdf. The UN commission concluded that roof knocks cannot be considered an effective warning, given the confusion they often cause to building residents and the short time allowed to evacuate before the actual strike. The Palestinian writer Adania Shibli told me how, during the 2014 Gaza war, she was in Ramallah, but still received warning calls to evacuate her building. Presumably her phone was mistakenly thought to be in Gaza. The story demonstrates the fact that the targeting of the warning messages can be as imprecisely targeted as the missile that follows.

33 For Forensic Architecture: Eyal Weizman, Susan Schuppli, Jacob Burns, Steffen Kraemer, Reiner Beelitz, Samir Harb, Zahra Hussain, Francesco Sebregondi. For Situ Research: Bradley Samuels, Akshay Mehra, Charles Perrault, Xiaowei Wang, McKenna Cole. Collaborators: Office of the United Nations Special Rapporteur on Counter-Terrorism and Human Rights (Ben Emmerson QC, Annie O'Reilly, Sarika Arya), Al Mezan Center for Human Rights (Nuriya Oswald), Amnesty International (Mustafa Qadri), Al-Jazeera (Ana Naomi de Sousa), Chris Cobb-Smith (munitions expert and consultant), Myra Macdonald (freelance journalist).

34 Lorraine Daston and Peter Galison, *Objectivity* (New York: Zone Books, 2010). Objectivity, Daston and Galison showed, is based on the negation of whatever constitutes subjectivity — the personality and position of the scientists, perceived as an obstacle to knowledge.

35 For one of many such examples, see the reaction of NGO Monitor, an organization that covers the NGO community from a pro-Israel perspective, to the July 2015 launch of Amnesty Inter-

national and our Gaza Platform: "For this project, Amnesty is partnering with a group by the name of Forensic Architecture, headed by Eyal Weitzman [sic.]. Weitzman is a former board member of the Israeli political NGO B'Tselem and signed a petition during the 2009 Gaza conflict calling for the UN Security Council and the EU to impose sanctions on Israel." NGO Monitor, "Amnesty's 'Gaza Platform': All Window Dressing, No Substance," July 7, 2015, http://www .ngo-monitor.org/press-releases/nothing_but_window_dressing_amnesty_international_s_new _gaza_platform_; Gerald Steinberg, "EU Research Funds Wasted on Amnesty's Hollywood-Style CSI Adventure," NGO Monitor, August 13, 2015, http://www.ngo-monitor.org/in-the-media/eu _research_funds_wasted_on_amnesty_s_hollywood_style_csi_adventure.

36 On March 5, 2013, our report on white phosphorous was submitted to Israel's High Court in the context of a petition demanding the ban of the use of such munitions in urban environments. Its admission as evidence encountered strong objections by the Israeli military and the state's attorney, who questioned the competence of a team of architects to provide expertise on the military matters at stake in the case.

37 Sheera Frenkel, "Israel Backs Down over White Phosphorus," *Times* (London), April 23, 2009, http://www.thetimes.co.uk/tto/news/world/middleeast/article2604703.ece.

38 For Forensic Architecture: Eyal Weizman, Francesco Sebregondi. For Situ Research: Bradley Samuels, Akshay Mehra, Charles Perrault. Collaborators: Michael Sfard Law Office (Michael Sfard, Emily Schaeffer), Human Rights Watch—Arms Division (Stephen Goose, Bonnie Docherty, Mary Wareham), Chris Cobb-Smith (munitions expert and consultant). The report, *The Use of White Phosphorus Munitions in Urban Environments: An Effects-Based Analysis*, was published in two versions. The online interactive version can be accessed at http:// forensic-architecture.org/White Phosphorus. The printable PDF version can be accessed at http://www.forensic-architecture .org/wp-content/uploads/2014/05/WP-print-report-FINAL.pdf. It supported an ongoing campaign demanding amendment of existing international humanitarian law to close a loophole that did not consider it among the banned "incendiary weapons," an initiative led by Human Rights Watch and the Harvard Law School International Human Rights Clinic. Protocol III of the Convention on Prohibitions or Restrictions on the Use of Certain Conventional Weapons Which May Be Deemed to Be Excessively Injurious or to Have Indiscriminate Effects, adopted in 1980, prohibits the deployment of incendiary weapons in densely populated areas. Yet in its article 1, incendiary weapons are defined as weapons "primarily designed" to set fire to objects. Because white phosphorus munitions are designed as smoke munitions whose incendiary effects are considered only "secondary" or "incidental," white phosphorus is said not to fall within the category of weapons regulated by the protocol. See "Protocol on Prohibitions or Restrictions on the Use of Incendiary Weapons (Protocol III)," Geneva, October 10, 1980, https://www.icrc.org/ihl/PT1RO/515; "Israel Used White Phosphorus in Gaza Civilian Areas," Amnesty International, January 19, 2009, https://www.amnesty.org/en/latest/news/2009/01/israel-used-white-phosphorus-gaza-civilian -areas-20090119/; Human Rights Watch, *Rain of Fire: Israel's Unlawful Use of White Phosphorus in Gaza*, March 25, 2009, https://www.hrw.org/report/2009/03/25/rain-fire/israels-unlawful -use-white-phosphorus-gaza. For the Israeli position, see "IDF White Phosphorus Use Not Illegal," *Jerusalem Post*, January 13, 2009, http://www.jpost.com/Israel/IDF-white-phosphorus-use -not-illegal.

39 The court case is HCJ 4146/11, with the opinion delivered on May 13, 2013: "Because of our decision [to dismiss the petition] we have not authorized the request to admit the report as evidence. Nevertheless if the question will rise again and it would be necessary to examine the fine details of the case, we shall reexamine the dispute between the parties concerning the relevance of the

expertise of the report's authors." The full judgment is available, in Hebrew, at http://elyon1
.court.gov.il/files/11/460/041/b10/11041460.b10.htm.

40 Idan Landau, "Israel Gives Up White Phosphorus, Because 'It Doesn't Photograph Well.'" +972,
April 28, 2013, http://972mag.com/israel-gives-up-white-phosphorus-because-it-doesnt
-photograph-well/70063; Gili Cohen, "IDF to Stop Using Shells with White Phosphorus in
Populated Areas, State Tells High Court," Haaretz, May 13, 2013, http://www.haaretz.com/israel
-news/idf-to-stop-using-shells-with-white-phosphorus-in-populated-areas-state-tells-high-court
.premium-1.523852; Human Rights Watch, Rain of Fire.

41 There are of course several precedents to the work of the EAAF. During World War II, it was the Nazis
who organized one of the first mass exhumations, when the remains of Polish officers massacred by
the Soviets in Katyn were displayed for propaganda purposes. Karel Berkhoff, "Bykivnia: How Grave
Robbers, Activists, and Foreigners Ended Official Silence about Stalin's Mass Graves near Kiev," in
Human Remains and Identification: Mass Violence, Genocide and the 'Forensic Turn,' eds. Élisabeth
Anstett and Jean-Marc Dreyfus (Manchester: Manchester University Press, 2015), pp. 72–73.

42 Keenan and Weizman, Mengele's Skull, p. 19. Snow had arrived in Argentina in February 1984 with
a group of other forensic scientists assembled by the American Academy for the Advancement of
Science (AAAS) at the invitation of the National Commission on the Disappeared (CONADEP).
This followed an appeal from the Asociación Civil Abuelas de Plaza de Mayo. Snow then trained
the first team of the Equipo Argentino de Antropología Forense. See Christopher Joyce and Eric
Stover, Witnesses from the Grave: The Stories Bones Tell (Boston: Little, Brown, 1991), pp. 215–49;
Eyal Weizman, "Osteobiography: An Interview with Clyde Snow," Cabinet 43 (Fall 2011); Adam
Rosenblatt, Digging for the Disappeared: Forensic Science after Atrocity (Stanford: Stanford Uni-
versity Press, 2015), pp. 3–4. See also Luis Fondebrider "Forensic Architecture and the Investiga-
tion of Political Violence: Lessons Learned from Latin America and the Balkans," and Antonius
C. G. M. Robben, "Exhumations, Territoriality, and Necropolitics in Chile and Argentina," in Nec-
ropolitics: Mass Graves and Exhumations in the Age of Human Rights, eds. Francisco Ferrándiz and
Antonius C.G.M. Robben (Philadelphia: University of Pennsylvania Press, 2015), pp. 41–52, 53–75.

43 Rosenblatt, Digging for the Disappeared, p. 4.

44 Anselm Franke, "The Forensic Scenography," in Forensis, p. 494.

45 Luis Moreno Ocampo, Keynote lecture at the Architecture of Public Truth Conference, March 16,
2014, HKW, Forensis, https://www.youtube.com/watch?v=QH3601ETeuA.

46 Roxana Ferllini and Alexandra M. Croft, "The Case of an Armenian Mass Grave," Journal of Human
Rights 8.3 (June 2009), pp. 229–44.

47 After exhumations organized by Spain's Asociación para la Recuperación de la Memoria Histórica
(ARMH) were considered illegal, on October 16, 2008, Spanish judge Baltasar Garzón considered
the 1977 amnesty law for crimes committed during the civil war to be not applicable to the disappeared resting in thousands of mass graves and declared the court competent to investigate the
massacres. The controversy led to the institution of other judiciary processes meant to stop exhumations. On May 2010, Garzón was suspended from judicial activity. Ferrándiz and Robben, "Introduction: The Ethnography of Exhumations," in Necropolitics, pp. 1–38. In regard to the exhumations, see also the work of the Asociación para la Recuperación de la Memoria Histórica, http://
memoriahistorica.org.es. On the problems and difficulties of exhuming the bodies of victims of
Stalinist terror in the Voronezh region some 500 kilometers south of Moscow, see Viacheslav Bitu-
itcki, "State Secrets and Concealed Bodies: Exhumations of Soviet-Era Victims in Contemporary
Russia," in Human Remains and Identification, pp. 98–116. On the exposure of the photographic
process involved in the purges, see Tomasz Kizny, "The Great Terror in the USSR: Portraits of the

Victims of a State Crime," in *Images of Conviction: The Construction of Visual Evidence,* ed. Diane Dufour (Paris: Le-Bal and Éditions Xavier Barral, 2015), pp. 109–29.

48   Michal Givoni, "Witnessing in Action: Ethics and Politics in a World without Borders," in *The Power of Inclusive Exclusion: Anatomy of Israeli Rule in the Occupied Palestinian Territories*, eds. Adi Ophir, Michal Givoni, and Sari Hanafi (New York: Zone Books, 2009); Michal Givoni, *The Ethics of Witnessing: A History of a Problem* (Jerusalem: The Van Leer Jerusalem Institute and Hakibbutz Hameuchad Publishing, 2015), in Hebrew.

49   Felman and Laub, *Testimony: Crises of Witnessing in Literature, Psychoanalysis and History* (London: Routledge, 1991); Annette Wieviorka, *The Era of the Witness*, trans. Jared Stark (Ithaca: Cornell University Press, 2006). According to Hannah Arendt, the Eichmann trial relied too much on victim testimonies. See Weizman, *The Least of All Possible Evils*, chap. 4; Keenan and Weizman, *Mengele's Skull*, pp. 11–12.

50   Yve-Alain Bois, Michel Feher, Hal Foster, and Eyal Weizman, "On Forensic Architecture: A Conversation with Eyal Weizman," *October* 156 (Spring 2016), pp. 116–40.

51   Weizman, *The Least of All Possible Evils*, p. 113; Michal Givoni, "Witnessing in Action," in *The Power of Inclusive Exclusion*.

52   If popular entertainment is any indicator of the cultural shift toward forensic fetishism, then it is significant that from the television *CSI* series to the novels of Patricia Cornwell and the former forensics expert Kathy Reichs, the scientist-detective has gradually taken the place of the psychologist/psychoanalyst-detective popular in TV dramas throughout the 1980s and 1990s, which often reflected the emphasis on psychology by such novelists as Agatha Christie.

53   Haglund, working in Rwanda, was quoted saying: "The dead are speaking to us. We are interpreting for the dead. The dead are telling us the same story that the living told the investigators. But this is the first time on this scale that they have been allowed to speak." James C. McKinley, Jr., "From a Grave in Rwanda, Hundreds of Dead Tell Their Tale," *New York Times*, February 16, 1996, quoted in Keenan, "Getting the Dead to Tell Me What Happened," pp. 35–40. For Snow's quote, see Weizman, "Osteobiography: An Interview with Clyde Snow."

54   Keenan and Weizman, *Mengele's Skull*, pp. 18–19.

55   Shela Sheikh, "Forensic Theater: Grupa Spomenik's Pythagorean Lecture. Mathemes of Reassociation," in *Forensis*, pp. 166–88; When more than 70 percent of the bone mass of a single person was collected, the bones were formally considered a single individual worthy of reburial, according to Islamic beliefs. Some of the victims who were shot and put into mass graves considered themselves to be secular Yugoslavs, but were inhumed with a religious identity. This reflected the process of Yugoslav's ethic division.

56   *The Mineral Geology of Genocide*, directed by Paulo Tavares and Eyal Weizman (2012), http://archive.forensic-architecture.org/audio-video/the-mineral-geology-of-genocide.

57   For Forensic Architecture: Eyal Weizman, Christina Varvia, Hania Jamal, Lawrence Abu Hamdan, Ana Naomi de Sousa, Gochan Yildirim — 1635film-istanbul, Stefan Laxness, Pierre-Francois Gerard, Samaneh Moafi, Hana Rizvanolli, Simone Rowat, George Clipp, Yamen Albadin, Hala Makhlouf, Mihai Meirosu, Yamen Albadin, Hala Makhlouf, Ghias Aljundi, and Nestor Rubio.

58   Amnesty International, "'It Breaks the Human': Torture, Disease and Death in Syria's Prisons," August 17, 2016, http://www.amnestyusa.org/research/reports/%E2%80%98it-breaks-the-human-torture-disease-and-death-in-syria-s-prisons.

59   Abu Hamdan, quoted in Oliver Wainwright, "'The Worst Place on Earth': Inside Assad's Brutal Saydnaya Prison," *Guardian*, August 18, 2016, https://www.theguardian.com/artanddesign/2016/aug/18/saydnaya-prison-syria-assad-amnesty-reconstruction.

60 See, for one example, Alain Badiou, *Ethics: An Essay on the Understanding of Evil*, trans. Peter Hallward (London: Verso, 2001).

61 Michael Sfrad, a human rights lawyer and a frequent collaborator, explained that "architects were now those able to show lawyers things that lawyers can't see." Michael Sfrad, in conversation at his office, January 2013. He repeated a similar point in a conversation with Susan Schuppli at The Architecture of Public Truth conference at the Haus der Kulturen der Welt, Berlin, organized alongside the opening of the *Forensis* exhibition, March 2014, http://www.hkw.de/en/programm /projekte/veranstaltung/p_100468.php.

62 Keenan and Weizman, *Mengele's Skull*, p. 24.

63 Bruno Latour, "The Anthropocene and the Destruction of the Image of the Globe," Latour's fourth Gifford Lecture, delivered February 25, 2013, http://www.ed.ac.uk/humanities-soc-sci/news -events/lectures/gifford-lectures/archive/series-2012-2013/bruno-latour/lecture-four.

64 Whitehead, *Process and Reality*, pp. 3–4, 249. "Non-sensuous perception" for Whitehead is limited to living entities, but it is suggestive of the possibility of its extension because perception, for him, is not limited to the human or even to the living, but is a property of all material forms. See also Melanie Sehgal, "A Situated Metaphysics: Things, History, and Pragmatic Speculation in A.N. Whitehead," in *The Allure of Things*, eds. Roland Faber and Andrew Goffey (London: Bloomsbury, 2014). See also John Durham Peters, *The Marvelous Clouds: Toward a Philosophy of Elemental Media* (Chicago: University of Chicago Press, 2015), p. 4.

65 In the opening pages of *Matter and Memory*, Henri Bergson writes: "Matter is an aggregate of 'images.' And by 'image' we mean a certain existence which is more than that which the idealist calls a representation, but less than that which the realist calls a thing—an existence placed halfway between the 'thing' and the 'representation.'" Henri Bergson, *Matter and Memory*, trans. Nancy M. Paula and W. Scott Palmer (New York: Zone Books, 1988), p. 9.

66 Susan Schuppli examines the procedures by which media artifacts in the archive of the ICTY were turned into evidence. As she follows the movement of videotapes, satellite images, maps, and recording devices through a juridical matrix that sorts, archives, catalogs, and presents them, these objects become what she calls "material witnesses": that is, they bear witness not only to the alleged criminal events, but to the very sorting process they underwent in order to qualify as evidence. Susan Schuppli, "Entering Evidence: Cross-Examining the Court Records of the ICTY," in *Forensis*, pp. 263–300. See also Susan Schuppli, *A Material Witness: Forensic Media and the Making of Evidence* (Cambridge, MA: MIT Press, forthcoming).

67 The Model Court collective describes the ways in which new audio-visual and telecommunication technologies, their material presence, digital properties, interruptions, and breakdowns outline the contemporary sphere of universal jurisdiction. Their film and installation *Resolution 978HD* (2013) follows the genocide trial of François Bazaramba, a Rwandan national, in a district court of Porvoo, Finland. The court was set up in a local basketball court. Because the trial necessitated the remote interrogation of the accused via teleconference, the legal principle of habeas corpus, which usually demands the physical presence of the accused, was reinterpreted as the threshold condition of various technologies—bandwidth, resolution, and automatic light detectors—that would allow the remotely assembled court to see a person blush or sweat. Lawrence Abu Hamdan, Sidsel Meineche Hansen, Lorenzo Pezzani, and Oliver Rees (Model Court), "Resolution 978HD: A Visual Essay," in *Forensis*, pp. 310–17, http://www.forensic-architecture.org/file/resolution-978hd. In the 1945 Nuremberg trials, in which twenty-one major Nazi war criminals faced judgment, films were screened as part of the process, and the proceedings were themselves filmed. American architect Dan Kiley supervised the refurbishment of the old Nuremberg court. The innovation was that the

judges were placed to one side, facing the accused, while the central perspective was occupied by the screen, allowing the public a direct view of it. The screen served as a link between the accused, the judges, and the public. During his opening address Judge Jackson said, "We will show you these concentration camps in motion pictures, just as the Allied armies found them when they arrived." A film, shot at Dachau on May 5, 6, and 7, 1945, by the Special Coverage Unit (SPECOU) was screened on November 29, 1945. Christian Delage, "The Nuremberg Trials: Confronting the Nazis with the Images of Their Crimes," in *Images of Conviction*, pp. 131–49. For more on the use of media in the Nuremberg trials, see Cornelia Vismann, "Tele-Tribunals: Anatomy of a Medium," *Grey Room* 10 (Winter 2003). The 1961 Eichmann trial in Jerusalem saw the first use of video cameras in this process. See Rony Brauman and Eyal Sivan, *Adolf Eichmann: The Nazi Criminal Who Organized the Destruction of the Jewish People* (Turin: Einaudi, 2003). And see their film *The Specialist: Portrait of a Modern Criminal* (1999). In the context of the more recent process of the tribunals of the ICTR and the ICTY, videos are used extensively. On the media architecture of the ICTY, see Laura Kurgan, "Residues: ICTY Courtroom No. 1 and the Architecture of Justice," in *Alphabet City 7: Social Insecurity*, eds. Cornelius Heesters and Len Guenther (Toronto: House of Anansi, 2000), pp. 112–29; Susan Schuppli, "Entering Evidence," in *Forensis*. For more recent changes to the British court system, see BBC, "TV Cameras Allowed into Court of Appeal," October 31, 2013, http://www.bbc.co.uk/news/uk-24744684. The new building of the ICC, which opened in early 2016, was designed to closely integrate physical and media architecture.

68 Harun Farocki, *Eye/Machine III*, www.harunfarocki.de/installations/2000s/2003/eye-machine-iii; Thomas Elsaesser, "Harun Farocki: Filmmaker, Artist, Media Theorist," in *Harun Farocki: Working the Sight-Lines*, ed. Thomas Elsaesser (Amsterdam: Amsterdam University Press, 2004), pp. 11–41. See also Jimena Canales, *Harun Farocki and Trevor Paglen: Visibility Machines (Issues in Cultural Theory)*, ed. Niels Van Tomme (University of Maryland, Baltimore County: Center for Art, Design and Visual Culture, 2015). For a critique of the term, see Trevor Paglen, "Operational Images," *e-flux* 59 (November 2014), http://www.e-flux.com/journal/operational-images.

69 Laura Kurgan, *Close Up at a Distance: Mapping, Technology, and Politics* (New York: Zone Books, 2013); Andrew Herscher, "Envisioning Exception: Satellite Imagery, Human Rights Advocacy, and Techno-Moral Witnessing," lecture at the Centre for Research Architecture, Goldsmiths, University of London, March 4, 2013. For this and other recorded lectures on remote sensing, see http://www.forensic-architecture.org/seminars/sensing-injustice. Andrew Herscher, "Surveillant Witnessing: Satellite Imagery and the Visual Politics of Human Rights," *Public Culture* 26.3 (2014); Lisa Parks, *Cultures in Orbit: Satellites and the Televisual* (Durham: Duke University Press, 2005). In the human rights context, satellite images are always exclusively presented in pairs of "before and after" images, as in the following: In 2002, Eritrea used satellite images to document village destruction in a case it brought against Ethiopia in the International Court of Justice in The Hague. In 2003, the United States Committee for Human Rights in North Korea released a report based on satellite images of prison camps in North Korea titled *The Hidden Gulag: Exposing North Korea's Prison Camps*. In 2004, Human Rights Watch's report *Raising Rafah: Mass Home Demolitions in the Gaza Strip* used satellite images in order to document the number of buildings destroyed by Israel. In 2007, Eyes on Darfur, a project pursued by Amnesty International and the American Academy for the Advancement of Science, documented eighteen sites of destroyed villages in Darfur.

70 Kurgan, *Close up at a Distance*, p. 117. Andrew Herscher has suggested that the fact that these surveillance technologies originate in military technologies, and are equally used by militaries—a hybrid visual practice of surveillance and human rights witnessing that he has called "surveillant witnessing"—coupled with the fact that human rights violations are sometimes noted by states

and militaries as among the justifications for war, compromises the work of human right groups. Herscher, "Surveillant Witnessing."

71   During the 2001 US attack on Afghanistan, the Pentagon bought exclusive rights to pictures of the country produced by American Imaging's satellites, especially those made by the provider Ikonos. US spy satellites, Keyholes, take photographic images estimated to be six to ten times sharper than the 1.0-meter resolution available from Ikonos in 2001. Duncan Campbell, "US Buys Up All Satellite War Images," *Guardian*, October 17, 2001, https://www.theguardian.com/world/2001/oct/17/physicalsciences.afghanistan.

72   See Ariella Azoulay's definition of the "event" of photography in Ariella Azoulay, *The Civil Contract of Photography* (New York: Zone Books, 2008), p. 14. The event of photography, according to Azoulay, is a set of political relations between those photographing, those being photographed, and those reproducing, circulating, interpreting, and making claims on behalf of images. For her, the photographic image is a material diagram through which it is possible to reconstruct the power relations at work in the photographic encounter.

73   The Lebanese artist Rabih Mroué showed what price photographing or videoing soldiers could entail. He collected videos from the Syrian civil war. One of them shows a group of soldiers moving along a street corner. One of these soldiers is seen locking sight with the videographer, raising his gun, and then the camera records its own fall to the ground. Shouts are heard before the clip abruptly ends. *The Pixelated Revolution* is a lecture-performance by Mroué about the use of mobile-phone images during the Syrian revolution. Rabih Mroué, *The Pixelated Revolution* (2012), https://vimeo.com/119433287. See also Hito Steyerl, *The Wretched of the Screen* (Berlin: Sternberg Press, 2012).

74   In the early 2000s, human rights groups such as Witness and B'Tselem in Palestine began distributing hand-held cameras within conflict zones, but the widespread availability of smart phones in more recent years has made that practice redundant. Keller Easterling, "Broadband," *Extrastatecraft: The* Power *of Infrastructure Space* (London: Verso, 2015).

75   Susan Sontag, *Regarding the Pain of Others* (New York: Picador, 2003); Azoulay, *The Civil Contract of Photography*. See also *Antiphotojournalism*, an exhibition curated by Carles Guerra and Thomas Keenan, La Virreina Centre de l'Imatge, Barcelona, July 5 – October 10, 2010, http://antiphotojournalism.blogspot.co.uk.

76   Jacques Derrida and Bernard Steigler, "The Archive Market: Truth, Testimony, Evidence," *Echographies of Television: Filmed Interviews* (London: Polity, 2002), pp. 82–99.

77   See the work of Eliot Higgins, alias Brown Moses, a citizen journalist and blogger who uses open sources and social media to investigate conflict worldwide: https://www.bellingcat.com. His best-known cases are the Syrian civil war, 2014–2015, Russian military intervention in Ukraine, and the downing of Malaysia Airlines Flight 17. On Higgins and Forensic Architecture, see Ian Steadman: "Future Proof," *New Statesman*, September, 11, 2014, http://www.newstatesman.com/future-proof/2014/09/returning-gaze-everyone-s-war-reporter-always-connected-world.

78   The term "image complex" was proposed by Meg McLagan and Yates McKee, eds., *Sensible Politics: The Visual Culture of Nongovernmental Activism* (New York: Zone Books, 2012), pp. 12, 22, 23. For them, it is the multiplicity of visual evidence, including photographs, maps, videos, reports, charts, spaces, and bodies, through which politics is brought to visibility.

79   Ines Weizman and Eyal Weizman, *Before and After*: *Documenting the Architecture of Disaster* (Moscow: Strelka Press, 2014).

80   This text was first published in Weizman and Weizman, *Before and After*. The Paris scene is described in Mary Warner Marien, *Photography—A Cultural History* (London: Laurence King, 2006), pp. 44–45.

81 "Phnom Penh, Cambodia: 1973, 1985," in *Earthshots: Satellite Images of Environmental Change*, 8th ed., ed. Robert Wellmann Campbell (Sioux Falls, S.D.: USGS EROS Data Center, 2008), now available at https://cityofwater.wordpress.com/tag/mapping; *Kampuchea: Decade of the Genocide. Report of a Finnish Inquiry Commission*, ed. Kimmo Kiljunen (London: Zed Books, 1984). The Finnish Inquiry Commission estimated that about six hundred thousand people in a population of over seven million died during the bombing, while two million people became refugees. Between seventy-five thousand and one hundred and fifty thousand Cambodians were executed by the Khmer Rouge, while roughly one million died from hunger, disease, and overwork. For more about the Finnish Commission, see Edward S. Herman and Noam Chomsky, *Manufacturing Consent: The Political Economy of the Mass Media* (London: Vintage Books, 1994), p. 260. During these years, a political debate emerged within the Western Left between the "anti-imperialists" opposing the US bombing in Vietnam and Cambodia and the "antitotalitarians" who saw the Khmer Rouge as a totalitarian menace that called for international intervention. These two images suggest that these events represent one continuous and entangled disaster.

82 This project was coordinated and produced by Christina Varvia.

83 This project was coordinated by Stefan Laxness, with Christina Varvia as advisor.

84 For Forensic Architecture: Eyal Weizman. For Situ Research: Bradley Samuels, Therese Diede, Robert Beach. Collaborating organizations: Michael Sfard Law Office (Michael Sfard, Emily Schaeffer), B'Tselem (Sarit Michaeli). See also Forensic Architecture and Situ Research, "Bil'in: Reconstructing the Death of a Palestinian Demonstrator via Video Analysis," http://www.forensic-architecture.org/case/bilin; *Forensis*, pp. 83–91; IDF response: Lieut. Col. Naftali XXXXX, April 3, 2014. The Abu Rahma case is still ongoing.

85 Emad Burnat and Guy Davidi, *Five Broken Cameras* (2011).

86 The quote is attributed by Siegfried Kracauer to Marc Bloch in Carlo Ginzburg, "Microhistory: Two or Three Things That I Know About It," trans. John and Anne C. Tedeschi, *Critical Inquiry* 20.1 (Autumn 1993), p. 27.

87 Henri Lefebvre, *Rhythmanalysis: Space, Time and Everyday Life*, trans. Stuart Elden (London: Continuum, 2004). For a critique of militarized rhythmanalysis, see Derek Gregory, "From a View to a Kill: Drones and Late Modern War," *Theory, Culture and Society* 28.7–8 (2011), p. 188.

88 M.E. Tardu, "United Nations Response to Gross Violations of Human Rights: The 1503 Procedure," *Santa Clara Law Review* 20 (1980), p. 582; L. Fisler Damrosch, "Gross and Systematic Human Rights Violations," *Max Planck Encyclopaedia of Public International Law* (February 2011); C. Medina Quiroga, *The Battle of Human Rights: Gross, Systematic Violations and the Inter-American System* (Dordrecht: Martinus Nijhoff, 1988), pp. 8–9.

89 Dan McQuillan, "Algorithmic States of Exception," *European Journal of Cultural Studies* 18.4–5 (August–October 2015), pp. 564–76.

90 PATTRN is an open-source project hosted at Goldsmiths, University of London. The PATTRN project was initiated thanks to a Proof-of-Concept Grant from the European Research Council in the framework of Forensic Architecture (2014–2015). Project architect: Francesco Sebregondi; project coordinators: Nick Axel and Andrea Rota; major contributing authors: TEKJA Data (PATTRN front end) and Digital Consolidation (PATTRN editor).

91 Dipesh Chakrabarty, "The Climate of History: Four Theses," *Critical Inquiry* 35.2 (Winter 2009), pp. 197–222.

92 Environmental violence rests on the dual exploitation of humans and nature. See Chris Williams, "On the Nature and Causes of Environmental Violence," *Climate and Capitalism*, December 8, 2013, http://climateandcapitalism.com/2013/12/08/the-nature-and-causes-of-environmental-violence;

Stefania Barca, "Telling the Right Story: Environmental Violence and Liberation Narratives," *Environment and History* 20.4 (November 2014), pp. 535–46; Andrea Carmen and Viola Waghiyi, *Indigenous Women and Environmental Violence*, report submitted to the United Nations Permanent Forum on Indigenous Issues, January 18–20, 2012, http://www.un.org/esa/socdev/unpfii/documents/EGM12_carmen_waghiyi.pdf.

93 Rob Nixon, *Slow Violence and the Environmentalism of the Poor* (Cambridge, MA: Harvard University Press, 2011), p. 2.

94 While pathology deals with the individual body, epidemiology is concerned with the statistical measurement and spatial mapping of patterns of public health, disease, and mortality at the level of populations. What epidemiologists refer to as "indirect mortality" is the result of the destruction of the environmental conditions that sustain life. In a seminar organized by Forensic Architecture and Médecins Sans Frontières-France, we focused on the way in which emergent techniques for collecting, analyzing, and presenting conflict-related mortality data have been used as tools of political advocacy, supporting calls for intervention or abstention in recent debates around conflicts such as those in Sudan, Darfur, Burma, the Democratic Republic of Congo, and Iraq, among others. The sessions showed that despite being based on medical science and quantitative analysis (and because of its high political stakes), epidemiological figures are highly contested. Statistics in this field are based upon choices regarding whose deaths should be measured and calculated, what is to be left outside calculations, and what is deemed incalculable. See Forensic Epidemiology: Mortality Research in the Field and Forums of Contemporary Conflict, workshop organized by CRASH/MSF and the Centre for Research Architecture/Goldsmiths, December 7–8, 2012, http://www.forensic-architecture.org/seminar/forensic-epidemiology.

95 Nixon, *Slow Violence*, pp. 9, 41.

96 Meeting between Dr. Eric Baccard and a team from Forensic Architecture (including the author), International Criminal Court in The Hague, March 4, 2012.

97 Commission for Historical Clarification, *Guatemala: Memory of Silence*, http://www.aaas.org/sites/default/files/migrate/uploads/mos_en.pdf, pp. 33–57; Audrey R. Chapman and Patrick Ball, "The Truth of Truth Commissions: Comparative Lessons from Haiti, South Africa, and Guatemala," *Human Rights Quarterly* 23.1 (2001), pp. 1–43; Priscilla B. Hayner, *Unspeakable Truths: Facing the Challenge of Truth Commissions* (New York: Routledge, 2002).

98 Greg Grandin, *The Last Colonial Massacre: Latin America in the Cold War* (Chicago: University of Chicago Press, 2011).

99 For Forensic Architecture: Eyal Weizman, Paulo Tavares, Daniel Fernandez-Pascual, Hannah Meszaros-Martin. For Situ Research: Bradley Samuels, Akshay Mehra, Charles Perrault. Collaborators: CALDH — Centro para la Acción Legal en Derechos Humanos (Rodrigo Salvadó, Edwin Cannil), ODHAG — Oficina de Derechos Humanos del Arzobispado de Guatemala (Raul Nájera, Ana Carolina).

100 On May 10, 2013, Ríos Montt was convicted of genocide and crimes against humanity. The court found that under his regime, the "Ixils were considered public enemies of the state and were also victims of racism, considered an inferior race," and it sentenced Ríos Montt to eighty years in prison. The Constitutional Court of Guatemala overturned the conviction just ten days later, on May 20, 2013, and forced a retrial. In November 2013, in an attempt to bypass the legal blockage in Guatemala itself, Guatemalan prosecutors presented a petition at the Inter-American Commission on Human Rights in Washington. Forensic Architecture's investigation was presented in this context. Trial International, "Efrain Ríos Montt, https://trialinternational.org/latest-post/efrain-rios-montt.

101 Commission for Historical Clarification, *Guatemala: Memory of Silence*. Human rights statistician Patrick Ball estimated that the number of fatalities among the Ixil Maya during these years to be between 1,996 and 2,325. Rodrigo Baires Quezada, Oswaldo J. Hernández, and Patrick Ball, "Por qué los datos casan con la hipótesis de que hubo genocidio," *Plaza Pública*, April 23, 2013, https://www.plazapublica.com.gt/content/por-que-los-datos-casan-con-la-hipotesis-de-que-hubo -genocidio, in Spanish. The date for the Montt trial is continually postponed and has not yet been set. Amnesty International, "Ríos Montt's Trial Is the Ultimate Test for Guatemala's Justice system," January 7, 2016, http://www.amnestyusa.org/news/press-releases/rios-montt-s-trial-is-the -ultimate-test-for-guatemala-s-justice-system.

102 On the Ecuadorian constitution of the rights of nature see Paulo Tavares, "Nonhuman Rights," in *Forensis*, pp. 553–71; Paulo Tavares, "Murky Evidence," *Cabinet* 43 (Fall 2011), pp. 101–105. A central reference in this discussion is Christopher Stone, "Should Trees Have Standing?—Toward Legal Rights for Natural Objects," *Southern California Law Review* 450 (1972). There are other precedents such as rights to ecosystems granted in New Zealand. The first was the Whanganui River which, in a framework agreement between the Crown and the Māori people, was recognized as a person when it comes to the law. Sandra Postel, "A River in New Zealand Gets a Legal Voice," *National Geographic*, September 4, 2012.

103 For Forensic Architecture: Eyal Weizman, Samir Harb, Nicola Perugini, Juan P. Brockhaus, Steffen Kraemer. Collaborators: Michael Sfard Law Office (Michael Sfard, Emily Schaeffer). Forensic Architecture, "The Wall in Battir: Landscape and Heritage against the Logic of Separation," http://www.forensic-architecture.org/case/wall-battir; UNESCO, "Palestine: Land of Olives and Vines—Cultural Landscape of Southern Jerusalem, Battir," June 20,2014, http://whc.unesco.org /en/list/1492. On the outcome, see Nir Hasson, "Palestinians, Settlers, Greens Declare Victory in Court Ruling on Separation Barrier," *Haaretz*, January 4, 2015, http://www.haaretz.com/israel -news/.premium-1.635293. For further information regarding Forensic Architecture's involvement, see "Legal Ruptures: A Conversation with Michael Sfard," in *Forensis*, pp. 97–108. Forensic Architecture's team included Nicola Perugini and Samir Harb, who previously worked on the Palestinian submission to UNESCO.

PART TWO: COUNTERFORENSICS IN PALESTINE

1 Aristotle, *Poetics*, trans. Ingram Bywater, 4.1449b.

2 Sari Hanafi, "Spatio-cide, réfugiés, crise de l'État-nation," *Multitudes* 18 (Autumn 2004), https:// www.cairn.info/revue-multitudes-2004-4-page-187.htm.

3 Sigmund Freud, *The Standard Edition of the Complete Psychological Works of Sigmund Freud,* vol. 4, *The Interpretation of Dreams (Part 1)*, trans. A.A. Brill (London: Hogarth Press, 1986), pp. 119–20. A man accused by his neighbor of having returned a kettle in a damaged condition explains that he had returned the kettle undamaged, that it was already damaged when he borrowed it, and that he had never borrowed it in the first place. For a recognition of the historical fact of the Nakba, and an explanation of its necessity, see the recent book by centrist columnist Ari Shavit, *My Promised Land: The Triumph and Tragedy of Israel* (New York: Spiegel and Grau, 2013) and Benny Morris's position as articulated after the publication of his groundbreaking *The Birth of the Palestinian Refugee Problem* (Cambridge: Cambridge University Press, 1988). The interview in question is Coby Ben-Simhon, "Benny Morris on Why He's Written His Last Word on the Israel-Arab Conflict," *Haaretz*, September 20, 2012, http://www.haaretz.com/israel-news/benny-morris-on-why -he-s-written-his-last-word-on-the-israel-arab-conflict-1.465869.

4   Eyal Weizman, *The Least of All Possible Evils: Humanitarian Violence from Arendt to Gaza* (London: Verso, 2012); Nicola Perugini and Neve Gordon, *The Human Right to Dominate* (New York: Oxford University Press, 2015); Aeyal Gross, *The Writing on the Wall: Rethinking the International Law of Occupation* (Cambridge: Cambridge University Press, 2017).

5   In mid-2016, the human rights organization B'Tselem reached a similar conclusion. B'Tselem, "The Occupation's Fig Leaf: Israel's Military Law Enforcement System as a Whitewash Mechanism," report summary, May 25, 2016, http://www.btselem.org/publications/summaries/201605 _occupations_fig_leaf. It claims that it demanded an investigation in 739 cases, but since 2000, only in 25 instances were charges brought. Gili Cohen, "Citing IDF Failure to Bring Soldiers to Justice, B'Tselem Stops Filing Complaints on Abuse of Palestinians," *Haaretz*, May 25, 2016, http://www .haaretz.com/israel-news/.premium-1.721332.

6   B'Tselem, "A Palestinian Charged in a Military Court Is as Good as Convicted," June 21, 2015, http:// www.btselem.org/press_releases/20150622_presumed_guilty: "Every year, thousands of Palestinians are brought before military courts on various charges, including entering Israel without a permit, stone-throwing, membership in an illegal association, violence, firearms-related offenses and traffic violations. The military court has jurisdiction over residents of the entire West Bank, including areas over which partial control was transferred to the Palestinian Authority." Noam Sheizaf, "Conviction Rate for Palestinians in Israel's Military Courts: 99.74%," +972, November 29, 2011, http://972mag .com/conviction-rate-for-palestinians-in-israels-military-courts-99-74-percent/28579.

7   "The International Criminal Court (ICC) is a court of 'last resort' and will step in where national jurisdictions have failed to address international crimes." Coalition for the International Criminal Court, "Complementarity," http://www.iccnow.org/?mod=complementarity.

8   The High Court of Justice (HCJ) intervenes in very few cases, and controversially so, leading legal scholars to claim that its rulings have helped regulate and systematize the occupation and make it more efficient. David Kretzmer, *The Occupation of Justice: The Supreme Court of Israel and the Occupied Territories* (Albany: State University of New York Press, 2002). Forensic Architecture has helped provide evidence that was presented in the High Court of Justice. The case for banning the use of white phosphorous munitions (see Part 1, pp. 76–77) was presented there in 2012–2013. Legal battles regarding our report were still left unresolved when the military suddenly retreated and explained it will no longer use these munitions. In 2014, in the same court, we provided evidence in the case against the wall in Battir (see Part 1, pp. 125–27). Evidence in the case of the killing of Palestinian protestor Bassem Abu Rahma was presented there, beginning with the opening of proceedings in 2010, though the process is still ongoing.

9   Yehezkel Lein and Eyal Weizman, *Land Grab: Israel's Settlement Policy in the West Bank* (Jerusalem: B'Tselem, 2002); Eyal Weizman, *Hollow Land: Israel's Architecture of Occupation* (London: Verso, 2007).

10   In order to gain wide public support, the BDS movement has cast its campaign in legal terms, successfully conceptualizing the regime currently in place in Israel-Palestine as one that violates international law and requires a measure of transnational enforcement. The BDS movement used the ICJ case as its starting point. The original Palestinian civil-society call for BDS is BDS Movement, "Palestinian Civil Society Call for BDS," July 9, 2005, https://bdsmovement.net/call. It begins: "One year after the historic Advisory Opinion of the International Court of Justice (ICJ) which found Israel's Wall built on occupied Palestinian territory to be illegal" and continues: "We, representatives of Palestinian civil society, call upon international civil society organizations and people of conscience all over the world to impose broad boycotts and implement divestment initiatives against Israel similar to those applied to South Africa in the apartheid era."

11   Lein and Weizman, *Land Grab*. Eyal Weizman, *Jewish Settlements in the West Bank: Built Up Areas and Land Reserves*, 2002, can be found at https://www.btselem.org/download/settlements_map_eng.pdf.

12   Edward Said, "Yeats and Decolonization," in *Nationalism, Colonialism, and Literature*, eds. Terry Eagleton, Fredric Jameson, Edward W. Said (Minneapolis: University of Minnesota, Press, 1990), p. 77. See also the work of the architecture collective DAAR (Decolonizing Architecture Art Residency) that I have coestablished in Palestine with Sandi Hilal and Alessandro Petti. Alessandro Petti, Sandi Hilal, and Eyal Weizman, *Architecture after Revolution* (Berlin: Sternberg Press, 2014).

13   Edward Said, "Palestinians under Siege," *London Review of Books* 22.24 (December 14, 2000), pp. 9–14, http://www.lrb.co.uk/v22/n24/edward-said/palestinians-under-siege.

14   Dahlia Scheindlin, "Truth, Tapes and Two Dead Palestinians," *+972*, May 22, 2014, http://972mag.com/truth-tapes-and-two-dead-palestinians/91215.

15   Marc Garlasco, interviewed by Eyal Weizman, New York City, September 27, 2009.

16   Eyal Weizman, "Forensic Architecture: Only The Criminal Can Solve the Crime," *Radical Philosophy* 164 (November–December 2010), pp. 9–24.

17   Charles J. Dunlap, "Lawfare: A Decisive Element of 21st-Century Conflicts?," *Joint Force Quarterly* 3 (2009), p. 39. Charles J. Dunlap, "Law and Military Interventions: Preserving Humanitarian Values in 21st-Century Conflicts," paper delivered at the conference Humanitarian Challenges in Military Intervention, Carr Center for Human Rights Policy in the Kennedy School of Government, Harvard University, November 29, 2001, http://people.duke.edu/~pfeaver/dunlap.pdf. See also Charles Dunlap, "Lawfare amid Warfare," *Washington Times*, August 3, 2007.

18   The strand of legal scholarship known as "critical legal studies" emerged together with other poststructuralist discourses at the end of the 1980s. Critical legal studies scholars aimed to expose the way the law is made, the workings of power in the making and enactment of law, and to challenge law's normative account and offer an insight into its internal contradictions and indeterminacies. It was, broadly speaking, a critical, left-leaning practice that attempted to deploy law at the service of a socially transformative agenda.

19   Daniel Ayalon, "Challenges to Israeli Foreign Policy," an article adapted from his talk before the Israel Council on Foreign Relations, January 6, 2010, http://www.israelcfr.com/documents/4-1-3-Daniel-Ayalon.pdf.

20   Israel Ministry of Foreign Affairs, "FAQ: The Campaign to Defame Israel," November 10, 2010, http://mfa.gov.il/MFA/ForeignPolicy/FAQ/Pages/FAQ_Attack_Israeli_Values.aspx, quoted in Perugini and Gordon, *The Human Right to Dominate*, p. 62.

21   Caroline Wyatt, "Legal Claims 'Could Paralyse' Armed Forces," BBC News, October 18, 2013, http://www.bbc.co.uk/news/uk-24576547. On the conception of threat posed by legal action, see Thomas Keenan and Eyal Weizman "The Third Strategic Threat," *openDemocracy*, June 7, 2010, http://www.opendemocracy.net/thomas-keenan-eyal-weizman/israel-third-strategic-threat.

22   Perugini and Gordon, *The Human Right to Dominate*, esp. "The Human Rights to Colonize," pp. 101–26.

23   Gerald M. Steinberg, "EU Research Funds Wasted on Amnesty's Hollywood-Style CSI Adventure," August 13, 2015, http://www.ngo-monitor.org/in-the-media/eu_research_funds_wasted_on_amnesty_s_hollywood_style_csi_adventure; NGO Monitor, "Amnesty's 'Gaza Platform': All Window Dressing, No Substance," July 07, 2015, http://www.ngo-monitor.org/press-releases/nothing_but_window_dressing_amnesty_international_s_new_gaza_platform.

24   Uri Blau, "Did Israeli Settler Group Use Government Funds to Spy on Human-rights NGOs?," *Haaretz*, January 19, 2016, http://www.haaretz.com/israel-news/1.698201.

25   John Brown, "Hebron Shooter Called to 'Kill Everyone in Gaza,'" *+972*, April 29, 2016, http://972mag.com/hebron-shooter-called-to-kill-everyone-in-gaza/118869.

26   Amira Hass, "Using Black Ops against Palestinian NGOs," *Haaretz*, August 18, 2016, http://www
     .haaretz.com/opinion/.premium-1.737221.

27   Michael Hodges, "Forensic Architecture is Unravelling Conflict from Gaza to Guatemala," *Wired*,
     January 25, 2016, http://www.wired.co.uk/article/gaza-data-forensics.

28   For Forensic Architecture: Eyal Weizman, Nick Axel, Steffen Kraemer, Lawrence Abu Hamdan. See
     http://www.forensic-architecture.org/case/nakba-day-killngs.

29   Jillian Kestler-D'Amours, "Israel Criminalizes Commemoration of the Nakba," *Electronic Intifada*,
     March 29, 2011, https://electronicintifada.net/content/israel-criminalizes-commemoration-
     nakba/9289.

30   The unedited six-hour-long footage has been shared with a number of news agencies and sev-
     eral human rights organizations who have verified the video as accurately portraying events on
     that day. As a children's rights organization, DCI–Palestine explained that their first priority is the
     best interests of the child. Publicly releasing the full video could allow others to identify specific
     children where faces are visible. Given the widespread and systematic ill-treatment that exists in
     the Israeli military detention system, DCI–Palestine does not feel that it can responsibly release
     the full-length CCTV footage. Eyewitnesses at the scene, including journalists and photographers,
     have provided statements verifying that the video accurately depicts the day's events. See https://
     www.youtube.com/user/DCIPS.

31   The Obama administration on May 21, 2014, called on Israeli officials to "conduct a prompt and
     transparent investigation." *Haaretz*, "U.S. Urges Restraint by Both Sides After Killing of Palestin-
     ian Teens," May 21, 2014, http://www.haaretz.com/israel-news/1.591912. On May 23, the UN Office
     of the High Commissioner for Human Rights declared that the killings may amount to "extrajudi-
     cial executions" or "willful killings" under international law, and Human Rights Watch recently
     found that the killings constitute an apparent war crime. UN News Centre, "Killing of Palestinian
     Teenagers in West Bank Elicits UN Call for Prompt Investigation," June 9, 2014, www.un.org/apps
     /news/story.asp?NewsID=47875#.U6Gbm_mSySp; Human Rights Watch, "Israel: Killing of Chil-
     dren Apparent War Crime," June 9, 2014, https://www.hrw.org/news/2014/06/09/israel-killing
     -children-apparent-war-crime.

32   On June 11, Al-Quds University's Institute of Forensic Medicine in Abu Dis undertook the exhuma-
     tion in the presence of US, Danish, and Israeli pathologists. No bullet was found in the body, but
     the examination identified both the entry and exit wounds of live fire as the cause of death. DCI–
     Palestine, "Use of Live Ammunition Confirmed in Nawarah Shooting," June 12, 2014, http://www
     .commondreams.org/newswire/2014/06/12/use-live-ammunition-confirmed-nawarah-shooting.

33   B'Tselem, "Investigation of Bitunya Shooting Leading to Arrest of Border Police Officers Confirms
     B'Tselem's Finding That the Youths Were Killed by Live Fire," November 12, 2014, http://www
     .btselem.org/press_releases/20141112_bitunya_killings_investigation.

34   Peter Beaumont, "Video Footage Indicates Killed Palestinian Youths Posed No Threat," *Guard-
     ian*, May 20, 2014, http://www.theguardian.com/world/2014/may/20/video-indicates-killed-
     palestinian-youths-no-threat-israeli-forces; Mitch Ginsburg and Lazar Berman, "Film of Pal-
     estinians' Killing Likely Doctored, Top Official Says," *Times of Israel*, May 21, 2014, http://www
     .timesofisrael.com/top-official-film-of-palestinians-killing-likely-doctored.

35   Robert Tait, "Israel Asked to Investigate Shooting of Palestinian Teenagers," *Telegraph*, May 21,
     2014, http://www.telegraph.co.uk/news/worldnews/middleeast/israel/10845721/Israel-asked-to
     -investigate-shooting-of-Palestinian-teenagers.html; Avi Issacharoff, "An Itchy IDF Trigger Finger
     or a 'Pallywood' Movie?," *Times of Israel*, May 23, 2014, http://www.timesofisrael.com/an-itchy
     -idf-trigger-finger-or-a-pallywood-movie; Larry Derfner, "Day of Catastrophe for 'Pallywood'

Conspiracy Theorists," *+972*, November 13, 2014; Human Rights Watch, "Israel: Killing of Children Apparent War Crime," June 9, 2014, https://www.hrw.org/news/2014/06/09/israel-killing-children-apparent-war-crime.

36 Ivan Watson, Kareem Khadder, and Mike Schwartz, "Father Blames Israeli Military in Palestinian Teens' Deaths," CNN, May 22, 2014, http://edition.cnn.com/2014/05/22/world/meast/israel-west-bank-shooting.

37 Human Rights Watch, "Israel: Stop Threatening Witness to Killings. Forces Target Man Whose Cameras Recorded Deaths," June 19, 2014, https://www.hrw.org/news/2014/06/19/israel-stop-threatening-witness-killings.

38 Israeli TV Channel 2, "Israeli TV Analysis of CNN Coverage of Beitunia Incident," May 23, 2014, https://www.youtube.com/watch?v=OgPEhjT5u7k&feature=youtu.be.

39 As Human Rights Watch noted: "The Israeli military has used at least one type of assault-rifle attachment, produced by Israel Military Industries, that allows forces to fire rubber bullets, but also to fire live ammunition without removing the attachment. A brochure states that the 22-centimeter-long 'launcher' can be 'attached to any rifle with NATO flash suppressor' and allows 'immediate 5.56-mm lethal firing capability without removing adapter.'" Human Rights Watch, "Israel: Killing of Children Apparent War Crime."

40 *Ibid.*

41 William Kherbek, "Artist Profile: Lawrence Abu Hamdan," *Rhizome*, August 21, 2015, http://rhizome.org/editorial/2015/aug/21/artist-profile-lawrence-abu-hamdan.

42 On August 18, 2015, our report was presented in the presence of Siam Nawara in a special event convened at the US Congress by Betty McCollum, a Democratic representative from Minnesota, who had also, in what was described as "probably the statement most in support of Palestinian rights to have been made on the capitol," sent a letter to the State Department: "The murders of Nadeem Nawara and Mohammad Daher only highlight a brutal system of occupation that devalues and dehumanizes Palestinian children. The letter is available at http://mccollum.house.gov/sites/mccollum.house.gov/files/15.0818%20State-Patterson-Malinowski_Palestinian%20Nadeem%20Nawara%20Shooting.pdf.

43 Yonah Jeremy Bob, "Judge Recuses Himself in Ex-Border Cop's Manslaughter Trial for Death of Palestinian," *Jerusalem Post*, October 12, 2015, http://www.jpost.com/Israel-News/Judge-recuses-himself-in-ex-border-cops-manslaughter-trial-for-death-of-Arab-422661.

44 According to the Israeli human rights group Yesh Din, since 2000, only 5 percent of complaints submitted to the Military Police Criminal Investigations Division (MPCID) have led to an indictment. Of the five thousand Palestinians killed by the IDF since 2000, only seven soldiers have been convicted, and none spent more than several months in prison. Yesh Din, "MPCID Investigations into the Circumstances Surrounding the Death of Palestinians: Convictions and Penalties," July 2013, http://www.yesh-din.org/userfiles/file/datasheets/Law%20Enforcement%20upon%20-%202012.pdf. The only person convicted was in the case of the Gaza killing of a journalist who was a European national. The shooter was a Bedouin soldier. DCI–Palestine, "New Forensic Architecture Evidence Identifies Nadeem Nawara's Killer," November 20, 2014, http://www.DCI–Palestine.org/new_forensic_architecture_evidence_identifies_nadeem_nawara_s_killer; Robert Mackey, "Video Analysis of Fatal West Bank Shooting Said to Implicate Israeli Officer," *New York Times*, November 24, 2014, http://www.nytimes.com/2014/11/25/world/middleeast/video-analysis-of-fatal-west-bank-shooting-said-to-implicate-israeli-officer.html.

45 Gili Cohen, "Israeli Military Shuts Investigation into Fatal 2014 Shooting of Palestinian Teen," *Haaretz*, March 30, 2016, http://www.haaretz.com/israel-news/.premium-1.711848.

46 Yonah Jeremy Bob, "Judge Recuses Himself in Ex-Border Cop's Manslaughter Trial for Death of Palestinian," October 12, 2015, http://www.jpost.com/Israel-News/Judge-recuses-himself-in-ex -border-cops-manslaughter-trial-for-death-of-Arab-422661.

47 Orlando Crowcroft, "Palestinians Freed in 2011 Gilad Shalit Prisoner-Swap Back in Custody," *Guardian*, June 18, 2014, https://www.theguardian.com/world/2014/jun/18/palestinians-freed -2001-gilad-shalit-custody.

48 Forensic Architecture and Amnesty International, *The Gaza Platform: An Interactive Map of Israeli Attacks during the 2014 Gaza Conflict*, http://gazaplatform.amnesty.org.

49 United Nations Development Programme, Programme of Assistance to the Palestinian People, "One Year After—House Reconstruction Begins in Gaza," http://www.ps.undp.org/content /papp/en/home/ourwork/crisispreventionandrecovery/successstories/one-year-after-_-house -reconstruction-begins-in-gaza.html. The figures are from the Gaza Ministry of Public Works.

50 When the ratification documents were signed, it was the only point of consensus between all Palestinian factions, which are otherwise bitterly divided. The ICC can try persons of any nationality for crimes committed on the territory of the states that have signed its Rome Statute. Now that Palestine has joined the court, Israeli politicians and officers could be prosecuted for war crimes and crimes against humanity committed in the West Bank and Gaza, even though Israel is not a member of the ICC. Opening the way to this ratification, the UN General Assembly recognized the state of Palestine in 2012, upgrading it from "permanent observer" to "non-member observer state," thus opening up the possibility of its membership in the court. See George Bisharat, "Palestinian Considerations for Accession to the Rome Statute," *Journal of Palestine Studies*, October 20, 2014, http://www.palestine-studies.org/institute/fellows/palestinian-considerations-accession -rome-statute. Mubarak Awad and Jonathan Kuttab, "Nonviolent Resistance in Palestine: Pursuing Alternative Strategies," *Electronic Intifada*, March 29, 2002, https://electronicintifada.ne t/content/nonviolent-resistance-palestine-pursuing-alternative-strategies/4584. A poll by the Palestinian Center for Policy and Survey Research in June 2014 found that 80 percent of Gazans and the majority of West Bank residents wanted the Palestinian Authority to go to the ICC. Popular pressure on the PA to join the ICC increased after the breakdown in peace talks in April 2014 and certainly after the 2014 Gaza war.

During the 2014 war, all Palestinian factions agreed on a declaration stating that they are all prepared to deal with the personal and national repercussions of joining the ICC. The heads of the Islamist organizations (Hamas and Islamic Jihad) signed last, but they signed, extending the court's jurisdiction over the occupied Palestinian territories in order to allow charges to be brought against Israel, in full recognition of the fact that this might involve the risk that charges also will be brought against Palestinians. George Bisharat, panel discussion, "Operation Protective Edge: Legal and Political Implications of ICC Prosecution," George Mason University, October 20. 2014, *Status Hour* 3.1, http://www.statushour.com/operation-protective-edge-the-icc.html. Previously, Israel and its Western allies had threatened to withdraw financial aid from the PA if it pursued membership. The US Senate, for example, debated legislation in 2012 that would cut off millions of dollars in assistance to the PA, and the EU has reportedly said it will withhold aid for rebuilding Gaza after the latest assault if the PA were to bring a case against Israel. Donna Cassata, "US Lawmakers Threaten to Halt Aid to Palestinians If They Use UN Upgrade against Israel," *Times of Israel*, November 29, 2012, http://www.timesofisrael.com/us-lawmakers-threaten-cutoff -of-palestinian-aid-if-they-use-un-upgrade-against-israel; David Hearst, "Exclusive: Hamas Pushes Abbas to Join ICC," *Middle East Monitor*, August 11, 2014, https://www.middleeastmonitor .com/20140811-exclusive-hamas-pushes-abbas-to-join-icc.

51 Bloggers such as Jehad Saftawi posted a large amount of audio-visual material. "During the war," he said, "we started the idea to have a live stream…we were searched for a way to make people try to understand what the Gaza people are living in." "The 'Forensic Architects' Investigating Gaza," video, Reuters, July 31, 2015, http://uk.reuters.com/video/2015/07/31/the-forensic-architects-investigating-ga?videoId=365136621; Tristran Martin, "Gaza Destruction Comes under Forensic Lens in Amnesty Report," Reuters, July 29, 2015, http://www.reuters.com/article/2015/07/29/us-mideast-gaza-amnesty-report-idUSKCN0Q30U120150729.

52 But, suffering from a great shortage of living space, when bombardments end, residents of the Gaza Strip immediately start clearing up the rubble and use whatever can be salvaged to rebuild their homes. Life is more important than evidence. For instance, some individuals pick up fragments of munitions as souvenirs or to use to make practical or decorative objects. See, for example, *Business Insider*, "Remnants of War Become Art in Gaza," October 2014, http://www.business insider.com/afp-remnants-of-war-become-art-in-gaza-2014-10?IR=T.

53 *Breaking the Silence: Israeli Soldiers Talk about the Occupied Territories*, http://www.breakingthe silence.org.il.

54 Investigation by Forensic Architecture and Amnesty International with Al Mezan, the Palestinian human rights group in Gaza. For Forensic Architecture: Eyal Weizman, Christina Varvia, Nick Axel, Francesco Sebregondi, Camila E. Sotomayor, Vere Van Gool, Shourideh C. Molavi, Gustav A. Toftgaard, Dorette Panagiotopoulou, Jamon Van Den Hoek, Rosario Güiraldes, Hania Halabi, Jacob Burns, Mohammed Abdullah, Kent Klich, Ana Naomi de Souza, Susan Schuppli, and Chris Cobb-Smith. The report was published close to the first anniversary of the event. Amnesty International, *'Black Friday': Carnage in Rafah During 2014 Israel/Gaza Conflict*, https://blackfriday .amnesty.org. It was also submitted and referred to in the UN Independent Commission of Inquiry on the Gaza conflict as well as the preliminary investigation of the Gaza Conflict by the International Criminal Court in The Hague (ICC).

55 United Nations, "Joint Statement by the Secretary-General and US Secretary of State John Kerry on Humanitarian Ceasefire Announcement," New York, July 21, 2014, http://www.un.org/sg /statements/index.asp?nid=7899; Sudarsan Raghavan, William Booth, and Griff Witte, "How a 72-Hour Truce in Gaza Fell Apart in Less Than 2 Hours," *Washington Post*, August 1, 2014, https://www.washingtonpost.com/world/israel-hamas-agree-to-72-hour-humanitarian-cease -fire/2014/08/01/059f1ff8-194e-11e4-9e3b-7f2f110c6265_story.html. Qatar and Turkey confirmed Hamas's agreement, and the United Nations also had assurances "received directly from the Hamas leadership." Israel later claimed that John Kerry has misinformed Israel about Hamas's agreement to the terms requested by Israel—that it could still look for tunnels within the areas it held.

56 "Press Release Al Qassam Brigades Regarding Breach of Ceasefire and Alleged Capture of Israeli Soldier," *Occupied Palestine*, August 1, 2014, https://occupiedpalestine.wordpress.com/2014 /08/01/gazaunderattack-press-release-al-qassam-brigades-regarding-breach-of-truce-and-alleged -capture-of-israeli-soldier.

57 Breaking the Silence, *This Is How We Fought in Gaza 2014: Soldiers' Testimonies and Photographs from Operation "Protective Edge,"* testimony 42, pp. 108–109, http://www.breakingthesilence.org .il/pdf/ProtectiveEdge.pdf.

58 Max Blumenthal and Allison Deger, "Who Broke the Ceasefire?: Obama Blames Hamas against the Evidence," *Mondoweiss*, August 2, 2014, http://mondoweiss.net/2014/08/ceasefire-against -evidence#sthash.0RIE1a14.dpuf.

59 Interview by Amnesty International fieldworker with Dr. Majed Abu Taha, August 14, 2014.

60 This was in line with the ceasefire terms, which stated: "During this period, civilians in Gaza will receive urgently needed humanitarian relief, and the opportunity to carry out vital functions, including burying the dead, taking care of the injured and restocking food supplies. See United Nations, "Joint Statement by the Secretary-General and US Secretary of State John Kerry on Humanitarian Ceasefire Announcement."

61 The Qassam Brigades, Hamas's military wing, claimed that the encounter took place at 7:30 a.m. At 7:34 a.m., they tweeted: "at 7:00 am a group [of Hamas fighters] clashed with [Israeli] forces east of Rafah and caused many injuries and death to them." Quoted in Blumenthal and Deger, "Who Broke the Ceasefire?" The capturing of the Israeli fighter took place during this fire fight, they later explained, before the ceasefire had come into effect: "Zionist Enemy Forces used the talks about a humanitarian ceasefire to advance troops more than two kilometers inside the Gaza Strip to the east of Rafah. Our assessment is that one of our deployed ambushes clashed with the advancing troops." "Statement Clarifying the Zionist Enemy's Violation of the Humanitarian Ceasefire, the Claim of the Disappearance of One Soldier, and the Clashes East of Rafah," in "Press Release Al Qassam Brigades Regarding Breach of Ceasefire and Alleged Capture of Israeli Soldier."

62 Yoav Zeitun, "Givati Commanders from the Rafah Battle 'Clear Conscience,'" Ynet, September 24, 2014, http://www.ynet.co.il/articles/0,7340,L-4568410,00.html, in Hebrew; Tal Lev Ram, "Exclusive: New Details," IDF Radio, April 14, 2015, http://glz.co.il/1138-61304-he/Galatz.aspx, in Hebrew; Uri Misgav, "Hannibal Comes Out of the Closet: 'Better a Body Than a Captured Soldier,'" Haaretz, September 29, 2014, in Hebrew, http://www.haaretz.co.il/blogs/misgav/.premium -1.2445759.

63 An Israeli soldier already had been captured on July 19, 2014, causing celebration on the Palestinian side, but the military declared that he was dead when taken.

64 Those parts of it made public by the military were released in order to convince the Israeli public that an IDF criminal investigation into "possible war crimes" committed by the Givati Brigade that day would be redundant. "Exclusive: New Details about the Rafah Battle," IDF Radio (Gali Tzahal), April 14, 2015, http://glz.co.il/1138-61304-he/Galatz.aspx, in Hebrew; Amos Harel and Gili Cohen, "You Will Not Hear from Me That the IDF Is the Most Moral Army in the World," Haaretz, April 9, 2015, http://www.haaretz.co.il/news/politics/.premium-1.2610618, in Hebrew.

65 Ilana Dayan, "From Deep Under," Uvda (a documentary series accesses through Mako.co.il), April 19, 2015, http://www.mako.co.il/mako-vod-keshet/uvda#/mako-vod-keshet/uvda-2015 /VOD-eaea8aa6a91dc41006.htm?sCh=440c3cc15d499410&pId=957463908, in Hebrew.

66 Dayan, "From Deep Under"; further details in Amir Bohbot, "Interview with Lieutenant Ethan: I Declared 'Hannibal' and Ran into the Tunnel," Walla, August 10, 2014, http://news.walla.co.il /item/2773902, in Hebrew; Gili Cohen, "Givati Inquiry into the Battle in Rafah: Fire was Disproportionate, but Soldiers Were Not Properly Secured in the Area," Haaretz, April 14, 2014, http://www .haaretz.co.il/news/politics/1.2613390, in Hebrew; Yohai Ofer, "Army Assessed That Goldin Alive and Taken to Hospital," NRG, April 14, 2014, http://www.nrg.co.il/online/1/ART2/688/909.html.

67 Zitun, "Givati Commanders Who Fought in Rafah: Clear Conscience."

68 "Israeli Fire on Gaza Town Raises War Crimes Claim," Daily Mail (UK), August 31, 2014, http://www .dailymail.co.uk/wires/ap/article-2739001/Israeli-fire-Gaza-town-raises-war-crimes-claim.html.

69 In 2002, Israel instituted the "Incarceration of Unlawful Combatants Law." In an imitation of the similar American law, prisoners were no longer treated according to criminal law, but could be held "as long as the hostile acts of such force against the State of Israel have not yet ceased." Incarceration of Unlawful Combatants Law, 5762-2002, https://www.jewishvirtuallibrary.org/jsource /Politics/IncarcerationLaw.pdf. Only a few were charged according to this law. "The Third Geneva

Convention for the arrangement of care of prisoners of war or Convention [III] Relative to the Treatment of Prisoners of War (Geneva, 12 August 1949) declared combatants, though they have killed intentionally, are not individually responsible for the killing they have done, and could not be tried and made liable for the death and destruction they caused." Merav Mack, introduction to *Captives,* ed. Merav Mack (Jerusalem: The Van Leer Jerusalem Institute and the Zalman Shazar Center for Jewish History, 2014), p. 24, in Hebrew.

70   Gush Emunim claimed that those released contributed to the eruption of the "first Intifada" in 1987. Ronen Bergman, "Prisoners of War and Those Reported Missing: Conclusions Drawn from the Israeli Cases," in *Captives*, p. 204, in Hebrew.

71   In 1996, the bodies of two Israeli soldiers were exchanged for the bodies of 123 Lebanese fighters. In 1998, the remains of a single Israeli soldier were exchanged for sixty-five Lebanese prisoners and the bodies of forty. In 2004, an Israeli civilian and the bodies of three IDF soldiers, captured in 2000, were exchanged for over 430 Palestinian and Lebanese prisoners and the bodies of fifty-nine Lebanese. In 2007, the remains of an Israeli civilian were exchanged for a Lebanese civilian, two Hezbollah prisoners, and the remains of two Hezbollah fighters. In June 2008, Israel released a Lebanese prisoner in exchange for the partial remains of up to twenty Israeli soldiers killed during the 2006 Lebanon War. In July 2008, the bodies of two Israeli soldiers, captured in a cross-border raid in July 12, 2006, were exchanged for a Lebanese prisoner, four Hezbollah fighters, and the bodies of 199 fighters. In October 2011, an IDF soldier was exchanged for 1,027 Palestinian prisoners held in Israel.

72   Yossi Peled, Gabi Ashkenazi, and Yaakov Amidror drafted the original command. The order generated a protest within the IDF. At least one battalion commander refused to transmit it to his soldiers, arguing that it was flagrantly illegal, and in a number of units, lively debates took place about the morality of the order. Some soldiers said they would refuse to open fire on their comrades. Nevertheless, some soldiers say that even after the command was revised, they were briefed in the spirit of the original procedure. Sara Leibovich-Dar, "The Hannibal Procedure," *Haaretz*, May 21, 2003, http://www.haaretz.com/the-hannibal-procedure-1.9412.

73   See the video on the website of Israeli journal *The Seventh Eye* dated August 14, 2014, http://www.the7eye.org.il/121821, in Hebrew.

74   The Third Geneva Convention, which deals with the treatment of prisoners of war by those who imprison them, does not regulate the military's duties in relation to its own combatants.

75   In 1999, a tank commander said: "In the briefings, we were told more than once that the military goal in the event of an abduction is the death of the soldier, because the IDF prefers a dead soldier to an abducted soldier." *The Seventh Eye*, August 14, 2014, http://www.the7eye.org.il/121821, in Hebrew. See also Amos Harel, "After Shalit, Some IDF Officers See a Dead Soldier as Better Than Abducted," *Haaretz*, November 1 2011, http://www.haaretz.com/after-shalit-some-idf-officers-see-a-dead-soldier-as-better-than-abducted-1.393039.

76   Before the 2008 incursion into Gaza, a commander of an infantry battalion made clear that he expected his soldiers to commit suicide rather than be abducted: "No soldier in the 51st Battalion can be kidnapped at any cost, not in any circumstance. That can mean that a soldier should detonate his hand grenade and blow himself up [together] with the person trying to abduct him." Anshel Pfeffer "IDF Warns Soldiers of Kidnappings Ahead of Gilad Shalit's release," *Haaretz*, September 18, 2011, http://www.haaretz.com/idf-warns-soldiers-of-kidnappings-ahead-of-gilad-shalit-s-release-1.390520. A video report broadcast on Israel Television Channel 2 News, "The IDF Hannibal Protocol—IDF Commander Briefing Troops," is available at https://www.youtube.com/watch?v=BvlP6yM15ws.

77 Ronen Bergman, *By Any Means Necessary* (Tel Aviv: Kinneret Zmora-Bitan Dvir, 2009), in Hebrew; Leibovich-Dar, "The Hannibal Procedure"; Uri Misgav, "From Defensive Shield to Lt Eitan," *Haaretz*, August 11, 2014, http://www.haaretz.co.il/blogs/misgav/.premium-1.2402935, in Hebrew; Ariel Colonomos, "Hostage Dilemmas: Learning from Hamas to Use against ISIS," *Haaretz*, September 10, 2014, http://www.haaretz.com/opinion/.premium-1.615122. The "official" and the "oral" version of the Hannibal Directive formulate the relation between the target and the collateral differently. The officially written version, seeking to be within the domain of Israeli and international humanitarian law (IHL), states that the fire must be aimed at the captors in the likelihood that it would also hurt the captured. If the captured soldier dies, it would then be seen as "collateral damage" to attempts to stop the acts of capture. This was publically confirmed by the chief of staff during the Gaza war, Benny Gantz, who framed this as the "double-effect doctrine," according to which the "bad result" (the killing of a captive soldier) is morally permissible only as a side effect of promoting a good action (stopping his captors). Following the 2006 capture of Gilad Shalit, the IDF's Gantz, modified the directive. It now allows field commanders to act without awaiting confirmation from their superiors. At the same time, the directive's language was tempered to make clear that it does not call for the willful killing of captured soldiers.

In response to a letter written by the Association for Civil Rights in Israel dated January 12, 2015, Israel's attorney general reaffirmed: "The operational Directive concerning foiling an attempt to abduct an Israeli soldier or citizen is classified, and therefore its stipulations cannot be divulged. Over the past few years, the Directive has been thoroughly subject to staff work. Within such staff work, the issue of the risk to the abductee...was examined by the highest-ranking officials. The stipulation that was adopted within the framework of this Directive reflects, in our opinion, a suitable balance between the different considerations involved in this matter.... However, we would like to emphasize that the Directive prohibits executing an attack aimed at causing the death of the abductee." Office of the Attorney General, letter re: Inquiry regarding "The Hannibal Directive and Its Implementation in Highly Populated Areas" to Dan Yakir, Adv., Tamar Feldman, Adv., The Association for Civil Rights in Israel, January 12, 2015.

78 Quoted in Ronald Mellor, *The Roman Historians* (London: Routledge, 1999), p. 70.

79 Colonomos, "Hostage Dilemmas."

80 Grégoire Chamayou, "The Manhunt Doctrine," *Radical Philosophy* 169 (September–October 2011), https://www.radicalphilosophy.com/commentary/the-manhunt-doctrine.

81 Interview with Colonel Ofer Winter by Yossi Yehoshua, *Yedioth Ahronoth*, August 15, 2014 (paper-only edition), in Hebrew.

82 Protocol Additional to the Geneva Conventions of 12 August 1949, and relating to the Protection of Victims of International Armed Conflicts (Protocol I), 8 June 1977, article 51, paragraph 4, 1953, https://www.icrc.org/ihl/INTRO/470; Martti Koskenniemi, "'Human Rights Mainstreaming as a Strategy for Institutional Power," *Humanity: An International Journal of Human Rights, Humanitarianism, and Development* 1.1 (Fall 2010), pp. 48–49; Weizman, *The Least of All Possible Evils*, pp. 11–17.

83 The UN disagrees that such calculations are legal. "The commission emphasizes that policy considerations and remote strategic objectives informed by political goals—such as denying armed groups the leverage they could obtain over Israel in negotiations for the release of a captured soldier—are not valid considerations in conducting the proportionality analysis required under international humanitarian law." United Nations High Commissioner for Human Rights, *Report of the Detailed Findings of the Commission of Inquiry on the 2014 Gaza Conflict*, A/HRC/29/CRP.4, http://www.ohchr.org/EN/HRBodies/HRC/CoIGazaConflict/Pages/ReportCoIGaza.aspx#report, p. 15.

84 Hannibalism was the very reason and logic of the Gaza war, a war intended "to extract a price" and

deter "Lebanon" from future capture attempts. Israel Ministry of Foreign Affairs, "PM Olmert: Lebanon Is Responsible and Will Bear the Consequences," July 12, 2006, http://www.mfa.gov.il/mfa/pressroom/2006/pages/pm%20olmert%20-%20lebanon%20is%20responsible%20and%20will%20bear%20the%20consequences%2012-jul-2006.aspx.

85   Uri Misgav, "Israel Should Get God Out of the Army," *Haaretz*, August 8, 2014, http://www.haaretz.com/opinion/.premium-1.609495.

86   Breaking the Silence, *This Is How We Fought in Gaza 2014*, testimony 60, pp. 145–46.

87   *Ibid*. Testimony 93, pp. 202–203.

88   Targets that were not previously authorized because the "population officers" in the military intelligence determined their bombing would involve too high a level of civilian casualties were authorized after Hannibal was launched. There are three levels of fire. The first anticipates a "low level of civilian harm," the second refers to a "moderate level," and the third to a "necessary level," where a high level of harm to civilians is expected. According to the testimonies, after Hannibal was declared, many targets that were classified as the highest level — multistory buildings or structures located in densely populated areas — were approved. Breaking the Silence, *This is How We Fought in Gaza 2014*, testimony 107, pp. 226–27; testimony 95, pp. 204–205; testimony 107, pp. 226–27; testimony 91, pp. 198–99; testimony 95, pp. 204–205.

89   "Interview by Amnesty International fieldworker with Abdel-Rahim Lafi, September 24, 2014," Amnesty International, *'Black Friday,'* p. 28.

90   "Interview by Amnesty International fieldworker with Saleh Abu Mohsen, September 9, 2014," *ibid.*, p. 27.

91   "Interview by Amnesty International fieldworker with Mohammed Khalil Mohammed Abu Duba (son of the deceased Khalil Abu Duba and brother of the deceased Munir Abu Duba), September 28, 2014," *ibid.*, p. 28 (the Amnesty report did not include all the quotes used here); "Interview by Amnesty International fieldworker with Ahmad Ziyad Qassem al-Qadi, October 24, 2014" (the interview was not included in the report).

92   "Interview by Amnesty International fieldworker with Dr Majed Abu Taha, August 14, 2014," *ibid.*, p. 40.

93   Dolev Ohayon, "I Must Take the Thoughts of Dying Out of My Head," April 23, 2015, http://news.walla.co.il/item/2847705, in Hebrew.

94   Ofer Winter and his deputy, Eli Gino, directed the attack. They intended to surround and isolate the neighborhood north of Salah al-Eddin Street. "Tank commanders were given permission in principle to shoot at 'suspicious points' — buildings, people or vehicles — without warning. What constituted a 'suspicious point' was left to the discretion of the commanders, and soldiers interpreted it as any building close to the tanks or overlooking them. Almost every object or structure within the forces' eyeshot had the potential to be considered suspicious and thus targeted." Amnesty International, *'Black Friday,'* p. 35.

95   *Ibid.*, p. 36.

96   Forensic Architecture and Amnesty International, *The Gaza Platform*.

97   Breaking the Silence, *This Is How We Fought in Gaza 2014*, testimony 66, p. 156.

98   "From Deep Under," *Uvda*.

99   Tal Lev Ram, "Exclusive: New Details," IDF Radio, April 14, 2015, http://glz.co.il/1138-61304-he/Galatz.aspx, in Hebrew.

100 Interview with Colonel Ofer Winter by Yossi Yehoshua, in Hebrew.

101 Interview by Amnesty International fieldworker with Mohammed Khalil Mohammed Abu Duba, September 28, 2014, Amnesty International, *'Black Friday,'* p. 37.

102 We constructed our models based on satellite images as well as on OpenStreetMap, a free online map, a kind of Wikipedia of maps, a crowd-sourced project that allows activists to contribute their time and skills to drawing plans of uncharted cities. We approximated the height of the buildings based on the length of their shadows as seen in different satellite photographs.

103 "Interview by Amnesty International fieldworker interview with Saleh Abu Mohsen, October 7, 2014," Amnesty International, *'Black Friday,'* pp. 27, 38.

104 *Ibid.*, p. 38.

105 Further analysis of Pléiades and other satellite data was undertaken with Dr. Jamon Van Den Hoek, a scientist working on remote sensing who was based at the at the National Aeronautics and Space Administration (NASA) Goddard Space Flight Center in Washington. He is also a "geo-spatial intelligence leader" in the geography program at Oregon State University.

106 Breaking the Silence, "Those Guys Were Trigger Happy, Totally Crazy," http://www.breakingthe silence.org.il/testimonies/database/103279.

107 In another diary entry, Ohayon looks at a mushroom cloud that "rose hundreds of meters high. When we left the [Gaza] strip they told us that they could see this mushroom in Beer Sheva almost 40 kilometres away." Ohayon, "I Must Take the Thoughts of Dying Out of My Head."

108 Hubert Damisch, *A Theory of /Cloud/: Toward a History of Painting*, trans. Janet Lloyd (Stanford: Stanford University Press, 2002), p. 15; John Durham Peters, *The Marvelous Clouds: Toward a Philosophy of Elemental Media* (Chicago: University of Chicago Press, 2015), p. 259. John Ruskin "recommended daily quarter-hour contemplation of the dawn clouds as part of morning devotions, keeping pencil and brush to hand to record particularly beautiful occasions." Ashmolean, "Cloud Studies," http://ruskin.ashmolean.org/collection/9006/9037/9357.

109 Luke Howard, "On the Modification of Clouds, and on the Principle of Their Production, Suspension, and Destruction; being the Substance of an Essay read before the Askesian Society in the Session 1802–1803," *Philosophical Magazine and Journal of Science* 16 (1803) and 17 (1804).

110 Forensic Architecture, in consultation with Houston-based blast consultant Robert Scates, at Rimkus Consulting Group in Houston, July 3, 2015.

111 In his poem "The House as Casualty," Palestinian poet Mahmoud Darwish (in the translation of Catherine Cobham) lists the contents of a destroyed house: "stone, wood, glass, iron, cement…cotton, silk, linen, papers, books…. Plates, spoons, toys, records, taps, pipes, door handles, fridges, washing machines, flower vases, jars of olives and pickles, tinned food…. Salt, sugar, spices, boxes of matches, pills, contraceptives, antidepressants, strings of garlic, onions, tomatoes, dried okra, rice and lentils…. Rent agreements, marriage documents, birth certificates, water and electricity bills, identity cards, passports, love letters…. Photographs, toothbrushes, combs, cosmetics, shoes, underwear, sheets, towels." The dust that remained after the collapse of the twin towers on 9/11 had to be analyzed to identify the different substances it contained. In her essay "Impure Matter," Susan Schuppli reproduces a chart with the results. It lists 45.1 percent rockwool/fiberglass, 31.8 percent composites such as plastic and concrete, 7.1 percent charred wood, 2.1 percent paper fibers, 2 percent synthetic fibers, 1.4 percent glass fragments, 1.4 percent natural fibers, 1.3 percent of human remains, and drugs (from the bodies), paint, foam, and asbestos each under 1 percent.

112 When the military uses controlled detonation of tunnels, using about fifty kilograms of explosives, "the shock waves move through it and collapse the entire tunnel. And then a kilometer away, on the other side, you see the tunnel's other shaft fly up in the air. You blow up a house here, and sometime you see the effects half a kilometer away." Breaking the Silence, *This Is How We Fought in Gaza 2014*, testimony 31, p. 85. Another testimony referred to more munitions: "You

insert ten mines — 100–150 kilos — and it blows up the shaft. It simply collapses in on itself." *Ibid.*, testimony 53, p. 132. Still, this is much less than the effect that a one-ton bomb would have.

113 Basim Dudeen, "The Soils of Palestine (The West Bank and Gaza Strip)," in *Soil Resources of Southern and Eastern Mediterranean Countries,* eds. P. Zdruli, P. Steduto, C. Lacirignola, and L. Montanarella (Bari: CIHEAM, 2001), pp. 203–25, http://ressources.ciheam.org/om/pdf/b34 /01002095.pdf.

114 Human Rights Watch, *Razing Rafah: Mass Home Demolitions in the Gaza Strip*, October 17, 2004, https://www.hrw.org/report/2004/10/17/razing-rafah/mass-home-demolitions-gaza-strip.

115 Amnesty International, "Egypt: End Wave of Home Demolitions, Forced Evictions in Sinai amid Media Blackout," November 27, 2014, https://www.amnesty.org/en/latest/news/2014/11/egypt -end-wave-home-demolitions-forced-evictions-sinai-amid-media-blackout/; *Cairo Observer*, "The Erasure of Gaza and the Normalisation of 'Gazafication,'" April 25, 2015, http://cairobserver.com /post/117284479799/the-erasure-of-rafah-and-the-normalization-of#.VTzSkRfgP-a.

116 Nicholas Pelham, "Gaza's Tunnel Phenomenon: The Unintended Dynamics of Israel's Siege," *Journal of Palestine Studies* 41 (2011–2012), pp. 6–31. The tunnels are supported by reinforced concrete walls and arched roof elements that are manufactured locally in adjacent workshops. See Eado Hecht, "Gaza: How Hamas Tunnel Network Grew," BBC News, July 22, 2014, http://www .bbc.co.uk/news/world-middle-east-28430298; Marissa Newman, "Hamas Said to Have Executed Dozens of Tunnel Diggers," *Times of Israel*, August 11, 2014, http://www.timesofisrael.com/hamas -said-to-have-executed-dozens-of-tunnel-diggers.

117 Bohbot, "Interview with Lieutenant Ethan."

118 "Interview by Amnesty International fieldworker with Inam Ouda Ayed bin Hammad, September 4, 2014," Amnesty International, *'Black Friday,'* p. 32.

119 The interview with Fund was included in "From Deep Under," *Uvda*.

120 Ram, "Exclusive: New Details."

121 Ohayon, "I Must Take the Thoughts of Dying Out of My Head."

122 "Press Release Al Qassam Brigades Regarding Breach of Ceasefire and Alleged Capture of Israeli Soldier."

123 Zeitun, "Givati Commanders from the Rafah Battle 'Clear Conscience.'"

124 Ido Efrati and Anshel Pfeffer, "Between Forensics, Religion and Politics: How Israel Determines a Missing Soldier Is Dead in the Absence of a Body," *Haaretz*, August 3, 2014, http://www.haaretz .com/news/diplomacy-defense/.premium-1.608676 (subscription required).

125 *Ibid.*

126 According to Israel Weiss, the former chief military rabbi, "even when we don't have physical evidence, there are halakhic [Jewish-theological] parameters that allow us to pronounce death without a body or other remains." *Ibid.*

127 Yair Ettinger, "For IDF Chief Rabbi, Some Decisions Mean Life or Death," *Haaretz*, October 8, 2014, http://www.haaretz.com/news/national/.premium-1.619892 (subscription required).

128 Zvi Barel, "A Nightmare Called Hannibal," *Haaretz*, August 6, 2015, in Hebrew, translated and quoted in full in English in Richard Silverstein, "A Nightmare Called Hannibal," *Tikun Olam*, August 7, 2014, http://www.richardsilverstein.com/2014/08/07/a-nightmare-called-hannibal.

129 "Interview by Amnesty International fieldworker with Ahmad Abdel Wahhab, October 14, 2014," Amnesty International, *'Black Friday,'* p. 58.

130 There were many other bombings during and after the capture of Lieutenant Goldin that were allowed according to what Amnesty International has called Israel's "gloves-off policy" by which targets that were previously not authorized because of the expectation for high levels of collateral

damage were allowed under the logic of the Hannibal Directive's attempt to generate deterrence. In one such case, on August 3, the military attacked a UN compound in Rafah where three thousand civilians had taken refuge, killing eleven, five of them children.

131 "Interview by Amnesty International fieldworker with Mohammed Khalil Mohammed Abu Duba," Amnesty International, 'Black Friday,' p. 52.

132 See Gili Cohen, "Trial of Soldier Who Shot Dead Wounded Palestinian Assailant in Hebron Opens," *Haaretz*, May 9, 2016, http://www.haaretz.com/israel-news/1.718637.

133 Isabel Kershner, "Israeli Military Revokes Use of Force to Foil Captures," *New York Times*, June 28, 2016, http://mobile.nytimes.com/2016/06/29/world/middleeast/israel-hannibal-procedure.html.

PART THREE: GROUND TRUTHS

An earlier version of this text was published Eyal Weizman and Fazal Sheikh as *The Conflict Shoreline: Colonialism as Climate Change* (Göttingen and New York: Steidl and Cabinet Books, 2015), translated into Hebrew as *Kav Hamidbar, Sav Ha'Imut* (Tel Aviv: Babel Books and Zochrot, 2016). Thanks are due to Nūri al-'Uqbi, Sayāh and Salim al-Tūri, Oren Yiftachel, Haia Noach, Neve Gordon, Jamon Van Den Hoek, Eduardo Cadava, Shela Sheikh, Liz Jobey, and Adrian Lahoud for their help. Jacob Burns provided good insight throughout. For help in interpreting the aerial images thanks go to Eli Atzmon and another prominent aerial photography analyst who prefers to remain anonymous. Michael Komem and his team at Orientation in Jerusalem provided the transliteration.

1 Members of the al-Tūri tribe had bought land in the eastern part of al-'Araqīb from the al-'Uqbis in 1905 and had begun to use it as a cemetery in 1914.

2 The association has dealt with a host of different matters beyond those of land rights, including, after the Israeli technician Mordechai Vanunu's exposure of Israel's nuclear program in 1986, antinuclear activism.

3 Israeli High Court of Justice Civil Case 7161/06, in Hebrew.

4 Nūri al-'Uqbi, interview, July 20, 2014.

5 On May 14, 2015, the appeal was rejected in a harshly written decision that denied each and every one of the historical and legal arguments. "Despite the claims of the appellants, no physical evidence was presented to support claims for the existence of a permanent Bedouin settlement," wrote Judge Esther Hayut, who went on to recommend that the Bedouins accept the latest of the long-rejected proposals by the state to move to Bedouin towns. See Civil Case 02242/12, May 14, 2015, p. 38, article 55, in Hebrew. Ten days earlier, on May 4, 2015, the court had decided to evict the 350 residents of Khirbet Susya, in the South Hebron Hills of the West Bank, just past the Wall from al-'Araqīb. A day later, on May 5, 2015, the same court authorized the destruction of the Bedouin village of Umm al-Ḥīrān and the plan to construct a new settlement for Jewish national-religious families on its ruins. See Ilene Prusher, "Susya, the Next Outrage in the Israeli-Palestinian Dance of Build-and-Destroy," *Haaretz*, August 4, 2015, http://www.haaretz.com/israel-news/.premium-1.669360; Mairav Zonszein, "Palestinian Village of Susya Faces Imminent Demolition," *+972*, May 7, 2015, http://972mag.com/palestinian-village-of-susya-faces-imminent-demolition-threat/106501; Charlotte Silver, "Israel Destroys Bedouin Village for 84th Time," *Electronic Intifada*, May 22, 2015, https://electronicintifada.net/blogs/charlotte-silver/israel-destroys-bedouin-village-84th-time; Shirly Seidler, "Supreme Court Allows State to Replace Bedouin Village with Jewish One," *Haaretz*, May 6, 2015, http://www.haaretz.com/news/israel/1.655145.

6 Yehezkel Lein and Eyal Weizman, *Land Grab: Israel's Settlement Policy in the West Bank* (Jerusalem: B'Tselem, 2002). We wrote: "Land collectively owned by several villagers was often registered

to the one villager that could read and write. Land merchants and local Ottoman administrators took the opportunity to register large areas of land to their own names. Fallahs and Bedouin farmers who cultivated lands for generations became tenants of absentee owners. It was from the absentee owners that the first wave of Zionist land purchase took place, and farmers were 'legally' displaced from their lands." See http://www.btselem.org/download/200205_land_grab_eng.pdf.

7   State of Israel, Ministry of Justice, "Summary Report of the Experts Team on Land Settlement on the Siyag and the Northern Negev," October 20, 1975.

8   What Oren Yiftachel has called the "dead Negev doctrine" is an Israeli version of the colonial principle of *terra nullius* ("empty land," void of sovereignty or ownership)—a legal principle originating at the 1884–1855 Berlin Conference that disregarded native forms of government cultivation and settlement and dispossessed indigenous people in Africa, Australia, and other places throughout the colonial world, based on the argument that they were "part of the natural environment." Oren Yiftachel, Sandi Kedar, and Ahmad Amara, "Challenging a Legal Doctrine: Rethinking the Dead Negev Ruling, Law and Government," *Mishpat U-Mimshal* 20.1 (2012), pp. 7–147, in Hebrew. The *terra nullius* law was revoked in Australia in a milestone judgment handed down on June 3, 1992, in the landmark case of Mabo v. Queensland in the Australian High Court. The court determined that under certain circumstances, indigenous land rights (native title) had not been extinguished by white European settlement and indeed, under common law, still existed in some parts of what is now called Australia in the latter years of the twentieth century. On *terra nullius*, see Sven Lindqvist, *Terra Nullius: A Journey Through No One's Land*, trans. Sarah Death (New York: New Press, 2007). The legal battles of the Bedouins are thus related, Yiftachel explains, to those of indigenous peoples in countries such as Australia, Canada, South Africa, India, and Brazil. For comparison, see also Patrick Wolfe, "Settler Colonialism and the Elimination of the Native," *Journal of Genocide Research* 8.4 (December 2006), pp. 387–409, and Yiftachel, Kedar, and Amara, "Challenging a Legal Doctrine," p. 27.

9   Ground Truth was curated by Debby Farber for Zochrot. The structure where it was held was built by Aziz al-Tūri and Sharon Rotbard. Zochrot, "Ground Truth: Records of Displacement, Return and Environmental Destruction in the Negev/Naqab Displacement, Return and Environmental Destruction in the Negev/Naqeb Event in Al-Araqi," January 1– February 1, 2016, http://zochrot .org/en/gallery/55860.

10 Zochrot, "Truth Commission on the Responsibility of Israeli Society for the Events of 1948–1960 in the South," http://zochrot.org/en/keyword/45328.

11 This part of the book—making the case for the Bedouins of al-ʿAraqīb—evolved from *The Conflict Shoreline*, an earlier text I wrote around Fazal Sheikh's aerial photographs of the Negev. What follows here is an extended version that includes more research, as well as archaeological, documentary, cartographic, and photographic evidence. Some of the aerial photographs in what follows were produced by cameras connected to kites flown by Public Lab and the inhabitants of al-ʿAraqīb. See Weizman and Sheikh, T*he Conflict Shoreline*. Fazal Sheikh's "Desert Bloom" series can be found in Fazal Sheikh, *Erasure* (Göttingen: Steidl, 2015).

12 There are various other methods of establishing the border of aridity based on different modes of calculating average levels of rainfall and distribution of temperature and evaporation (or evapotranspiration—water lost in the atmosphere from plants). Almost all maps of Palestine from the nineteenth century mark the threshold of the desert in one way or another. Most often the map of Palestine is framed in such a way as to leave out the desert south of Beersheba. One of the first attempts at annotating the threshold of the desert was on Heinrich Kiepert's 1891 *Map of Palestine* (*Neue Handkarte von Palaestina*), where the desert is colored in yellow in contrast with the green

colors above it. There, this takes place roughly around the 300-millimeter aridity line. Some other maps drew a thick red line around the location of the same isohyet.

13 Wladimir Köppen and Alfred Wegener, *The Climates of the Geological Past*, facsimile of the German original and English translation of *Die Klimate der Geologischen Vorzeit*, ed. Jörn Thiede, Karin Lochte, and Angelika Dummermuth, trans. Bernard Oelkers (Stuttgart: Schweizbart, 2015). Danny M. Vaughn, s.v. "Arid Climates," *Encyclopedia of World Climatology*, ed. John E. Oliver (Dordrecht: Springer, 2005).

14 See Bureau of Investigative Journalism, "BIJ: Drone Strikes in Pakistan," http://wherethedrones strike.com, a platform produced by Forensic Architecture in collaboration with Situ Research and the Bureau of Investigative Journalism in 2014.

15 Harari writes: "Wheat didn't like rocks and pebbles, so Sapiens broke their backs clearing fields. Wheat didn't like sharing its space, water, and nutrients with other plants, so men and women labored long days weeding under the scorching sun. Wheat got sick, so Sapiens had to keep a watch out for worms and blight. Wheat was defenseless against other organisms that liked to eat it, from rabbits to locust swarms, so the farmers had to guard and protect it. Wheat was thirsty, so humans lugged water from springs and streams to water it. Its hunger even impelled Sapiens to collect animal feces to nourish the ground in which wheat grew." Yuval Noah Harari, *Sapiens: A Brief History of Humankind* (New York: HarperCollins, 2015), p. 80; James Scott, "Beyond the Pale: The Earliest Agrarian States and 'their Barbarians,'" lecture at the University of London School of Oriental and African Studies, May 12, 2016.

16 In an implicit recognition of Bedouin land ownership, the Ottomans purchased land from the 'Azāzmah tribe in order to build the city of Beersheba. See Ismael Abu-Saad and Cosette Creamer, "Socio-Political Upheaval and Current Conditions of the Naqab Bedouin Arabs," in *Indigenous (In)Justice: Human Rights Law and Bedouin Arabs in the Naqab/Negev,* eds. Ahmad Amara, Ismael Abu-Saad, and Oren Yiftachel (Cambridge, MA: Harvard University Press, 2012), p. 19. On Zionist land purchases see Chanina Porat, *From Wasteland to Inhabited Land: Land Purchase and Settlement in the Negev 1930–1947* (Jerusalem: Yad Izhak Ben-Zvi Press, 1996), in Hebrew. The Ottomans did not venture to register land there unless it was primarily the Zionists and non-Bedouin Arab land owners who registered the land they had purchased from the Bedouins.

17 "Colonial Secretary Churchill approved that which was promised to the sheiks in the area of Beersheba by the High Commissioner Herbert Samuel; that no harm will be done to the customs and special rights of the Bedouin tribes," in Yiftachel, Kedar, and Amara, "Challenging a Legal Doctrine," p. 182.

18 David J. Dean, "Air Power in Small Wars: The British Air Control Experience," *Air University Review* 34.5 (July–August 1983), pp. 24–31; David Omissi, *Air Power and Colonial Control: The Royal Air Force 1919–1939* (Manchester: Manchester University Press, 1990); David MacIsaac, "Voices from the Central Blue: The Air Power Theorists," in *Makers of Modern Strategy, From Machiavelli to the Nuclear Age*, ed. Peter Paret (Oxford: Oxford University Press, 1986), pp. 624–47, esp. p. 633.

19 In 1922, Churchill asked the British Royal Air Force to take over from the army control of Mesopotamia's (Iraq's) Shia areas. Sven Linqvist, *A History of Bombing*, trans. Linda Haverty Rugg (New York: New Press, 2000), entry 101. Sir Percy Cox, the high commissioner in Baghdad, reported that by the end of 1922, "on [at least] three occasions demonstrations by aircraft" had been sufficient to bring "tribal feuds to an end. On another occasion planes…dropped bombs on a sheik and his followers who refused to pay taxes, held up travellers and attacked a police station." Philip Anthony Towle, *Pilots and Rebels: The Use of Aircraft in Unconventional Warfare, 1918–1988* (London: Brassey's, Defence Publishers, 1989), p. 17. See also David Willard Parsons, "British Air Con-

trol: A Model for the Application of Air Power in Low-Intensity Conflict?," *Airpower Journal* 8.2 (Summer 1994), pp. 28–39.

20 The Arab states that were formed in the first part of the twentieth century continued the policy of concentrating and settling the Bedouins within their borders. Dawn Chatty, "The Bedouin in Contemporary Syria: The Persistence of Tribal Authority and Control," *Middle East Journal* 64.1 (Winter 2010), pp. 29–49.

21 For the Egyptian example, see "Making the Desert Bloom: Away from the Crowded Nile," *Economist*, March 18, 1999, http://www.economist.com/node/191156.

22 J.R.W., "Will the Libyan Desert Bloom Again?," *Milwaukee Journal*, January 8, 1932. See also "Making the Libyan Desert Bloom," *Milwaukee Journal*, December 20, 1938. In one of the most embarrassing quotes for Zionist history, Abba Ahimeir, a right-wing Jewish writer in prestate Palestine, called upon Zionists to learn from "Fascist praxis and its psycho-politics." In fact, at least in its pre–World War II years, the visual culture, energy, and enthusiasm of both Fascists and Zionists were very similar. Ahimeir also called Ze'ev Jabotinsky "our Duce," but later retracted. Tom Segev, "Words That Can't be Retracted," *Haaretz*, April 20, 2012, in Hebrew. By the time the camps were dismantled in 1933, the Italians had killed about 60 percent of the local population. See Christopher Duggan, *The Force of Destiny: A History of Italy Since 1796* (New York: Houghton Mifflin, 2007), p. 496; Simonetta Falasca Zamponi, "Storytellers and Master Narratives," in *States of Memory: Continuities, Conflicts, and Transformations in National Retrospection,* ed. Jeffrey K. Olick (Chapel Hill: Duke University Press, 2003), pp. 43–71.

23 Eyal Weizman, *Hollow Land: Israel's Architecture of Occupation* (London: Verso, 2007), pp. 221–36.

24 See B'Tselem's ongoing account on Hebron, "Hebron City Center, http://www.btselem.org/topic /hebron.

25 Gideon Levy, "The Sewage of Ma'ale Edumim," *Haaretz*, February 22, 1998. Available in English at http://www.wrmea.org/1998-april/the-sewage-of-ma-ale-edumim-an-article-written-by-gideon -levy-in-the-feb.-22-1998-ha-aretz.html.

26 United Nations Office for the Coordination of Humanitarian Affairs, "Humanitarian Fact Sheet on the Jordan Valley and Dead Sea Area," February 2012, http://www.europarl.europa.eu/meet docs/2009_2014/documents/dplc/dv/dead_sea_/dead_sea_en.pdf. Israel is now planning a new town in the Jordan Valley. Bedouins will be relocated there. Amira Hass, "Israeli Government Plans to Forcibly Relocate 12,500 Bedouin," *Haaretz*, September 16, 2014, http://www.haaretz.com/israel-news/.premium-1.615986.

27 The cycle of droughts, starting in 2006, led to the movement of two-million impoverished farmers into the outskirts of cities. Syrian water reservoirs, which could have alleviated the situation, were depleted by half between 2002 and 2008, following Assad's policy of cultivating water-costly cotton and cereals. See a report by Integrated Regional Information Networks (IRIN), a service of the UN Office for the Coordination of Humanitarian Affairs, "Syria: Drought Driving Farmers to the Cities," September 2, 2009, http://www.irinnews.org/report/85963/syria-drought-driving -farmers-to-the-cities. See also The Center for Climate and Security, "One-Stop List of Resources on Syria, Drought, Climate Change and Unrest," updated, January 23, 2014, http://climateand security.org/2014/01/23/updated-one-stop-list-of-resources-on-syria-drought-climate-change -and-unrest.

28 Francesco Femia and Caitlin Werrell, "Climate Change Before and After the Arab Awakening: The Cases of Syria and Libya," in *The Arab Spring and Climate Change*, eds. Caitlin E. Werrell and Francesco Femia (Washington, DC: Center for American Progress, Stimson, and The Center for Climate and Security, 2013); Russell Sticklor, "Syria: Beyond the Euphrates," *New Security Beat*, September

28, 2010, http://www.newsecuritybeat.org/2010/09/syria-at-the-crossroads-beyond-the-euphrates; Robert F. Worth, "Earth Is Parched Where Syrian Farms Thrived," *New York Times*, October 13, 2010, http://www.nytimes.com/2010/10/14/world/middleeast/14syria.html; Wadid Erian, Bassem Katlan, and Ouldbdey Babah, "Drought Vulnerability in the Arab region: Special Case Study: Syria" (2010), United Nations Global Assessment Report on Disaster Risk Reduction, 2011, http://www.preventionweb.net/english/hyogo/gar/2011/en/bgdocs/Erian_Katlan_&_Babah_2010.pdf; Forensic Architecture, "Drone Strikes: Investigating Covert Operations through Spatial Media," http://www.forensic-architecture.org/case/drone-strikes; Global Assessment Report on Disaster Risk Reduction 2011, "Revealing Risk, Redefining Development," http://www.preventionweb.net/english/hyogo/gar/2011/en/home/index.html.

29 Femia and Werrell, "Climate Change Before and After the Arab Awakening," pp. 25–27.

30 Security experts now refer to the Sahel as the "corridor of terror," pointing to the loss of agricultural land as the "underlying cause of social, economic and environmental problems that feed recruitment for violent extremist organizations" such as "Al Qaeda-linked groups." Mark Sexton and Shafi Saiduddin, "Desertification and Insurgency: A Global Crisis," *Army Magazine*, July 2014, p. 50; Kim Sengupta and Brian Brady, "West Turns Sights on Threat in the Desert," *Independent*, January 20, 2013, http://www.independent.co.uk/news/world/africa/west-turns-sights-on-threat-in-the-desert-8458857.html. Adrian Lahoud provides a strong counternarrative: "For decades, it was assumed that desertification in the Sahel was primarily caused by poor farming practices — that unsophisticated local farmers could not adapt to changing environmental conditions as quickly as they needed to, leading to overgrazing, deforestation, and erosion.... More recently, however, anthropogenic climate change has forced a reexamination of these alleged causes." Adrian Lahoud, "Floating Bodies," in *Forensis: The Architecture of Public Truth*, ed. Forensic Architecture (Berlin: Sternberg Press, 2014), p. 504; Miles Amoore, "Kew's Great Green Wall to Hold Back Saharan Terror," *London Sunday Times*, July 20, 2014, http://www.thesundaytimes.co.uk/sto/news/world_news/Africa/article1436532.ece. It includes the following sentence: "Scientists are planting millions of trees across Africa to fight the spread of the desert and alleviate the poverty that Islamists feed on." Ever sensitive to global trends, Israel has also started to explain the need to settle the Negev Bedouins in towns as a local chapter in the global war on terror. In this scenario, the Bedouins need to be brought under control because as "nomads," they are involved in the smuggling of weapons from the disintegrating Libyan military into Gaza and the West Bank. The Bedouins of Sinai, neglected and disenfranchised by the Egyptian state, have indeed been involved in such smuggling activities, but they, like the Negev Bedouins, have long since ceased to be nomads. Ron Ben-Yishai, "Sinai Panic Creates Terror," *Ynet*, June 18, 2012, http://www.ynetnews.com/articles/0,7340,L-4244057,00.html.

31 *Atlas of the Negev*, eds. Eliahu Stern, et al. (Sde Boker: Ben-Gurion University of the Negev, 1986).

32 Noam Levin, Ruth Kark, and Emir Galilee, "Maps and the Settlement of Southern Palestine, 1799–1948: An Historical/GIS Analysis," *Journal of Historical Geography* 36.1 (December 2009), p. 11.

33 Franz Mauelshagen, "Redefining Historical Climatology in the Anthropocene," *Anthropocene Review* 1.2 (August 2014), pp. 171–204.

34 Jeremiah 13:19 .

35 Isaiah 35:7.

36 In 1911, a Zionist organization purchased six thousand dunams (roughly fifteen hundred acres) from the Bedouins in Jammama (Ruchama). By 1947, the Jewish National Fund and Jewish individuals had purchased ten times that, about sixty thousand dunams (fifteen thousand acres) of Negev land from Bedouin tribes. Chanina Porat, *The Negev: From a Desert to Cultivatable Land. Negev*

Development and Settlement 1949–1956 (Beersheba: Ben-Gurion Heritage Institute, Ben-Gurion University of the Negev, 1996), p. 3, in Hebrew.

37 Meron Benvenisti, *Sacred Landscape: The Buried History of the Holy Land since 1948* (Berkeley: University of California Press, 2002), pp. 59–62.

38 *Ibid.*, p. 61.

39 D.H.K. Amiran, "The Pattern of Settlements in Palestine," *Israel Exploration Journal* 2.2 (1953), pp. 67–71.

40 *Ibid.*, p. 78.

41 The fluctuations are between 31°25′N and 31°10′N. See *Atlas of Israel: Cartography, Physical and Human Geography*, 3rd ed. (New York: Macmillan, 1985), p. 18; see especially map 3, "Fluctuations of the Annual 200 mm Isohyet, September 1931 – September 1976."

42 Walid Khalidi, *All That Remains: The Palestinian Villages Occupied and Depopulated by Israel in 1948* (Washington, DC: Institute for Palestine Studies, 1992), p. 127.

43 Neve Gordon, "In the Negev," *London Review of Books* 34.6, March 22, 2012.

44 Benvenisti, *Sacred Landscape*, p. 19.

45 Jewish Telegraphic Agency, "Israel Inaugurates Yarkon-Negev Pipeline Amid Great Festivities," July 20, 1955, http://www.jta.org/1955/07/20/archive/israel-inaugurates-yarkon-negev-pipeline -amid-great-festivities.

46 Gadi Elgazi, response to Kav Hamidbar, *Sav Ha'Imut*, Tola'at Sfarim bookshop, April 4, 2016.

47 The Jewish National Fund is an international organization that for the past one hundred years has been in charge of planting trees in the "land of Israel." The designation of the zone of operation as the "land of Israel" marks the fact that this organization predates the state, but the persistence of this designation after the establishment of Israel and the occupation of the West Bank also became a code name for afforestation in areas in which state law did not apply. Furthermore, not being a state agency allowed the JNF to act on behalf of "world Jewry," rather than citizens of the state, which would also include Arabs. Shaul Ephraim Cohen, *The Politics of Planting* (Berkeley: University of California Press, 1993). During the 1948 war, Weitz was also the leading figure in the notorious three-member "Transfer Committee" that sought to expedite the expulsion of Palestinians from areas occupied by the Israeli military. *Ibid.*, p. 75.

48 Alon Tal, *Pollution in a Promised Land: An Environmental History of Israel* (Berkeley: University of California Press, 2002), p. 92.

49 These cities were an economic and social failure and now have the highest unemployment levels of all Jewish cities in Israel. Zvi Efrat, *The Israeli Project: Building and Architecture 1948–1973* (Tel Aviv: Tel Aviv Museum of Art, 2004), in Hebrew. Forthcoming in English as *Project Israel*, Spector Books, Leipzig.

50 In 2004, after independent researchers found radioactivity in areas beyond and around the site, Israeli authorities distributed potassium iodide antiradiation tablets to thousands of residents living in Dimona and in the Bedouin settlements in the vicinity of the reactor. AFP news agency, "Israel Distributes Radiation Pills to Residents Near Nuclear Reactor," August 8, 2004, http://www.abc.net.au/cgi-bin/common/printfriendly.pl?http://www.abc.net.au/news/news items/200408/s1171510.htm.

51 Doron Efrati, "Wheat and Drought," Shlomi: The Center for Teacher Training in Science and Technology, http://www.shlomi.org.il/amitim/AOL/articles/bread/bazoret.htm, in Hebrew.

52 Avner Ben Amos, "From Dayan to Almog: The Bedouins Are the Same Bedouins," *Haokets*, December 10, 2013, https://enghaokets.wordpress.com/2013/12/10/the-military-face-behind-the-prawer -plans-civilian-mask. The original quote comes from *Haaretz*, in August 31, 1963.

53 Tal, *Pollution in a Promised Land*, pp. 53–54, 206–209.

54 *Ibid.*

55 A recent UN report expressed grave concern about the situation of these displaced: "The number of Bedouins living below the poverty line, their living and housing conditions, their levels of
malnutrition, unemployment and infant mortality are all significantly higher than the national
averages. They have no access to water, electricity and sanitation and are subjected on a regular
basis to land confiscations, house demolitions, fines for building 'illegally,' destruction of agricultural fields and trees, and systematic harassment and persecution." "Israel, Additional Information
(2001)," in *Concluding Observations of the UN Committee on Economic, Social and Cultural Rights:
Eighth to Twenty-Seventh Sessions (1993–2001)*, ed. Leif Holmström (The Hague: Kluwer Law International, 2003), pp. 317–20.

56 Nevatim, one of the busiest of Israeli military air force bases, has been expanded in the middle of
the former *siyag*, still the most densely populated Bedouin area.

57 This military megabase is currently under construction between the development towns of Dimona
and Yeruḥam. Planned for thirty thousand army personnel, it was named after Ariel Sharon. Parts
of the base are already operative. When completed, the base will house the Israeli Defense Force's
Armaments School, Logistics Training School, Military Police School, and other military training
centers. The base will include training facilities, sports areas, a shopping mall, synagogues, hotels,
cinemas, and entertainment facilities. Peter Arga, "Another Step to the South: Training Campus
Headquarters Founded," in Hebrew, Israel Defense Forces, November 13, 2014 http://www.idf
.il/1133-21463-he/Dover.aspx, in Hebrew. There are Bedouin villages that have been declared illegal
east of the site and also a Jewish-owned ranch. The site is bounded by a closed military zone with
some families of the unrecognized Bedouin village of al-Mshash contained within it. The government plans to move the residents to Segev Shalom/Shgēb al-Salām, one of the Bedouin townships.

58 Hanna Hamdan, "The Settlement Policy and the 'Judiazation' of Space in the Negev," Adalah
electronic sheet no. 11.3.2005, in Hebrew; Gadi Algazi, "The State of Israel vs. Citizens of Israel,"
Tarabut, July 28, 2010, http://www.tarabut.info/en/articles/article/al-arakib-demolished.

59 Gordon, "In the Negev."

60 Nūri al-ʿUqbi, interview, July 20, 2014.

61 *Ibid.*, p. 347.

62 Farkhan Shlebe, quoted in *ibid.*, p. 349.

63 Chaim Levinson, Ido Efrati, Jack Khoury, and Revital Hovel, "Man Killed in Rocket Strike on Negev
Bedouin Community," *Haaretz*, July 19, 2014, http://www.haaretz.com/israel-news/.premium
-1.606027.

64 Jewish National Fund, "Desertification — A Global Issue," http://www.kkl.org.il/eng/forestry-and
-ecology/combating-desertification/desertification-a-global-issue; "Combating Desertification,"
http://www.kkl.org.il/eng/forestry-and-ecology/combating-desertification; "Turning the Desert Green," http://www.kkl.org.il/eng/forestry-and-ecology/afforestation-in-israel/turning-the
-desert-green.

65 Jonathan Cook, "Bedouins defiant despite Israel eviction plan," Al Jazeera, June 14, 2014, http://
www.aljazeera.com/news/middleeast/2014/06/bedouins-defiant-despite-israel-eviction-plan-negev
-201461474220183274.html.

66 Abu-Madigam v. Israel Land Authority, HCJ 2887/04, in Hebrew. Al-ʿAraqīb was sprayed with her-
bicide on February 14, 2002; April 2, 2003; June 17, 2003; January 15, 2004; and February 10, 2004.
Fields of wheat, barley, corn, and watermelon were destroyed. Negev Coexistence Forum for Civil
Equality, http://www.dukium.org.

67 Algazi, "The State of Israel vs. Citizens of Israel."

68 The decisive moment in the trial happened when the plaintiffs' lawyer read out the producer's own label: "Precaution…wear gloves, avoid breathing in the fumes…wash with water and soap any part of the body that came into contact with the chemical. Avoid animal feeding over an area sprayed by the chemical or their entry for seven days from the time of the spraying." Abu-Madigam v. Israel Land Authority.

69 The former South African ambassador to Israel, Ismail Coovadia, explained: "I have supported the struggle against apartheid South Africa and now I cannot be a proponent of what I have witnessed in Israel, and that is, a replication of apartheid." "South African diplomat rejects gift from Israeli Ministry of Foreign Affairs," *Middle East Monitor*, June 18, 2013, https://www.middleeastmonitor.com/news/middle-east/6323-south-african-diplomat-rejects-gift-from-israeli-ministry-of-foreign-affairs.

70 Jewish National Fund, "Desertification — A Global Issue"; Jewish National Fund, "Combating Desertification"; Jewish National Fund, "Turning the Desert Green."

71 Contemporary environmental research recognizes that grazing, now excluded from most of the desert for ecological reasons, increases soil productivity by breaking through the saline crust of the soil and allowing seeds to take hold and germinate, while droppings act as fertilizers. Tal, *Pollution in a Promised Land*, p. 351. Grazing goats have also been returned to forest areas such as the Carmel after it was recognized that by eating the small bushes between the trees, they make it harder for fires to proliferate.

72 Amir Ben-David, "Report: Planting by JNF Causes Ecological Damage," *Ynet*, March 28, 2013, in Hebrew.

73 Guy Rotem, Amos Bouskila, and Alon Rothschild, *Ecological Effects of Afforestation in the Northern Negev*, report by the Society for the Protection of Nature in Israel, May 2014, http://www.teva.org.il/_Uploads/dbsAttachedFiles/forestration_northern_NegevSPNI_Eng_finalMay2014.pdf, p. 47. The authors refer to Eyal Rotenberg and Dan Yakir, "Contribution of Semi-Arid Forests to the Climate System," *Science* 327.5964 (January 2010), pp. 451–54.

74 The complete quote is: "The trees at Sde Boker speak to me differently than do the trees planted elsewhere. Not only because I participated in their planting and in their maintenance, but also because they are a gift of man to nature and a gift of the Jews to the compost of their culture." David Ben-Gurion, *Memoirs* (Cleveland: World Publishing, 1970), p. 150. Human-induced climate change, caused to a large extent by intensive farming and water-use policies, was a major factor in the more frequent droughts that have been afflicting the wider Mediterranean region. Katy Human, "Human-Caused Climate Change a Major Factor in More Frequent Mediterranean Droughts," National Oceanic & Atmospheric Administration, October 27, 2011, http://www.boulder.noaa.gov/?q=node/16; Sonja J. Vermeulen, Bruce M. Campbell, and John S. I. Ingram, "Climate Change and Food Systems," *Annual Review of Environment and Resources* 37 (November 2012), pp. 195–222. In 2005, agriculture covered 37 percent of the earth's terrestrial surface. Changes in land cover are a major source of CO_2 to the atmosphere, contributing from 12 to 17 percent of global emissions. Large agribusiness cattle ranching, soybean farming, and plantation agriculture have become more important as drivers of climate change. R. Lal, "Soil Carbon Sequestration Impacts on Global Climate Change and Food Security," *Science* 304.5677 (June 2004), pp. 1623–27; Zafrir Rinat, "Experts Discuss Middle East Climate Change at JNF Workshop," *Haaretz*, July 3, 2014, http://www.haaretz.com/israel-news/science/.premium-1.602741. See also D. J. Eldridge, Eli Zaady, and Moshe Shachak, "Infiltration through Three Contrasting Biological Soil Crusts in Patterned Landscapes in the Negev, Israel," *Catena* 40.3 (July 2000), pp. 323–36.

75 In 2013, to reduce the number of asylum seekers, Israel completed the fencing-up of the entire

length of its border to Egypt. Many desert thresholds are being fenced up. This process takes place not only in the Negev, Gaza, and the West Bank, but also along other aridity lines in such places as Saudi Arabia, the western Sahara, and the US–Mexico border (an aridity line separates the American Southwest from Mexico through the notorious frontiers of El Paso/Ciudad Juarez and San Diego/Tijuana). Guatemalan architect Teddy Cruz has called these bends of conflict zones "the political equator." *Political Equator*, http://politicalequator.blogspot.com.

76 Geographic determinism is the theory that the characteristics of culture (sometimes also of race) are shaped by geographic conditions. Ellsworth Huntington, one of the most visible proponents of geographic determinism, proposed that the fall of the Roman Empire was precipitated by reductions in agriculture output caused by shifts in the aridity line. Ellsworth Huntington, *World Power and Evolution* (New Haven: Yale University Press, 1919).

77 Fernand Braudel, *The Mediterranean and the Mediterranean World in the Age of Philip II: Vol. 1*, trans Siân Reynolds (Berkeley: University of California Press, 1996), p. 20. Quoted in Dipesh Chakrabarty, "The Climate of History: Four Theses," *Critical Inquiry* 35.2 (Winter 2009), p. 204 (quotation modified as per original).

78 See the "Ecologies" section in *Forensis*, pp. 483–633.

79 The term "Anthropocene" was proposed by Paul Crutzen in 2000. Since 2008, geologists have proposed the formal adoption of the Anthropocene epoch (still pending).

80 An algorithmically made estimation of civilian casualties is now presented to commanders by various computer programs before a mission to determine the correct "proportion" of collateral damage and to try to avoid "excessive death." But as has become apparent from Pakistan through Iraq to Gaza and Lebanon, the supposedly unintentional killing of civilians can also be used by militaries as an effective strategy, a mode of leveraging power, articulated through fear, punishment, deterrence, and retribution. "We will wield disproportionate power against every village from which shots are fired on Israel, and cause immense damage and destruction.... This is not a suggestion. This is a plan that has already been authorized." Gabriel Siboni, "Disproportionate Force: Israel's Concept of Response in Light of the Second Lebanon War," Institute for National Security Studies *Insight* 74, October 2, 2008, http://www.inss.org.il/index.aspx?id=4538&articleid=1964. The United Nations Fact Finding Mission on the Gaza Conflict (the Goldstone report) also insisted that Israel waged "a deliberately disproportionate attack designed to punish, humiliate and terrorize a civilian population, radically diminish its local economic capacity both to work and to provide for itself, and to force upon it an ever-increasing sense of dependency and vulnerability." United Nations, *Human Rights in Palestine and Other Occupied Arab Territories: Report of the United Nations Fact-Finding Mission on the Gaza Conflict*, A/HRC/12/48, September 29, 2009, p. 409, http://www2.ohchr.org/english/bodies/hrcouncil/docs/12session/A-HRC-12-48.pdf. Eyal Weizman, *The Least of All Possible Evils: Humanitarian Violence from Arendt to Gaza* (London: Verso, 2011), pp. 20–21.

81 An exception to this argument has been the position of the Indigenous Environmental Network in Paris, where indigenous peoples staged a direct action. "We, Indigenous Peoples, are the redline. We have drawn that line with our bodies against the privatisation of nature, to dirty fossil fuels and to climate change. We are the defenders of the world's most biologically and culturally diverse regions. We will protect our sacred lands. Our knowledge has much of the solutions to climate change that humanity seeks. It's only when they listen to our message that ecosystems of the world will be renewed." Tom Goldtooth, executive director of the Indigenous Environmental Network, quoted in *Play and Ideas*, "Reclaiming Streets from Paris to the World, #D12, #COP21, Paris Blog Part Two of Three," December 16, 2015, http://benjaminheimshepard.blogspot.com/2015/12

/reclaiming-streets-from-paris-to-world.html. Similarly, the slogan of several low-lying island nations is "1.5 to stay alive." As Naomi Klein tells it, "At the last minute, a clause was added to the Paris Agreement that says countries will pursue 'efforts to limit the temperature increase to 1.5°c.' Not only is this non-binding but it is a lie: we are making no such efforts. The governments that made this promise are now pushing for more fracking and more tar sands development — which are utterly incompatible with 2°c, let alone 1.5°c." Klein, "Let Them Drown."

82   Franz Mauelshagen, "Modernity's Decline? The Return of Catastrophism in the Anthropocene," in *Decline and Declinism*, eds. William O'Reilly and Richard Miles (Budapest: Central European University Press, forthcoming); James Rodger Fleming, *Historical Perspectives on Climate Change* (Oxford: Oxford University Press, 1998), pp. 11–20.

83   Hugh Williamson, "An Attempt to Account for a Change in Climate Which has been Observed in the Middle Colonies in North-America," *Transactions of the American Philosophical Society* 1 (January 1, 1769 – January 1, 1771), http://www.jstor.org/stable/1005036?seq=2#page_scan_tab_contents. Williamson was the first to have used the term "change of climate." He also proposed a programmatic change of climate by landscape modifications. "In order then that we may be able to form an estimate of the heat of any country, we must not only consider the latitude of the place, but also the face and situation of the country, and the winds which generally prevail there, if any of these should alter, the climate must also be changed. The face of the country may be altered by cultivation, and a transient view of the general cause of winds will convince us, that their course may also be changed" (p. 273). Jefferson claimed that "a change in our climate…is taking place very sensibly." Thomas Jefferson, *Notes on the State of Virginia*, ed. William Peden (Chapel Hill: University of North Carolina Press, 1955), p. 80. Noah Webster provided a rebuttal in two speeches collected and published as Noah Webster, *On the Supposed Change in the Temperature of Winter* (Connecticut Academy of Arts and Science, 1810). For more on the Webster-Jefferson debate, see Joshua Kendall, "America's First Great Global Warming Debate," *Smithsonian.com*, July 14, 2011, http://www.smithsonianmag.com/history/americas-first-great-global-warming-debate-31911494. Nineteenth-century forest polices were based on "dessicationist" (extreme dryness) beliefs that deforestation caused local, regional, and even continental drought. None of these theories were thought through about the planet as a whole. See J.R. Fleming, *Historical Perspectives on Climate Change* (Oxford: Oxford University Press, 1998); Richard Grove, *Ecology, Climate and Empire: Colonialism and Global Environmental History, 1400–1940* (Winwick, UK: White Horse Press, 1997).

84   Eduardo Cadava, *Emerson and the Climates of History* (Stanford: Stanford University Press, 1997), pp. 40–41.

85   In an implicit continuation of these climatic experiments, American Cold War scientists tried to develop ways of weaponizing the weather by artificially generating clouds for floods or driving them away to make droughts. There were also stranger contemporaneous NASA studies that sought to find ways of making different planets and moons — including Venus and Mars — open to human inhabitation by instigating climate-changing events there. These debates, undertaken from the late eighteenth century to the late twentieth, are at the root of today's earth-system science. On the weaponization of the environment: "between 1967 and 1972, a US Air Force effort called Operation Popeye attempted to wash out parts of the North Vietnamese resupply route known as the Ho Chi Minh Trail by seeding clouds over Laos during monsoons. Among the largest efforts was Project Stormfury, which tested techniques for steering or extinguishing tropical cyclones." Paul N. Edwards, *A Vast Machine: Computer Models, Climate Data, and the Politics of Global Warming* (Cambridge, MA: MIT Press, 2010), pp. 359–60.

86   Richard Grove, *Green Imperialism: Colonial Expansion, Tropical Island Edens and the Origins of Environmentalism, 1600–1860* (Cambridge: Cambridge University Press, 1996), pp. 163–68.

87   Paulo Tavares, *Over the Ruins of Amazonia: Territorial Politics at the Frontiers of Climate Change* (New York: Verso, forthcoming).

88   James C. Scott, *Seeing Like a State: How Certain Schemes to Improve the Human Condition Have Failed* (New Haven: Yale University Press, 1998), p. 262.

89   An anthropology of such liminal spaces is described in Anna Lowenhaupt Tsing, *Friction: An Ethnography of Global Connection* (Princeton: Princeton University Press, 2004), as well as in her later book, *The Mushroom at the End of the World: On the Possibility of Life in Capitalist Ruins* (Princeton: Princeton University Press, 2015). See also Hannah Martin, "Outlaw Earth," PhD diss., Centre for Research Architecture, Goldsmiths, University of London (forthcoming, 2017); Tavares, *Over the Ruins of Amazonia*.

90   Tavares, *Over the Ruins of Amazonia*.

91   Tal, *Pollution in a Promised Land*, p. 69.

92   *Ibid.*, p. 266.

93   Human Rights Watch, *Prison Conditions in Israel and the Occupied Territories, 1991: Middle East Watch Report*, pp. 18 and 64, https://www.hrw.org/reports/pdfs/i/israel/israel.914/israel914 .pdf. Because by international law Israel is forbidden to remove the occupied population from the Occupied Territories, the prisons have been defined, for operational and legal purposes, as extraterritorial islands of occupied territory inside Israel.

94   Catrina Stewart, "Israelis Build the World's Biggest Detention Centre," *Independent*, March 10, 2012, http://www.independent.co.uk/news/world/middle-east/israelis-build-the-worlds-biggest-detention-centre-7547401.html; Bill Van Esveld and Arthur Helton, *Sinai Perils: Risks to Migrants, Refugees, and Asylum Seekers in Egypt and Israel*, report by Human Rights Watch, November 12, 2008, https://www.hrw.org/reports/2008/egypt1108. Israel's laws were changed to enable it to imprison migrants arriving after December 2013 for up to one year without trial. Those who arrived before that date now receive an "invitation to attend a residence facility," otherwise known as an "open detention center," where migrants can be held in indefinite detention without judicial review. Allison Deger, "African Asylum Seekers in Israel Reject 'Invitation' to Desert Prison," *Mondoweiss*, March 28, 2014, http://mondoweiss.net/2014/03/african-seekers-invitation.html.

95   Gilead Natan, "The Treatment of Infiltrators from the Egyptian Border," Knesset Research and Information Centre, May 26, 2010, http://www.knesset.gov.il/mmm/data/pdf/m02524.pdf, in Hebrew. See also Stewart, "Israelis Build the World's Biggest Detention Centre," and Van Esveld and Helton, *Sinai Perils*. The story of Ktzi'ot manifests much of the history of Zionist colonization in the Negev. It was established in 1953 as a military agrarian (Nahal) settlement point after the military expelled thirty-five hundred members of the Bedouin al-'Azāzme tribe. The settlement was abandoned in the 1960s. In the late 1980s, its infrastructure was converted to serve as a detention camp for Palestinian prisoners arriving in large numbers during the first Intifada. In recent years, Ktzi'ot has gradually been converted into the world's largest migrant detention center. A recent UN report estimated that by 2020, south-to-north migration between the drying Sahel and Europe will affect more than sixty million people. *Desertification: the Invisible Frontline*, report by The United Nations Convention to Combat Desertification, 2014, http://www.unccd.int/Lists /SiteDocumentLibrary/Publications/Desertification_The%20invisible_frontline.pdf. For the consequences of migration through the Mediterranean, see Charles Heller, Lorenzo Pezzani, and Situ Research, "The Left-to-Die Boat: The Deadly Drift of a Migrants' Boat in the Central Mediterranean," Forensic Architecture, 2012, http://www.forensic-architecture.org/case/left-die-boat. See

also Heller and Pezzani, "Liquid Traces: Investigating the Deaths of Migrants at the EU's Maritime Frontier," in *Forensis,* pp. 637–84.

96   Arie S. Issar and Mattanyah Zohar, *Climate Change — Environment and Civilization in the Middle East* (Berlin: Springer, 2004), p. 23. Issar and Zohar reconstruct the paleoclimatic scenario for the post–Roman-Byzantine period as follows: "a series of dry years with an annual average precipitation of less than 40 mm over the surface drainage basin caused the olive crop to diminish to a level where it was no longer economical to cultivate. A few consecutive years of drought may even have caused many trees to dry up and die. Thus, the olive plantations on the terraces were abandoned and the natural vegetation of dwarf oak, pistachios, etc., returned to dominate the landscape. With the return of the natural *maqui* type vegetation, the permanent inhabitants could shift to an economy of raising goats and sheep, and in good years to sow the terraces for grain and fodder" (p. 26). See also H.J. Bruins, "Ancient Desert Agriculture in the Negev and Climate-Zone Boundary Changes During Average, Wet and Drought Years," *Journal of Arid Environments* 86 (November 2012), p. 26; Rehav Rubin, "The Romanization of the Negev, Israel: Geographical and Cultural Changes in the Desert Frontier in Late Antiquity," *Journal of Historical Geography* 23.3 (July 1997), pp. 267–83.

97   Michael Evenari, Leslie Shanan, and Naphtali Tadmor, *The Negev: The Challenge of a Desert* (Cambridge, MA: Harvard University Press, 1971). "In those days field trips were made in convoy style, with about one-fifth of the party acting as security guards in case of an attack by marauders…. Many of us grew beards" and "would look like gun-packing frontiersman in the Wild West" (p. 1).

98   Edward Henry Palmer, *The Desert of the Exodus: Journeys on Foot in the Wilderness of the Forty Years' Wanderings,* 2 vols. (Cambridge: Deighton, Bell and Co, 1871), vol. 2, p. 287. Quoted in Evenari, Shanan, and Tadmor, *The Negev,* p. 27.

99   Gideon Avni, "Early Mosques in the Negev Highlands: New Archaeological Evidence on Islamic Penetration of Southern Palestine," *Bulletin of the American Schools of Oriental Research* 294 (May 1994), pp. 83–100. For a more recent interdisciplinary approach, reading the military, agrarian, economic (human), and climate (desertification) history against each other, see the Ancient Deserts Agricultural Systems Revived (ADASR) project, http://www.mnemotrix.com/adasr /home.html.

100 "We asked a neighboring Bedouin sheikh to assist us. He promised to send seven of his Bedouins with their camels. On the morning of December 4, twenty-one Bedouins appeared with their camels and plows! Soon the farm, which had been abandoned for many centuries, came to life as the camels began to drag their antiquated wooden plows…. Soon the whole field was green and now we felt that we had made the first step on the road to our goal." Evenari, Shanan, and Tadmor, *The Negev,* p. 4.

101 Civil Case 7161/06, Al-Uqbi v. The State of Israel, December 7, 2009 (my summary of some of the contents of the testimony).

102 *Ibid.* (my translation from Hebrew).

103 See also the summary of the case in Noa Kram, "Clashes over Recognition: The Struggle of Indigenous Bedouins for Land Ownership Rights Under Israeli Law," PhD diss., California Institute of Integral Studies, 2013.

104 Bruce Granville Mille, *Oral History on Trial: Recognizing Aboriginal Narratives in the Courts* (Vancouver: University of British Columbia Press, 2011). Al-'Uqbi's new representative, the human rights lawyer Michael Sfard, who took over from Gabso in early 2010 in an attempt to turn the tide, responded to this allegation by stating that by hearing land claims for the first time almost sixty years after dispossession, a period during which the village elders who could have personally

testified had passed away, the state was responsible for "evidentiary damage." Interview with Michael Sfard, Tel Aviv, April 9, 2014. This argument made no impression on Dovrat.

105 Roy S. Fischel and Ruth Kark, "Sultan Abdülhamid II and Palestine: Private Lands and Imperial Policy," *New Perspectives on Turkey* 39 (Fall 2008), pp. 129–66; Ruth Kark, "The Agricultural Character of Jewish Settlement in the Negev: 1939–1947," *Jewish Social Studies* 45.2 (Spring 1983), pp. 157–74.

106 Al-Uqbi v. The State of Israel, May 13, 2010 (my translation from Hebrew).

107 *Ibid.*

108 In its summation of the al-'Araqīb case, the state added: "It is not enough to have a tent encampment, temporary accommodation, a few dwellings, or scattered buildings that are not continuous and contiguous in order to qualify as a settlement." Dovrat, final verdict in Al-Uqbi v. The State of Israel. However, as Yiftachel et al. explain, nowhere did the Ottoman law mention "a village" but rather used the term "inhabited location" and therefore did not define what a settlement is. Yiftachel, Kedar, and Amara, "Challenging a Legal Doctrine," p. 92.

109 Dovrat, final verdict in Al-Uqbi vs. The State of Israel, pp. 20–21.

110 Yiftachel, Kedar, and Amara, "Challenging a Legal Doctrine," p. 176.

111 Interview with Michael Sfard, Tel Aviv, April 9, 2014.

112 Literary critic Franco Moretti has developed a distant reading approach. See Moretti, *Distant Reading* (London: Verso, 2013).

113 The original sources are: Henry Baker Tristram, *The Land of Israel: A Journal of Travels in Palestine (Undertaken with special reference to its physical character)* (London: Clay and Taylor; Society for Promoting Christian Knowledge, 1865), p. 372; Edward Hull, *Mount Seir, Sinai and Western Palestine* (London: Richard Bentley and Son, 1885), pp. 138–39; William M. Thomson, *The Land and the Book* (New York: Harper and Brothers, 1910), p. 556. All quotes are in Yiftachel, Kedar, and Amara, "Challenging a Legal Doctrine," pp. 76–80.

114 Palmer, *The Desert of the Exodus*, vol. 2, pp. 298–99.

115 Edward Said, *Orientalism* (London: Penguin Books, 2003), p. 286.

116 Dovrat, final verdict in Al-Uqbi v. The State of Israel.

117 Civil Appeal 218/74, Salim Al-Hawashleh v. State of Israel, P.D. 38(3): 141 (1984), final verdict, August 2, 1984, in Hebrew.

118 Palmer, *The Desert of the Exodus*, vol. 2, p. 392.

119 *Ibid.*, p. 390.

120 Yifa Yaakov, "6th-Century Byzantine Monastery Excavated in Negev," *Times of Israel*, April 1, 2014, http://www.timesofisrael.com/6th-century-byzantine-monastery-excavated-in-negev.

121 Palmer, *The Desert of the Exodus*, vol. 2, p. 393.

122 *Ibid.*

123 It was only in April 1870 that the British consulate general to "Beyrout" was pleased to report to the Queen that the prohibition on the export of grain from Syria and Palestine had finally been removed. "Report by Her Majesty's Consulate General in Beyrout," *London Gazette*, April 25, 1870, issue 23610, 2302. Another account describes the situation thus: "Between 1869 and 1871 Hebron was plagued with a severe drought. Food was so scarce that the little available sold for ten times the normal value. Although the rains came in 1871, there was no easing of the famine, for the farmers had no seed to sow. The [Jewish] community was obliged to borrow money from non-Jews at exorbitant interest rates in order to buy wheat for their fold. Their leaders finally decided to send their eminent Chief Rabbi Eliau [Soliman] Mani to Egypt to obtain relief." Isaac Samuel Emmanuel and Suzanne A. Emmanuel, *History of the Jews of the Netherlands Antilles*, 2 vols. (Cincinnati: American Jewish Archives, 1970), vol. 2, p. 754.

124 Palmer, "The Desert," *The Desert of the Exodus*, vol. 2, pp. 389, 392.

125 In the spring of 2014, American photographer Fazal Sheikh first showed me the series of aerial images of the Negev he had taken in the fall of 2011.

126 In 1913, Frederick Laws was the first to develop the practice of aerial reconnaissance for the British military. Looking from a light aircraft at a moist patch of grass in the air force base in southeast England from which his light aircraft took off, Laws could make out the imprint of "a dog, following a parade of soldiers, being chased off by the Sergeant" shortly after they had all moved on. F. C. V. Laws, "Looking Back," *Photogrammetric Record* 3.13 (April 1959), pp. 28–29.

127 C. Donald Ahrens, *Meteorology Today: An Introduction to Weather, Climate, and the Environment*, 8th ed. (Belmont, CA: Thomson Higher Education, 2007), p. 110. A similar phenomenon is observed by Patricio Guzmán in his film *Nostalgia for the Light (Nostalgia de la Luz)*, 2010. The relation between humidity and resolution is captured by a photographic term known as "dimensional stability," which measures the size-changes of objects caused by small deflections generated by different levels of humidity and temperature. High-altitude photography and the demands of photo interpretation thus require special media. For information on Kodak Aerocon High Altitude Film see http://www.kodak.com/ek/uploadedFiles/Content/Manufacturing_Services/Aerial_Products /Literature_and_Publications/ti2344.pdf.

128 Sheikh, "Desert Bloom," in *Erasure*. Weizman and Sheikh, *The Conflict Shoreline*.

129 The US Coast Guard and the Federal Aviation Administration (FAA) implemented a 2,300-square-kilometer temporary flight restriction zone over the spill area. Citing BP's authority, they further denied access to members of the press attempting to document the spill. See "About Public Lab," https://publiclab.org/about.

130 A. G. Macmunn and Cyril Falls, *Military Operations Egypt and Palestine*, vol. 2, part 2 (London: HM Stationary Office, 1930), pp. 84–85. Military reports of this battle included in this text note the water shortage and the problem of obtaining drinking water for the thirty thousand horses, mules, and camels employed by the EEF. Some charges were delayed so the horses could be taken back to Beersheba for watering. In other occasions, horses were thrown into battle without drinking for three days.

131 They had arrived in Beersheba in early October 1917 — their planes packed in parts on freight trains — just in time to see the British storm through the town on October 31. The squadron managed to fly out and to land at a Gaza airfield, but a few days later, the city fell, too. The aviators managed to escape again, relocating this time to the north of Palestine. Some pilots, among them several Jews, were shot down and are buried in the German military cemetery in Nazareth. Squadron 304 was one of the first to record systematically archaeological sites from the air. Sites included Christian churches in Jerusalem, Bethlehem, and Nazareth, as well as older ruins in Jericho, Caesarea, Acre, and the Dead Sea. The sorties were also part of the Heritage Commando (Denkmalschutzcommando), which undertook numerous scientific surveys of ancient monuments. The organization was led by Theodor Wiegand, who also employed aerial photographs obtained from specially equipped kites. The images became important for aerial archaeology, because many places in Lebanon, Syria, Israel, and the Palestinian territories have since been built over. See *Image Collection Palestine*, ed. Lothar Saupe (Munich: Bavarian State Archives, 2010), photographs of Palestine recorded 1917–18 by the Bavarian Squadron 304.

132 Nada Atrash, "Mapping Palestine: The Bavarian Air Force WWI Aerial Photography," *Jerusalem Quarterly* 56 (Winter–Spring 2014), p. 95, http://www.palestine-studies.org/sites/default/file s/jq-articles/JQ%2056-57%20Mapping%20Palestine.pdf.

133 Alon Tal refers to this presentation in *Pollution in a Promised Land*, p. 350. The photographs were presented by Aviva Rabinovich, a JNF botanist.

134 In *The Conflict Shoreline*, I wrote, erroneously, that "PS" meant Palestine Survey. The survey had a crucial part to play in the history of the area: less than a year after the photographs were taken, the Anglo-American Committee of Inquiry used these aerial images to calculate population numbers and levels of cultivation in order to draft one of the proposed lines of partition of Mandatory Palestine. In the Beersheba district alone, they identified 8,722 tents and 3,389 stone houses (*bāykat*) belonging to the Bedouin tribes of the area. Yiftachel, Kedar, and Amara, "Challenging a Legal Doctrine," p. 100. A map, "Distribution of the Nomad Population of the Beersheba Subdistrict" was compiled from information that included the aerial photographs of 1945. Background information on the compilation of this map can be found in Appendices 3 and 4 of United Nations, General Assembly, *Ad Hoc Committee on the Palestinian Question, Report of Sub-Committee 2* (1947), A/AC.14/32, https://unispal.un.org/pdfs/AAC1432.pdf.

135 Dov Gavish, *A Survey of Palestine under the British Mandate 1920–1948* (London: Routledge, 2005), pp. 245–48.

136 Ian Black and Benny Morris, *Israel's Secret Wars: A History of Israel's Intelligence Services* (London: Hamish Hamilton, 1991), p. 129; Gil Eyal, *The Disenchantment of the Orient — Expertise in Arab Affairs and the Israeli State* (Stanford: Stanford University Press, 2006), p. 85. For a good, accessible introduction to aerial photography and image resolution in World War II, see Denis Cosgrove and William L. Fox, *Photography and Flight* (London: Reaktion Books, 2010).

137 Yosef Ben Shlomo, "Expert Report for the Analysis of Aerial Imagery," September 15, 2009, sent to Nūri al-'Uqbi.

138 In 1945, in the area of the photographs, there was an extensive and continuous Bedouin agricultural settlement, save for a small percentage of the land where the slopes of the streams were too steep. Along the streams there are wells and cisterns. An extensive network of routes connect the clusters of houses, including stone houses, tent encampments, farmyards, small gardens, livestock pens and shelters, storage for agricultural produce, and piles of hay and other produce. In her March 15, 2010, verdict against the plaintiffs, Judge Dovrat claimed that the photographs were inconclusive in proving the existence of a permanent Bedouin settlement. The people, she suggested, could have just passed by and cultivated temporarily: "Although the expert claimed that there was a continuous agricultural settlement on site, it became apparent that it was of very low density." Dovrat, final verdict in Al-Uqbi v. The State of Israel, p. 17.

139 The following is a more detailed technical explanation: For the making of the Port Said survey series, the RAF reconnaissance airplanes were photographing at an altitude of 15,000 feet. The focal length of the lens was 12 inches or 1 foot. The scale of the film is obtained by dividing the altitude by focal length. The scale of the negative film is thus 1:15,000, which means that every millimeter on the film represents 15 meters on the ground. Because the size of the negative film is 9 inches or 228.6 millimeters, the area captured on each separate negative film is about 3.4 by 3.4 kilometers, or 11.5 square kilometers. The resolution of the film used by the RAF is 35 line pairs per millimeter. This unit, lp/mm, measures how many pairs of alternating black and white lines would fit within a millimeter on a negative. If there are 35 line pairs, each the width of at least a single grain, then in a single millimeter on the film there are 70 grains. The size of a silver salt grain is 0.014 millimeters. At a scale of 1:15,000 the size of the grain represents 214 millimeters of ground. However, given the atmosphere, the effective resolution is 50 centimeters per grain.

140 Eli Atzmon, interview, April 29, 2014.

141 Eyal Weizman, "Matter against Memory," in *Forensis*, pp. 361–378, 365.

142 Regavim, "Bedouin Myth #2 — Are The Bedouin Villages Historical?," December 16, 2013, http://

regavim.org.il/en/bedouin-myth-2-are-the-bedouin-villages-historical, in Hebrew; Regavim, "The Negev Bedouins: The Real Story," November 2013, http://174.137.191.60/~regavimo/wp-content /uploads/2013/11/5balloons.pdf. Political theorists Nicola Perugini and Neve Gordon explain that, "according to the organization's human rights narrative, Jewish settlers are victims of discrimination and the colonized Palestinians are the 'invaders' and 'silent conquerors' of Israeli national lands as well as the perpetrators of human rights violations against Jewish citizens of Israel." Nicola Perugini and Neve Gordon, *The Human Right to Dominate* (Oxford: Oxford University Press, 2015). A good resource for thinking about the politics of NGOs can be found in *Nongovernmental Politics*, ed. Michel Feher (New York: Zone Books, 2007).

143 Besides the 1945 photographs, the Regavim report also presented Israeli Air Force photographs from 1956, 1965, and 1987 and a satellite image from 2010. It is only in the 1965 photograph, and from that date on, Regavim's report claimed, that it was possible to notice the cemetery in its early stages and a single tent next to it. Regavim's conclusion is that "the 'historic' village al-'Araqīb, which the Bedouin claimed was established during the Ottoman period, was built at the end of the 1990s and thereafter." They wrote that in "the area where al-'Araqīb is today, in 1945, no village or cemetery [existed] whatsoever." Regavim, *The Truth about the Bedouins in the Negev*, December 2013.

144 Interview with Sheikh Sayāh al-Tūri in the cemetery of al-'Araqīb, September 27, 2014.

145 David Rosenberg, "Officer murdered in Negev terror attack," Arutz 7: Israel National News, January 18, 2017: "A terrorist belonging to the Islamic movement sped toward our forces with intent to kill as many police as possible even before the evacuation"; "Police: a terrorist from the Islamic movement run over policemen during the evacuation in the Negev," Ynet, January 18, 2017, http://www.ynet.co.il/articles/0,7340,L-4909098,00.html.

146 For Forensic Architecture: Oren Ziv, Ariel Caine, Stefan Laxness, Christina Varvia, Nichola Czyz, and Omar Ferwati.

147 Hila Azoulay, "The Autopsy shows: the runaway driver from the Negev was wounded from a shot in the knee that was on the gas pedal," Channel 10, January 20, 2017, http://news.nana10.co.il /Article/?ArticleID=1228683; John Brown, "First release: Visual analysis of the events in Umm al-Hiran refutes the police version of events," mekomit.co.il, January 19, 2017, and John Brown, "Abu al-Qi'an's autopsy shutters the police version," mekomit.co.il, January 21, 2017.

Design and production by Julie Fry, New York

Printed and bound by Die Keure, Bruges

RELATED TITLES

The Civil Contract of Photography
Ariella Azoulay

Close Up at a Distance: Mapping, Technology & Politics
Laura Kurgan

Contemporary States of Emergency:
The Politics of Military and Humanitarian Interventions
Didier Fassin and Mariella Pandolfi, eds.

Nongovernmental Politics
Michel Feher, ed., with Gaëlle Krikorian and Yates McKee

Outlaw Territories:
Environments of Insecurity/Architectures of Counterinsurgency
Felicity D. Scott

The Power of Inclusive Exclusion:
Anatomy of Israeli Rule in the Occupied Palestinian Territories
Adi Ophir, Michal Givoni, and Sari Hanafi, eds.

Sensible Politics: The Visual Culture of Nongovernmental Activism
Meg McLagan and Yates McKee, eds.

Walled States, Waning Sovereignty
Wendy Brown